ACADIA
NATIONAL PARK

HILARY NANGLE

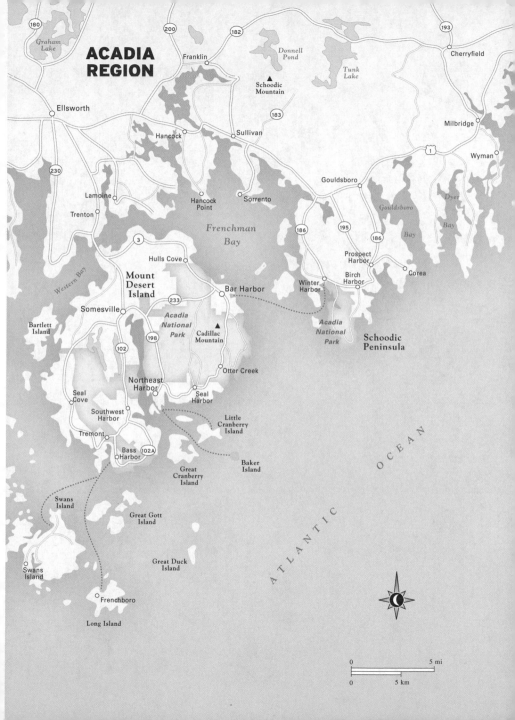

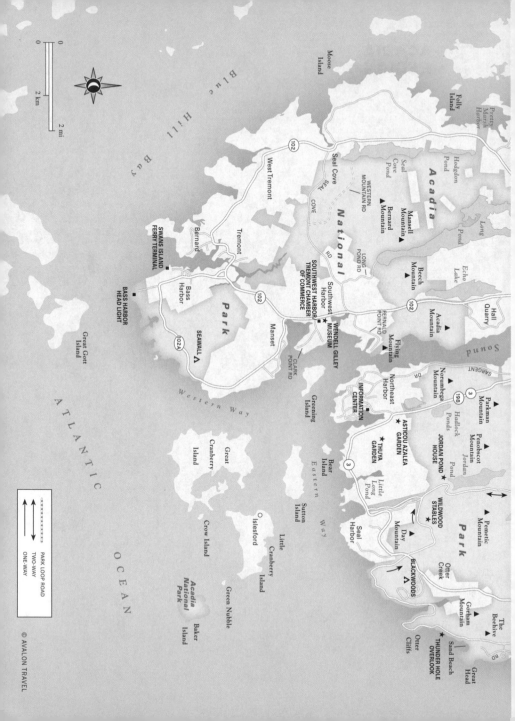

Contents

Acadia National Park

Mount Desert Island has been luring visitors since French explorers first answered the island's siren song in 1604. Raw, remote, and seductive, it dangles like a pendant into the Atlantic, flashing its voluptuous profile to passing navigators and mainland drivers. Although only 15 miles from north to south and 12 miles from west to east, the island is home to about 30,000 of Acadia National Park's roughly 46,000 acres. It's a miniature masterpiece, a gem of a natural and cultural resource that's laced with hiking trails and carriage roads, etched by a craggy coastline, sprinkled with ponds, and lorded over by bald peaks.

Acadia's appeal is contradictory: It's accessible, and yet it's not. More than two million visitors annually arrive on Mount Desert by car, bus, plane, or cruise ship, all eager to view the park's icons. The park loop road makes that easy. But even on the most crowded days, it's possible to slip away and find solitary peace on a hike or a paddle or a bike ride. Step off the major thoroughfares, and birdsong replaces idle chatter, pine perfumes the air, and signs of civilization disappear from view. Off-the-beaten-path gems might lack the drama of the icons, but they feed the soul, ease the mind, and restore much-needed balance to a hectic life.

Clockwise from top left: wharf in Corea; Bass Harbor Head Light; *Lulu* lobster boat tour; Acadia ferry; granite steps on one of Acadia's trails; granite shores viewed from Acadia's Wonderland Trail.

Truth is, there is no one Acadia. Beyond Mount Desert Island, more sections of the park beckon. Islesford and Baker Island are connected by passenger ferries and excursion boats, as is the mainland Schoodic section of the park; oh-so-remote Isle au Haut lets the curious view from the safe confines of a boat while inviting the hardy to hike and camp in near solitude; and Schoodic's pink granite shores receive far fewer visitors than Mount Desert Island.

While the park is the region's flawless gem, it's set amid other precious ones. If stretched taut, Hancock County—with Acadia as its centerpiece—would have more than 1,000 miles of coastline. No saltwater locale on the entire eastern seaboard can compete with the region's variety of scenery or its natural resources, which include the Maine Coastal Islands National Wildlife Refuge, the Donnell Pond Public Reserved Land, three scenic byways, and countless preserves. It's inspiring scenery that feeds dozens of artists and artisans, whose galleries and studios pepper the region's byways.

A recent quotation put this area in its proper contemporary perspective: "Maine is so lovely," a British visitor to Acadia sighed nostalgically, "I do wish England had fought harder to keep it."

Clockwise from top left: live lobsters; Schoodic Peninsula; Flying Mountain Trail; Isle au Haut.

Planning Your Trip

Where to Go

Acadia on Mount Desert Island

Mountains tumbling to the sea, ocean waves crashing upon granite ledges, serene ponds, and wildflower-filled meadowlands—the Mount Desert Island section of the park has it all, in spades. Watch the sun rise out of the Atlantic from **Cadillac Mountain's summit,** drive along the icon-rich **Park Loop Road,** hike trails through forestlands and up coastal peaks, scale granite cliffs, or paddle the coastline's nooks and crannies. Intimate yet expansive, wild yet civilized, Acadia is as accessible or as remote as you desire.

Mount Desert Island Communities

Excursions into the park depart from the surrounding communities, which have attractions of their own: museums, gardens, shops, and theaters. **Bar Harbor** is the island's hub; tony **Northeast Harbor** is located at the mouth of Somes Sound, a rare fjord; **Southwest Harbor** is the heart of the island's quiet side. All edge sections of the park, and, of course, these communities, along with the smaller fishing villages, are where you'll find a **lobster dinner** with all the fixings.

Schoodic Peninsula

Everything changes when you continue north on Route 1: the pace slows, fast-food joints and even stoplights disappear, and independence reigns. **Schoodic Point's pink granite shores** are undoubtedly the highlight of the park's only mainland section, but there are other reasons to mosey **off the beaten track.** Back roads and

Lobster boats anchor in protected coves and harbors on the Schoodic Peninsula.

© AVALON TRAVEL

and back-to-the-landers, have worked diligently to preserve not only the landscape but also the heritage. It's a fine place to kick back, relax, and savor the good life.

Deer Isle and Isle au Haut

If Deer Isle isn't the end of the world, there's a sense that you can see it from here. Tethered to the mainland by a soaring bridge over Eggemoggin Reach, Deer Isle and Little Deer Isle are fishing communities accented by a **vibrant arts community.** Depart the island's tip by ferry for Isle au Haut, where the most **remote and rugged** piece of Acadia National Park awaits **hikers** and those for whom even Deer Isle is a bit too crowded.

scenic byways loop through fishing villages, bisect a mountain- and lake-speckled wilderness preserve, access a national wildlife refuge, and edge those pink shores. It's a bonanza for **hikers, bikers, anglers, boaters,** and **bird-watchers.**

Blue Hill Peninsula

Water, water everywhere. Around nearly every bend is a **river** or **stream,** a **cove,** a **boat-filled harbor,** or a **serene pond.** It's an inspired and inspiring landscape dotted with **historic homes and forts.** The locals, a blend of summer rusticators, genteel retirees, artists, boatbuilders,

Ellsworth and Trenton

To visit Mount Desert Island, you must pass through the madness of Ellsworth and Trenton, a traffic-clogged, curse-inducing strip of mini malls and big-box stores. There are a few gems hidden amid the sprawl, including **historic buildings,** trails for **hiking,** and lakes for **boating.** Perhaps most delightful is **Birdsacre,** the former home of ornithologist Cornelia Stanwood, now a preserve with nature and bird rehab centers. It's a fine place to refuel your soul.

When to Go

If you yearn to be car-free on Mount Desert, plan to be here in summer, particularly between **late June and mid-October,** when Acadia's **Island Explorer shuttle service** operates.

If you plan to visit the Isle au Haut section of the park, time a visit for **early June-mid-September** to coincide with the **Isle au Haut passenger ferry service** to the park dock; otherwise you'll have nearly a 10-mile round-trip hike to Duck Harbor.

High Season (July-Aug.)

Summer means plentiful **festivals** and **fairs, nightlife** in Bar Harbor, **nature tours,**

concerts (jazz, classical, and pop), **carriage rides, hiking,** and **whale-watching** trips. The downside is the crowds, although the surrounding towns on Mount Desert Island as well as those on the Schoodic and Blue Hill Peninsulas and on Deer Isle are far quieter.

Mid-Season (late Apr.-June and Sept.-Oct.)

Spring tends to be something of a blip in Maine; the park starts reawakening around **mid-late April,** when the entire **Park Loop Road reopens** (including the Cadillac Mountain Road). Even then, some of the

- **Bicycling:** Pedaling Acadia's famed **carriage roads** takes you to the heart of the park. Forty-five of the 57 miles of gravel roads are open to bicyclists, and many are accented with rough stone bridges. All are mapped and signposted, so you won't get lost. While there are some ups and downs, none of the roads are very steep.

- **Birding:** Twenty warbler species are among the 338 bird species that have been sighted on Mount Desert Island. Plan a day with **Down East Nature Tours** to sight eagles, ospreys, peregrine falcons, shorebirds, and warblers as well as rare birds such as the Nelson's sharp-tailed sparrow.

- **Camping:** Make advance reservations for Acadia's **Blackwoods Campground** on Mount Desert Island, which has the greatest concentration of trails, with options for all abilities. Consider adding three nights on **Isle au Haut** for a primitive escape.

- **History:** Don't miss **Castine,** a seemingly bucolic town fought over by the French, British, and Dutch thanks to its strategic location.

- **Rock Climbing:** No experience is required to climb Acadia's cliffs, but you will need a guide or a lesson. **Acadia Mountain Guides Climbing School** and **Atlantic Climbing School,** both in Bar Harbor, will tailor instruction to your needs and help you find the perfect route.

- **Scenic Driving Tour:** Drive the **Park Loop Road** on Mount Desert Island and then loop together the **Schoodic National Scenic Byway,** wrapping around the Schoodic Peninsula, with the inland **Black Woods Scenic Byway.**

For a backcountry experience, camp in the Isle au Haut section of Acadia National Park.

- **Sea Kayaking:** One of the best ways to see Acadia is from the water, and paddling a sea kayak along the shoreline allows you to explore all the nooks and crannies. Outfitters in Bar Harbor, Southwest Harbor, and Stonington offer **guided trips.** Experienced kayakers seeking island-hopping experiences should join the Maine Island Trail Association.

- **Solitude:** Plan well in advance to book a campsite on **Isle au Haut,** home to a remote section of Acadia National Park that sees fewer than 130 visitors daily.

- **Whale-Watching:** Whale-watching excursions go up to 20 miles out to sea, which means not only will you likely spot whales, seals, and seabirds, but you'll also get grand views of the island-salted seascape.

Climbers prepare to scale Acadia's granite cliffs.

carriage roads tend to be fragile and open only for foot traffic, not for bicycles. **Trails can be muddy,** and ice still coats some of the rocks, but you'll be rewarded by hardy **wildflowers** poking up here and there. Until about mid-May, you'll also be spared the annoying blackflies. In May the **weather can be unpredictable,** and many **businesses still haven't opened** for the season.

Fall is fantastic in the park and on the island; it's my favorite season here. **Nights are cool** (mid-40s to mid-50s), days are often brilliant, and the **fall foliage** vistas are dramatic (see www.mainefoliage.com). The word has spread through the grapevine, though, and fall is **popular with cruise lines,** so you won't be alone—but the visitor head count is still far lower than in July and August.

Low Season (Nov.-mid Apr.)

Although Acadia is open in winter for **cross-country skiing, snowshoeing, snowmobiling** (with some restrictions), **hiking,** and even camping, there are few services and no programs; even the surrounding towns all but roll up the sidewalks.

Before You Go

Park Fees and Passes

The entrance fee is **$25 per vehicle** ($20 for motorcycles) late June-mid-October, and it is valid for seven days. Acadia's other fee options include:

- **Individual Pass** ($12): Valid for seven days.

- **Acadia Annual Pass** ($50): Valid for one year from the day of purchase.

- **Interagency Annual Pass** ($80): Allows unlimited entrance for one year to all national parks.

- **Access Pass** (free): Lifetime access to all national parks for any blind or permanently disabled U.S. citizen or permanent resident.

- **Senior Pass** ($10): Lifetime entrance to more than 300 national parks for U.S. citizens and permanent residents age 62 or older.

- **Interagency Volunteer Pass:** Accumulate 250 service hours for this one-year pass.

Reservations

There is **no lodging within Acadia National Park.** Reservations for Acadia National Park's **Seawall and Blackwoods Campgrounds on Mount Desert Island** are available online at www.recreation.gov or 877/444-6777. Reservations for the park's **Duck Harbor Campground on Isle au Haut** open April 1; contact the park for a reservation form (207/288-3338, www.nps.gov/acad). Reservations for the new **Schoodic Woods Campground on the Schoodic Peninsula,** opening in July 2015, should be available online in 2016; until then, call the park for more information.

In the Park

Visitors Center

Hulls Cove Visitors Center (Rte. 3, Hulls Cove, 207/288-3338, 8am-4:30pm daily Apr. 15-June 30 and Sept. 1-Oct. 31, 8am-6pm daily July-Aug.) is eight miles southeast of the head of Mount Desert Island. Day-trippers can leave their cars in the lot and hop on the Island Explorer bus, which stops at the base of the stairway from the parking lot to the center.

Where to Stay

MOUNT DESERT ISLAND

Blackwoods Campground (open year-round; primitive walk-in camping only Dec.-Mar.): Advance reservations are recommended. **Seawall Campground** (open late May-Sept.): About half the sites are first-come, first-served, but plan on arriving as early as 8:30am if trying to secure an unreserved site in midsummer.

The island has **hotels, motels, inns, B&Bs, cottages,** and a dozen **private campgrounds.** Lodging can be scarce at the height of summer, particularly during the first two weeks in August, when room rates also spike. Off-season rates are always lower. Only a handful of accommodations remain open year-round.

ISLE AU HAUT

Duck Harbor Campground (open May 15-Oct. 15): Advance reservations and permit are required. There is only one small inn on the island.

SCHOODIC PENINSULA

Schoodic Woods Campground is expected to open in 2015. A handful of inns and B&Bs peppers the Schoodic Peninsula and surrounding region; it's best to make advance reservations, especially in August.

Getting Around

The free **Island Explorer** (www.exploreacadia.com) shuttle bus runs **June-mid-October.** The hub is the Bar Harbor Village Green, where all of the routes (except Schoodic) begin or end. The service covers most of the island as well as the Bar Harbor Airport in Trenton. From **mid-June-late September,** the **Bar Harbor Ferry** connects with the Island Explorer's Schoodic Peninsula route.

From **early June-mid-September,** the **Isle au Haut Boat Company** operates a passenger ferry to the park's Duck Harbor dock in addition to its year-round service to the Town Dock.

The Best of Acadia National Park

Ready to hit the Park Loop Road running? You can pack a lot into three days, taking in the highlights and actually experiencing the park with hikes, bike rides, boat trips, or ranger-led programs. You might even include the Schoodic section of the park. For easiest park access, base yourself in Bar Harbor; even better, stay at one of the park's campgrounds.

Day 1

Pack a picnic, head to the park's Hulls Cove Visitors Center, purchase a pass, pick up a schedule of ranger-led activities, then drive or pedal the **Park Loop.** Now, you can complete the loop itself in about two hours, but it'll take the better part of the day if you stop at all the sights, including the Acadia Nature Center, Wild Gardens of Acadia, and Abbe Museum at **Sieur du Monts Spring,** as well as **Sand Beach, Thunder Hole, Jordan Pond House,** and **Cadillac Mountain** (best at

sunset or save that for sunrise tomorrow). Make it a whole day by adding a hike. Perhaps stretch your legs with a **walk along the Ocean Path** or ascend Great Head or Gorham Mountain. If time permits, visit the Seawall area and **Bass Harbor Head Light.** In the evening, if you're not completely exhausted, perhaps attend a ranger-led program at either Blackwoods or Seawall Campgrounds.

Day 2

Rise early and catch sunrise from the summit of **Cadillac Mountain.** Spend the morning and early afternoon exploring one of the park's outlying holdings, taking either the ranger-narrated cruise to **Baker Island** or **Islesford** or catching the ferry to Winter Harbor and exploring the **Schoodic** section of the park either by bicycle or on the Island Explorer. On returning, if time permits, head to the **Jordan Pond House** for tea

view of Bar Harbor and the Porcupine Islands from the summit of Cadillac Mountain

If you only have one day to explore Acadia National Park, spend it on Mount Desert Island. Rise early and welcome the day from the summit of **Cadillac Mountain.** Descend to Bar Harbor for breakfast, and pick up a picnic lunch to enjoy during your park explorations. Begin at the **Hulls Cove Visitors Center,** where you can purchase a park pass, watch a film, check out exhibits, and pick up copies of the park map, carriage road map, and ranger program schedule. If you're traveling with children, plan around one of the family-oriented ranger-led activities.

Spend the morning driving the coast-hugging section of the **Park Loop Road,** stopping to take in the sights at **Sieur du Monts Spring,** including the **Abbe Museum** and **Wild Gardens of Acadia;** to wriggle your toes in the sands of **Sand Beach;** perhaps hike the **Ocean Path, Great Head,** or **Gorham Mountain;** and view **Thunder Hole.** Continue to Jordan Pond House for a walk or pedal on the **carriage roads,** followed by popovers on the lawn.

Loop over to the quiet side of the island, perhaps stopping to visit **Asticou** or **Thuya Gardens** in Northeast Harbor, then edging around the shoreline of **Somes Sound** on Sargent Drive. Loop out through Southwest Harbor to the **Seawall** section of the park to view **Bass Harbor Head Light,** perhaps hiking **Wonderland** or **Ship**

Thuya's formal English gardens

Harbor Nature Trail en route. End the day with a sunset paddle, a dinner cruise to **Islesford,** or a **ranger-led program** at one of the park's campgrounds. If you didn't rise early to catch sunrise from Cadillac's summit—or even if you did—consider returning for sunset.

and popovers on the lawn. Work it off with a walk or pedal on the carriage roads.

Day 3

Pursue your interests, mixing and matching any of the following: Take a guided **sea kayaking** tour exploring the western side of the island, departing from Pretty Marsh; take a guided **bird-watching** tour with Michael Good of Down East Nature Tours; **hike** Acadia, St. Sauveur, or Flying Mountain, followed by a refreshing swim in Echo Lake; reserve a **horse-drawn carriage ride** to the Day Mountain summit; pedal or walk the **Eagle Lake** and **Witch Hole Pond** carriage roads; scale Acadia's cliffs on a climbing lesson; or join one or more ranger-led programs.

A 15-Day Road Trip

Spend 15 days here and you'll have enough time to visit all sections of Acadia National Park, browse the studios of mega-talented artisans, go whale-watching, hike magnificent trails, kayak along undeveloped coastline, and view working lobstering villages and lighthouses. This driving tour begins in the Schoodic region, and then takes in Mount Desert Island before heading to the Blue Hill Peninsula via Ellsworth, with Isle au Haut as the grand finale.

The best air access is via Bangor International Airport. Book your first two nights' lodging in the Schoodic region, nights 3 through 10 on Mount Desert Island (perhaps the first four on the east side of the island and the rest on the west side), nights 11 and 12 on the Blue Hill Peninsula, and nights 13 and 14 on Deer Isle.

Schoodic Peninsula
DAY 1
Begin with a drive or bicycle loop around the **Schoodic section of Acadia National Park.**

watching the surf on Schoodic Point

Depending on your interests, day hike the Schoodic Head Loop or spend the rest of the day sea kayaking.

DAY 2
Drive to either **Maine Coastal Islands National Wildlife Refuge,** on Petit Manan, for bird-watching and easy hiking, or to the **Donnell Pond Public Reserved Land** for a day hike followed by a swim. Don't forget a picnic lunch.

Mount Desert Island
DAY 3
Browse the numerous **artisans' galleries** tucked in all corners of the Schoodic Peninsula as you make your way to Mount Desert Island. Begin at Lee Fusion Art Glass and move on to Lunaform, Barter Gallery, Spring Woods Gallery, and Hog Bay. Stop by the park's Hulls Cove Visitors Center when you arrive on Mount Desert Island to purchase a park pass and pick up a schedule of ranger-led activities.

one of Acadia's prettiest carriage road bridges, near Seal Harbor

DAY 4

Spend the day in **Acadia National Park.** Begin by driving or bicycling the **Park Loop** to take in the park's highlights. Stop for a hike along the way—perhaps an easy stroll along the **Ocean Path,** a moderate hike up Great Head or Gorham Mountain, a challenging hike up one of the trails that start at Sieur de Monts Spring, or a strenuous climb up a ladder trail. Reward your efforts with tea and popovers at the **Jordan Pond House.**

DAY 5

Another day in the park: Get up early and catch sunrise from atop **Cadillac Mountain,** then indulge your passions: hiking, sea kayaking, or bicycling. Check the schedule of ranger-led activities to see what naturalist programs are scheduled, and make it a point to take part in one that intrigues you.

DAY 6

Spend the day in **Bar Harbor.** Reserve a spot on a **whale-watching trip.** Visit the **Abbe Museum,** shop the downtown shops, and stroll the **Shore Path.** End the day with a sunset carriage tour in the park.

DAY 7

Explore **Northeast Harbor.** Visit the **Asticou and Thuya Gardens,** and perhaps wander out the back gate of Thuya and up Eliot Mountain. Shop downtown and gawk at the yachts in the harbor. Bicycle or drive Sargent Drive along the shores of **Somes Sound.**

DAY 8

Choices, choices: Pack a picnic lunch and either take to the **carriage roads** on foot or bike or hop aboard a passenger ferry to the **Cranberry Isles.** If you want to have a sunset dinner on Islesford, make advance reservations and either go on a day when there's a late boat or arrange for a water taxi.

DAY 9

Head for the western side of the island and visit pretty **Somesville** and **Southwest Harbor,** allowing time to tour the **Wendell Gilley Museum.** In the afternoon, hike Acadia, St. Sauveur, or Flying Mountain, then refresh yourself with a dip in **Echo Lake,** followed by dinner at Thurston's Lobster Pound.

Acadia National Park is a great place to introduce kids to the great outdoors. Between park visits, you'll find plenty of other activities with real kid appeal. Here are a few sure bets.

IN THE PARK

Before arriving, register either by phone or online for Acadia Quest, an experiential scavenger hunt in the park. At park headquarters, sign kids up as Junior Rangers. Then pick and choose from the ranger-led activities that appeal to your family's interests and abilities. Good choices for easy family hikes include the Ocean Path, Jordan Pond Nature Trail, Ship Harbor Nature Trail, and Wonderland. If you're into geocaching, ask about the park's EarthCache Program (www.nps.gov/acad/earthcache.htm).

SLIMY SEA CREATURES

You can't beat the wow appeal of Diver Ed's Dive-in Theater Boat Cruise (207/288-3483 or 800/979-3370, www.divered.com). Ed dives to the depths with an underwater camera while you wait onboard and watch the action. When he re-surfaces, he brings along with him a variety of creatures from the depths for passengers to see, feel, and learn about.

LOBSTER LORE

Even if the kids won't eat lobster, they'll be fascinated by Captain John Nicolai, who tells all during two-hour cruises aboard the Lulu (56 West St., Bar Harbor, 207/963-2341 or 866/235-2341, www.lulu-lobsterboat.com).

HANDS-ON NATURE

"Please touch" is the philosophy at the George B. Dorr Museum of Natural History (105 Eden St./Rte. 3, Bar Harbor, 207/288-5015, www.coa.edu, 10am-5pm Tues.-Sat., donation), a small museum on the College of the Atlantic campus in Bar Harbor. Kids have the opportunity to touch fur, skulls, and even whale baleen.

FERRY HOPPING

Spend the better part of a day on the Cranberry Isles, visiting both Big and Little Cranberry and either walking or biking around, or take the passenger ferry to Winter Harbor, and hop on the Island Explorer bus to visit the Schoodic section of Acadia National Park. En route, watch for seals, seabirds, and lobster boats hauling traps.

NATIVE AMERICAN CULTURE

Check with the Abbe Museum (26 Mt. Desert St., Bar Harbor, 207/288-3519, www.abbemuseum.org, 10am-5pm daily late May-early Nov., call for off-season hours, $6 adults, $2 ages 6-15) about scheduled special programs for kids, and time your visit to take advantage of them. There's a resource room for children downstairs and a few other kid-friendly exhibits at this Native American history museum, but the events bring it all to life.

NATURALIST'S NOTEBOOK

Bookstore? Museum? Arts space? Exploratorium? The Naturalist's Notebook (16 Main St., Seal Harbor, 207/801-2777, www.thenaturalistsnotebook.com) is all that and more, with three floors of kid-friendly engaging exhibits, books, and treasures.

LAUGH FEST

Improv Acadia (15 Cottage St., Bar Harbor, 207/288-2503, www.improvacadia.com, $15 adults, $10 under age 13) stages a family-friendly show every evening.

I SCREAM, YOU SCREAM

The ultimate kid-in-a-candy-store experience is at Ben & Bill's (66 Main St., Bar Harbor, 207/288-3281 or 800/806-3281), where you can buy not only chocolates made on-site but also to-die-for ice cream in both adult- and kid-pleasing flavors.

OLYMPICS OF THE FOREST

Expert lumberjack Tina Scheer and her crew perform the most amazing skills at The Great Maine Lumberjack Show (Rte. 3, Trenton, 207/667-0067, www.mainelumberjack.com, 7pm daily mid-June-early Sept., 4pm Sat. and 2pm Sun. early Sept.-mid-Oct., $12 adults, $11 over age 62, $7.50 ages 4-11). During the 75-minute performance, two teams compete in 12 events, including ax throwing and log rolling. You can participate in some and even arrange for your youngster to learn how to log roll. Talk about a great story for that "What I did on my summer vacation" assignment.

Bar Harbor's Shore Path

the pond at Asticou Azalea Garden

DAY 10

Drive out to **Bass Harbor Head Light,** then continue to the village and take the luncheon nature cruise to **Frenchboro** with Island Cruises (be sure to make advance reservations). Or, if you're an experienced cyclist, take a bike aboard the state ferry to **Swans Island** for the day.

Blue Hill Peninsula
DAY 11

Depart Mount Desert for the Blue Hill Peninsula. En route, visit **Birdsacre,** a peaceful preserve and bird refuge. You could also put the region in perspective with a plane or glider flight. Spend the afternoon in **Blue Hill,** beginning with a tour of the **Parson Fisher House.** Afterward, if time permits, visit some of the many **galleries** in town. Do ask locally to see if the **Flash! In the Pans** are performing during your days on the peninsula, and make it a point to hear them.

DAY 12

Your choice: Hike **Blue Hill Mountain,** followed by more time for visiting galleries; hike **Great Pond Mountain,** followed by a visit to the **Craig Brook National Fish Hatchery;** or

mosey over to **Castine** and pick up a brochure for a self-guided walking or bicycling tour followed by a guided sea kayaking tour.

Deer Isle and Isle Au Haut
DAY 13

Explore **Deer Isle** and **Stonington,** allowing plenty of time to browse the galleries along the way. Hike the **Edgar Tennis** or **Barred Island Preserves** and, if your timing is right, visit the **Haystack Mountain School of Crafts.**

DAY 14

Another day in the park, this time the **Isle au Haut** section. Plan in advance and book a seat on the early boat, then spend the day hiking. Don't forget a picnic lunch and water; supplies are limited on the island.

Back to Bangor International Airport
DAY 15

Visit **Fort Knox** and the **Penobscot Narrows Bridge and Observatory** in the morning before heading home. If you're flying out of Bangor, you can either mosey up Route 15 or connect via Route 174 to U.S. 1A north.

Lobster, Lighthouses, and L.L.Bean

Yes, you can hit the three L's in the Acadia region. Book your first three nights on Mount Desert, nights four and five in the Blue Hill region, and nights six and seven on Deer Isle.

Day 1

Make your first stop on **Mount Desert Island** the park's Hulls Cove Visitors Center to purchase your park pass, pick up a schedule of ranger-led activities, and chat with a ranger. In the evening, head to **Thurston's Lobster Pound** for a lobster dinner with all the fixings.

Day 2

Rise early and beat the crowds on the **Park Loop Road.** In the afternoon, take a cruise aboard the *Lulu,* and learn everything there is to know about lobsters. Afterward, stroll up Main Street to **Ben & Bill's** for a lobster ice cream cone (it's a good idea to ask for a taste first).

Thurston's Lobster Pound

Day 3

Take a spin out to **Bass Harbor** to see the lighthouse, then board Island Cruises' *R. L. Gott* for the luncheon tour to **Frenchboro.** There's no finer place for a lobster or lobster roll than **Lunt's Dockside Deli.**

Day 4

Book a morning whale- and puffin-watching cruise that includes **Petit Manan Light** on its itinerary. Afterward, leave Mount Desert Island for the Blue Hill Peninsula, stopping at the **L.L.Bean Factory Store** in Ellsworth. It's nowhere near as big or as complete as the mother ship in Freeport, but it will provide a taste of what the gigunda outdoor-oriented retailer offers. After your shopping spree, it's on to the Blue Hill region. En route, detour down Newbury Neck in Surry to **Perry's,** the real deal when it comes to lobster shacks.

Lobster fishing anchors Stonington's economy.

Day 5

Head to **Castine,** pick up a walking tour brochure at a local business, and take a leisurely stroll around town, making sure to see **Dyce's Head Lighthouse.** Spend the afternoon pursuing your interests: perhaps a hike up Blue Hill Mountain, a sea kayaking tour, or gallery browsing throughout the peninsula.

Day 6

On to **Deer Isle.** When you cross the bridge onto Little Deer Isle, bear right at the info booth and head to the end of the road for views of **Pumpkin Island Light.** Then mosey on down the peninsula to **Stonington,** a bona fide lobstering community. Spend the afternoon with Captain Walter Reed's **Guided Island Tours** (be sure to book in advance and tell him what you want to see—lighthouses and lobster fishing). Finding a lobster dinner in these parts is easy.

Day 7

Pack a picnic lunch and take the ferry to **Isle au Haut,** passing **Robinson Point Light,** and spend the day hiking in **Acadia National Park.** Go for one last lobster dinner in Stonington or Deer Isle before heading home tomorrow.

Best Hikes

Mount Desert Island

OCEAN PATH

This popular trail is both easy and easy to reach. Best to time an early morning arrival for this **4.4-mile round-trip** that mirrors the shore, taking in Sand Beach, Thunder Hole, Otter Cliffs, and Monument Cove (page 49).

JORDAN POND SHORE PATH

A mostly level **3.2-mile loop,** the shore path navigates a counterclockwise circuit of **Jordan Pond.** Plan your hike for fall, for a supremely colorful palette, and reward your efforts with popovers at **Jordon Pond House** (page 51).

GORHAM MOUNTAIN TRAIL

This **1.8-mile round-trip** hike covers the trail directly to the summit of 525-foot **Gorham Mountain,** with a return via **Cadillac Cliffs** for views of Sand Beach, Egg Rock Light, the Beehive, and Champlain Mountain (page 53).

BEACHCROFT PATH

Fifteen-hundred beautifully engineered pink-granite steps and slabs ease the moderate **2.4-mile round-trip** climb to **Huguenot Head** on the west side of Mount Desert's **Champlain Mountain.** Savor the views over Frenchman Bay before the more difficult ascent to the summit, where the views are even more spectacular (page 54).

PENOBSCOT AND SARGENT MOUNTAINS

This **6-mile round-trip** hike takes in two summits on the west side of Mount Desert Island. The terrain is difficult to strenuous, but you can take a swim break between peaks in **Sargent Pond,** and the views are worth the effort (page 54).

FLYING MOUNTAIN TRAIL

Despite being the lowest of Acadia's 26 peaks, this west-side mountain delivers gorgeous views over the mouth of Somes Sound via this **1.5-mile loop.** The descent brings you to **Valley Cove,** a

Beachcroft Path

a rocky beach off the Schoodic Head Loop

One highlight of the Flying Mountain Trail is a dip in Valley Cove.

place to cool tootsies, before the easy walk back to the parking lot (page 57).

Schoodic Peninsula
SCHOODIC HEAD LOOP
The Schoodic Head Loop connects three trails for a **2.7-mile round-trip** hike that travels from woods to the summit for expansive views (page 144).

SCHOODIC MOUNTAIN
Not to be confused with the Schoodic Head Loop, this moderately difficult **2.8-mile loop** in the Donnell Pond Public Reserved Land rewards hikers with panoramic views of Acadia's peaks on Mount Desert Island across Frenchman Bay (page 144).

Blue Hill Peninsula
BLUE HILL MOUNTAIN TRAIL
On a clear day, head for the summit of **Blue Hill** and take in the wraparound view—encompassing Penobscot Bay, the hills of Mount Desert, and the Camden Hills—on this easy-to-moderate **2-mile round-trip** hike (page 181).

Isle au Haut
WESTERN HEAD AND CLIFF TRAILS
For terrific shoreline scenery, day trip to Isle au Haut, and hike these two trails for a nice loop around **Western Head.** The route follows the coastline, ascending to ridges and cliffs and descending to rocky beaches, with some forested sections (page 224).

Acadia on Mount Desert Island

Look for ★ to find recommended sights, activities, dining, and lodging.

Highlights

★ **Sieur de Monts Spring:** This lovely oasis is home to the Wild Gardens of Acadia, the Acadia Nature Center, the Sweet Waters of Acadia spring, and the original Abbe Museum, as well as the base for hiking Dorr Mountain (page 40).

★ **Sand Beach:** Spread a blanket on one of the few beaches in this part of Maine (page 41).

★ **Thunder Hole:** Time your visit right to see the tide surge and explode through this geological formation (page 42).

★ **Jordan Pond House:** Come for tea, popovers, and ice cream on the lawn, but allow time to walk or ride the carriage roads or explore the nature trail (page 43).

★ **Cadillac Mountain:** Acadia's prime feature is the highest point on the eastern seaboard, allegedly where the sun's first rays land. Drive, bike, or hike to the 1,530-foot summit for stunning views (page 43).

★ **Carriage Roads:** Fifty-seven miles of meandering crushed-stone paths crossing 17 handsome stone bridges welcome walkers, bikers, horseback riders, snowshoers, and cross-country skiers (page 44).

★ **Eagle Lake:** A mountain backdrop and undeveloped shores contribute to Eagle Lake's popularity. A small-boat launch and a carriage road make it easy to explore (page 45).

★ **Park Ranger Programs:** Join one of the numerous programs, from guided hikes and photography tours to natural history programs and children's activities, offered daily by park rangers (page 35).

★ **Park Loop Road:** If you do nothing else on Mount Desert Island, drive this magnificent road that takes in many of Acadia National Park's highlights (page 37).

★ **Gorham Mountain Trail:** This trail requires a minimum amount of effort to produce maximum rewards. It's an excellent family hike—kids love the Cadillac Cliffs (page 53).

Rather like an octopus, or perhaps an amoeba, Acadia National Park extends its reach here and there and everywhere on Mount Desert Island. The park was created from donated parcels—a big chunk here, a tiny chunk there—and

slowly but surely fused into its present-day size of more than 47,000 acres (35,332 acres are owned by the National Park Service; the balance is privately owned land under conservation easements managed by the park). Permanent boundaries do exist—Congress certified them in 1986—but they can be confusing to visitors. One minute you're in the park, the next you've stepped into one of the island's towns. This symbiotic relationship is a reminder that Acadia National Park, covering a third of the island, is the major presence on Mount Desert. It affects traffic, indoor and outdoor pursuits, and in a way, even the climate.

Acadia's history is unique among national parks and is indeed fascinating. Several books have been written about the high-minded (in the positive sense) and high-profile personalities who provided the impetus and wherewithal for the park's inception and never

flagged in their interest and support. To spotlight a few, we can thank George B. Dorr, Charles W. Eliot, and John D. Rockefeller Jr. for the park we have today.

The National Park Service began keeping track of Acadia's visitors in 1919, when 64,000 people were counted. Given Acadia's complicated boundary, an exact count is impossible, but park officials estimate an average of 2.5 million visits annually. A big bump in numbers is expected in 2016, when Acadia celebrates the 100th anniversary of its creation.

In 2014, the park began implementing a comprehensive plan to reopen and maintain the planned vistas from the historic carriage roads and motor roads in the park, so don't be surprised to find tree-cutting crews at work over the next few years. The reward is enjoying the views that were purposefully designed into the systems.

Previous: Jordan Pond to the Cranberry Isles from the South Bubble ledges; view from the summit of South Bubble. **Above:** Jordan Pond House.

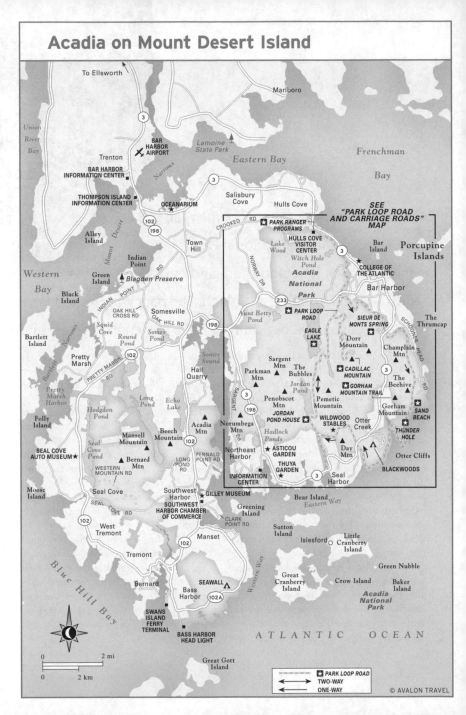

Acadia on Mount Desert Island

Exploring the Park

INFORMATION CENTERS

There are two major centers on Mount Desert Island for Acadia National Park information. Some Acadia information is also available from the Bar Harbor Chamber of Commerce's two offices (one on Route 3 in Trenton, as you approach the island; the other at the corner of Main and Cottage Streets in Bar Harbor), the Southwest Harbor Chamber of Commerce, and the Mount Desert Island Chamber in Northeast Harbor. The park also maintains a small info center facing the Village Green in Bar Harbor.

Thompson Island Information Center

As you cross the bridge from Trenton toward Mount Desert Island, you might not even notice that you arrive first on tiny Thompson Island, site of **Thompson Island Information Center** (8am-6pm daily mid-May-mid-Oct.), established jointly by the Mount Desert Island Chamber of Commerce and Acadia National Park.

The rustic building, on your right as you head south on Route 3, has walls lined with brochures for accommodations, restaurants, and activities. There are also restrooms. Across Route 3 is a picnic area overlooking Mount Desert Narrows.

If you've arrived without a place to stay (particularly in July-Aug.), the welcoming staffers here are incredibly helpful. They keep track of lodging vacancies throughout Mount Desert Island and will go to great lengths to funnel you somewhere. In high season, don't expect to be overly choosy, though—room rates are high, vacancies are few, and you take your chances.

In season, a park ranger is usually posted on Thompson Island to answer questions and provide basic advice on hiking trails and other park activities, but consider this a stopgap—also be sure to continue on to the park's main visitors center. You can purchase your Acadia pass here as well.

Hulls Cove Visitors Center

The modern **Hulls Cove Visitors Center** (Rte. 3, Hulls Cove, 207/288-3338, 8am-4:30pm daily Apr. 15-June 30 and Sept. 1-Oct. 31, 8am-6pm daily July-Aug.) is eight miles southeast of the head of Mount Desert Island and is well signposted. Here you can buy your park pass; rendezvous with pals; make reservations for ranger-guided natural and cultural history programs; watch a 15-minute film about Acadia; study a relief map of the park; buy books, park souvenirs, and cassette-tape guides; and use the restrooms. Pick up a copy of the **park's event calendar,** which lists activities along with tide calendars, and the schedule for the excellent **Island Explorer** shuttle bus system, which operates late June-Columbus Day. The Island Explorer is supported by park entrance fees as well as by Friends of Acadia and L.L.Bean. If you have children, enroll them in the park's free **Junior Ranger program.** To earn a Junior Ranger patch, they must complete the activities in an age-appropriate workbook, attend ranger-led programs, and promise to take care of Acadia.

Parking is usually ample at the visitors center, although the lot gets mighty full in midsummer, when as many as 9,000 people visit each day. Day-trippers also leave their cars in the lot and hop on the Island Explorer bus. The bus stops at the base of the winding stairway from the parking lot to the center.

Bar Harbor Village Green

The park maintains a small **information center** (8am-5pm, late June-mid Oct.) in downtown Bar Harbor on the Village Green, adjacent to the Island Explorer bus stop on Firefly Lane. Park and bus information, as well as visitor passes, are available here.

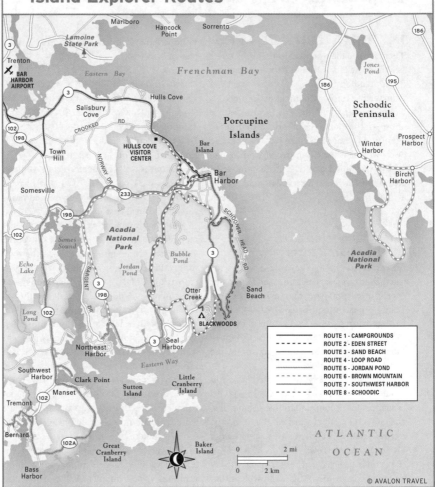

Island Explorer Routes

ROUTE 1 - CAMPGROUNDS
ROUTE 2 - EDEN STREET
ROUTE 3 - SAND BEACH
ROUTE 4 - LOOP ROAD
ROUTE 5 - JORDAN POND
ROUTE 6 - BROWN MOUNTAIN
ROUTE 7 - SOUTHWEST HARBOR
ROUTE 8 - SCHOODIC

© AVALON TRAVEL

Acadia Park Headquarters

Information is available at **Acadia National Park Headquarters** (Eagle Lake Rd./Rte. 233, Bar Harbor, 207/288-3338, www.nps.gov/acad, 8am-4:30pm daily Mar. 1-mid-Apr. and Nov.-Dec., 8am-4:30pm Mon.-Fri. Jan.-Feb. and mid-Apr.-late Oct., closed Thanksgiving Day, Dec. 24-25), located in a former Civilian Conservation Corps camp about 3.5 miles west of downtown Bar Harbor.

Park headquarters is also the meeting point for the volunteer work projects organized three times per week by the park and Friends of Acadia.

PARK ENTRANCE FEES

A single glance at the map of Acadia National Park immediately raises the question: How do you sell passes and count heads in a park that has patches of land here and there and everywhere—even on a section of the mainland and on offshore islands? The answer: not easily.

Park Rules

Most rules at Acadia are just common sense; some are specific to Acadia's situation and needs.

- It's forbidden to disturb or remove any **public property**—plants, minerals, artifacts, animals, etc. This extends to the rocks on the beaches.

- **Pets** are allowed in Acadia, with some exceptions, but they must be on a leash (6 feet or shorter). They must not be left unattended. Pets are not allowed on Sand Beach or at Echo Lake May 15-Sept. 15; in the Wild Gardens of Acadia, on ranger-led programs, or in the Duck Harbor Campground on Isle au Haut. They are also banned from the park's ladder trails and from the visitors centers and other public buildings. Service dogs, of course, are always exempt from the rules.

- **In-line skating, roller skiing,** and **skateboarding** are allowed only on roads closed to automobiles.

Be sure to purchase a park pass before entering Acadia.

- **Bicycles** are not allowed on any hiking trails. They're allowed on 45 miles of park carriage trails, but not on 12 miles of signposted (Green Rock Company) private carriage roads.

- **Motorized vehicles** are not allowed on park trails and carriage roads; **ATVs** are not allowed anywhere in the park. **Electric wheelchairs** are allowed on the carriage roads.

- **Camping** within park boundaries is allowed only at the park's two campgrounds on Mount Desert Island, one on Isle au Haut, and one on the Schoodic Peninsula. There is no backcountry camping in the park or anywhere else on Mount Desert Island, but outside the park, there are commercial campgrounds.

- **Camp stoves** and **grills** are allowed only in designated campgrounds and picnic areas; fires are allowed only in fire rings and fireplaces at these sites.

- **Alcohol** use is not allowed in the public buildings or facilities, at parking lots and pullouts, at Sand Beach, Echo Lake Beach, along the Lake Wood shoreline, or within a 0.25 mile of the swimming areas at the southeastern end of Long Pond.

- **Hunting** is not allowed in the park.

- **Fireworks** are not allowed in the park.

- **Feeding of wildlife,** including gulls, is prohibited.

- Federal law requires the use of **seatbelts** by drivers and passengers in all national parks.

So, let's look at the picture another way. It's important to know that 100 percent of the entrance fees stays in the National Park Service: Half goes to support the Island Explorer, $8 goes directly to the park for visitor services and improvements (not resource management, research, or planning), and the last $2 is shared by National Park Service sites that don't charge fees in the region, such as Maine's St. Croix Island National Historic Site, just south of Calais. The private Friends of Acadia organization and other donors often match these funds to make the money even more effective.

Consider just a few of the projects your pass helps fund:

- Trail and carriage road reconstruction and rehabilitation
- The Island Explorer bus system
- New and improved restroom facilities
- Repairs to historic stone bridges
- New and improved informational exhibits
- Rock wall reconstruction
- Campground rehabilitation

At many of the project sites, you'll see brown National Park Service signs that read "This Project Funded by Your Park User Fee." Think of them as Acadia's thank-you note for your support.

Where to Buy Your Park Pass

- **Hulls Cove Visitors Center,** the park's visitors information center mid-April-October; no entrance fees are collected November-mid-April.
- The Acadia National Park information office on Firefly Lane, opposite the **Village Green** in downtown Bar Harbor; it also faces the hub for the propane-powered Island Explorer bus system.

- **Sand Beach Park Entrance Station,** on Park Loop Road between the Schooner Head Overlook and Sand Beach.
- **Blackwoods and Seawall Campgrounds,** the park's only camping areas.
- **Thompson Island Information Center** (Rte. 3, Trenton).
- Inside the park, you can purchase your pass at the **Jordan Pond Gift Shop** and the **Cadillac Mountain Gift Shop.**
- Local **chambers of commerce** and some **accommodations** also sell passes.

Park Fees and Passes

- **Entrance fee:** $25 per car or RV, $20 per motorcycle late June-mid-October, when the Island Explorer is running. It covers everyone in the vehicle and is valid for seven days. If want to buy an individual pass that will not cover a car (best if you're traveling on foot or by bicycle or using the Island Explorer for transportation), the fee is $12 for seven days.
- **Acadia Annual Pass:** $50, valid for one year from the day of purchase. If you're in Acadia more than one week in any given

Acadia National Park operates a small information center in downtown Bar Harbor.

year, this is the cheapest option. It covers the pass holder and passengers in a non-commercial vehicle.

- **Interagency Annual Pass:** $80, allowing unlimited entrance for one year to all national parks and other federal recreation sites that have entrance or vehicle fees.

- **Senior Pass:** $10, an incredible bargain for U.S. citizens and permanent residents who are age 62 or older, allowing lifetime entrance to more than 300 national parks, historic sites, and monuments. It also entitles you to half-price camping. Purchase must be made in person with proof of age (a driver's license, passport, etc.). The pass covers everyone in the pass holder's vehicle. You will need to show an ID at the park's gate.

- **Access Pass:** free for any U.S. citizen or permanent resident who is blind or permanently disabled (a temporary disability, such as a broken arm or leg, does not qualify). It allows lifetime entrance to all national parks as well as Fish and Wildlife, Forest Service, and Bureau of Land Management sites. It also allows half-price camping. The pass covers everyone in the pass holder's vehicle.

- **Interagency Volunteer Pass:** Accumulate 250 service hours and you'll be rewarded with a one-year pass valid for federal recreation sites.

GUIDED TOURS

The variety of guided activities in the park and nearby is astonishing: There are park ranger walks and talks and cruises, bus tours, bicycling tours, sea kayaking tours, birding expeditions, guided hikes, horse-drawn carriage rides, and even deluxe camping outfitters.

★ Park Ranger Programs

When you stop at the Hulls Cove Visitors Center, pick up the current schedule of ranger-led programs (or download ahead of time at www.nps.gov/acad). You'll find a whole raft of possibilities for learning more about the park's natural and cultural history.

The park ranger programs, lasting 1-3 hours, are great—and most are free. During July-August there are dozens of programs each week. Included are 7am birding walks; moderate-level mountain hikes; tours of the historic Carroll Homestead, a 19th-century farm; Cadillac Mountain summit natural-history tours; children's expeditions to learn about tide pools and geology (an adult must accompany kids); trips for wheelchair users; and even a couple of tours a week in French. Some tours require reservations, and others do not; reservations can be made up to three days in advance.

Reservations are required and fees charged for several different boat cruises with park rangers, who provide natural-history narration. The specific cruises can vary from year to year, but they usually include **Baker Island, Dive-in Theater, Frenchman Bay,** and **Islesford.**

Park rangers also give evening lectures during the summer in the amphitheaters at Blackwoods and Seawall Campgrounds. And best of all, you can join almost every ranger program via an Island Explorer bus (late June-mid-Oct.).

Bus and Trolley Tours

The veteran of the Bar Harbor-based bus tours is **Acadia National Park Tours** (ticket office Testa's Restaurant, Bayside Landing, 53 Main St., Bar Harbor, 207/288-0300, www.acadia-tours.com, May-Oct., $30 adults, $15 under age 13). A 2.5-3-hour naturalist-led tour of Bar Harbor and Acadia departs at 10am and 2pm daily from Testa's Restaurant, across from Agamont Park near the Bar Harbor Inn, in downtown Bar Harbor. Reservations are advised in midsummer and during fall-foliage season (late Sept.-early Oct.); pick up reserved tickets 30 minutes before departure.

If you have a time crunch, take the one-hour trolley-bus tour operated by **Oli's Trolley** (ticket office 1 West St., Bar Harbor, 207/288-5443 or 866/987-6553, www.

acadiaislandtours.com, 4 trips 10am-3:30pm daily July-Aug., $16 adults, $11 ages 5-12, $6 younger than 5), which includes Bar Harbor mansion drive-bys and the Cadillac Mountain summit. The ticket office is downtown at Harbor Place, next to the town pier on the waterfront. Dress warmly if the air is at all cool; it's an open-air trolley. Reservations are advised. The trolley also does 2.5-hour park tours (10am, 11am, 1pm, and 2pm daily May-Oct., $30 adults, $16 ages 5-12, $6 younger than 5). The bus and trolley routes both include restroom stops. Tours depart from the boardwalk at the Harborside Hotel, 55 West Street.

While the Island Explorer buses do reach a number of key park sights, they are not tour buses. There is no narration, the bus cuts off the Park Loop at Otter Cliffs, and it excludes the summit of Cadillac Mountain.

Bird-Watching and Nature Tours

Oli's Trolley offers narrated tours of the park.

For private tours of the park and other parts of the island, contact Michael Good at **Down East Nature Tours** (150 Knox Rd., Bar Harbor, 207/288-8128, www.downeastnaturetours.com). A biologist and Maine Guide, Good is simply batty about birds. He has spent more than 25 years studying the birds of North America and has even turned his home property on Mount Desert Island into a bird sanctuary. Good specializes in avian ecology in the Gulf of Maine, giving special attention to native and migrating birds. Whether you're a first-timer wanting to spot eagles, peregrine falcons, shorebirds, and warblers or a serious bird-watcher seeking to add to your life list, perhaps with a Nelson's sharp-tailed sparrow, Good is your man. Prices begin at $75 per person for four hours and include transportation from your lodging; kids are half price. Bring your own binoculars; Good supplies a spotting scope. He also offers a two-hour wetland ecology tour ($40 adults, $20 kids).

Carriage Tours

To recapture the early carriage roads era, take one of the horse-drawn open-carriage tours run by **Carriages of Acadia** (Wildwood Stables, Park Loop Rd., Seal Harbor, 877/276-3622, www.carriagesofacadia.com), one mile south of the Jordan Pond House. Six one- and two-hour trips start at 9am daily mid-June-mid-October. Reservations are not required, but they're encouraged, especially in midsummer. The best outing is the two-hour **Day Mountain Summit** ($26 adults, $12 ages 6-12, $7 ages 2-5) ride at 4pm. The one-hour loop around Day Mountain is $20 for adults, $10 for children, and $6 for little kids.

You can also arrange for a private 1-4-hour carriage road tour. A one-hour trip is $180 for up to four passengers, plus $35 for each additional passenger; two hours is $240 plus $50; three hours is $360 plus $50; and four hours is $480 plus $50. Wildwood has no trail rides, but you can bring your own horse and stable it here ($25 per night for a box stall). A basic campground has sites ($15) for stall renters.

DRIVING TOURS

The ideal way to fully appreciate Acadia is to hike the miles of trails, bike the carriage roads, canoe the ponds, swim in Echo Lake, and camp overnight. It seems rather a shame to treat Acadia as a drive-through park, but circumstances—time, health, and other factors—sometimes dictate that.

★ Park Loop Road

Logically, a driving tour of Acadia would follow the 20-mile Park Loop Road (Apr. 15-Nov. 30, weather permitting). It begins at the Hulls Cove Visitors Center, winds past several of the park's scenic highlights (with parking areas), ascends via a 3.5-mile spur to the summit of Cadillac Mountain, and provides overlooks of magnificent vistas. Over the years, growing trees had obscured many of the vistas, but a new vista management plan is restoring them to their original design. Allow a couple of hours so you can stop along the way. You can rent an audio tour on cassette or CD ($13, including directions, an instruction sheet, and a map) at the Hulls Cove Visitors Center. Another option is to pick up the drive-it-yourself tour booklet, *Motorist Guide: Park Loop Road* ($4), available at the Thompson Island and Hulls Cove Visitors Centers.

Start at the parking lot below the Hulls Cove Visitors Center and follow the signs; part of the loop is one-way, so you'll be doing the loop clockwise. Traffic gets heavy at midday in the height of summer, so aim for an early-morning start if you can. The maximum speed is 35 mph, but be alert for gawkers and photographers stopping without warning and pedestrians dashing across the road from stopped cars or tour buses. If you're out at midday in summer, don't be surprised to see cars and RVs parked in the right lane in the one-way sections; it's allowed when the designated parking lots are filled, and drivers do it even when they aren't.

Along the route are trailheads and overlooks as well as **Sieur de Monts Spring,** home to the Acadia Nature Center, Wild Gardens of Acadia, Abbe Museum summer site, and the convergence of several spectacular hiking trails; **Sand Beach; Thunder Hole; Otter Cliffs; the Fabbri Picnic Area,** with one wheelchair-accessible picnic table; **Jordan Pond House; Bubble Pond; Eagle Lake;** and the summit of **Cadillac Mountain.** Just before you get to Sand Beach, you'll see the Park Entrance Station, where you'll need to purchase a pass if you haven't already done so. If you're here during nesting and fledging season—April-mid-August—be sure to stop in the Precipice Trail Parking Area to view the peregrine falcons with telescopes provided by park staff.

Island Tour

If you still have time for and interest in more driving after you've done the loop, take a spin around the rest of the island. Exit the Park Loop Road near Bar Harbor onto Route 233, heading west. Continue to Route 198 and turn left (south). After just over one mile, watch for a smallish sign for **Sargent Drive.** Only cars are allowed on this road—no RVs. Take Sargent Drive, skirting gorgeous **Somes Sound,** into Northeast Harbor.

Leave Northeast Harbor via Route 198 northbound, and drive until you reach the head of Somes Sound. Go left around the head of the sound to **Somesville,** a gem of a historic hamlet, then continue south on Route 102 to Southwest Harbor. If you have time, take the Route 102A loop, which offers a chance to see **Bass Harbor Head Light.** You'll want to walk from the parking lot to get the best view; one trail has you scampering down steps to the ledges and rocks below it, while the other is a paved drive to near the light's base. Otherwise, continue on Route 102 to Tremont, with a possible detour into Bernard for great lobster on the wharf, then go clockwise around to West Tremont, Seal Cove, Pretty Marsh, and back to Somesville. From here, you can go directly north to leave the island via Route 102/198, or go to Bar Harbor by heading east.

Park Loop Road and Carriage Roads

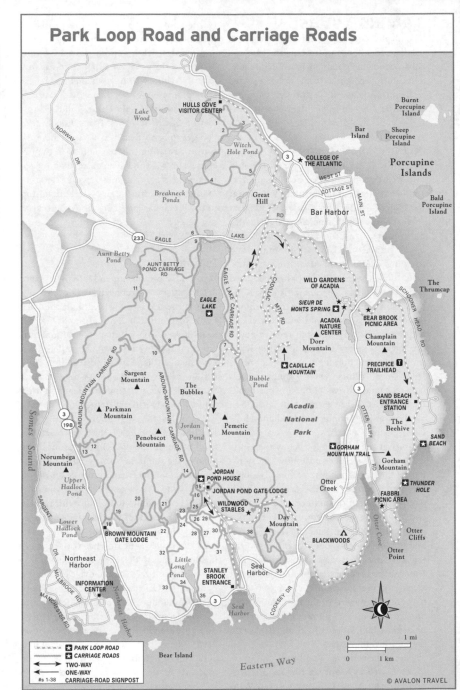

© AVALON TRAVEL

Peregrine Falcons

One of Acadia's great success stories is that of a seasonal mountain dweller, the peregrine falcon. DDT and other pollutants caused a decline in the number of falcons until the last breeding pair in Acadia was observed in 1956. Even before DDT, trappers, hunters, and nest robbers depleted peregrines. The peregrine was listed as a federal endangered species in the early 1970s and was removed from that list in 1999; it remains an endangered species in Maine.

In 1984, biologists reintroduced the falcons to Acadia, and in 1991, a breeding pair settled on the east-facing cliffs of Champlain Mountain and produced young. By 2014, more than 120 chicks had fledged from Acadia, including nesting sites on Jordan Cliffs, Valley Cove cliffs on Somes Sound, the Beech Cliffs above Echo Lake, and on privately owned Ironbound Island, where the park has a conservation easement.

Peregrines nest between late March and early August. Their nests, or scrapes, are shallow ledges on cliff sides, which provide them with an unimpeded view of potential prey (other birds) below. Their high-speed pursuits of prey—they can reach speeds of more than 200 mph—thrill those who are lucky enough to witness them.

Park staff usually is stationed at the **Precipice Trail Parking Area** (9am-noon Mon.-Thurs. spring-summer, weather permitting) with spotting scopes to help anyone who stops by view the peregrines and their scrapes and to provide information about their habits. Check the park's event schedule for the latest information.

During breeding and fledging season (Apr.-mid-Aug.), the trailhead for the Precipice Trail is gated, with an informational sign explaining the history and status of peregrines in the park. Other trails may be closed for the same reason; check at the Hulls Cove Visitors Center.

ACADIA QUEST

Acadia Quest (207/288-3340, www.friend-sofacadia.org) is terrific way for families to explore the park. The free, annual scavenger hunt encourages participants to collect experiences in Acadia. Teams must include at least one adult older than 18 and one child younger than 18. To complete the quest, teams undertake and document activities in a variety of categories; the theme and specifics change each year. Doing so immerses you in the park, engaging all in fun and in some cases educational activities. The quest runs from late spring until early November, but is designed so that it can be completed in a one-week vacation. Children who successfully complete the hunt earn a Quest patch, but here's the big prize: The team earns an Acadia pass valid for the following year and is also entered into a grand prize drawing. Register either by phone or online to receive a Quest package including permission slip, park map, program details, and a Quest card.

The Car-Free Park

Since 1999, when the fare-free, propane-fueled buses began running throughout Mount Desert Island, more than five million riders have used the **Island Explorer** bus system, reducing car and RV usage and their resultant pollutants and greenhouse gases. The Island Explorer transports passengers to ferry landings, saves hikers and bikers from backtracking, gets commuters to work, and has revolutionized the summertime traffic patterns on Mount Desert Island.

Since the service began on an experimental basis, it has been dramatically expanded, in great part thanks to the backing of L.L.Bean. Service now begins in late June and lasts until Columbus Day—the Schoodic Peninsula route, which coordinates with the Bar Harbor-Winter Harbor ferry, continues through August; the Ellsworth Express operates once a day in each direction through early September.

Why spend valuable vacation time looking for a place to park your car? Why be disappointed when you reach a hiking trailhead and find the parking lot full? Take the bus. Feeling unsteady and unable to hike or bike? Tour the park and the island on the bus. Each bus can handle up to six bikes and a wheelchair, and there are even dedicated bike shuttles operating between the Bar Harbor downtown hub and Eagle Lake.

The nonprofit **Downeast Transportation** (207/667-5796, www.exploreacadia.com) operates the fleet, with support from your park entrance fees, Friends of Acadia, L.L.Bean, and area towns and businesses.

Two caveats: First, these aren't tour buses, and there is no narration, nor do they climb Cadillac Mountain, so don't use them as a substitute for a guided tour or as a way to see all park highlights. Second, although the buses are free, riders traveling into the park must have a park pass.

The Island Explorer hub is the Bar Harbor Village Green, where all of the routes (except Schoodic) begin or end. Late June-Labor Day, service begins at 6:45am daily, although not every route starts that early. The last bus leaves downtown Bar Harbor about 10pm for the campgrounds at the northern end of the island. A geolocation system provides tracking information at the Village Green, at the Hulls Cove Visitors Center, and online.

Specific stops are listed on the schedule, but drivers will pull over and pick you up or drop you off anywhere they feel it's safe. Don't hesitate to request a stop or flag down a bus.

So pick up a schedule—copies are everywhere on Mount Desert—and use the Island Explorer to explore the island.

Sights

The **Park Loop Road** will lead you to the major sights on the east side of the park—Sieur de Monts Spring, Sand Beach, Thunder Hole, Otter Cliffs, and the summit of Cadillac Mountain—but there's also the fantastic carriage-road system. As you explore the rest of the park acreage on Mount Desert, particularly its west side, you'll come upon still more surprising spots.

★ SIEUR DE MONTS SPRING

About two miles from Bar Harbor and close to the often-busy Park Loop Road, Sieur de Monts Spring is an oasis in a tranquil woodland setting. Named after 17th-century French explorer Pierre Dugas, Sieur de Monts, the spring is the centerpiece of a 10-acre parcel donated in 1916 for a future national park by George Bucknam Dorr, known as the father of Acadia. It was Dorr who erected the pretty Italianate Spring House and dubbed this "The Sweet Waters of Acadia"—after the Sweet Waters of Europe and the Sweet Waters of Asia, two springs that had deeply impressed him on a visit to Constantinople. (The water here, incidentally, is not safe to

the original Abbe Museum at Sieur de Monts Spring

now supported by the park and the Friends of Acadia and maintained by volunteers as well as a park-sponsored college student during the summer months.

An important feature of this lovely area is the privately run **Abbe Museum** (207/288-3519, www.abbemuseum.org, 10am-5pm daily late May-mid-Oct., $3 adults, $1 ages 11-17), the original home of Dr. Robert Abbe's extensive personal collection of prehistoric and historical archaeological artifacts, some dating back 11,000 years. Opened in 1928, the museum outgrew this building, which is on the National Register of Historic Places, and now has a handsome year-round home in downtown Bar Harbor. Inside are exhibits on Maine archaeology and the history of the museum. Tickets purchased here can be applied toward admission to the main campus of the museum in Bar Harbor.

The Sieur de Monts Spring area provides access to several Acadia hiking trails. Moderate to strenuous trails, many with granite stairs, ascend **Dorr Mountain** (originally Dry Mountain, then Flying Squadron Mountain). The easy **Jesup Path**—just over a mile between Park Loop Road and The Tarn and partially wheelchair accessible—is a delightful stroll. In spring, the boardwalk area of the path is a birder's feast. The path in its entirety is particularly spectacular during the fall foliage season. You can also access the Tarn and Hemlock Trails at Sieur de Monts.

Sieur de Monts Spring is on the Island Explorer bus Route 3/Sand Beach and Route 4/Blackwoods.

★ SAND BEACH

Below the Park Loop Road and the Park Entrance Station, Sand Beach is the park's only large sandy beach on saltwater—*cold* saltwater (about 55°F). Well, it's not really sand, as a sign posted here will tell you—it's composed of zillions of crushed shells, pulverized so they look like sand. If you haven't purchased your park entrance pass by this point, you'll need to do it here. Sand Beach is about

drink—nor, for that matter, is the water in those Istanbul springs.)

Also here is the **Acadia Nature Center** (9am-5pm daily June-Aug., 9am-4pm daily Sept.-early Oct., free), containing hands-on exhibits on flora and fauna and explanations of the ongoing efforts to preserve the park's natural resources.

While at the nature center, take time to walk through the adjacent **Wild Gardens of Acadia** (9am-5pm daily July-Aug., shorter hours mid-May-June and Sept.-Oct., donation appreciated), touted as "an outdoor field guide" to the island's plant life. George B. Dorr acquired and named the land in 1909, and in 1961 then-park superintendent Harold Hubler proposed the wildflower garden. The Bar Harbor Garden Club initially sponsored it, and the book *Wild Flowers of Mount Desert Island*, published in 1918, was used to determine the plantings. Walking paths lace the gardens, which are divided into a dozen different habitats containing more than 400 indigenous wildflower species. It's

Acadia Facts

- Acadia National Park was **established by Congress in 1929,** after previous incarnations as Lafayette National Park (1919) and Sieur de Monts National Monument (1916).

- Acadia covers nearly **50,000 acres** on the mainland and islands, including more than 14,000 acres protected by conservation easements. Acadia's permanent boundaries were established by Congress in 1986, but it is allowed to acquire offshore easements between from the Penobscot Bay shipping channel east throughout Hancock County and mainland easements on the Schoodic Peninsula. No other U.S. national park has as large an easement program in terms of percentage of total acreage.

- Acadia has **26 mountains** ranging in height from 284 feet (Flying Mountain) to 1,530 feet (Cadillac Mountain). Cadillac is the highest point on the eastern seaboard of the United States.

- Nine **"great ponds"** (covering more than 10 acres) lie within the park boundaries. Five others abut parkland. The depths of these lakes and ponds range from 7 feet (Aunt Betty Pond) to 150 feet (Jordan Pond). Mount Desert Island's lakes and ponds have restrictions on swimming and personal and motorized watercraft.

- Acadia has more than 130 miles of **hiking trails.** At the height (so to speak) of trail construction, in the early 20th century, there were some 230 miles. Some of the discontinued trails are being rehabilitated via the Acadia Trails Forever program, a joint project of the park and Friends of Acadia.

- Acadia officials estimate an average of more than **2.5 million park visits** each year, most in the months of July, August, and September.

- The **"creature counts"** in Acadia, on Mount Desert Island, and in the surrounding waters include 338 species of birds, 17 species of amphibians, 5 reptile species, 28 species of fish, 47 species of terrestrial mammals, and 12 species of marine mammals.

- The **Park Loop Road** is 20 miles, with an additional 3.5-mile spur to the visitors center, 1 mile spur to Jordan Pond House, and 7 miles for a round-trip to the summit of Cadillac Mountain.

- The park has 45 miles of car-free, broken-stone **carriage roads** for walking, biking, and horseback riding as well as cross-country skiing and snowshoeing in winter; 12 miles of privately owned carriage roads south of Jordan Pond are usable by walkers and horses but not bicycles.

- Acadia has three **campgrounds**—two on Mount Desert Island, one on Isle au Haut. Only one, Blackwoods, is open all year. Backcountry camping is not allowed in Acadia. Commercial campgrounds are located on Mount Desert Island beyond park boundaries.

- The Schoodic Peninsula is the only park acreage that's on the mainland; all other park properties are on **islands.** A bridge connects Mount Desert Island to the mainland town of Trenton, but other parcels must be reached by boat.

25 minutes from Bar Harbor via the Island Explorer bus (Route 3/Sand Beach). It's a bit quicker by car before and after the bus season. You can access the **Great Head Trail** and **Ocean Path** from here.

★ THUNDER HOLE

Thunder Hole gets pumped up as a spectacular attraction, and it is—but only if your timing is right. If not, as one ranger snickered, it's more of a gurgling gulch. When the wind is coming from the south or southeast, when a storm has churned up the sea, or when the tide is rushing inward, you'll hear and feel

Sand Beach

with a trail and stairway on the ocean side. Descend the stairs to a cobble beach, where the incoming tide rumbles as it rolls over the smooth, rounded stones. The stairway parallels a cascading stream that disappears into the beach only to resurface a few feet below. Cliffs fringed with spruce trees frame the beach. A trail near the top of the stairway leads out to a point, where views of the surf are especially fine when the tide is surging. Be careful on the path, as erosion has taken its toll, and resist the urge to remove any rocks from the beach area. Not only is it against park rules, but it also threatens the beach's continued existence.

★ JORDAN POND HOUSE

The only restaurant within the park is the **Jordan Pond House** (Park Loop Rd., 207/276-3316, www.acadiajordanpondhouse.com, 11:30am-8pm daily mid-May-late June and late Aug.-late Oct., 11:30am-9pm daily late June-late Aug.), a modern facility in a spectacular waterside setting. Jordan Pond House began life as a rustic 19th-century teahouse; wonderful old photos still line the walls of its current incarnation, built after a disastrous fire in 1979. Afternoon tea is still a tradition, with tea, popovers, and extraordinary strawberry jam served on the lawn until 5:30pm daily in summer, weather permitting. It is not exactly a bargain at around $12, but it's worth it. Jordan Pond is far from a secret, however, so expect to wait for seats at the height of summer. Better yet, plan ahead and make reservations. Jordan Pond House is on Route 5 of the Island Explorer bus.

A health note: Perhaps because of all the sweet drinks and jam served outdoors, patrons at the lawn tables sometimes find themselves pestered by bees. They don't usually sting unless you pester them back, but be alert if anyone in your party is allergic to bee stings.

how Thunder Hole got its name. As the water rushes into a narrow slot in the rocks, it creates a powerful roar, shoots into the air, and often showers the closest bystanders.

If your schedule is flexible, check the tide tables in the local paper and try to be here for the incoming tide, preferably about mid-tide.

Because of the sea spray, the steps leading down toward Thunder Hole are often very slippery. Take particular care with small children and anyone who tends to be unsteady. Stay well back from the shoreline when the surf is rough. People have been swept away by rogue waves, and rescue is extremely difficult.

The park operates an information station (9am-5pm daily May-late Oct.) at Thunder Hole.

LITTLE HUNTERS BEACH

Sh, don't tell too many people about this small treasure, just before Hunters Head on the Park Loop Road. It is unsigned but is designated on the park map. Watch for a stream crossing

★ CADILLAC MOUNTAIN

As the highest point in Acadia, at 1,530 feet, the summit of Cadillac Mountain receives the day's first rays of sunlight. A couple of trails will get you to the summit, including one from Blackwoods Campground, and you can get a good road- or mountain-bike workout on the road (bikes aren't allowed on trails), but in the end, most summiteers tend to get there by car—a seven-mile round-trip on a paved road. The Island Explorer bus does not go to the Cadillac Mountain summit.

Formerly named Green Mountain, Cadillac was once topped by the wooden Summit Hotel, built by an ambitious developer who eventually fell on hard times and went bankrupt. Some might say he deserved it for blighting the landscape. Before its decline in the late 19th century, however, the 6,000-foot Green Mountain Cog Railway transported guests to the summit, where the view was just as spectacular as it is today. (Photos of the cog railway era are part of the collection at the Bar Harbor Historical Society on Ledgelawn Street.) The summit road was built in 1931.

At the height of summer, the busiest times on the summit are sunrise, midday, and sunset; if you don't have your heart set on seeing the sunrise or sunset, the crowds are thinner an hour or two after sunrise or an hour or two before sunset. The best sunset views aren't from the summit, but from the Blue Hill pullout, with parking, and from some of the small pullouts as you descend the road. Go early to snag a parking space.

At the top are head-swiveling vistas along with a gift shop and restrooms. Be sure to walk the paved 0.3-mile Summit Trail loop for the full effect, but stay on the trail to preserve the summit's fragile plants and soil.

The park runs the **Hawkwatch** program (9am-2pm Mon.-Fri. late Aug.-mid-Oct., weather permitting) near the Cadillac summit. The observation site is on the Cadillac North Ridge Trail, about 600 feet from the summit parking lot. Park interpreters are on hand to help you identify the various species of hawks, falcons, eagles, and ospreys that migrate through Acadia each fall. Since the Hawkwatch project began in 1995, the annual raptor count during the migration season has averaged about 2,500, but 2007 witnessed a record-breaking 3,697.

★ CARRIAGE ROADS

Bare summits, woodlands, gem-like ponds, 17 handsome stone bridges, and dazzling vistas—you'll see them all as you walk or bike the fantastic 57-mile carriage road network that makes Acadia unique among the nation's national parks.

Most folks head to Cadillac's summit for sunrise, but sunset is equally alluring.

Mr. Rockefeller's Roads

Between 1913 and 1940, petroleum heir John D. Rockefeller Jr. was involved in the purchase of acreage and the design and construction of more than 57 miles of carriage roads on Mount Desert Island. Today, thanks to him, we can all walk and bike these roadways, and even go for our own horse-drawn carriage rides. Forty-five miles of these roads are now within Acadia National Park boundaries and 12 are on private land but open to the public. Not only did Rockefeller conceptualize the project, finance it, and consult on every aspect of the road and bridge designs, he was on hand during the construction and landscaping phases. No detail escaped his scrutiny.

The carriage road system is one of Acadia's most valued cultural resources—listed since 1979 on the National Register of Historic Places. Distinctive features of the roads are 17 handsome rough-stone bridges (with single, double, and triple arches; no two are alike), 16-foot-wide broken-stone roadbeds that required countless hours of labor, and tasteful carved trail markers. A holdover from Rockefeller's previous carriage road experience was the use of roadside borders of squared-off granite coping stones—known at Acadia as "Mr. Rockefeller's teeth."

And then there are the two stone gate lodges or gatehouses—Brown Mountain Gate Lodge (near Northeast Harbor) and Jordan Pond Gate Lodge (near Jordan Pond)—heralding entrances to the original carriage road system (many more access points exist today). Designed by Grosvenor Atterbury in a whimsical French Romanesque style, the handsome structures are startling, to say the least. It's hard not to smile when you come upon them. During the carriage road building, engineer Paul Simpson and his family occupied the Jordan Pond Gate Lodge.

Until his death in 1960, when Acadia National Park assumed responsibility for 45 miles of the carriage road system, John D. Rockefeller Jr. continued his magnanimity by financing the maintenance of the carriage road network. By the early 1990s, however, the roads, bridges, and drainage systems had seriously deteriorated, and the fabulous vistas had become overgrown. Enter Friends of Acadia (FOA), an amazing nonprofit organization that helped the park obtain federal funding and then maximized the grant with matching private funds—generating enough to cover the $6 million face-lift and begin a carriage road endowment. Annual contributions from FOA and a portion of park user fees fund maintenance. In addition, volunteers log countless hours.

Mr. Rockefeller's Roads: The Untold Story of Acadia's Carriage Roads & Their Creator, written by Rockefeller's granddaughter, Ann R. Roberts, tells the story of Acadia's car-free carriage roads and relates a fascinating saga of benevolence, sensitivity, talent, and organization.

Forty-five miles of the broken-stone roads—all on the east side of the island, between the Hulls Cove Visitors Center in the north and Seal Harbor in the south—are open for walking, bicycling, and horseback riding, and in winter for cross-country skiing and snowshoeing. Twelve additional miles of roads on private land owned by the Green Rock Company are open for walking and horseback riding but not cycling—be alert for the No Bikes signs when you're cycling; all of the private roads are south of the Jordan Pond House.

★ EAGLE LAKE

The largest lake on the eastern half of the island, Eagle Lake is entirely within the park, so its shoreline is undeveloped. Cadillac, Pemetic, and Sargent Mountains and the Bubbles surround it. You can pedal or walk around Eagle Lake on a carriage road, launch a canoe or kayak and paddle its waters, or just find a rock to sit on and enjoy the scenery. You might spot ospreys, eagles, great blue herons, loons, and other wildlife. Two parking lots off Route 233 make access easy—one is by the boat launch, and a larger one is on the other side of the road—but during peak season, these are often filled. Consider taking the Island Explorer bus, which offers a Bicycle Express route between Bar Harbor's Village Green and Eagle Lake.

SEAWALL

The remote Seawall section of the park, on the island's west side, is not heavily visited. Two easy shore walks are great for kids, and a picnic area is a fine place to watch waves crash on the rugged pink granite shoreline. The best time to visit, however, is at night: It's one of the best places in the country for stargazing.

BASS HARBOR HEAD LIGHT

At the southern end of Mount Desert's western "claw," follow Route 102A to the turnoff toward Bass Harbor Head. Drive or bike to the end of Lighthouse Road, walk down a steep wooden stairway, and look up and to the right. Voilà! For the best views, scramble carefully to the lower rocks. Bass Harbor Head Light, its red glow automated since 1974, stands sentinel at the eastern entrance to Blue Hill Bay. A paved path with interpretive signage starts from the other end of the parking lot and leads to near the tower's base. Built in 1858, the 26-foot tower and light keeper's house are privately owned, but the dramatic setting is a photographer's dream. Winter access to the parking lot may be limited, but otherwise the area is open year-round. Not far from the light (east along Rte. 102A) are the trailheads for the easy Ship Harbor and Wonderland Nature Trails, part of Acadia National Park. The lighthouse is a short walk from Route 102A, on the Island Explorer bus Route 7/ Southwest Harbor.

BASS HARBOR MARSH

The Marshal Brook fire road, off the Seal Cove Road in Southwest Harbor, provides the best access to the marsh for bird-watching.

PRETTY MARSH PICNIC AREA

Picnic spots are everywhere on Mount Desert, but an Acadia National Park site that many people miss is the Pretty Marsh Picnic Area, overlooking Pretty Marsh Harbor, on the opposite side of the island from Bar Harbor. Dense woods shelter grills and tables, and you can walk down to the shoreline and even launch a sea kayak. Kids love this place, but come prepared with insect repellent. The picnic area is just west of Route 102 (Pretty Marsh Rd.) on the westernmost shore. Pretty Marsh is not on an Island Explorer bus route; you'll need a car or bike to get here.

Experience Acadia's carriage roads on a horse-drawn carriage ride up Day Mountain.

ISLESFORD HISTORICAL MUSEUM

Orphaned from the main sections of the park, the **Islesford Historical Museum** (207/288-3338, www.nps.gov/acad, free), on Little Cranberry Island and operated by the National Park Service since 1948, displays collections pertinent to the island's history and heritage. Accessing the island requires taking one of the passenger ferries, excursion boats, or private boats that depart from Southwest Harbor or Northeast Harbor. The best choice is the ranger-narrated Isleford Historic and Scenic Cruise aboard the *Sea Princess,* departing from Northeast Harbor (207/276-5352, www.barharborcruises.com, $28 adults, $18 ages 5-11, $7 age 5 and younger).

BAKER ISLAND

The best way to get to—and to appreciate— history-rich Baker Island is on the ranger-narrated Baker Island Acadia National Park Tour aboard the *Miss Samantha,* booked through **Bar Harbor Whale Watch Co.** (1 West St., Bar Harbor, 207/288-2386 or 888/942-5374, www.barharborwhales.com, mid-June-mid-Sept., $46 adults, $27 ages 6-14, $5 under age 6). The half-day tours include access via motorized skiff to the 130-acre island, which has a farmstead, a lighthouse, and intriguing rock formations. The return trip provides a view of Otter Cliffs from the water (bring binoculars and look for climbers), Thunder Hole, Sand Beach, and Great Head. Call or check the website for departure times.

History buffs, lighthouse lovers, and naturalists will love this trip. Hannah and William Gilley, who rowed here from Mount Desert Island accompanied by their three young children, goats, and household goods, settled Baker Island in the early 1800s. They built a home and a farm and reared 12 children, with Hannah schooling them in the three R's and rowing them to church in Southwest Harbor every Sunday. When the lighthouse was built on the island in 1828, William became its first keeper, at an annual salary of $350. He was removed from that post in 1848 for political reasons, and that's where the story gets really interesting.

Note that because the National Park Service contracts with an independent boat company, there have been years when this tour hasn't been available. In that case, the only way to reach Baker Island is via charter or your own boat. In any case, pack a lunch. Check the park's ranger program schedule or a visitors center for tour status.

Hiking

It would take weeks of nonstop all-day hiking to cover every trail in the Mount Desert Island acreage of Acadia National Park, and it would consume most of this book to write about them. It's not a bad idea, but few of us have enough free time to manage such a feat. It's best to do as much as you can when you're here, and return as often as possible to do more.

This section contains a selection of choice hikes, ranging from very easy to strenuous. Evaluate your schedule and your skills and limitations (especially the capabilities of your least-sturdy hiking partners), gather your gear, pack a picnic and plenty of water, and head out.

As you take your first step on your first trail, however, keep in mind the Leave No Trace philosophy that governs all recreation in the park. Stick to it for yourself and for the generations to come.

Until the establishment of the Island Explorer bus system, hikers had to do loop trails in order to return to their cars or bikes, or they had to make elaborate arrangements for pickup or shuttling. The bus schedule has created all kinds of other options. It allows you to skip the backtracking—and in some cases lets you pick up transport along the way if you or the kids wear out earlier than expected. This holds true only during the bus season (late June-early Oct., reduced schedule early Sept.-early Oct.). Even if your destination or locale isn't a scheduled bus stop, you can request a stop or flag down a bus anywhere that's safe for the driver to pull over. Pick up the latest schedule at the Hulls Cove Visitors Center or download it before you leave home at www.exploreacadia.com.

The hikes are divided here into two sections—the east side of Mount Desert Island and the west side. Because Somes Sound nearly bisects the island, none of the trails cross from one side of the island to the other, and almost every one of the peaks' ridgelines runs north-south. The hikes are listed in order of difficulty, from very easy to strenuous; trail lengths vary within each category. Ratings are based on park advisories and personal experience.

Bear in mind that most visitors tend to spend more time on the east side of the island, for a variety of reasons—there are more trails, a range of easy-to-moderate trails, the carriage road network, the auto road to the Cadillac Mountain summit, the Park Loop Road, the park's only restaurant (Jordan Pond House), and so on. Heading for the west-side trails, even at the height of summer, can provide quieter spaces and some truly great hikes.

A number of commercial maps are available. I like the *Acadia National Park Hiking and Biking Trail Map* ($5), published by Map Adventures (www.mapadventures.com), because it's easy to read. The only drawback is that it doesn't include the entire island, making it a bit difficult to figure out locations if you're not familiar with the area. There's also a waterproof version ($10). Another good choice is the waterproof *Appalachian Mountain Club Acadia National Park Discovery Map* ($9.95), a GPS topographic map that includes all of Mount Desert Island and has insets for Isle au Haut and the Schoodic Peninsula.

Note: The park is in the process of changing trail names to their historical ones, which can make for some confusion when hiking. Park rangers will have the latest information.

EAST-SIDE TRAILS
Jordan Pond Nature Trail
Distance: 1-mile loop
Duration: 30-45 minutes
Elevation gain: Minimal
Effort: Very easy

Acadia's trails are clearly marked.

Trailhead: Jordan Pond Parking Area (Island Explorer Route 5/Jordan Pond)

This oh-so-easy trail is perfect for little ones. You can pick up a brochure ($0.50 donation) at the trailhead detailing 10 numbered sites, so you can pepper the walk with fun info and quiz the kids along the way. Reward them afterward with ice cream at the Jordan Pond House.

The trail loops from the Jordan Pond overflow/hikers parking lot through the woods and down to the pond, following the shore for a bit before looping back to the starting point.

Ocean Path

Distance: 4.4 miles round-trip
Duration: 1.5-2 hours
Elevation gain: Level
Effort: Very easy
Trailhead: Take the Park Loop Road to either the Sand Beach or the Otter Point parking lots. The Island Explorer bus (Route 3/Sand Beach) stops at Sand Beach and Otter Cliffs Parking Areas, so you can begin the walk at either end. If you want to do the trail in one direction only rather than backtracking, get off the bus at one end or the other, then pick up another bus when you're ready to continue onward.

Because this trail is so easy and easy to reach, it's extremely popular. In fact, lovely as it is, you'd have to be crazy to be on it 10am-3pm at the height of summer. At the risk of divulging the solution, the last time I walked it, at 7am on a bright June day, I had the path all to myself—a minor miracle, actually—and the tide was at just the right height for Thunder Hole to live up to its name.

The trail runs close to the shore for about half its length and takes in several of the Park Loop Road's highlights—Sand Beach, Thunder Hole, Otter Cliffs, and the giant sea stack in Monument Cove—not to mention gorgeous sea-level views of Frenchman Bay.

Along here, it's especially tempting to "liberate" rocks from the shore, but resist the urge. Remember the slogan, "Leave the rocks for the next glacier." If you forget, a few judiciously placed National Park Service signs will remind you.

Compass Harbor

Distance: 1 mile round-trip
Duration: 30 minutes
Elevation gain: Level
Effort: Very easy
Trailhead: Compass Harbor section of the park, off Bar Harbor's Main Street approximately one mile south of the intersection with Mount Desert Street

This is an easy stroll through an often-ignored section of the park. You can easily walk from downtown, if you want to lengthen the hike without adding any difficulty. The path loops through old-growth forest to a point on Compass Harbor and by the ruins of George B. Dorr's summer cottage. There are plenty of nice spots for a picnic here, and at low tide you might even brave a swim from the pebbly beach area. The loop at Compass Harbor also connects to the Schooner Head trail into the main section of the park.

Great Head Trail

Distance: 1.7-mile loop
Duration: 1 hour
Elevation gain: 145 feet
Effort: Moderate
Trailhead: Take the Park Loop Road to the Sand Beach Parking Area (Island Explorer Route 3/Sand Beach)—the lower parking area is closer to the beach, but it fills up first. Walk down the steps to the beach and across it to the far (eastern) side, where you'll see the trailhead marker. You'll need to cross a rivulet here to reach the trailhead. If you're not here at low tide and you don't have waterproof shoes, remove your shoes so you won't be hiking with wet feet.

First take the trail to the right, which climbs a few dozen steps (the "moderate" part), then continue right toward the headland ("head"), from which you can see the beach and the prominent mound of the Beehive. Out in Frenchman Bay is Egg Rock Light and beyond it is Schoodic Point. Continue on the trail counterclockwise, following the perimeter of the head, perhaps pausing for a picnic near the ruins of a stone teahouse, constructed in 1915. Continue the loop around the head, then return back to Sand Beach.

Tips for Day Hiking

Since Acadia has no backcountry camping, all the hikes in the park are day hikes—guaranteeing, at least, a load off your back. You need little gear for a daylong hike, but use common sense and be prepared for emergencies. Even for experienced hikers and backcountry campers, it's worth noting the "maps and guides" information specific to Acadia.

In general, the gear you carry (and the size of your day pack) depends on your plans for the day—following a short nature trail and then calling it quits; hiking for a few hours and then stopping for a swim; or hiking all day with a noontime picnic. Here's a checklist to help you get organized:

- **Identification,** such as a driver's license. Even if you don't carry your regular wallet, be sure you have your health insurance card.

- **Maps and guides.** Purchase a trail map at the park's visitors center. The National Park Service map of Acadia that's available free at the visitors center will give you the lay of the land and useful general info, and it's serviceable if you're planning only to drive or bike the Park Loop Road, but do not rely on it for hiking. On the east side of the island, even if you are planning to stick to the hiking trails, be sure also to carry a map of the park's carriage roads to avoid confusion where carriage and hiking trails meet and cross. For trail guides, I recommend *A Walk in the Park* ($12) by Tom St. Germain and *Hiking Acadia National Park* ($17) by Dolores Kong and Dan Ring. Both provide useful detailed maps and elevations for each hike. Also valuable is the Appalachian Mountain Club's *Discover Acadia National Park* ($17) by Jerry and Marcy Monkman, which comes with a foldout map (contour interval 100 feet). Besides hikes, the Appalachian Mountain Club guide includes information on bike and paddling routes as well as other recreational activities in the park.

- Between late June and Columbus Day, carry a copy of the **Island Explorer bus schedule,** which you can find almost anywhere on the island or download before you leave home (www.exploreacadia.com). Stuff it in your day pack, even if you're getting to your trailhead by car. If someone in your hiking party wants to quit early, you'll want to know the nearest spot (and time) to catch a bus.

- **Water and food.** Even though some ponds in the park are used as drinking-water sources for surrounding towns, it's treated before they get it. Don't risk intestinal problems; carry your own water. If you're worried about carrying weight, and can tolerate the taste, include iodine tablets. To avoid excessive thirst, don't bring salty snacks—carry gorp or energy bars (without chocolate, so you don't have to deal with a melting mush). If you're carrying picnic fare, don't be overambitious or greedy if you're planning a strenuous hike. Be sure to pack any mayo-based food in a flexible insulated bag; peanut butter and jam (jelly for the kids) sandwiches are a safer bet.

- A couple of wastebasket-size **trash bags**—carry in, carry out. A spare bag can also come in handy for protecting maps, a camera, and binoculars in the event of a sudden squall (not unheard of during a Maine summer).

You can reach Sand Beach (and therefore the Great Head Trail) via the Island Explorer bus, but since the Park Loop Road is one-way at this point, you won't be able to return to Bar Harbor the way you came. You'll need to grab a bus and continue the loop back to Bar Harbor, but the time is the same: 25 minutes from Bar Harbor to Sand Beach, 25 minutes back to the Village Green from Sand Beach.

If you're staying in Bar Harbor, consider bicycling to the trail via the relatively quiet Schooner Head Road, off Route 3 just south of town.

Option: Another easier way to hike Great Head is to begin on the north side of the head and go in a clockwise direction. Take Main Street (Rte. 3) south out of Bar Harbor, and about 0.8 mile after the athletic field, bear

- A **compass or GPS receiver,** particularly if you're directionally challenged or are planning a lengthy hike. If you own a cell phone, carry it, but turn it off and use it only in an emergency. Wireless service can be iffy in some parts of Acadia; check when you arrive.

- A small **first-aid kit** (in a waterproof or ziplock bag) containing a few basic items: adhesive bandages, aspirin or acetaminophen, ibuprofen, perhaps an elastic bandage. Even though bees don't tend to be a problem in Acadia (except perhaps on the lawn at Jordan Pond House), be sure you're carrying a prefilled epinephrine syringe to prevent anaphylaxis if you're allergic to bee stings (or, for that matter, shellfish). Include a few wooden matches and a whistle in case of emergency.

- **Moist towelettes** for various cleanup tasks, or for cleansing minor scrapes.

- A **Swiss Army knife.** Carry the kind with a corkscrew if you're planning on having wine with a picnic. Or you could decant white wine into a plastic water bottle to save weight—but go easy on the alcohol. Not only will it dehydrate you, but also you're more prone to tripping and falling.

- A full-brimmed **hat** and decent **hiking shoes** (not sandals, which provide no ankle support).

- **Sunblock, lip balm** (the kind with UV protection), and **insect repellent.** Lewey's, a natural repellent, is a good choice, especially for children. Ben's and Cutter's tend to be widely available.

- A **camera** (with a spare battery and memory card) and **binoculars.** Most of the island's summits are bare, allowing fabulous views.

- A **mini flashlight** and spare batteries.

- **Clothing.** Depending on your plans for the day, carry a change of socks, a rain jacket or windbreaker, maybe a fleece vest, and perhaps a swimsuit for a hike such as Penobscot and Sargent Mountains, where you can pause for a swim in Sargent Pond.

- Most importantly, **don't hike alone,** or if you do, tell someone—a friend, a relative, your lodging manager, a campground ranger, your shrink, anyone—or leave a note to say where you are headed. If for any reason you don't return, the park rangers at least will know where to start looking.

- Remember, **bikes are banned** from all hiking trails. **Dogs must be leashed** (not always convenient on strenuous scrambles), and they are banned from Sand Beach and hiking trails with ladders ("ladder trails"). Best advice: Don't bring a dog. If you do, hike only the shorter, easier trails—and do come equipped to clean up after your pet.

- Lyme disease has been reported here, so when you return, **check for ticks.**

left onto Schooner Head Road, which roughly parallels the Park Loop Road. Continue just beyond the turn for the Schooner Head Overlook, park at the dead end, and begin your hike from this end of Great Head. There are actually two loops, which could end up taking you 1.8-2 miles. Keep bearing left (clockwise) to skirt the perimeter of Great Head.

Jordan Pond Shore Path

Distance: 3.2-mile loop

Duration: 1 hour minimum

Elevation gain: Level

Effort: Easy to moderate

Trailhead: Jordan Pond. By car from Bar Harbor, take the Park Loop Road (the two-way west side of the loop) to the Jordan Pond parking lot, or take Island Explorer bus Route 4/Loop Road or Route 5/Jordan

Pond. In midsummer, another auto option is to take Route 3 south from Bar Harbor to Seal Harbor, then take the Stanley Brook entrance to the park, going north toward Jordan Pond. Park and head toward the boat-launching ramp; you'll see the trailhead to the right.

This mostly level, counterclockwise circuit of Jordan Pond is a great way to walk off a Jordan Pond House lunch (including those popovers). Or do the hike first and reward yourself with afternoon tea. Start on the east side, the easiest; the west side has the only moderate section—rocky and rooty and, depending on recent weather, possibly a bit squishy. Log bridges have been installed in a number of spots.

Jordan Pond is part of the island's drinking-water supply, so no swimming (or even wading) is permitted here.

As if the summer setting here weren't enough, this trail is even more beautiful in the fall, when stands of birches add gold to the palette. Plus, the trail is far less crowded in late September-early October (except perhaps for Columbus Day weekend).

Option: The giant glacial erratic known as **Bubble Rock** is enough of a phenomenon that you may want to detour from the shore trail to see it via the Bubbles Divide Trail, at the northeast corner of the pond. It's a 1-mile round-trip, up and back on the trail. At the risk of perpetuating a cliché, I'll add that the classic photo here is a Sisyphus imitation—the mythological fellow relentlessly pushing the boulder up a mountain, only to have it roll back. Fortunately, this one doesn't move, since it's the size of an SUV. There must be thousands of photo albums all over the world containing this image. Needless to say, kids love it. (For an easier hike, use the Bubble Rock trailhead off the Park Loop Road.)

In the summer of 2003, trail areas around Jordan Pond House and Jordan Pond were upgraded for wheelchair access, part of a major public-private collaborative effort to increase accessibility in the park. The improved access is on the east side of Jordan Pond.

One reward for hiking South Bubble is the opportunity to snap this classic shot.

South Bubble Trail

Distance: 1 mile round-trip
Duration: 1 hour
Elevation gain: 250 feet
Effort: Easy to moderate
Trailhead: Bubble Parking Area on the Park Loop Road, approximately 2.3 miles south of the Cadillac Mountain turnoff.

This relatively easy ascent of South Bubble rewards hikers with views from its scoured granite summit over Jordan Pond and beyond to the Cranberry Isles to the south, Pemetic Mountain to the west, and over Eagle Lake toward Cadillac Mountain to the north. From the parking lot, follow the Bubbles Divide Trail, passing the Jordan Pond Carry trail and the junction with the North Bubble Trail, and then turning left onto the South Bubble Trail. From the summit, follow a path to the left to find Bubble Rock, a glacial erratic that appears ready to tumble off the cliff and drop onto cars far below. Return to the main trail and continue on to the ledges overlooking Jordan Pond. Be sure to keep an eye on

With a Little Help from Our Friends

As we watch federal funding for national parks lose headway year after year, every park in the United States needs a safety net like **Friends of Acadia** (FOA, 207/288-3340 or 800/625-0321, www.friendsofacadia.org), a dynamic organization headquartered in Bar Harbor. Propane-powered shuttle-bus service needs expanding? FOA finds a multimillion-dollar donor. Well-used trails need maintenance? FOA organizes volunteer work parties. New connector trails needed? FOA gets them done. No need seems to go unfilled.

Friends of Acadia was founded in 1986 to preserve and protect the park for resource-sensitive tourism and myriad recreational uses. Since then, FOA has contributed more than $20 million to the park and surrounding communities for trail upkeep, carriage road maintenance, seasonal park staff funding, and conservation projects. FOA also cofounded the Island Explorer bus system and instigated the Acadia Trails Forever program, a joint park-FOA partnership for trail rehabilitation.

You can join FOA and its 3,700 members; memberships start at $35 per year. You can also lend a hand while you're here: FOA and the park organize volunteer work parties for Acadia trail, carriage road, and other outdoor maintenance three times weekly (8:20am-12:30pm Tues., Thurs., and Sat.) between June and Columbus Day. Call the recorded information line (207/288-3934) for the work locations, or visit the website. The meeting point is park headquarters (Eagle Lake Rd./Rte. 233, Bar Harbor), about three miles west of town. This is a terrific way to give something back to the park, and the camaraderie is contagious. Take your own water, lunch, and bug repellent. Dress in layers and wear closed-toe shoes. More than 10,000 volunteer hours go toward this effort each year.

Each summer, Friends of Acadia also sponsors a handful of **Ridge Runners,** who work under park supervision and spend their days out and about on the trails repairing cairns, watching for lost hikers, and handing out Leave No Trace information. FOA also hires more than a dozen area teens each summer for the Acadia Youth Conservation Corps, which does trail and carriage road work, and the Acadia Youth Technology Team, a youth-powered think tank coming up with new ways to get young people excited about the park.

If you happen to be in the region on the first Saturday in November, call the FOA office to register for the annual carriage road cleanup, which usually involves more than 400 volunteers. Bring water and gloves; there's a free hot lunch at midday for everyone who participates. It's dubbed Take Pride in Acadia Day—indeed an apt label.

little ones, especially near the cliffs. Return by backtracking via the same trail. For a longer, more strenuous hike, consider looping in North Bubble and/or descending to Jordan Pond, a steepish scramble over and through boulders, with a squeeze through one tight spot.

★ Gorham Mountain Trail

Distance: 1.8 miles round-trip
Duration: 1.5-2 hours
Elevation gain: 525 feet
Effort: Moderate
Trailhead: On the one-way section of the Park Loop Road, continue past Sand Beach and Thunder Hole to the Gorham Mountain Parking Area. The Island Explorer bus (Route 3/Sand Beach) can drop you off here, or walk a short distance along the Ocean Path

after getting off the bus at the Thunder Hole stop. The trailhead is at the back of the parking lot.

The round-trip distance specified covers the trail directly to the summit, then a return the same way with a short detour via Cadillac Cliffs. You can also continue onward from the Gorham summit, following part of the Bowl Trail down to the Park Loop Road, then walk along the Ocean Path back to your car, if you've left it in the Gorham lot.

Follow cairns across ledges up from the trailhead to a fork, where you'll see a plaque commemorating Waldron Bates, the ingenious path maker who instigated the strategic use of granite staircases and iron ladders for Acadia's trails.

Bates was a lawyer in his day job, but his summer avocation as head of the Roads and Paths Committee for the Bar Harbor Improvement Association (1900-1909) gave him the greatest pleasure. Think of him as you navigate the Cadillac Cliffs Trail, one of his projects.

For now, though, bear left, saving the Cadillac Cliffs route for the return, and head for the open-ledge summit, at 525 feet the third lowest of Acadia's peaks. A cairn marks the spot. From here, you'll see Sand Beach, Egg Rock Light in Frenchman Bay, the Beehive, Champlain Mountain, and lots more—a fabulous view.

Return via the same route, but make the short detour left onto the U-shaped Cadillac Cliffs Trail, featuring stairs, rocky footing, granite "tunnels," and even an ancient sea cave, now high and dry. This sea cave once was filled with beach cobbles, but slowly it has been cleaned out by hikers—a prime example of the damage done by removing "just one."

Beachcroft Path

Distance: 2.4 miles round-trip
Duration: 1.5-2 hours
Elevation gain: 1,100 feet
Effort: Moderate to difficult
Trailhead: The Tarn Parking Area, on Route 3, just south of the Sieur de Monts Spring park entrance and just north of The Tarn; or take the Island Explorer bus (Route 4/Blackwoods).

The Beachcroft Trail on Huguenot Head leads up the west side of Champlain Mountain. Also called the Beachcroft Path, the trail, constructed in 1915, is best known for its nearly 1,500 beautifully engineered pink granite steps and slabs. It's a moderate climb via switchbacks to the granite ledges of Huguenot Head and its views over Frenchman Bay. Take in the views and replenish yourself with a snack to prepare for the next section. The trail descends briefly before climbing steeply up stairs and over rocky ledges to the Champlain summit. The views are stupendous. From there, you can connect with the Bear Brook or Precipice Trails.

Option: For a shorter, less strenuous hike, instead of continuing up Champlain, scramble up the ledges to the true summit of Huguenot Head; it's worth it for the panoramic vistas. If you turn around here, the total distance is just over 1.2 miles round-trip.

Penobscot and Sargent Mountains

Distance: 6 miles round-trip
Duration: 4 hours
Elevation gain: 1,200 feet
Effort: Difficult to strenuous
Trailhead: Park your car in the overflow lot at Jordan Pond House, go left of the restaurant, and look for the carved trail signpost.

You'll cross Jordan Stream and a carriage road before starting on the rough part—heading upward rather steeply with rocky, ledgy footing. Handholds have been installed in strategic spots (this part is even less fun on the return route). But the rewards are worth the effort. Continue on to the Penobscot summit (1,194 feet, the fifth highest in the park), with wide-open views. In August, you'll have wild blueberries (but leave some for others) en route to the top.

The best feature of this hike is that you get to reach one summit and then go for a swim in gorgeous little Sargent Pond before tackling the next one. From Penobscot summit, it's only 10 minutes downhill to the pond. If you're retracing your route, you can even have a second swim on the way back. This is a long hike, however; if you're hiking with kids, be sure they're up to the challenge. For that matter, be sure you are.

From Sargent Pond, head upward on the South Ridge Trail to the summit of Sargent Mountain (1,373 feet, the second highest in the park).

Don't rush the return—the vistas are superb—but when you're ready, go back the same way.

Dorr Mountain via Homans, Emery, and Schiff Paths

Distance: 2.8 miles round-trip
Duration: 1.5-2 hours
Elevation gain: 1,200 feet

Effort: Difficult to strenuous

Trailhead: Take Hemlock Trail from the beginning of the Sieur de Monts Spring parking lot (look for the split-rail fence) and follow it to the intersection with the Jesup Path. Continue on the Hemlock Trail another few yards to the trailhead on your left. You can also take the Hemlock Trail from Bar Harbor to the trailhead.

Avid hiker Tom St. Germain, author of *A Walk in the Park,* rediscovered the Homans Path, originally built in 1915, while searching for abandoned trails in the early 1990s and wrote about it in another book, *Trails of History.* He deserves a big thanks, and Friends of Acadia and the Park Service also deserve accolades for restoring the trail, which reopened in 2004.

The Homans Path ascends rapidly via steps and switchbacks 0.3 mile to the intersection with the Emery Path, which later intersects the Schiff Path (the two were previously known as the East Face of Dorr Trail). It's a beautiful hike that weaves through narrow passages in the granite ledges and even under slabs of granite. Along the way and especially from the summit, expect nice views over Frenchman Bay.

Options: Instead of the Homans, you can also ascend via Emery from Sieur du Monts Springs; it's another dandy, with steps, balconies, and gorgeous vistas. On the return, follow the East Face Trail all the way down to the Sieur de Monts Spring parking lot or veer off on Kurt Diederich's Climb, which also returns to the lot. Diederich is the steepest and roughest of the three step trails from Sieur du Monts. Avoid it when ascending, and be careful on the descent. There are some loose slabs and rocks, and leaf cover in sections can be slippery. There are a few nice glimpses of The Tarn, but for the most part, the better views are on the Emery and Homans Trails.

Other Recommended East-Side Trails

In 2011, trail crews finished reworking the historic **Jesup Path,** one of the trails added by George Dorr, to make it partially wheelchair accessible. Trail crews replaced split logs and muddy sections with a 2,000-foot-long boardwalk section that passes through a large grove of white birches. When combined with the Hemlock Trail, it offers nearly 0.75 mile of accessible terrain near Sieur de Monts Spring.

The **Seaside Path,** or Seaside Trail, runs about two miles through the woods (use insect repellent) between Seal Harbor and the Jordan Pond House. Use the Island Explorer bus to make this a one-way hike, or retrace your route for a longer hike.

A choice moderate hike is **Conner's Nubble,** with superb views down to Eagle Lake and the mountains off to the east. For a moderate-to-strenuous hike, try **Parkman Mountain**—not too difficult, but difficult enough to make it worthwhile, especially with the views from the bald summit. It's what you might call an "all-purpose hike."

You can access the **Cadillac South Ridge Trail** from Blackwoods Campground. Start the trail at the entrance to the campground and do a 7.4-mile round-trip. The hike is moderate to strenuous, with a 1,530-foot elevation gain, but there are a couple of quite easy stretches; the last part is the steepest.

Experienced, serious hikers seeking real challenges in the "strenuous" category should consider the **Beehive** and **Precipice Trails.** These two "ladder trails" (no pets allowed) are the park's toughest routes, with sheer faces and iron ladders. Champlain Mountain's 1.6-mile round-trip Precipice Trail is often closed, usually from mid-April into August, to protect nesting peregrine falcons. Avid hikers consider the 0.8-mile round-trip Beehive a "must-do." If challenges are your thing, you're not acrophobic, and these trails are open (check beforehand at the Hulls Cove Visitors Center), go ahead. Both trailheads are on the Park Loop Road (Island Explorer Route 3/Sand Beach).

If you're looking to escape the sunset-viewing crowds on Cadillac, a short hike, about 20-30 minutes, up either **Parkman** or **Bald** will give you the same views.

WEST-SIDE TRAILS
Wonderland

Distance: 1.4 miles round-trip
Duration: 45 minutes
Elevation gain: Minimal
Effort: Easy
Trailhead: The Wonderland Trail begins on the south side of Route 102A, one mile west of the Seawall Campground. Walk from Seawall; if you're staying elsewhere, ask the Island Explorer bus driver (Route 7/Southwest Harbor) to drop you off (it's not a regular stop).

The shortest and easiest of the park's trails, Wonderland follows an old fire road and is more a walk than a hike—a great starter-upper for a family ensconced at Seawall Campground. Most of the route is wooded—trees gnarled from the wind, branches laden with moss—with the rugged shoreline and a small cobble beach as your reward at the end.

Across Route 102A from the Wonderland trailhead is the 420-acre Big Heath, considered one of Maine's "critical areas." Avoid it because of its sensitive peat land, wet and squishy and fragile underfoot (not to mention its battalions of mosquitoes). You'll be skirting its edges, though, if you walk the Hio Trail from the back of Seawall Campground.

Ship Harbor Nature Trail

Distance: 1.3-mile loop
Duration: 45-60 minutes
Elevation gain: Level
Effort: Easy, some uneven ground
Trailhead: The parking area (with restroom) for Ship Harbor is less than 0.5 mile west of the Wonderland Parking Area. The trail is on the south side of Route 102A. As with Wonderland, you can be dropped off by an Island Explorer bus (Route 7/Southwest Harbor), or flag one down after your hike.

The Ship Harbor Nature Trail, a figure-eight-shaped loop, isn't quite as easy as Wonderland—roots can snag you along the way, and rocks can be slippery if it has rained or the tide has receded—but it's even more educational as a family hike. At the Thompson Island Information Center, the Hulls Cove Visitors Center, or at Seawall Campground, pick up a copy of the park's 12-page *Ship Harbor Nature Trail* booklet and use it along the way.

Legend has it that the harbor earned its name during the Revolutionary War, when an American privateer, seeking refuge, became stranded here.

If the tide has gone out, follow the trail along the shore first (counterclockwise) so the kids can check out what's been left in the

Pink granite and crashing surf tip the Ship Harbor Nature Trail.

tide pools. If the tide is high, perhaps you'll want to follow the booklet's suggested clockwise route. Or you can do a figure-eight route. In any case, you won't get lost. If you want a quieter experience, plan a hike for early morning or late afternoon.

Option: Since Wonderland and Ship Harbor are so close together, consider doing both trails in a morning or afternoon. Carry a picnic, and enjoy it on the shore.

Flying Mountain Trail

Distance: 1.5-mile loop
Duration: 1-2 hours
Elevation gain: 200 feet
Effort: Moderate, some steep sections
Trailhead: The trail begins at the end of Fernald Point Road, 0.8 mile east of Route 102 at the northern edge of Southwest Harbor. If you're driving from the Bar Harbor area, slow down after passing Echo Lake and take the next left. Drive to the end of the road, park in the Valley Cove lot, and begin at the carved signpost. Fernald Point was the site of the early 17th-century St. Sauveur mission settlement established by French Jesuits. The Island Explorer bus headed to or from Southwest Harbor can drop you off or pick you up at the corner of Route 102 and Fernald Point Road; from here, walk down the road to the trailhead.

At 284 feet, Flying Mountain is the lowest of Acadia's 26 summits, so it shouldn't have one of the best views—but it does. With minimal effort (some minor scrambling up and over, but the trail is level at the end), you're surveying the mouth of Somes Sound, including Northeast and Southwest Harbors and Greening Island between them. It is pretty spectacular.

From the trailhead, the rise through the trees is a bit steep, with some stepped ledges, but it's quick and stairs make it easy. At the summit, relax and take photos, then descend toward Valley Cove. You'll encounter roots and rocks, and your knees may complain a bit, but again, it's really not strenuous, and it doesn't last long. At the bottom, bear left onto the Valley Cove Road and return to the parking area.

You can hike the Valley Cove Trail as an extension of the Flying Mountain Trail, but it may be closed mid-March-mid-August, as peregrine falcons have been nesting there in recent years.

Beech Mountain Trail

Distance: 1.1 miles round-trip
Duration: 1-1.5 hours
Elevation gain: 700 feet
Effort: Moderate

The view from the summit of Flying Mountain takes in the mouth of Somes Sound.

Trailhead: From Route 102 in Somesville, take Pretty Marsh Road west to Beech Hill Road. Turn left and continue to the end, climbing gradually to the parking area for Beech Cliff and Beech Mountain. This trail is not accessible via the Island Explorer.

Several hiking routes merge and converge in the Beech Mountain area. Some begin from a trailhead on the southern side of Beech and can be more strenuous than this one. This hike starts from the northern side. None of the Beech Mountain hikes are particularly convenient to the Island Explorer bus system.

A short distance from the beginning of the Beech Mountain Trail, you'll reach a fork—the Beech Mountain loop. Bear right to do the loop counterclockwise—the rewarding vistas over Long Pond come sooner, and it's less steep this way.

At the summit (839 feet) stands the park's only fire tower, now disused and rarely open. During unseasonably hot summers, when the ranger-posted fire-danger level is high, volunteers come up to keep an eye on things, but small charter planes do most of the fire patrols these days. Besides the great views of Long Pond, from here you can see as far as Blue Hill to the northwest and the Cranberry Isles to the south. A knob near the summit is a prime viewing spot for migrating hawks and other raptors in September.

From the summit, continue your counterclockwise route or backtrack the way you came, heading down to the trail junction and back to the parking area.

Option: If you're particularly fascinated by mosses and lichens (and have brought insect repellent), consider a three-mile round-trip to Beech Mountain that begins with a lovely walk in the woods starting at the same trailhead. Instead of taking the Beech Mountain Trail, follow the Valley Trail on fairly level ground for just under one mile. Then bear right onto the Beech Mountain South Ridge Trail and start climbing stone steps (lots of them) toward the summit. Descend from the summit via the Beech Mountain loop route, going clockwise (left) to take advantage of the Long Pond vistas.

Acadia Mountain Trail

Distance: 2.5 miles round-trip
Duration: 1.5-2 hours
Elevation gain: 1,050 feet
Effort: Difficult
Trailhead: From Somesville, west of Bar Harbor, take Route 102 south for just over three miles, alongside Echo Lake, until you see the signposted Acadia Mountain parking lot. Cross the road to the trailhead. The Island Explorer (Route 7/Southwest Harbor) goes along Route 102; request a stop to start your hike, and flag down the bus when you've finished the hike.

Climb the steps and continue to the junction with the St. Sauveur Mountain Trail. (If you're up for a much longer hike, combine Acadia with the St. Sauveur loop for a four-mile round-trip.) Continue left on the Acadia Mountain Trail, where it's briefly deceptively flat and lovely. After crossing a fire road (your eventual return route), begin the rocky, ledgy ascent, following the cairns.

It's less than one mile to the open summit—with fantastic views up and down Somes Sound. There's actually a sort of double summit, with the second one only slightly lower than the 641-foot maximum height. In summer you'll find wild blueberries. The descent toward the sound is longer and quite steep—take it slowly. At the bottom, when you reach the spur to Man o' War Brook, detour briefly to follow the brook to Somes Sound. Allegedly, Revolutionary War vessels stocked up on water here during their exploits along the Maine coast. Return to the trailhead via an easy walk on the mile-long fire road.

Biking

Bicycling on Mount Desert Island is a joy, but you have to pedal in the right locations. The island is mountainous, and that includes the roads; many have serious ups and downs. Dedicated and experienced road cyclists will have a blast. Mountain bikers, casual bikers, families, and everyone else will be more than pleased with the carriage roads. These gravel roads lace the heart of the park and are punctuated with beautiful stone bridges. They provide a variety of challenges, and you can create a ride of practically any length by linking them together.

You'll find a number of commercial maps available. I prefer the *Acadia National Park Hiking and Biking Trail Map* ($5 paper, $10 waterproof) published by Map Adventures (www.mapadventures.com), because I find it easiest to read, it details in-town roads, and it shows some of the dirt roads described below. One big drawback for cyclists is that this map doesn't include the entire island; the northern third is simply lopped off, so if you're cycling that section, you'll need another map as well.

ROAD BIKING

Road biking on Mount Desert Island is best left to the experienced. Roads are often narrow, shoulders frequently nonexistent or soft, and gawking drivers often aren't paying attention to the road. Families, once-a-year pedalers, and casual bicyclists will do best on the carriage roads. That said, serious road bikers do have a few choices. Stop in at one of Bar Harbor's bike shops for recommendations or to find out about group rides. If you go by yourself, timing is critical. For the best ride with the least traffic, get up at the crack of dawn and start pedaling once it's truly light outside. It's very important to wear reflective clothing on these roads. It's also wise to drive the roads before cycling them to check conditions. If it has been a while since they've

been resurfaced, you might be in for a very rough ride.

Park Loop Road

Since bikes are not allowed on hiking trails in Acadia, the Park Loop Road provides a good workout for mountain or road bikers. Its prime drawback is the volume of car and RV exhaust fumes you'll be inhaling if you take this route in the middle of the day at the height of summer—so don't. Park-wide ozone alerts are not common, but they do occur in Acadia. Nor are the Park Loop's shoulders as wide as they might be to comfortably accommodate many bikes. Besides, on most of the one-way sections of the Park Loop, overflow auto parking is allowed in the right lane, and dodging cars isn't fun. The 27-mile route is indeed spectacular, so if you want to bike it, plan your pedaling for early in the day (around 7am in summer), late in the day (around "happy hour," when everyone else has packed it in and headed for bars or restaurants), or during shoulder months (June, Sept., or even Oct.).

Southeast Quarter of the Island

This route dips in and out of the park. Begin in Bar Harbor and follow Route 3 to Schooner Head Road, then follow signs to Park Loop Road. Ride the Park Loop to the end of the one-way section in Seal Harbor, turn right onto Jordan Pond Road heading to Seal Harbor, and then pick up Route 3 to the intersection with Route 198 in Northeast Harbor. Go left on Route 198 into Northeast Harbor, taking Harborside Road to Joy Road to Manchester Road, and turn right. Manchester Road merges into Sargent Drive. Follow it until it meets Route 198, turn left, and continue to the intersection with Route 233. Turn right and follow Route 233 back to Bar Harbor.

You can increase the mileage by exploring

some of the back roads of Seal Harbor (watch out for Martha Stewart) or Northeast Harbor. Another option is to take the Duck Brook Road off Route 233, just after the Eagle Lake parking lots. The road meanders into Bar Harbor, merging onto West Street.

Routes 102/102A

Experienced cyclists who are accustomed to traffic might consider this loop around the western half of Mount Desert Island. It passes through Somesville, Southwest Harbor, Bass Harbor, Tremont, and Pretty Marsh. While little mileage on this route is actually in the park, quite a few offshoots do venture into it, in most cases on dirt roads. If you do the full loop, it's about 26 miles. Unless you're intent on getting in mileage, plan time to stop and explore along the way. Expect nonexistent or soft shoulders on much of the route and moderate to heavy traffic.

To add to the distance, venture down some of the side roads along the way, such as Ripples Road to Beech Hill Road (dead ends) or Hall Quarry Road (loop), or detour north in Pretty Marsh on Indian Point Road, which ends at Routes 198/102.

CARRIAGE ROADS

The better alternative for most aspiring bicyclists is to bring, borrow, or rent a bike and take advantage of the spectacular carriage road system—57 miles of crushed-rock roadways with nary a car in sight. Bikes are allowed on only 45 of the 57 miles; 12 miles are on private land, so be alert for signs.

At every junction in the carriage road system stands a tall wooden post with a number and directional signs. Use these numbers, together with the park's free carriage road map, to navigate the network. Also very helpful are a couple of portable books: *A Pocket Guide to the Carriage Roads of Acadia National Park* by Diana Abrell and *A Pocket Guide to Biking on Mount Desert Island* by Audrey Minutolo.

Periodically, carriage roads and their bridges undergo necessary repairs, and since such work is possible only in decent weather, you may encounter closures. When you obtain the carriage road map at the Hulls Cove Visitors Center, ask a ranger to indicate any sections that are under repair or closed.

Some sections of the carriage roads are fine for wheelchairs, particularly near Eagle Lake and Bubble Pond. Since these are multiuse roadways, bicyclists in particular should remember and adhere to the rules:

- **Bikes yield to everyone** (pedestrians, horses, wheelchairs, strollers); pedestrians yield to horses. Horses tend to become skittish around bikes, so be particularly cautious when you're pedaling near them. Better still, pull off to the right, stop, and let them pass.

- **Wear a helmet.**

- **Keep to the right** and signal clearly when passing on the left.

- **Do not speed;** speeders are a danger to pedestrians, horses, children, wheelchair users, and sometimes themselves.

- **Pets** must be leashed.

As with the park's hiking trails, it would take a whole book just to focus on all the options on the carriage roads. While the carriage roads make wonderful walking paths, they are the best places in the park for bikes, so most of the route suggestions that follow are geared to cyclists.

It cannot be said often enough: There is no off-road biking in Acadia, and bikes are not allowed on the hiking trails.

Eagle Lake and Witch Hole Pond

These two loops are probably the most popular in the park—they're not difficult (good for families) and they're close to Bar Harbor, where so many visitors stay. Thus, if you decide to do either in the middle of summer, get an early start. If you're planning to rent bikes, rent them the night before so you can be on your way right after breakfast.

If you're doing this anytime between late June and Columbus Day, check the schedule for the Island Explorer bus and use it to get to and from your starting and ending points. The Island Explorer Bicycle Express operates between the Bar Harbor Village Green and Eagle Lake.

For the Eagle Lake loop, the Route 6/ Northeast Harbor bus makes a stop at the head of Eagle Lake on Route 233, or you can pedal or drive from downtown Bar Harbor via Mount Desert Street. At the end of the street, cross over to Route 233 (Eagle Lake Rd.) and follow it to the beginning of this route. You can park in the Eagle Lake Parking Area, across Route 233 from the beginning of the carriage road.

To reach the Witch Hole Pond loop from downtown Bar Harbor by bike, take West Street to its end, cross Route 3, and then continue on West Street Extension. Take a right onto Duck Brook Road, and continue from here to the carriage road, starting at signpost 5.

Option: Drive to the Hulls Cove Visitors Center, park, and bike (or walk your bike) up the steep trail to the first carriage road intersection, signpost 1. From here, continue to signpost 2, and then veer right to make the circuit via the junctions at signposts 4 and 5 and then to 3, making a loop back to signpost 1. From here, it's pretty much downhill to your car.

Each of these rides is about six miles. If you'd prefer to double your biking mileage, park at the Eagle Lake Parking Area and do both loops.

Jordan Pond and Bubble Pond

To ride this loop, take the Island Explorer bus to the Jordan Pond Parking Area or drive here via the Park Loop Road (use the Jordan Pond parking lot, not the Jordan Pond House Parking Area). Pedal back along the Park Loop Road (follow bike rules and stay with the traffic; it's two-way here) to the handsome stone Jordan Pond Gate Lodge. From here you have two choices—a clockwise route or a counterclockwise one.

The counterclockwise route allows you a

downhill coast along Jordan Pond near the end of your 8.5-mile circuit. Enter the carriage road next to the gatehouse and continue to the junction at signpost 17. Head north, passing Bubble Pond along its west shore—practically in the water—to signpost 7. Bear left around the bottom of Eagle Lake, to signpost 8, continue to signpost 10, and then turn south, skirting Jordan Pond, to signpost 14. Continue south to signposts 15 and 16, exiting onto the Park Loop Road across from where you entered.

After these warm-up rides, you'll have a good sense of this amazing network.

Amphitheatre Loop

This is a fabulous 5.5-mile loop that takes you into the heart of the park, far from the noise of traffic and civilization. You'll pass over two bridges—the gently curving Amphitheatre Bridge, at 236 feet one of the longest in the system, and Little Harbor Brook Bridge, which must be one of the smallest. The route has some steady climbs, but the rewards are panoramic views to the Cranberry Islands. Follow a clockwise route beginning at the Brown Mountain Gatehouse parking lot on Route 198 (one mile north of Northeast Harbor). Enter the carriage road system and bear right at signposts 18 and 19, and keep straight or left at signpost 20. Keep right again at signposts 21 and 22. When you return to signpost 20, turn left and keep left until you're back at the parking area.

Option: Hikers can enjoy the 0.8-mile Amphitheatre Trail connecting the two bridges. It's a lovely walk in the woods paralleling and often crossing Harbor Brook as it babbles and descends over waterfalls into small pools—perfect for cooling hot, tired feet. Don't take this trail during spring runoff periods or after heavy rains, when that sweet brook might be a raging torrent.

Around the Mountain

This 11-mile loop is an outstanding ride for experienced mountain bikers. It circumnavigates several of the park's major peaks, including Sargent, Penobscot, Cedar Swamp, Parkman, and Gilmore, and it passes numerous bridges and waterfalls. The views are glorious. It's not an easy ride, however, as it climbs many hills. Begin at the Parkman Mountain parking lot on Route 198 by heading right. At signpost 13, go left, and then go left at signpost 12. You're now on the Around the Mountain Road. At signpost 10 turn right and keep right, staying on the Around the Mountain Road, at signposts 14, 21, 20, and 19. At signpost 12, turn left, then turn right at signpost 13 to return to the parking lot. You can also access this route from the Jordan Pond area.

Hadlock Brook Loop

The rewards for this 3.9-mile loop around Hadlock Pond include views out to the Cranberry Islands, three bridges, and one of the park's highest waterfalls. Begin at the Parkman Mountain parking lot on Route 198, heading right on the carriage road. At the first junction, signpost 13, go left. At the next, signpost 12, go right. The first section is the steepest—you'll reap the benefits of this short climb with a long downhill a bit later. The first bridge you'll come to is Hemlock Bridge over Maple Spring. Take a few

minutes and descend the stairs to the spring so you can view this lovely bridge from all angles. Continue on a few hundred yards to aptly named Waterfall Bridge, which crosses Hadlock Brook and provides fine views of a 40-foot waterfall. Again, be sure to hoof it down and under the bridge for the views. Now comes a grin-inducing downhill, a gentle descent to signpost 19; turn right here and again at signpost 18. While nowhere near as impressive as the other two bridges, the small Hadlock Brook Bridge is still lovely. At signpost 13, keep left to return to the Parkman Mountain lot.

Option: If you're on foot, you can connect to the lower section of the loop and Hadlock Pond by descending the Maple Spring Trail that passes Hemlock Bridge or the Hadlock Brook Trail, under Waterfall Bridge. Each is roughly 0.5 mile long.

FIRE ROADS
Hio Trail

This old Acadia fire road begins at the back of the Seawall Campground (behind Loop C) and goes over to Route 102. It's an easy four-mile round-trip. The path is mostly wooded, passing near the Big Heath, so if you take the trail late in the day, be sure to use insect

Experienced mountain bikers will enjoy the 11-mile Around the Mountain loop.

repellent. It's a great family ride, with plenty of bird- and wildlife-watching opportunities.

Long Pond Fire Road

This five-mile loop off Route 102 starts just south of Pretty Marsh Picnic Area, where you can park. It follows a dirt road to Long Pond and back, with a short section on Route 102

to close the loop. The terrain is moderate, with many long hills; spruce and fir trees line most of the route, and you'll pass boggy areas as well as a few ponds. This is prime moose territory, so be on the lookout for the gangly beasts. If you see one, observe it from a distance; if it starts coming toward you, move away quietly.

Other Recreation

CALM-WATER PADDLING

Both **Eagle Lake** and **Jordan Pond** have boat ramps. The Eagle Lake put-in is off Route 233; the Jordan Pond put-in is adjacent to the hiker parking lot near the Jordan Pond House, on the Park Loop Road. No swimming is allowed in either lake.

Another fine pond for paddling is **Seal Cove Pond** in Tremont. Route 102 skirts the western edge of the 1.5-mile-long pond, and the shoreline has plenty of houses, but most of the forested eastern shore is in the park. The primary access point is off Western Mountain Road. To find it, take Seal Cove Road from Seal Cove, go left on the first park road, and follow it to its intersection with Western Mountain Road. Turn right; the road ends at the put-in. You might also be able to find a parking spot or two with easy access on Route 102.

SWIMMING

Acadia has a limited number of swimming areas; their parking lots are mighty crowded on hot days. Go early in the day, or take your chances.

Don't assume you can swim in any freshwater pond or lake you encounter in the park or even elsewhere on the island. Six island locations—Upper and Lower Hadlock Ponds, Bubble and Jordan Ponds, Eagle Lake, and the southern half of Long Pond—are drinkingwater reservoirs where swimming and windsurfing are banned (but boating is allowed). Don't let your dog swim in these ponds either.

Five of the six are within the park; Long Pond borders the park.

Sand Beach

Located slightly below the Park Loop Road (take Island Explorer Route 3/Sand Beach), Sand Beach is the park's and the island's biggest sandy beach. Lifeguards are on duty during the summer, and even then the biggest threat can be hypothermia. The saltwater is terminally glacial—in mid-July it rarely exceeds 55°F. By September it's usually warmer, though the air will be cooler. Even though kids seem not to notice, they can become chilled quickly; keep an eye on their condition. The best solution is to walk to the far end of the beach, where a warmer, shallow stream meets the ocean. Also, if you arrive here at the incoming tide, after the sun has warmed up the sand, the water temperature is marginally higher. On a hot August day, arrive early; the parking lot fills up. Bring a picnic. There are changing rooms and restrooms. Dogs are not allowed on Sand Beach.

After hiking nearby Great Head on a hot day, go for a swim at Sand Beach—you'll be surprisingly grateful for the chilly water.

Echo Lake

The park's most popular freshwater swimming site, staffed with a lifeguard and inevitably crowded on hot days, is Echo Lake, south of Somesville on Route 102 and well signposted. Take the Island Explorer bus Route

7/Southwest Harbor. Pets are not allowed on the beach.

Swimming Holes

If you have a canoe, kayak, or rowboat, you can reach swimming holes in **Seal Cove Pond** and **Round Pond,** both on the western side of Mount Desert. Both have shorelines bordering the park. The eastern shore of **Hodgdon Pond,** also on the western side of the island, is accessible by car via Hodgdon Road and Long Pond Fire Road.

Another popular swimming hole is **Lake Wood,** at the northern end of Mount Desert. It has a small sand beach and a grassy area, a restroom by the parking area, and auto access. To get to Lake Wood from Route 3, head west on Crooked Road for just over 0.5 mile to Lake Wood Pond Road. Turn left and continue to the parking area, which will be crowded on a hot day, so arrive early.

ROCK CLIMBING

Acadia has a number of splendid sites prized by climbers: Otter Cliff, with 60-foot sea cliffs, Great Head sea cliffs, South Bubble Mountain, South Wall and the Central Slabs on Champlain Mountain, and Canada Cliff on the island's western side. Popular bouldering spots include the shoreline between Sand Beach and Otter Cliff and near Blackwoods Campground. The climbing season usually runs May-October. Occasionally it can start earlier or end later, but you'd have to be on or near the island to be able to catch the decent weather before it deteriorates. This can happen even in summer. Be aware of tides, especially when climbing Otter Cliffs or Great Head.

Some park regulations for Acadia climbing:

- Don't leave your **dog** tied up or on the loose while you're climbing.

- The park's **bridges** are off-limits for climbing or bouldering.

- While **peregrine falcons** are nesting (Apr.-mid-Aug.), the Central Slabs area on the Precipice and the Jordan Cliffs, as well as other areas, are almost always closed.

- Sign in at the registration box at climbing sites—**registration** is required at Otter Cliffs, the South Wall, and Canada Cliff.

- If you're part of an organized commercial or noncommercial group numbering six or more, a **permit** is required for Otter Cliffs. Download from www.nps.gov/acad.

- At Otter Cliffs, used the **fixed anchors,** not trees, to belay.

If you've forgotten any climbing gear or need replacements, the best source is **Cadillac Mountain Sports** (26 Cottage St., Bar Harbor, 207/288-4532, www.cadillacsports. com), on the ground floor next to Atlantic Climbing School.

Climbing Schools and Guides

If you haven't tried climbing, never do it yourself without instruction. The best advice is to contact one of Bar Harbor's two climbing operations. **Acadia Mountain Guides Climbing School** (228 Main St., Bar Harbor, 207/288-8186 or 888/232-9559, www.acadiamountainguides.com, mid-May-Oct.) offers all levels of instruction and guided climbs for individuals and families. School owner Jon Tierney has been climbing, guiding, and instructing in Acadia since 1983. Rates vary with the number of climbers, but a private full-day guided climb is $260 and a half-day is $155. Family rates ($300 half-day, $460 full-day for up to 4 people) are available for families with kids younger than 10.

Atlantic Climbing School (ACS, 24 Cottage St., 2nd Fl., Bar Harbor, 207/288-2521, www.climbacadia.com) provides half-day climbing courses for beginners by reservation. You'll learn just enough to introduce you to the sport and do an initial basic climb—with guides and in line with park rules. ACS also offers a series of courses for intermediate climbers and a half- or full-day guided course for experienced climbers. Half-day courses are $95 per person for three people, $105 per person for two, and $160 for a private course. Full-day guided courses are $135 per person for three, $165 per person for two, or $265 for a private outing.

Jeff Butterfield, former owner of ACS, wrote the must-have book for experienced climbers, *Acadia: A Climber's Guide,* which covers all the best-known routes as well as some lesser-known crags. Routes are described and rated, with maps and symbols and other essential information. For instance, the book recommends that South Bubble climbers wear helmets for protection from rocks dropped ("by yahoos," as he puts it) from hiking trails overhead. Unfortunately it's out of print, but Jeff has turned it over to Grant Simmons, who expects the second edition will be available in spring 2015. He's also produced an app, *Rock Climbs of Acadia* ($7.99, www.rakkup.com/climbing-guidebook) covering more than 175 routes at Otter Cliffs, Great Head, and the South Wall.

GEOCACHING

Although traditional geocaching, with hidden prizes, is forbidden in the park, if you have your own GPS unit, you can participate in Acadia's **EarthCache Program** (www.nps.gov/acad/earthcache.htm). Instead of directing you to stashes of trinkets, it leads to some of the park's significant geological sites. Full details, including coordinates for the first stop, are available on the website. It takes an estimated 4-6 hours to complete the program, which will cover much of the park.

WINTER ACTIVITIES

The miles of car-free carriage roads in Acadia are fantastic for cross-country skiing and snowshoeing. The only problem is that even though Acadia gets about five feet of snow during an average winter, it's not like a ski resort, where there's a base and more snow keeps piling on top of it. Here, it might snow one day and rain or thaw the next. But now and then, a large volume of snow creates a winter wonderland for days or even weeks. Acadia's proximity to the ocean and the Gulf Stream current means that you take your chances with snow.

January-February can be good for winter sports, but then again, you never know. The park publishes a very handy *Winter Activities Guide,* a foldout map-brochure that explains what you can and cannot do and where you can and cannot go.

For carriage road information and other visitor information about Acadia during the winter, when the Hulls Cove Visitors Center is closed, contact **park headquarters** (Eagle Lake Rd./Rte. 233, Bar Harbor, 207/288-3338, www.nps.gov/acad/, 8am-4:30pm daily Mar. 1-mid-Apr. and Nov.-Dec., 8am-4:30pm Mon.-Fri. Jan.-Feb. and mid-Apr.-late Oct., closed Thanksgiving Day, Dec. 24-25).

Forty-five miles of carriage trails are open to **cross-country skiing** and **snowshoeing,** and volunteers sometimes set tracks; check with the park or online for grooming reports. Carriage roads designated for grooming include Witch Hole Pond, Aunt Betty Pond and Seven Bridges, Eagle Lake, Upper Hadlock Loop, Amphitheater Loop, and Around the Mountain Lower and Upper Loops. **Dogsledding** and **skijoring** are permitted on all closed motor roads, but there are restrictions. Check with park officials or online for current info. Unplowed park roads also are open, but many of these are shared with snowmobilers, so use caution. **Snowmobilers** can ride the 27-mile Park Loop Road, most fire roads, and the road to the Cadillac summit. Winter **hiking** means navigating often icy and snow-packed trails. Be sure to read the park's *Winter Hiking Tips* before hitting the trail. Ponds and lakes are open for **ice fishing** usually from January into March, but check with local officials to be sure the ice is thick enough before venturing out on it.

Blackwoods Campground (Rte. 3, Otter Creek, 5 miles south of Bar Harbor), the park's only year-round campground, has limited sites for hardy souls up for experiencing Acadia in winter. A free permit, available from park headquarters, is required. Winter facilities include a hand pump for water and a portable toilet, bring your own toilet paper. It's a 0.5-mile hike in to the campground on an unplowed road, and all trash must be carried out. Snowmobiles are not permitted at the campground.

Winter toilets are available at the Brown Mountain, Parkman Mountain, and Sand Beach Parking Areas; the Eagle Lake and Jordan Pond boat ramps; Eagle Lake Carriage Road; and Fabbri Picnic Area.

Outfitters and Instruction

Cross-country skis ($18/day including skis, boots, and poles), snowshoes ($12-16), and ice skates ($8) are available for rent from **Cadillac Mountain Sports** (26 Cottage St., Bar Harbor, 207/288-4532, www.cadillacsports.com, year-round).

Atlantic Climbing School (ACS, 24 Cottage St., 2nd Fl., Bar Harbor, 207/288-2521, www.climbacadia.com) offers private **ice climbing** programs for all levels. Prices vary by course and number of participants, but expect to pay around $180 per person for two. ACS also offers half- and full-day **cross-country ski** excursions in the park; for two people, rates are $85 per person half-day, $140 per person full-day, including ski gear; a trail lunch is available for $25 per person. If you prefer **snowshoeing,** a guided trip for two is $100 per person half-day, $140 per person full-day, including snowshoes and trekking poles.

Practicalities

CAMPING

Mount Desert Island has at least a dozen private commercial campgrounds, but there are only two—**Blackwoods** and **Seawall**—within park boundaries on the island (a third park campground is on Isle au Haut, and a fourth is in the Schoodic section of the park).

Blackwoods and Seawall have no hookups. Most sites are for tents, but some do accommodate pop-ups, vehicle campers, and RVs up to 35 feet in length. Both campgrounds have seasonal restrooms (no showers) and dumping stations. Less than 0.5 mile from Blackwoods and even closer to Seawall are coin-operated hot showers and small markets for incidental supplies.

Both campgrounds are wooded and have no sea views but are not far from the water. In June, be prepared for blackflies; in July-August, bring insect repellent for mosquitoes. Maximum capacity at each site is six people, one vehicle, and one large tent or two small ones. Quiet time in both campgrounds is 10pm-6am.

Both campgrounds also have **amphitheaters,** where park rangers present free hour-long evening programs on a variety of natural and cultural history topics. Noncampers are also welcome at these events, and there's wheelchair access. Some of the programs have included "Forces of Nature," "Avian Mysteries," "Acadia's Treasures," "The French in Acadia," and "All Things Furry." Even sing-alongs are sometimes on the schedule. Blackwoods has programs several nights a week; Seawall programs tend to be on weekend evenings.

Collecting firewood is no longer allowed within Seawall's grounds. Rather than scrounge for what little duff remains around the campgrounds in order to build a campfire, stop on your way to Acadia and pick up a stash of firewood. All along Route 3 in Trenton and along Route 3 on Mount Desert, near the clusters of commercial campgrounds, you'll see signs for firewood for sale (around $3). Do not bring firewood from home, as it may contain bugs that threaten park resources.

The propane-powered Island Explorer buses serve both Blackwoods (Route 4/Blackwoods) and Seawall (Route 7/Southwest Harbor) late June-early October. Leave your vehicle at your campsite, and do your park and island exploring by bus.

Blackwoods Campground

With 306 campsites, Blackwoods Campground, just off Route 3, five miles south of Bar Harbor, is open all year. Because of its location on the east side of the island, it's also the more popular of the two campgrounds. Reservations, handled by the National Recreation Reservation Service (877/444-6777 or 518/885-3639 international, www.recreation.gov, credit or debit card required), can be made up to six months in advance and are suggested May 1-October 31. The fee is $30 per site per night May-October; you cannot reserve specific sites or adjoining sites. Campsites cost $10 in April and November, weather permitting; it's free December-March, but only a few primitive sites are available, with a portable toilet, a hand pump for water, and access only by hiking in from Route 3. No reservations are taken November-April. These dates and regulations are subject to change, so call to check so as not to be disappointed.

If you're staying at Blackwoods, consider adding the strenuous, seven-mile round-trip **Cadillac South Ridge Trail** to your hiking list. Of course, you can drive to the Cadillac summit and get the same fabulous 360-degree views, but this hike makes it feel like you earned them. Another plus: The park recently renewed the trail from Blackwoods to Gorham Mountain.

Seawall Campground

Reservations are accepted for about half of the 214 sites at Seawall Campground, on Route 102A in the Seawall district, four miles south of Southwest Harbor—it's first-come, first-served for the rest of the sites. But in midsummer, you'll need to arrive as early as 8:30am (when the ranger station opens) to secure one of those sites. Seawall is open late May-September. The cost is $30 per night for drive-in sites and $22 per night for walk-in sites. Make reservations up to six months in advance through the National Recreation Reservation Service (877/444-6777 or 518/885-3639 international, www.recreation.gov, credit or debit card required).

FOOD

The **Jordan Pond House** (Park Loop Rd., 207/276-3316, www.acadiajordanpondhouse. com, 11:30am-8pm daily mid-May-late June and late Aug.-late Oct., 11:30am-9pm daily late June-late Aug., $10-25). After a hike, pedal, or

The Island Explorer makes it easy to get around Acadia National Park without a car.

carriage ride, splurge on tea or lemonade and popovers (around $12), and request seating on the lawn. It's the only restaurant in the park, and it's wise to make reservations. Early and late in the season, it closes around 5pm. Note: A new concessionaire took over here in 2014, and consensus seems to be that tea and popovers are still worth it; ask locally about other meals.

EMERGENCIES

If you have an emergency while in the park, call **911**. The park's general information number is 207/288-3338. If you're in a remote location, it helps if you're carrying a cell phone, but keep it turned off while hiking or biking; save it for emergencies. The nearest hospital, in downtown Bar Harbor, is **Mount Desert Island Hospital** (10 Wayman Ln., 207/288-5081), with a 24-hour emergency room. The nearest major medical center is Eastern Maine Medical Center in Bangor, via a congested route that can take an hour or longer at the height of summer. Bangor, however, is one of the state's bases for a LifeFlight medevac helicopter.

The best advice for averting emergencies is to be cautious and sensible in everything you undertake in the park. Wear a helmet while biking. Don't hike alone or go off the trails—nearly every year someone is seriously injured or killed falling from the cliffs. Keep a sharp eye on children.

ACCESSIBILITY

The park publishes an *Accessibility Guide* (download from www.nps.gov/acad) that provides accessibility information about general facilities, programs, and services, including accessible trails, carriage roads, scenic sites, and ranger-led activities. Blackwoods Campground has 12 accessible drive-in sites; Seawall Campground has three RV, five drive-in, five walk-in, and a group site that are accessible. If you have other questions, call 207/288-3338, 8am-4:30pm Monday-Friday.

GETTING AROUND

The free **Island Explorer** (207/288-4573, www.exploreacadia.com) operates seven routes on Mount Desert Island that connect villages and campgrounds and access most areas of the park. It operates late June-early October.

Mount Desert Island Communities

Highlights

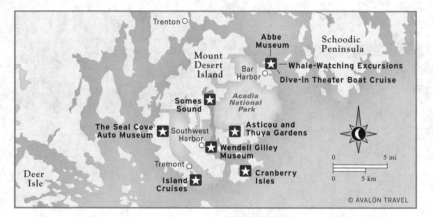

© AVALON TRAVEL

★ **Abbe Museum:** The Abbe Museum and its seasonal museum at Sieur de Monts Spring are fascinating places to learn about Maine's Native American heritage (page 73).

★ **Dive-in Theater Boat Cruise:** Got kids? Don't miss this tour, where Diver Ed brings the undersea world aboard (page 83).

★ **Whale-Watching Excursions:** Board a high-speed catamaran and cruise well offshore to view whales and the puffin colony at Petit Manan Light (page 84).

★ **Somes Sound:** It's worth the journey to the quiet side of the island to see this spectacular inlet, officially tagged a fjord (page 100).

★ **Asticou and Thuya Gardens:** Magical and enchanting best describe these two peaceful gardens. While Zen-like Asticou is best seen in

spring, Thuya delivers color through summer and also has hiking paths (page 100).

★ **Wendell Gilley Museum:** Gilley's intricately carved birds, from miniature shorebirds to life-size birds of prey, are a marvel to behold (page 108).

★ **The Seal Cove Auto Museum:** A must for fans of antique automobiles, the museum hosts one of the largest collections of Brass Era vehicles in the country, including a few extremely rare models (page 120).

★ **Island Cruises:** Adults and kids alike enjoy Captain Kim Strauss's extremely informative and fun nature cruises (page 121).

★ **Cranberry Isles:** Make it a point to cruise at least to Islesford for a taste of island life (page 124).

Perhaps no national park has as symbiotic a relationship with its feeder towns as Acadia National Park. Is it a chicken-and-egg situation? Not really. Whereas other national parks have served as magnets for the creation of

clusters of new towns, the towns that surround Acadia are longtime communities. These island towns made do and eked out a living from fishing and boat building long before the first 19th-century "rusticators" unloaded their families and steamer trunks, and long before the first chunk of pristine island real estate was donated to the nation.

Mount Desert Island's official towns (tax-collecting entities with all the bureaucracy that ensues) are Bar Harbor, Mount Desert, Southwest Harbor, and Tremont. Within each of these towns are villages—some with post offices and zip codes, some without. Bar Harbor, for instance, includes the villages of Hulls Cove, Salisbury Cove, Town Hill, and Eden, all in the northern part of the island, and part of the village of Otter Creek.

The town of Mount Desert can be the most confusing, since it includes the villages of Seal Harbor, Hall Quarry, Pretty Marsh, Beech Hill, Somesville, Northeast Harbor, and part of Otter Creek.

Be sure to drive or bike (or late June-Columbus Day, take the Island Explorer bus) around the smaller villages, especially Somesville, Bass Harbor, and Bernard. Views are fabulous, the pace is slow, and you'll feel you've stumbled on "the real Maine."

PLANNING YOUR TIME

Mount Desert Island is very seasonal, with most restaurants, accommodations, and shops open mid-May-mid-October. May and June bring the new greens of spring and blooming rhododendrons and azaleas in Northeast Harbor's Asticou Garden, but mosquitoes and blackflies are at their worst, and the weather is temperamental—perhaps sunny and hot one day, damp and cold the next, a packing nightmare. July and August bring summer at its best, along with the

Previous: Bar Harbor's waterfront; Thurston's Lobster Pound, in Bernard. **Above:** Bar Harbor's Shore Path.

Mount Desert Island Communities

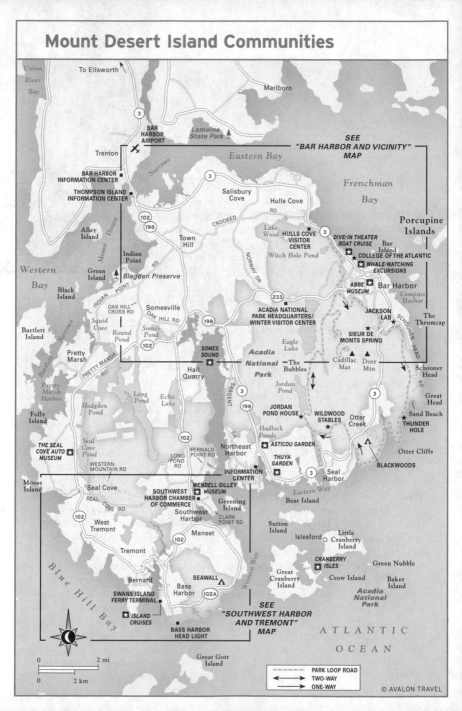

© AVALON TRAVEL

biggest crowds. September is a gem of a time to visit: no bugs, fewer people, less fog, and the golden light of fall. Foliage usually begins turning in early October, making it an especially beautiful time to visit (the Columbus Day holiday weekend brings a spike in visitors). Winter is Acadia's silent season, best left for independent travelers who don't mind making do or perhaps making a meal of peanut-butter crackers if an open restaurant can't be found.

The only road onto Mount Desert Island is Route 3. Unless you're traveling in the wee hours of the morning or late at night, expect traffic. Avoid it during shift changes on the island, 8am-9am and 3pm-4pm weekdays, when traffic slows to a crawl. On the island, use the Island Explorer bus system to avoid parking hassles.

Bar Harbor and Vicinity

In 1996, Bar Harbor (pop. 5,235) celebrated the bicentennial of its founding (as the town of Eden). In the late 19th century and well into the 20th, the town grew to become one of the East Coast's fanciest summer retreats.

In those days, ferries and steam yachts arrived from points south, large and small resort hotels sprang up, and exclusive mansions (quaintly dubbed "cottages") were the venues of parties thrown by summer-resident Drexels, DuPonts, Vanderbilts, and prominent academics, journalists, and lawyers. These "rusticators" came for the season with huge entourages of servants, children, pets, and horses. The area's renown was such that by the 1890s, even the staffs of the British, Austrian, and Ottoman embassies retreated here for the summer from Washington DC.

The establishment of the national park in 1919 and the arrival of the automobile changed the character of Bar Harbor and Mount Desert Island; two World Wars and the Great Depression took an additional toll in myriad ways; but the coup de grâce for Bar Harbor's era of elegance came with the Great Fire of 1947, a wind-whipped conflagration that devastated more than 17,000 acres on the eastern half of the island and leveled gorgeous mansions, humble homes, and more trees than anyone could ever count. Only three people died, but property damage was estimated at $20 million. Whole books have been written about the October inferno; fascinating scrapbooks in Bar Harbor's Jesup Memorial Library dramatically relate the gripping details of the story. Even though some of the elegant cottages have survived, the fire altered life here forever.

Bar Harbor often gets a bad rap for crowds. It's the island's largest town and the shopping hub; it's also where tour buses and cruise ships dock. That said, it's not hard to slip away to enjoy the town's sights and charms, of which there are many.

SIGHTS

Acadia National Park comes right up to the edge of town, but the Bar Harbor area has plenty of attractions of its own.

★ Abbe Museum

The fabulous Abbe Museum is a superb introduction to prehistoric, historic, and contemporary Native American tools, crafts, and other cultural artifacts, with an emphasis on Maine's Micmac, Maliseet, Passamaquoddy, and Penobscot people. Everything about this privately funded museum, established in 1927, is tasteful. It has two campuses: The **main campus** (26 Mt. Desert St., Bar Harbor, 207/288-3519, www.abbemuseum.org, 10am-5pm daily late May-early Nov., call for off-season hours, $8 adults, $4 ages 11-17) is home to a collection spanning nearly 12,000 years. Museum-sponsored events include crafts workshops, hands-on children's programs, archaeological field schools, and the **Native**

Bar Harbor and Vicinity

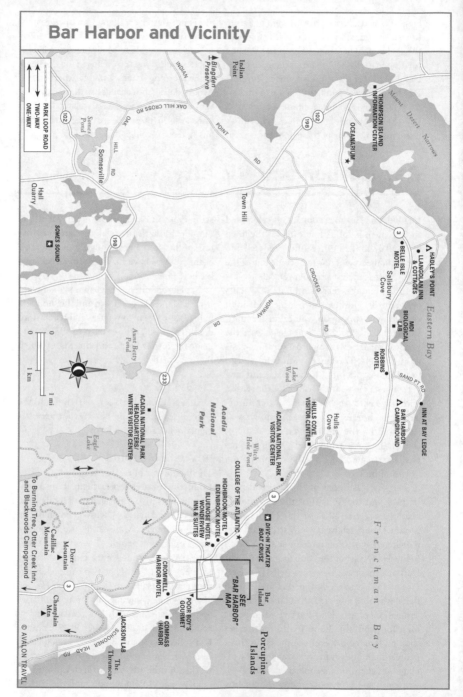

PARK LOOP ROAD
TWO-WAY
ONE-WAY

Indian Point
Blagden Preserve
INDIAN
OAK HILL CROSS RD
POINT
OAK
HILL
RD
Somesville
Somes Pond
Hall Quarry
SOMES SOUND
Mount Desert Narrows
THOMPSON ISLAND INFORMATION CENTER
OCEANARIUM
102
198
102
RD
Town Hill
Town Hill
3
HADLEY'S POINT
BELLE ISLE MOTEL
LLANGOLAN INN & COTTAGES
INN AT BAY LEDGE
Salisbury Cove
Eastern Bay
CROOKED
NORWAY
MDI BIOLOGICAL LAB
RD
DR
ROBBINS MOTEL
SAND PT RD
BAR HARBOR CAMPGROUND
198
Aunt Betty Pond
Lake Wood
Hulls Cove
233
Acadia National Park
ACADIA NATIONAL PARK HEADQUARTERS/ WINTER VISITOR CENTER
HULLS COVE VISITOR CENTER
ACADIA NATIONAL PARK VISITOR CENTER
Witch Hole Pond
Eagle Lake
COLLEGE OF THE ATLANTIC
HIGHBROOK MOTEL
EDENBROOK MOTEL
BLUENOSE HOTEL & WONDERVIEW INN & SUITES
3
DIVE-IN THEATER BOAT CRUISE
To Burning Tree, Otter Creek Inn, and Blackwoods Campground
Cadillac Mountain
Dorr Mountain
CROMWELL HARBOR MOTEL
SEE "BAR HARBOR" MAP
Bar Island
Frenchman Bay
3
Champlain Mtn
JACKSON LAB
SCHOONER HEAD RD
POOR BOY'S GOURMET
COMPASS HARBOR
The Thrumcap
Porcupine Islands

© AVALON TRAVEL

0   0
1 km   1 mi

St. Saviour's Episcopal Church

St. Saviour's Episcopal Church

St. Saviour's (41 Mt. Desert St., Bar Harbor, 207/288-4215, 7am-dusk daily), close to downtown Bar Harbor, boasts Maine's largest collection of Tiffany stained-glass windows. Ten originals are here; an 11th was stolen in 1988 and replaced by a locally made window. Of the 32 non-Tiffany windows, the most intriguing is a memorial to Clarence Little, founder of The Jackson Laboratory and a descendant of Paul Revere. Images in the window include the laboratory, DNA, and mice. In July-August, volunteers regularly conduct free tours of the Victorian-era church, completed in 1878; call for the schedule or make an appointment for an off-season tour. The church is open for self-guided tours 8am-8pm daily—pick up a brochure in the back. If old cemeteries intrigue you, spend time wandering the 18th-century town graveyard next to the church.

American Festival (held at the College of the Atlantic, usually the first Sat. after the Fourth of July).

Admission to the in-town Abbe also includes admission to the **museum's original site** (9am-4pm daily mid-May-mid-Oct.), in the park about 2.5 miles south of Bar Harbor at Sieur de Monts Spring, where Route 3 meets the Park Loop Road. Inside a small but handsome building listed on the National Register of Historic Places are displays from a 50,000-item collection. Admission to only the Sieur de Monts Spring Abbe is $3 adults, $1 ages 11-17, and admission paid here can be credited to admission to the main museum.

While you're at the original Abbe Museum site, take the time to wander the paths in the adjacent **Wild Gardens of Acadia,** a 0.75-acre microcosm of more than 400 plant species native to Mount Desert Island. Twelve separate display areas, carefully maintained and labeled by the Bar Harbor Garden Club, represent native plant habitats; pick up the map-brochure that explains each.

Bar Harbor Historical Society

The **Bar Harbor Historical Society** (33 Ledgelawn Ave., Bar Harbor, 207/288-0000, www.barharborhistorical.org, 1pm-4pm Mon.-Fri. mid-June-mid-Oct., free), in a Jacobean Revival-style building listed on the National Register of Historic Places, has fascinating displays, stereopticon images, and a scrapbook about the 1947 fire that devastated the island. The photographs alone are worth the visit. Also here are antique maps, Victorian-era hotel registers, and other local memorabilia. In winter it's open by appointment.

For a sample of Bar Harbor before the great fire, wander over to upper West Street, which is on the National Register of Historic Places thanks to the remaining grand cottages that line it.

College of the Atlantic

A museum, a gallery, and a pleasant campus for walking are reasons to visit the **College of the Atlantic** (COA, 105 Eden St./Rte. 3, Bar Harbor, 207/288-5015, www.coa.edu),

Bar Harbor

Bar Harbor

(passable by foot only at low tide)

0   0.1 mi
0   0.1 km

TOWN PIER
WHALE-WATCHING
EXCURSIONS

HARBORSIDE HOTEL
AND MARINA

OLI'S
TROLLEY

CHAMBER OF
COMMERCE
INFO OFFICE

SONG OF
THE SEA

BAR HARBOR
CLUB

EDEN

GALYN'S

BAR HARBOR
INN

NATIONAL
PARK
KAYAK
TOURS

SHERMAN'S
BOOK STORE

ALL FIRED UP

CRITERION
THEATRE

BASS
COTTAGE
INN

ULLIKANA
B&B

ISLAND
ARTISANS

ROSALIE'S PIZZA

CADILLAC
MTN
SPORTS

COASTAL KAYAKING/
ACADIA BIKE & CANOE

LOMPOC
CAFÉ

MAGGIE'S
RESTAURANT

BAR HARBOR
BICYCLE SHOP

MORNING
GLORY BAKERY

GEORGE'S

SEACROFT INN

ACADIA
INFORMATION

RUPUNUNI

REEL PIZZA

ISLAND EXPLORER
BUS HUB

Village Green

ST. SAVIOUR'S
EPISCOPAL CHURCH

CAFÉ THIS
WAY

ABBE
MUSEUM

MIRA MONTE
INN

VILAGER INN

BAR HARBOR
HISTORICAL
SOCIETY

MCKAYS
PUBLIC HOUSE

Agamont
Park

Shore Path

THE FIELD

STEPHENS LN

ALBERT MEADOW

Grant
Park

DERBY LN

ATLANTIC AVE

HANCOCK ST

To Havana

© AVALON TRAVEL

which specializes in human ecology, or humans' interrelationship with the environment. In a handsome renovated building that originally served as the first Acadia National Park headquarters, the **George B. Dorr Museum of Natural History** (10am-5pm Tues.-Sat., donation) showcases regional birds and mammals in realistic dioramas made by COA students. The biggest attraction for children is the please-touch philosophy, allowing them to reach into a touch tank and to feel fur, skulls, and even whale baleen. The museum gift shop has a particularly good collection of books and gifts for budding naturalists.

Across the way is the **Ethel H. Blum Gallery** (207/288-5015, ext. 254, 11am-4pm Mon.-Sat. summer, 9am-5pm Mon.-Fri. during the academic year), a small space that hosts some intriguing exhibits.

Also on campus is the **Beatrix Farrand Garden,** behind Kaelber Hall. The garden, designed in 1928, contained more than 50 varieties of roses and was the prototype for the rose garden at Dumbarton Oaks in Washington DC. Both are known for

Changing the World, One Mind at a Time

Wherever you turn on Mount Desert Island, you'll find evidence of **College of the Atlantic** (COA). The students are highly visible; graduates have established numerous island businesses; and the college itself is an integral part of the year-round island community. In addition to its Bar Harbor campus, COA owns marine research facilities on two offshore islands with lighthouses, Mount Desert Rock and Great Duck Island; Beech Hill Farm, an 85-acre Maine Organic Farmers and Gardeners Association-certified organic farm in Mount Desert, dedicated to sustainable agriculture, which provides produce for the school's kitchen as well as for local businesses and its own farm stand; and the Peggy Rockefeller Farms, a 125-acre farm donated by the Rockefeller family and dedicated to agricultural, conservation, and educational programs.

a finback whale skull outside the George B. Dorr Museum of Natural History

Founded in 1969, COA is an accredited four-year independent college with a graduate program. Despite being a small school—about 360 students—it has a far-reaching reputation; with approximately 17 percent of students coming from abroad. The school and the curriculum are built around the principles of close faculty-student connections and learning by doing in an interdisciplinary setting. COA awards two degrees, the bachelor of arts and the master of philosophy. Both are in human ecology, which the college defines as "the study of the interconnected relationships between people and our natural, social, and constructed environments." That translates to programs designed for long-term results that help people and nature flourish.

Many of the innovative school's alumni remain on the island to start new businesses or take over existing ones. COA alumni are behind the Dive-in Theater Boat Cruise, Reel Pizza Cinerama, Bar Harbor Ghost Tours, Natural History Center, and several restaurants, including Burning Tree, Cafe This Way, Havana, Lompoc Café, Morning Glory Bakery, and Guinness. That's just skimming the top. Town Hill Market, Sunflower Gardens & Greenhouses, Bar Harbor Cellars Winery, House Wine, and more than a dozen services are COA-graduate initiatives. And that's just on the island.

The college's admission policy, like its curriculum, is geared to the individual student, and interested students are encouraged to visit the campus, take a tour, and talk with faculty and staff. Even if you're not interested in pursuing the COA's educational opportunities, the gorgeous 35-acre oceanfront campus is well worth a visit. It houses a museum, a gallery, gardens, and a shorefront path.

Farrand's use of garden rooms, such as the walled terraces in this garden.

The 1st floor of **The Turrets,** a magnificent 1895 seaside cottage that's now an administration building, can be explored. Don't miss **Turrets Sea Side Garden,** fronting on the ocean, which was restored by a student in 2005. The central fountain, created by alumnus Dan Farrenkopf of Lunaform Pottery, was installed in 2009. Adjacent to The Turrets is a

sunken garden, created in a foundation and restored in 2009 by two students.

The college also offers excellent and very popular weeklong sessions of **Family Nature Camp** (800/597-9500, www.coa. edu/summer, July-early Aug., $940 adults, $480 ages 15 and younger covers almost everything). It's essential to register well in advance; ask about early-season discounts. Families are housed and fed on the campus, and explore Acadia National Park with expert naturalist guides.

Check the college's calendar of events for lectures, conversations, and other events.

The college and its museum are 0.5 mile northwest of downtown Bar Harbor; take Island Explorer Route 2/Eden Street.

Oceanarium and Maine Lobster Hatchery

At the northern edge of Mount Desert Island, 8.5 miles northwest of downtown Bar Harbor, is the understated but fascinating **Oceanarium and Maine Lobster Hatchery** (1351 Rte. 3, Bar Harbor, 207/288-5005, www.theoceanarium.com, 9am-5pm Mon.-Sat. mid-May-late Oct.). This low-tech, high-interest operation awes the kids, and it's pretty darn interesting for adults too. David and Audrey Mills have been at it since 1972 and are determined to educate visitors while showing them a good time. Visitors on tour view thousands of tiny lobster hatchlings, enjoy a museum, finger sealife in a touch tank, and meander along a salt marsh walk, where you can check out tidal creatures and vegetation. All tours begin on the hour and half hour. Allow 1-2 hours to see everything. Tickets are $15 adults, $10 ages 4-12, covering admission to the lobster hatchery, lobster museum, and touch tank; an expanded program includes a 45-minute Marsh Walk for $17 adults, $11 children.

Garland Farm

Fans of landscape architect Beatrix Farrand will want to visit **Garland Farm** (475 Bayview Dr., Bar Harbor, 207/288-0237, www.beatrixfarrandsociety.org), the ancestral home of Lewis Garland, who managed her Reef Point property. When Farrand dismantled that property in 1955, she moved here with the Garlands, engaging an architect to build an addition to the original farmhouse and barn using architectural elements from Reef Point. The property was sold a few times, and greatly reduced in size, until the Beatrix Farrand Society was formed in 2002 and

purchased it in 2004. The society's goal is to restore Garland Farm to its Farrand-era design and condition and create a center for the study of design and horticulture. The property, now listed on the National Register of Historic Places, hosts special events and programs. Garland Farm is open for visits one or two days per week and tours by appointment.

Hulls Cove Tool Barn and Sculpture Garden

Part shop, part nature center, part art gallery, the **Hulls Cove Tool Barn and Sculpture Garden** (17 Breakneck Rd., Hulls Cove, 207/288-5126, www.jonesport-wood.com, 9am-5pm Wed.-Sat., noon-5pm Sun, free), behind Hulls Cove General Store, is just one of creative Skip Brack's enterprises. Inside the barn is an extensive selection of old tools, with an emphasis on woodworking hand tools. Paths run through perennial gardens, woods, and fields at the Davistown Museum Sculpture Garden, which surrounds the barn and continues across the street. Throughout the garden are sculptures by noted Maine artists and found-object creations by Brack. Take the Island Explorer bus Route 1/Campgrounds and request a stop at the Hulls Cove General Store, then walk up the road.

Research Laboratories

Some of the world's top scientists live year-round or come to Bar Harbor in summer to work at two prominent scientific laboratories.

World renowned in genetic research, scientists at **The Jackson Laboratory for Mammalian Research** (600 Main St./Rte. 3, Bar Harbor, 207/288-6000, www.jax.org) study cancer, diabetes, muscular dystrophy, heart disease, and Alzheimer's disease, among others—with considerable success. The nonprofit research institution, locally called JAX or just "the lab," is also renowned for its genetics databases and for producing genetically defined laboratory mice, which are shipped to research labs worldwide. Free summer public tours (limited to 15 people; preregistration required) begin in the lab's visitors lobby

Adopt a Whale

Here's a trump card: When everyone else is flashing photos of kids or grandkids, you can whip out images of your very own adopted whale. And for that, you can thank Allied Whale's **Adopt-a-Whale** program at College of the Atlantic (COA) in Bar Harbor.

In 1972, COA established Allied Whale, a marine-mammal laboratory designed to collect, interpret, and apply research on the world's largest mammal. Although Allied Whale's primary focus is the Gulf of Maine, its projects span the globe, involving international scientific collaboration. Since 1981, part of the research has involved assembling an enormous photo collection (more than 25,000 images) for identification of specific humpback and finback whales (with names such as Quartz and Elvis) and tracking of their migration routes. The photo catalog of finbacks already numbers more than 1,000.

And here's where the adoption program comes in—it's a way to support the important research being done by Allied Whale and its colleagues. If you sign up as an adoptive "parent" for a year, you'll receive a Certificate of Adoption, a large color photo and a biography of your whale, its sighting history, an informational booklet, and an Adopt a Whale-Allied Whale bumper sticker. It's a superb gift for budding scientists. The adoption fee is $30 for a single humpback or finback or $40 for a mother and calf.

For further information, contact **Allied Whale** (207/288-5644, www.barharborwhalemuseum.org/adopt2.php).

and visit the lab's three main research wings. These show the evolution of facilities over the decades, beginning with the 1980s, and the guide discusses the genetic research occurring in each. The lab is 1.5 miles south of downtown Bar Harbor. Note: If this is something that's on your must-do list, plan ahead as the tours do sell out, often well in advance.

No less impressive is the **Mount Desert Island Biological Laboratory** (MDIBL, 159 Old Bar Harbor Rd., Salisbury Cove, 207/288-3605, www.mdibl.org), one of the few scientific research institutions in the world dedicated to studying marine animals to learn more about human health and environmental health. It is the only comprehensive effort in the country to sequence genomes. Tours are offered by advance reservation, with at least one week's notice. **Science Café** is a comfortable community science forum offered every other week at an off-site location. **Family Science Night,** held once or twice each summer, is an interactive program of performances, demonstrations, and hands-on science; reservations are recommended. In 2012, the lab won a $250,000 grant to work with the National Park Service and the Schoodic

Education and Research Center to create a **Pathway to BioTrails,** a hands-on program to involve park visitors in scientific research. The program will monitor park flora and fauna using a genetic technique called DNA barcoding. Ultimately, the program will offer a range of citizen science projects organized around hiking, cycling, and sea kayaking trails, allowing visitors, research scientists, and park staff to work together to assess the effect of environmental changes. The lab is six miles north of Bar Harbor off Route 3.

RECREATION
Parks and Preserves
BAR ISLAND

Check local newspapers or the Bar Harbor Chamber of Commerce visitors booklet for the times of low tide, then walk across the gravel bar to wooded Bar Island (formerly Rodick's Island) from the foot of Bridge Street in downtown Bar Harbor. Shell heaps recorded on the eastern end of the island indicate that Native Americans enjoyed this turf in the distant past. You'll have the most time to explore the island during new-moon or full-moon low tides, but no more than four hours—about two hours before and two hours after low tide. Be sure to wear a watch so you don't get trapped (for up to 10 hours). The foot of Bridge Street is also an excellent kayak-launching site.

Every summer, local papers carry stories of people trapped on the island by the tide, and about cars parked on the sandbar and forgotten, then flooded by the incoming tide. Don't let it happen to you.

COMPASS HARBOR

About a mile from downtown along Main Street (Rte. 3) is Compass Harbor, a section of the park where you can stroll through woods to the water's edge and explore the overgrown ruins of Acadia National Park cofounder George Dorr's home. This little pocket section of the park is a great place to escape crowds in town or at the big-ticket sights.

INDIAN POINT BLAGDEN PRESERVE

In the far northern corner of the island, still within the Bar Harbor town limits, is the lovely **Indian Point Blagden Preserve** (207/729-5181, dawn-6pm daily year-round), owned by The Nature Conservancy. From the junction of Route 3 and Route 102/198,

continue 1.8 miles to Indian Point Road and turn right. Go 1.7 miles to a fork and turn right. Watch for the preserve entrance on the right, marked by a Nature Conservancy oak leaf.

Five trails wind through the forested 110-acre preserve, a rectangular parcel with island, hill, and bay vistas and more than 1,000 feet of frontage on Western Bay. Seal-watching and birding are popular—there are harbor seals on offshore rocks, six species of woodpeckers, and 12 species of warblers, plus more than 100 other bird species in blowdown areas. To spot the seals, plan your hike around the time of low tide, when they'll be sprawled on the rocks close to shore. Wear rubberized shoes or boots. Bring binoculars or use the telescope installed here for that purpose. To avoid disturbing the seals, watch quietly and avoid jerky movements. Park near the preserve entrance and follow the Big Woods Trail, which runs the length of the preserve. A second parking area is farther in, but then you'll miss walking through much of the preserve. When you reach the second parking area, just past an old farm field, bear left along the Shore Trail to see the seals. Register at the caretakers' house, which is just beyond the first parking lot, where you can pick up bird and flora

At low tide, the sand bar connecting Bar Harbor to Bar Island is popular with sea kayakers and hikers.

checklists, and respect the private property on either side of the preserve.

Walks

SHORE PATH

A real treat is a stroll along downtown Bar Harbor's **Shore Path** (6:30am-dusk daily), a well-trodden granite-edged byway built around 1880. Along the craggy shoreline are granite-and-wood benches, town-owned **Grant Park** (great for picnics), birch trees, and several handsome mansions that escaped the 1947 fire. Offshore are the four Porcupine Islands. Leashed pets are allowed. Allow about 30 minutes for the one-mile loop, beginning next to the town pier and the Bar Harbor Inn and returning via Wayman Lane.

GREAT MEADOW LOOP

This easy walk connects downtown Bar Harbor with the park's Jesup Path, which leads to Sieur de Monts Spring. From there, you have access to the Dorr Mountain trails. It's a fine early-morning walk and a gentle introduction to hiking for those nervous about straying too far from civilization.

To find the Great Meadow Loop trailhead, walk up Mount Desert Street from the Village Green to Spring Street. Follow Spring Street to Cromwell Harbor Road and turn left. At the edge of Ledgelawn Cemetery, you'll see the signed trail. It meanders through the woods for a bit before emerging on Ledgelawn Avenue. Turn right and walk along the road until the trail reenters the woods across the road. The trail never strays too far from pavement. It parallels the road for a bit before recrossing it and shadowing the Park Loop Road; the Kebo Valley Golf Club will be on the right. Just before the trail crosses Harden Farm Road, you'll see the Jesup Path trailhead on the left, across the Park Loop Road. Take that if you want to head to Sieur de Monts Spring (0.6 mile). Otherwise, continue along the trail as it follows and crosses Harden Farm Road and wraps around the golf course (there's a portable toilet near one green).

At the intersection with Cromwell Harbor Road, turn right, return to Spring Street, and follow it back to Mount Desert Street and the Village Green. It's just shy of two miles round-trip.

Biking

With all the great biking options, including 45 miles of carriage roads (12 of the total 57 miles are off-limits to bicycles) and some of the best roadside bike routes in Maine, you'll want to

The Shore Path edges Bar Harbor's waterfront.

bring a bike or rent one. Two rental firms based in downtown Bar Harbor also handle repairs. Expect to pay around $25 per day for a rental bike, including a helmet, a lock, and a map, and more for a performance model. It's wise to make advance reservations.

The Minutolo family's **Bar Harbor Bicycle Shop** (141 Cottage St., Bar Harbor, 207/288-3886, www.barharborbike.com), on the corner of Route 3, has been in business since 1977. If you have your own bike, stop here for advice on routes—the Minutolos have cycled everywhere on the island and can suggest the perfect mountain-bike or road-bike loop based on your ability and schedule. The shop has rentals varying from standard mountain bikes to full-suspension models and even tandems as well as all the accessories and gear you might need. The shop also can give you the schedule for local rides organized by the **Downeast Bicycle Club** (www.downeastbicycleclub.ning.com).

Acadia Bike & Canoe (48 Cottage St., Bar Harbor, 207/288-9605 or 800/526-8615, www.acadiabike.com) also rents bikes.

For a low-key insider bicycle tour of the region, you can't do better than **Maine Coast Bicycle Tours** (48 Cottage St., Bar Harbor, 207/288-0050 or 888/412-2453, www.mainecoastbicycletours.com). Locally owned and operated, Maine Coast specializes in all-inclusive bicycle tours of Mount Desert Island, with forays to Schoodic Point and Swans Island. These folks know the island and are willing to share their insider info. The six-day tour costs about $1,900, which covers most meals (usually in top-rated restaurants), a 24-speed rental bicycle and related gear, a guide and a support vehicle, an afternoon guided sea-kayak or hiking tour, a guided walking tour of downtown Bar Harbor, a welcome reception at an oceanfront private home, a sunset tour of Cadillac, the round-trip ferry to Swans Island, and five nights of upscale inn lodging. This is not for very serious cyclists; trips cover a mere 15-25 miles each day, allowing plenty of time to enjoy the scenery and relax.

If you're headed to Southwest Harbor, perhaps for a day trip to Swans Island, see the information on Southwest Cycle in the *Southwest Harbor and Vicinity* section farther on in this chapter.

Sea Kayaking and Canoeing

If you've brought your own kayak, one place to launch it is **Hadley Point Beach** (Hadley Point Rd., Bar Harbor). This pebbly beach on Mount Desert Narrows has a couple of picnic tables, a portable toilet, and parking. Careful, though—the currents are very strong. To find the put-in, continue south from the Thompson Island Information Center on Route 3 for about four miles. The Hadley Point Road is on the left; follow it to the end.

GUIDED TOURS

Sea kayaking is wildly popular along the Maine coast, and Bar Harbor has become a major kayaking destination. No experience is necessary to join tours operated by any of the firms in Bar Harbor.

Since 1993, **National Park Kayak Tours** (39 Cottage St., Bar Harbor, 800/347-0940, www.acadiakayak.com) has offered Registered Maine Guide-led tours, each limited to a maximum of six tandem kayaks per trip. Four-hour morning, midday, afternoon, or sunset paddles ($48 pp July-Aug., $44 off-season) are offered, including shuttle service, a paddle and safety lesson, and a brief stop. Paddlers are shuttled to the quiet west side of the island (usually Western or Blue Hill Bay, occasionally Somes Sound), with the location determined by wind and weather. Most trips cover about six miles. Multiday camping trips also are offered. It's best if you make reservations at least one day in advance. Trips are offered Memorial Day weekend-early October.

Half-day, full-day, and multiday sea-kayak tours are on the schedule organized by **Coastal Kayaking Tours** (48 Cottage St., Bar Harbor, 207/288-9605 or 800/526-8615, www.acadiafun.com). The best option for beginners is the 2.5-hour morning harbor tour ($39 pp). A half-day family tour, departing at 1pm, can handle kids age eight and over ($49 pp). A

2.5-hour sunset cruise ($39 pp) begins around 5pm, depending on season; a full-day tour ($74 pp, lunch not included) covers about 10 miles; and a three-day island-camping adventure is $429 per person, including equipment and meals. All trips are weather dependent, and reservations are essential.

Golf

Duffers first teed off in 1888 at **Kebo Valley Golf Club** (100 Eagle Lake Rd./Rte. 233, Bar Harbor, 207/288-5000, www.kebovalleyclub.com, May-Oct.), Maine's oldest club and the eighth-oldest in the nation. The 17th hole became legendary when it took President William Howard Taft 27 tries to sink the ball in 1911. Kebo is very popular, with a gorgeous setting, an attractive clubhouse, and decent food service, so booking tee times is essential; you can reserve up to six days in advance.

Mount Desert Island YMCA

Here's a lifesaver on a stormy day: The **Mount Desert Island YMCA** (21 Park St., Bar Harbor, 207/288-3511, www.mdiymca.org, 5:30am-8:30pm Mon.-Fri., 7am-4pm Sat., 7am-2pm Sun. summer) has an indoor pool, a gym, a track, a fitness room, and a recreation room. Rates are $10 ages 19-59, $5 full-time

students and seniors, and $18 per family, covering two adults and up to three kids.

EXCURSION BOATS

Note that prices are given as a guide and will fluctuate with the cost of fuel.

★ Dive-in Theater Boat Cruise

You don't have to go diving in these frigid waters; others will do it for you. When the kids are clamoring to touch slimy sea cucumbers and starfish at various touch tanks in the area, they're likely to be primed for Diver Ed's **Dive-in Theater Boat Cruise** (207/288-3483 or 800/979-3370, www.divered.com), departing from the College of the Atlantic pier (105 Eden St., Bar Harbor). Ed Monat, former Bar Harbor harbormaster and College of the Atlantic grad, heads the crew aboard the 46-passenger *Starfish Enterprise*, which goes a mile or two offshore where Ed, a professional diver, goes overboard with a video camera and a mini-Ed, who helps put things in proportion. You and the kids stay on deck, all warm and dry, along with Captain Evil, who explains the action on a TV screen. There's communication back and forth, so the kids can ask questions as the divers pick up

Join a guided sea kayaking excursion for a paddle around Bar Harbor's waterfront.

urchins, starfish, crabs, lobsters, and other sealife. When Ed resurfaces, he brings a bag of touchable specimens—another chance to pet some slimy creatures (which go back into the water after show-and-tell). It's a great concept. Watch the kids' expressions—this is a big hit. The two-hour trips depart three times daily Monday-Friday, twice daily Saturday, and once on Sunday early July-early September; fewer trips are made in spring and fall. The cost is $40 adults, $35 seniors, $30 ages 5-12, $15 under age 5. Usually twice weekly there's a park ranger or naturalist on board and the tour lasts for three hours—check the park's *Beaver Log* newspaper or Diver Ed's website for the schedule and reservation information—these trips cost an additional $5. Advance reservations are strongly recommended.

★ Whale-Watching Excursions

Whale-watching boats go as far as 20 miles offshore, so no matter what the weather in Bar Harbor, dress warmly and bring more clothing than you think you'll need—even gloves, if you're especially sensitive to cold. I've been out on days when it's close to 90°F on the island but feels more like 30°F in a moving boat on the open ocean. Motion-sensitive children

and adults should plan in advance for appropriate medication, such as seasickness pills or patches. Adults are required to show a photo ID when boarding the boat.

Whale-watching, puffin-watching, and combo excursions are offered by **Bar Harbor Whale Watch Company** (1 West St., Bar Harbor, 207/288-2386 or 800/942-5374, www.barharborwhales.com), sailing from the town pier (1 West St.) in downtown Bar Harbor. The company operates under various names, including Acadian Whale Watcher, and has a number of boats. Most trips are accompanied by a naturalist (often from Allied Whale at the College of the Atlantic), who regales passengers with all sorts of interesting trivia about the whales, porpoises, seabirds, and other marine life spotted along the way. In season, some trips go out as far as the puffin colony on Petit Manan Light. Trips depart daily late May-late October, but with so many options it's impossible to list the schedule—call for the latest details. Tickets are around $65 adults, $35 ages 6-14, $9 under age 6. A portion of the ticket price benefits Allied Whale, which researches and protects marine animals in the Gulf of Maine.

Trips may extend longer than the time

Excursion boats depart from Bar Harbor's waterfront.

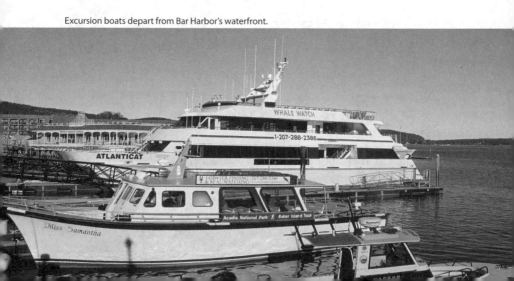

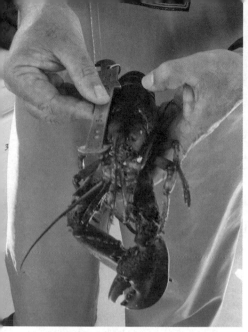
Join Captain John Nicolai aboard the *Lulu* to learn all about lobster fishing.

advertised, so don't plan anything else too tightly around the trip.

Scenic Nature Cruises (1.5-2 hours) and kid-friendly Lobster and Seal Watch Cruises (1.5 hours) are also offered. Rates for these are around $30 adults, $18 ages 6-14, and $5 or less for little kids.

Sailing

Captain Steve Pagels, under the umbrella of **Downeast Windjammer Cruises** (207/288-4585 or 207/288-2373, www.downeastwindjammer.com), offers 1.5-2-hour day sails on the 151-foot steel-hulled *Margaret Todd,* a gorgeous four-masted schooner with tanbark sails that he designed and launched in 1998. Trips depart at 10am, 2pm, and around sunset daily mid-May-mid-October (weather permitting) from the Bar Harbor Inn pier, just east of the town pier in downtown Bar Harbor. You'll get the best wildlife sightings on the morning trip, but better sailing on the afternoon trip; there's live music on the sunset one. A park ranger narrates some morning sails. Buy

tickets either at the pier, at 27 Main Street, or online with a credit card; plan to arrive at least half an hour early. The cost is $38 adults, $35 seniors, $28 ages 6-11, $5 ages 2-5. Dogs are welcome on all sails.

Sea Venture

Captain Winston Shaw's custom boat tour by **Sea Venture** (207/412-0222, www.svboattours.com) lets you design the perfect trip aboard *Reflection,* a 20-foot motor launch. Captain Shaw, a Registered Maine Guide and committed environmentalist, specializes in nature-oriented tours. He's the founder and director of the Coastal Maine Bald Eagle Project, and he was involved in the inaugural Earth Day celebration in 1970. He's been studying coastal birds for more than 25 years. You can pick from 10 recommended cruises lasting 1-8 hours, or design your own. In any case, the boat is yours. The boat charter rate is $120 per hour for up to two people, $140 for three or four, and $180 for five or six. Captain Shaw can also arrange for picnic lunches. On longer trips, restroom stops are available. The boat departs from the Atlantic Oakes Motel pier, off Route 3 in Bar Harbor.

Lobster Cruise

When you're ready to learn *the truth* about lobsters, sign up for a two-hour cruise aboard **Captain John Nicolai's *Lulu*** (56 West St., Bar Harbor, 207/963-2341, www.lululobsterboat.com), a traditional Maine lobster boat that departs up to four times daily from the Harborside Hotel and Marina. Captain Nicolai provides an entertaining commentary on anything and everything, but especially about lobsters and lobstering. He hauls a lobster trap and explains intimate details of the hapless critters. Reservations are required. Cost is $33 adults, $30 seniors and active U.S. military, $20 ages 2-12.

Ferry to Schoodic

If you want to visit the Schoodic section of Acadia National Park or spend some time on the Schoodic Peninsula, the **Bar Harbor**

Ferry (Bar Harbor Inn Pier, Bar Harbor, 207/288-2984, www.barharborferry.com, round-trip $32 adults, $22 children, $7 bicycles) operates five round-trips daily late June-August and twice daily mid-late June and September. The schedule coordinates with the Island Explorer bus, which circulates from Winter Harbor to Prospect Harbor and loops through the Schoodic section of the park late June-late August.

ENTERTAINMENT

At the height of the summer season, plenty of live entertainment includes pub music, films, and classical concerts.

The **Bar Harbor Town Band** performs for free at 8pm Monday and Thursday evenings July-mid-August in the bandstand on the Village Green (Main St. and Mt. Desert St., Bar Harbor).

The **Jesup Memorial Library** (www.jesuplibrary.org) regularly hosts author readings, concerts, and other activities.

Carmen Verandah/Bar Harbor Beerworks (119 Main St., Bar Harbor, 207/288-2766, www.restaurantsbarharbor.com) is the weekend place to be and be seen, with music, dancing, and more.

You never know quite what's going to happen at **Improv Acadia** (15 Cottage St., Bar Harbor, 207/288-2503, www.improvacadia.com, late May-mid-Oct., $17 adults, $12 under age 13). Every show is different, as actors use audience suggestions to create comedy sketches. Shows are staged once or twice nightly. Dessert, snacks, and drinks are available. The 8pm show in July and August is family-friendly.

The **Bar Harbor Music Festival** (207/288-5744 July-Aug., 212/222-1026 off-season, www.barharbormusicfestival.org, $25-40 adults, $15 students), a summer tradition since 1967, emphasizes up-and-coming musical talent in a series of classical, jazz, and pop concerts and even an opera, with most scheduled in July, at various island locations that include local inns and an annual outdoor concert in Acadia National Park. Tickets can be purchased at the festival office (59 Cottage St., Bar Harbor), and reservations are advised.

Every evening, 7pm-11pm, **pianist Bill Trowell** plays in the Great Room Piano Lounge at The Bluenose Hotel (90 Eden St., Bar Harbor, 207/288-3348, www.barharborhotel.com).

Theaters

Built in 1932 and listed on the National Register of Historic Places, the **Criterion Theatre** (35 Cottage St., Bar Harbor, 207/288-0829, www.criteriontheatre.org) is an 877-seat art deco classic, with an elegant floating balcony. Its recent history is a roller coaster of openings and closings, but with the help of an anonymous donor, the nonprofit Bar Harbor Jazz Festival (www.bhjf.org) purchased it late in 2014 with plans to restore it to its former glory and reopen in the spring as a year-round venue for movies and live performances.

Combine pizza with your picture show at **Reel Pizza Cinerama** (33 Kennebec Pl., Bar Harbor, 207/288-3811 for films, 207/288-3828 for food, www.reelpizza.net). Two films are screened nightly on each of two screens. All tickets are $6; pizzas start at $9. Doors open at 4:30pm; get there early for the best seats.

EVENTS

Bar Harbor is home to numerous special events; here's just a sampling. For more information, contact the Bar Harbor Chamber of Commerce (207/288-5103 or 888/540-9990, www.barharbormaine.com).

The mid-May **Taste of Bar Harbor** kicks off the season with cooking classes, brewery tours, tastings, competitions, and other culinary events.

In early June, the annual **Acadia Birding Festival** (www.acadiabirdingfestival.com) attracts bird-watchers with guided walks, boating excursions, tours, talks, and meals.

The **Fourth of July** is always a big deal in Bar Harbor, celebrated with a 6am blueberry-pancake breakfast, a 10am parade, an 11am seafood festival, a band concert, and fireworks. A highlight is the Lobster Race, a crustacean competition drawing contestants such as Lobzilla and Larry the Lobster in a four-lane saltwater tank on the Village Green. Independence Day celebrations in the island's smaller villages always evoke a bygone era.

The Abbe Museum, the College of the Atlantic, and the Maine Indian Basketmakers Alliance sponsor the annual **Native American Festival** featuring baskets, beadwork, and other handicrafts for sale as well as Indian drumming and dancing, held at College of the Atlantic on a Saturday in early July.

In even-numbered years, the **Mount Desert Garden Club Tour** presents a rare chance to visit some of Maine's most spectacular private gardens on the second or third Saturday in July; confirm the date with the Bar Harbor Chamber of Commerce (207/288-5103 or 888/540-9990, www.barharbormaine.com).

The **Directions Craft Show** fills a weekend in late July or early August with extraordinary displays and sales of crafts by members of the Maine Crafts Guild. You'll find it at Mount Desert Island High School (Rte. 233/ Eagle Lake Rd., Bar Harbor).

The **Acadia Night Sky Festival** (www.acadianightskyfestival.com) in September celebrates Acadia's stellar stargazing with arts and science events, presentations, and activities.

SHOPPING

Bar Harbor's boutiques—running the gamut from attractive to kitschy—are indisputably visitor-oriented; many shut down for the winter, even removing or covering their signs and blanketing the windows. Fortunately, the island has enough of a year-round community to support the cluster of loyal shopkeepers determined to stay open all year, but shop-till-you-droppers will be happiest here Memorial Day weekend-Columbus Day, and particularly in July-August. Remember also that Bar Harbor isn't Mount Desert's only shopping area.

Galleries

Downtown Bar Harbor's best crafts gallery is **Island Artisans** (99 Main St., Bar Harbor, 207/288-4214, www.islandartisans.com). More than 100 Maine artists are represented here, and the quality is outstanding—don't miss it. You'll find basketwork, handmade paper, woodcarvings, blown glass, jewelry, weaving, metalwork, ceramics, and more.

It's worth the brief detour off the beaten path to find **Rocky Mann Studio & Gallery** (38 Breakneck Rd., Bar Harbor, 207/288-5478, www.rockymann.com) to see Mann's porcelain and raku pottery.

Also worth a gander is the **Asticou Connection** (1302 Rte. 102, Town Hill, Bar Harbor, 207/288-2400, www.asticouconnection.com), the Savage family's gallery and workshop. Among the works by family members and area artists are furniture, sculpture, bronze castings, paintings, jewelry, and photography.

Gallery? Funky gift store? Museum? It's hard to categorize the **Rock & Art Shop** (13 Cottage St., Bar Harbor, 207/288-4800). Fossils, gems, minerals, bug-filled marbles, and preserved sea horses are part of the intriguing mix, most of which carries educational signs.

Books and Gifts

Toys, cards, and newspapers blend in with the new-book inventory at **Sherman's Book Store** (56 Main St., Bar Harbor, 207/288-3161). It's just the place to pick up maps and trail guides for fine days and puzzles for foggy days.

Find a whodunit at **Bar Harbor Mystery Cove Book Shop** (1 Dewey St., Hulls Cove, 207/288-4665), the overflow of an Internet business specializing in mysteries and detective fiction, from rare books to popular titles, but you'll find plenty of other choices in all genres.

An amazing selection of artisanal olive oils and vinegars, all available for tasting, along with other culinary treasures, fill the shelves of **Fiore** (8 Rodick Pl., Bar Harbor,

207/802-2580, www.fioreoliveoils.com). The store is located behind the police station.

Bark Harbor (150 Main St., Bar Harbor, 207/288-0404) is the place to pick up the perfect souvenir for your cat or dog.

Souvenir shops are everywhere on Mount Desert Island, so why single out one? If you need Maine-made mementos for Uncle Harry and Aunt Mary, or if the kids need trinkets for friends back home, the Acadia Corporation has several shops in downtown Bar Harbor that can cover it all. The price range is broad, quality is fairly high, and clerks are especially friendly at **The Acadia Shop** (85 Main St., Bar Harbor, 207/288-5600, www.acadiashops.com). Another branch, **Acadia Outdoors** (45 Main St., Bar Harbor, 207/288-2422), features sportswear and outdoor accessories.

Find field guides, books, nature-based games and toys, binoculars, and other must-haves for exploring the wild side of Acadia at **The Natural History Center** (6 Firefly Ln., Bar Harbor, 207/801-2617, www.thenaturalhistorycenter.com), which also offers naturalist-led tours.

ACCOMMODATIONS

If you're not planning to camp in one of Acadia National Park's two campgrounds (there are no other lodgings, and there's no backcountry camping), you'll need to search elsewhere on the island for a place to sleep. Bar Harbor alone has thousands of beds in hotels, motels, inns, B&Bs, and cottages—and the rest of the island adds to that total, with a dozen private campgrounds thrown into the mix. Nonetheless, lodgings can be scarce at the height of summer, particularly the first two weeks in August, a stretch that coincides with an outrageous spike in room rates (sort of like gasoline price hikes that just happen to occur just before long holiday weekends). Off-season, there's plenty of choice, even after the seasonal places shut down, and rates are always lower—often dramatically so. Rates noted here reflect peak season, usually July-August. Unless noted otherwise, properties are seasonal.

The Bar Harbor Chamber of Commerce (207/288-5103 or 888/540-9990, www.barharbormaine.com) and the Thompson Island Information Center (Rte. 3, Thompson Island, 207/288-3411) will give you a list of lodgings open year-round, and both offices are helpful for finding beds even at peak times.

Hostels

Not officially a hostel, but with a hostel-style

Independent shops line the streets of downtown Bar Harbor.

atmosphere, and only for women, the **MDI YWCA** (36 Mt. Desert St., Bar Harbor, 207/288-5008, $30-40/night, $75-100/week) has 2nd- and 3rd-floor single and double rooms, as well as a seven-bed solarium (dorm). Located in a historic downtown building next to the library and across from the Island Explorer bus hub, "the Y" has bathrooms on each floor, as well as a laundry room (coin-operated machines), a TV room, and shared kitchen facilities. There's zero tolerance for smoking, alcohol, and drugs (you'll need to sign an agreement). Reservations open on April 1; for summer and fall, call way ahead, as the Y is popular with the island's young summer workers.

Inns and Bed-and-Breakfasts

Few innkeepers have mastered the art of hospitality as well as Roy Kasindorf and Hélène Harton, owners of ★ **The Ullikana** (16 The Field, Bar Harbor, 207/288-9552, www. ullikana.com, $195-365), located in a quiet downtown location close to Bar Harbor's Shore Path. Roy and Hélène genuinely enjoy their guests. Hélène is a whiz in the kitchen; after one of her multicourse breakfasts, usually served on the water-view patio, you won't be needing lunch. She's also a decorating

genius, blending antiques and modern art, vibrant color with soothing hues, and folk art with fine art. Roy excels at helping guests select just the right hike, bike route, or other activity. Afternoon refreshments provide a time for guests to gather and share experiences. Alpheus Hardy, Bar Harbor's first cottager, built the 10-room Victorian Tudor inn in 1885. The comfortable rooms all have Wi-Fi and private baths (although one is detached); many have working fireplaces, and some have private terraces with water views. The innkeepers also speak French.

Right next door is the gorgeously renovated and rejuvenated ★ **Bass Cottage** (14 The Field, Bar Harbor, 207/288-1234 or 866/782-9224, www.basscottage.com, $230-380). Corporate refugees Teri and Jeff Anderholm purchased the 26-room 1885 cottage in 2003 and spent a year gutting it, salvaging the best of the old, and blending in the new to turn it into a luxurious and stylish 10-room inn. It retains its Victorian bones, yet is most un-Victorian in style. Guest rooms are soothingly decorated with cream- and pastel-colored walls and have phones, Wi-Fi, and flat-screen TVs with DVD players (a DVD library is available—valuable on a stormy day); many rooms have fireplaces and whirlpool tubs. The

The Ullikana is a beautifully renovated historical cottage just steps from Main Street.

spacious and elegant public rooms—expansive living rooms, a cozy library, porches—flow from one to another. Teri puts her culinary degree to use preparing baked goods, fruits, and savory and sweet entrées for breakfast and evening refreshments. A guest pantry is stocked with tea, coffee, and snacks.

Situated on one oceanfront acre in the West Street Historical District, **The Saltair Inn** (121 West St., Bar Harbor, 207/288-2882, www.saltairinn.com, $195-370) was originally built in 1887 as a guesthouse. Innkeepers Kristi and Matt Losquadro and their young family now welcome guests in eight guest rooms, most of which are quite spacious, and five of which face Frenchman Bay. Frills vary by room but might include whirlpool tubs, fireplaces, and balconies. All have TVs and Wi-Fi. A full breakfast is served either in the dining room or on the water-view deck. It's steps from downtown, but really, with a location like this, why leave?

Outside of town, in a serene location with fabulous views of Frenchman Bay, is Jack and Jeani Ochtera's ★ **Inn at Bay Ledge** (150 Sand Point Rd., Bar Harbor, summer 207/288-4204, www.innatbayledge.com, $175-400), an elegant, casual retreat tucked under towering pines atop an 80-foot cliff. Built in 1800 as a minister's home, it's been expanded and updated in the intervening years. Terraced decks descend to a pool and onto the lawn, which stretches to the cliff's edge. Stairs descend to a private stone beach below. Almost all guest rooms have water views; some have whirlpool tubs and/or private decks. A sauna and a steam shower are available. In the woods across the street are cottages, which lack the view but have use of the inn's facilities. Also on the premises is the Summer House ($475), a shingled cottage with a deck 25 feet from the edge of Frenchman Bay.

Much less pricey and a find for families is the **Seacroft Inn** (18 Albert Meadow, Bar Harbor, 207/288-4669 or 800/824-9694, www.seacroftinn.com, $109-149), well situated just off Main Street and near the Shore Path. All rooms in Bunny and Dave Brown's white multigabled cottage have air-conditioning, Wi-Fi, phones, TVs, refrigerators, and microwaves; a continental breakfast is available for $5 per person. Housekeeping is $10 per day. Some rooms can be joined as family suites.

Marian Burns, a former math and science teacher, is the reason everything runs smoothly at **Mira Monte Inn** (69 Mt. Desert St., Bar Harbor, 207/288-4263 or 800/553-5109, www.miramonte.com, $193-295), close (but not too close) to downtown. Born and raised here, and an avid gardener, Marian's a terrific resource for island exploring. Try to capture her during afternoon refreshments (5pm-7pm), and ask about her experience during the 1947 Bar Harbor fire. And don't miss her collection of antique Bar Harbor hotel photos. The 13 Victorian-style rooms have air-conditioning, cable TV, and either a balcony or a fireplace, and some have whirlpool tubs. Also available are four suites, some with kitchen or kitchenette. Rates include an extensive hot-and-cold breakfast buffet.

On a budget? Consider the pleasant but few-frills **Llangolan Inn & Cottages** (865 Rte. 3, Bar Harbor, 207/288-3016, www.llangolaninn.com), seven miles from downtown. The well-cared-for property includes a B&B and cottages. Five simple guest rooms ($80-90), one with a private bath and four sharing two baths, are comfortable and welcoming and include continental breakfast. Also available are basic housekeeping cottages ($100-149) sleeping 2-5, each with a kitchenette, a TV, and heat. Pets are permitted in cottages for $10 per night. This property is right on Route 3, so expect traffic noise. Ask for guest rooms facing the back or for a cottage well away from the road; even then, you'll probably hear the traffic.

Another budget choice is the **Otter Creek Inn** (Rte. 3, Otter Creek, 207/288-5151, www.ottercreekme.com), a well-maintained complex with a small motel-like inn ($90-125), a two-bedroom apartment ($145-180), and two housekeeping cabins ($105-140). Rooms have a mini-fridge, high-def TV, and Wi-Fi and include a continental breakfast at the adjacent

Mount Desert Island on a Budget

At first glance, Mount Desert Island might seem an expensive place to visit, especially if you're not a fan of camping. Truth is, you can afford to visit the island even if your budget is tight.

Consider this: Once you've paid for your park pass, your **recreation** is free. There are no further fees to hike, canoe, bicycle, or swim, unless you need to rent equipment. If so, plan ahead and ask about any deals. Some sports outfitters offer a discount for advance reservations or multiday rentals. Some will allow you to rent a bike after a certain time and keep it for the next day, charging you for only one day. That allows you to get in an extra evening ride—ideal at the peak of summer when daylight lasts well into the evening.

Outside the park, many of the recommended **sights** detailed here are free. Perhaps you can't afford to take the family to the Oceanarium, but you certainly can visit the MDI Biological Laboratory. Most of the park ranger programs are free (check the *Beaver Log*), including evening ones presented in the park's campgrounds. Free concerts and lectures are regularly presented at many locations around the island; check local newspapers or ask at information centers.

You must eat, but you can keep prices down, even when **dining out.** For starters, opt for lodging with an in-room refrigerator if possible. Then stock up on breakfast, sandwich, and salad staples (milk, cereal, bread, luncheon meats and cheeses, vegetables, fresh fruit, etc.) at the supermarket. If you don't have a refrigerator, a cooler will do, but remember to keep it stocked with ice. (Collapsible coolers are available and easy to pack or carry on an airplane, or you can purchase an inexpensive Styrofoam one.) You can survive on this; I've done so. Even better is to have access to boiling water to make instant soups or ramen noodles, to which you can add all kinds of vegetables for a healthful meal.

If you want to dine out, lunch is almost always less expensive than dinner. For dinner, look for restaurants with early-bird specials; many places have very reasonable meals available before 6 or 6:30pm. Or consider combining your meal with evening entertainment at Reel Pizza. When you do dine out, take home any leftovers (assuming you have a refrigerator or cooler). Other inexpensive options are public suppers; look for notices on bulletin boards and in local newspapers.

As for **lodging,** in general the farther you get from the key sights or town centers, the less it will cost. Look for accommodations within an easy walk of the Island Explorer bus so you won't have to drive (or perhaps even bring) a car. If you're staying for a week or longer, your best move is to find a cottage rental. (Hint: Prices for many rentals drop the week before Labor Day.) Another option is to consider a camping cabin. These rustic shelters generally do not have any plumbing—you'll have to walk to a shared bathhouse—but they are clean and dry and have real beds; some even provide linens or minimal cooking facilities. What you sacrifice in privacy is more than offset by the folks you'll meet from around the world.

Wherever you go, whatever you do, always ask about any applicable **discounts:** automobile clubs, seniors, military, family rates, etc. And finally, **ditch the car** and use the free Island Explorer bus to get around. Not only does doing so save you money on gasoline and avoid parking hassles, but—big bonus points—it benefits the environment.

market, which has everything from camping supplies to lobster and wine. Pets are $10 per day.

Hotels and Motels

One of the town's best-known, most visible, and best-situated hotels is the **Bar Harbor Inn** (Newport Dr., Bar Harbor, 207/288-3351 or 800/248-3351, www.barharborinn.com, $209-395), a sprawling complex on eight acres overlooking the harbor and islands. The 153 rooms and suites vary considerably in style, from traditional inn to motel, and are in three different buildings. Continental breakfast is included (Wi-Fi is extra), and special packages, with meals and activities, are available—an advantage if you have children. The kids will appreciate the heated outdoor pool; adults might enjoy the full-service spa. Also under the same management and ownership (www.bar-harbor-hotels.com) is the family-oriented **Acadia Inn** (98 Eden St., Bar Harbor, 207/288-3500, www.acadiainn.com, $200), located between the park entrance and downtown Bar Harbor. Facilities include an outdoor heated pool and Jacuzzi and a laundry. Rates include continental breakfast, Wi-Fi, and in-room fridge. It has direct trail access into the park.

The appropriately named **Harborside Hotel & Marina** (55 West St., Bar Harbor, 207/288-5033 or 800/238-5033, www.theharborsidehotel.com, from $359) fronts the water in downtown Bar Harbor. Most of the guest rooms, studios, and suites have a water view and semiprivate balcony. Some have large outdoor hot tubs. The $25 resort fee allows access to the beautifully restored Bar Harbor Club, with a full-service spa, fitness center, tennis courts, and oceanfront heated pool. Also on the premises are a second outdoor pool, an Italian restaurant, a pier, and a marina. Sharing use of those facilities is a sister property, the **West Street Hotel** (50 West St., 877/905-4498, www.theweststreethotel.com, from $289), a new and tony spot with a rooftop pool (ages 18 and older, only) overlooking downtown, harbor, islands, and ocean. Rooms have a nautical vibe, and those on the West Street-side have harbor views. All have Wi-Fi, flat-screen TVs, and in-room fridge.

the Bar Harbor Inn

On the edge of downtown, across from College of the Atlantic, are two adjacent sister properties tiered up a hillside: **Wonder View Inn & Suites** (55 Eden St., Bar Harbor, 888/439-8439, www.wonderviewinn.com, $130-279) and **The Bluenose Hotel** (90 Eden St., Bar Harbor, 207/288-3348 or 800/445-4077, www.barharborhotel.com, from $249). The pet-friendly ($20/pet/night) Wonder View comprises four older motels on 14 acres of estate-like grounds with grassy lawns and mature shade trees, an outdoor pool, and a restaurant. The estate was the home of famed mystery writer Mary Roberts Rinehart, who coined the phrase "The butler did it." Guest rooms vary widely, and rates reflect both style of accommodation and views; all have refrigerator, TV, Wi-Fi, and air-conditioning. The Bluenose, one of the island's top properties, comprises two buildings. Mizzentop is newest, and its guest rooms and suites are quite elegant, many with fireplaces, all with fabulous views and balconies. Also here are a spa, fitness center, indoor and outdoor pools, and a lounge with live music every evening. Stenna Nordica guest rooms, accessed from outdoor corridors, are more modest, but still have views.

On the edge of town, the **Cromwell Harbor Motel** (359 Main St., Bar Harbor, 207/288-3201 or 800/544-3201, www.cromwellharbor.com, $130-170) is set back from the road on nicely landscaped grounds with an outdoor pool. All guest rooms have Wi-Fi, air-conditioning, phones, TVs, microwaves, and refrigerators. The location puts all of downtown's sights within walking distance.

On the lower end of the budgetary scale are two neighboring motels: **Edenbrook Motel** (96 Eden St./Rte. 3, Bar Harbor, 207/288-4975 or 800/323-7819, www.edenbrookmotelbh.

com, $80-120), with panoramic views of Frenchman Bay from some rooms, and the wee bit fancier **Highbrook Motel** (94 Eden St./Rte. 3, Bar Harbor, 207/288-3591 or 800/338-9688, www.highbrookmotel.com, $119-179), with Wi-Fi, in-room mini-fridge, and continental breakfast. Both are about 1.5 miles from Acadia's main entrance, one mile from downtown.

Clean and affordable, the **Belle Isle Motel** (910 Rte. 3, Bar Harbor, 207/288-5726, www.belleislemotel.net, $80-95), a vintage mom-and-pop roadside motel, delivers on both counts. Darren and Camille Taylor purchased the Belle in 2011 and have spruced it up. The rooms are small, but all have air-conditioning, TV, free local calls, Wi-Fi, and refrigerators; deluxe rooms are more spacious, but closer to the road. Also on the premises are a heated pool, a playground, a picnic area, and a guest laundry. A microwave is available for guest use.

If all you want is a room with a bed, **Robbins Motel** (396 Rte. 3, Bar Harbor, 207/288-4659, www.robbinsmotel.com, $65), an older motel, has 30 small, unadorned (some might call them dismal) but clean, pine-paneled, queen-bed guest rooms. All have air-conditioning and TV; some have Wi-Fi. There

is no charm and it's not quiet, but it's cheap and clean. Off-season rates are as low as $36.

Seasonal Rentals

Contact **L. S. Robinson Co.** (337 Main St., Southwest Harbor, 207/244-5563, www.lsrobinson.com) or **Maine Island Properties** (Mount Desert, 207/244-4308, www.maineislandproperties.com) for listings of houses and cottages available by the week or month. In July-August, rates run $700-7,000 per week or more, plus tax and deposit. Both agencies handle rentals in all parts of Mount Desert. (If you decide to stay, they also have residential listings.) The Bar Harbor Chamber of Commerce's annual guide also has listings of cottages—some private, others that are part of cottage colonies.

Camping

Mount Desert Island's private campgrounds are located at the northern end of the island, down the center, and in the southwest corner. Most are also on the routes of the free Island Explorer bus service, making it easy and economical—and preferable—to leave your car or RV at your campsite and avoid the parking problems between late June and Columbus Day. The Thompson Island and Hulls Cove

West Street Hotel has a rooftop pool with panoramic harbor views.

Visitors Centers have a listing of private campgrounds.

Family-owned and operated, **Bar Harbor Campground** (409 Rte. 3, Bar Harbor, 207/288-5185, www.thebarharborcampground.com, $30-45) caters to families and offers a swimming pool, a recreation hall, and a play area. It doesn't accept advance reservation, nor does it take credit cards. Many of the 300 sites have ocean views. Hookups are available.

The Baker family has operated **Hadley's Point Campground** (33 Hadley Point Rd., Bar Harbor, 207/288-4808, www.hadleyspoint.com, May 15-mid-Oct., $29-44) since 1969. Tent sites are nicely spaced in the woods and have a sense of privacy; big-rig sites, located in fields, are tight. Camping cabins ($70), new in 2013, are furnished with one queen and two twin beds, a bathroom with toilet, sink, and metered shower, and Wi-Fi; pets are permitted for $10 per night. Facilities include a laundry, a heated pool, shuffleboard courts, horseshoes, and a playground. A public saltwater beach with a boat launch is within walking distance. The campground is eight miles from Bar Harbor.

FOOD

You won't go hungry in Bar Harbor, and you won't find chain fast-food places. The summer tourism trade and the College of the Atlantic students have created a demand for pizzerias, vegetarian bistros, brewpubs, and a handful of creative restaurants. But, of course, almost every restaurant has some kind of lobster dish. And even if you're using Bar Harbor as a base of operations, don't miss opportunities to explore restaurants elsewhere on the island.

The island's best collection of good, inexpensive restaurants, some open year-round, are along Rodick Street, from Reel Pizza down to Rosalie's, which actually fronts Cottage Street. You'll find a good ethnic mix. For sit-down restaurants, make reservations as far in advance as possible. Expect reduced operations during spring and fall; few places are open in winter.

Mount Desert Island is a seasonal community, and restaurant days and hours change frequently, so always call ahead. Also note that staffing is always a challenge in the region, and many businesses import workers from overseas. By the time waiters and waitresses have been fully trained, the season is almost over.

Local Flavors

Free tastings are offered daily at **Bar Harbor Cellars** (854 Rte. 3, Bar Harbor, 207/288-3907, www.barharborcellars.com). The winery, located at Sweet Pea Farm, is in the early stages of using organic techniques to grow hybrid grapes. In the meantime, it's making wines from European and California grapes. Also here is a Maine chocolate room and a small selection of complementary foods, such as olives, cheese, and crackers.

Only a masochist could bypass **Ben & Bill's Chocolate Emporium** (66 Main St., Bar Harbor, 207/288-3281 or 800/806-3281, www.benandbills.com), which makes homemade candies and more than 50 ice cream flavors (including a dubious lobster flavor); the whole place smells like the inside of a chocolate truffle. It opens daily at 10am, with closing dependent on the season and crowds, but usually late in the evening.

That said, the most creative flavors come from **MDI Ice Cream** (7 Firefly Ln., Bar Harbor, 207/288-0999, and 325 Main St., Bar Harbor, 207/288-5664, www.mdiic.com). It's made in small batches, just five gallons at a time, using the finest ingredients. We're talking creamy, rich, delicious, and wild flavors.

Probably the least-expensive lunch or ice cream option in town is **West End Drug Co.** (105 Main St., Bar Harbor, 207/288-3318), where you can get grilled-cheese sandwiches, PBJ, and other white-bread basics as well as shakes, egg creams, and sundaes at the fountain.

Equally inexpensive, but with a healthful menu, is the **Take-A-Break Cafe** (105 Eden St., Bar Harbor, 207/288-5015, www.coa.edu) in Blair Dining Hall, at College of the

Ben & Bill's sells lobster ice cream.

The Godfather, Manchurian Candidate. Reel Pizza opens daily at 4:30pm and has occasional Saturday matinees; closed Monday in winter. Arrive early; the best seats go quickly.

For breakfast or brunch, you can't beat **2 Cats** (130 Cottage St., Bar Harbor, 207/288-2808 or 800/355-2828, www.2catsbarharbor.com, 7am-1pm daily). Fun, funky, and fresh best describe both the restaurant and the food ($8-12). Dine inside or on the patio. Dinner is also served at 2 Cats—call for nights and hours. Three upstairs guest rooms are available for $165-195 ($125 in winter)—with breakfast, of course.

Escape the downtown madness at **Tea House 278** (278 Main St., Bar Harbor, 207/288-2781, www.teahouse278.com, 11am-7pm Wed.-Sun.), a traditional Chinese teahouse offering Gaiwan service, along with light fare (don't miss the tea-steeped eggs), and even Mahjong. The owners source all teas from small farms in China and Taiwan. Sit inside or in the tea garden, with dwarf trees and waterfall. The owners planned to open a gallery upstairs in 2015.

Choco-Latte (240 Main St., Bar Harbor, 207-801-9179, www.choco-lattecafe.com, 7am-9pm daily) aims to make all of its chocolates in house from organic Criollo cacao sourced from women-owned co-ops in Chiapas and Veracruz, Mexico. Pair it with an organic coffee or a hot chocolate.

Between Mother's Day and late October, the **Eden Farmers Market** operates out of the YMCA parking lot off Lower Main Street in Bar Harbor, 9am-noon each Sunday. You'll find fresh meats and produce, local cheeses and maple syrup, yogurt and ice cream, bread, honey, preserves, and even prepared Asian foods.

Picnic Fare

Although a few of these places have some seating, most are for the grab-and-go crowd.

For a light, inexpensive meal, you can't go wrong at **Morning Glory Bakery** (39 Rodick St., Bar Harbor, 207/288-3041, www.

Atlantic. If you find yourself on the college campus, perhaps for a boat tour or museum visit, consider eating here. The cafeteria-style café serves breakfast, lunch, and dinner on most weekdays, and although there are individual choices, the best deals are the all-you-can-eat meals ($5-10). There are always vegetarian, vegan, gluten-free, and meat choices, and the selection is organic and local whenever possible.

When it comes to pub-grub favorites, such as burgers and fish sandwiches, **The Thirsty Whale Tavern** (40 Cottage St., Bar Harbor, 207/288-9335, www.thirstywhaletavern.com, 11am-9pm daily, $7-16) does it right.

Combine a pizza with a first-run or art flick at **Reel Pizza Cinerama** (33 Kennebec Pl., Bar Harbor, 207/288-3811 for films, 207/288-3828 for food, www.reelpizza.net), where you order your pizza, grab an easy chair, and watch for your number to come up on the bingo board. Most films are screened twice nightly. Pizzas ($12-20 or by the slice) have cinematic names—Zorba the Greek, morninggclorybakery.com, 7am-5pm Mon.-Fri., 8am-5pm Sat.-Sun.). Fresh-baked goodies, breakfast and regular sandwiches, soups, and salads are all made from scratch.

Another good choice for take-out fare is **Downeast Deli** (65 Main St., Bar Harbor, 207/288-1001, www.downeastdeli.com, 7am-4pm daily). You can get both hot and cold fresh lobster rolls as well as other sandwiches, soups, and salads. Boxed lunches, including chips, cookie, and water, are available.

At **Adelmann's Deli & Grill** (224 Main St., Bar Harbor, 207/288-0455, 11am-8pm daily), build-your-own lunch sandwiches are $9.

Brewpubs and Microbreweries

Bar Harbor's longest-lived brewpub is the **Lompoc Café** (36 Rodick St., Bar Harbor, 207/288-9392, www.lompoccafe.com, 3pm-9pm Tues.-Sun. late Apr.-mid-Dec., entrées $10-21), with brews on tap. Go for pizzas, salads, and entrées, along with bocce in the beer garden and live entertainment on weekends. After 9pm there's just beer and thin-crust pizza until about 1am.

Lompoc's signature Bar Harbor Real Ale and about a half-dozen others are brewed by the **Atlantic Brewing Company** (15 Knox Rd., Town Hill, 207/288-2337 or 800/475-5417, www.atlanticbrewing.com), in the upper section of the island. Free brewery tours (2pm, 3pm, and 4pm daily late May-mid-Oct.), which include tastings, are available. Also operating here in summer is **Mainely Meat Bar-B-Q** (207/288-9200, 11:30am-8pm daily, $8-16), offering pulled pork, chicken, ribs, and similar fare for lunch and dinner.

Bar Harbor Brewing Company (8 Mt. Desert St., Bar Harbor, 207/288-4592, www.barharborbrewing.com), a sister of Atlantic Brewing, produces Thunder Hole Ale, Cadillac Mountain Stout, and True Blue. The microbrewery is located downtown in a spacious shop, where tours and tastings are held most afternoons; stop by or call for the schedule.

Visit Atlantic Brewing Company for tastings and tours.

Family Favorites

An unscientific but reliable local survey gives the best-pizza ribbon to **Rosalie's Pizza & Italian Restaurant** (46 Cottage St., Bar Harbor, 207/288-5666, www.rosaliespizza.com, 4pm-10pm daily), where the Wurlitzer jukebox churns out tunes from the 1950s. Rosalie's earns high marks for consistency with its homemade pizza, in four sizes or by the slice, along with calzones and subs; there are lots of vegetarian options. The Italian dinners—spaghetti, eggplant parmigiana, and others—are all less than $10, including a garlic roll. Beer and wine are available. Avoid the downstairs lines by heading upstairs and ordering at that counter, or call in your order.

Efficient, friendly cafeteria-style service makes **EPI's Pizza** (8 Cottage St., Bar Harbor, 207/288-5853, 6am-7pm daily Sept.-June, 6am-9pm daily July-Aug.) an excellent choice for subs, salads, pizzas, and even spaghetti. If the weather closes in, there are always the pinball machines in the back room.

Route 66 Restaurant (21 Cottage St.,

Bar Harbor, 207/288-3708, www.barharbor-route66.com, 11am-9pm daily, $9-25), filled with 1950s memorabilia and metal toys, is a fun restaurant that's a real hit with kids (check out the Lionel train running around just below the ceiling). The expansive menu includes sandwiches, burgers, pizza, steak, chicken, seafood, and kids' choices. No raves here, just okay food in a fun atmosphere.

Good food at a fair price reels them into **Poor Boy's Gourmet** (300 Main St., Bar Harbor, 207/288-4148, www.poorboysgourmet.com, from 4:30pm daily). Until 6pm it serves an early-bird menu with about nine entrées and again as many seconds-on-us pasta choices for $10-12. The price jumps just a bit after that, with most entrées running $12-20.

Savor the panoramic views over Bar Harbor, Frenchman Bay, and the Porcupine Islands along with breakfast or dinner at the **Looking Glass Restaurant** (Wonder View Inn, 50 Eden St., Bar Harbor, 207/288-5663, www.wonderviewinn.com, 7am 10:30am and 5:30pm-9pm daily, $12-38). It's quite casual, with choices ranging from sandwiches to rack of lamb. On Wednesday and Thursday nights, homemade pasta is the specialty, and there's live jazz on Thursday. It also offers a vegan menu as well as a children's menu, and the deck is pet-friendly.

Casual Dining

Once a Victorian boardinghouse and later a 1920s speakeasy, **Galyn's Galley** (17 Main St., Bar Harbor, 207/288-9706, www.galynsbarharbor.com, 11am-10pm daily Mar.-Nov., dinner entrées $13-35), has been a downtown dining mainstay since 1986. Lots of plants, modern decor, reliable service, and several indoor and outdoor dining areas contribute to the loyalty of the clientele. Reservations are advisable in midsummer. Be seated before 6pm to enjoy the Early Bird Lobster Special.

When you're craving fresh and delicious fare but not a heavy meal, the **Side Street Café** (49 Rodick St., Bar Harbor, 207/801-2591, www.sidestreetbarharbor.com, 11am-10pm

daily, $8-26) delivers. The lobster roll and the crab melt earn high fives, as do the burgers. It's open year-round.

Set back from the road behind a garden is the very popular **McKays Public House** (231 Main St., Bar Harbor, 207/288-2002, www.mckayspublichouse.com, 5pm-10pm daily, $11-26), a comfortable pub with seating indoors in small dining rooms or at the bar, or outdoors in the garden. The best bet is the classic pub fare, which includes shepherd's pie, burgers, and fish-and-chips. Fancier entrées, such as seafood risotto, are also available.

Casual, friendly, creative, and reliable defines **Cafe This Way** (14 Mt. Desert St., Bar Harbor, 207/288-4483, www.cafethisway.com, 7am-11:30am and 5:30pm-9:30pm Mon.-Sat., 8am-1pm and 5:30pm-9:30pm Sun., $16-25), where it's easy to make a meal out of the appetizers alone. Vegetarians will be happy here, and there's a gluten-free menu too. The breakfast menu is a genuine wake-up call ($5-9). It's not a choice for quiet dining.

Chef-owner Karl Yarborough is putting ★ **Mache Bistro** (321 Main St., Bar Harbor, 207/288-0447, www.machebistro.com, from 5:30pm Tues.-Sat., $20-28) on the must-dine list. His interpretations of rustic French and Mediterranean flavors are creative without being over the top. This place is justifiably popular, so do make reservations.

Most folks come to **Sweet Pea's Café** (854 Rte. 3, Bar Harbor, 207/801-9078, 7am-8pm Tues.-Sun., $9-16) for the wood-oven sourdough pizzas, topped with fresh greens, veggies, and local seafood, but the mussels and the oyster starters earn raves, as does the local cheese plate. Other options include sandwiches, salads, and sweets. Atlantic Brewing Company ales and Bar Harbor Cellars' wines are available. People love the breakfast popovers.

International Fare

For Thai food, **Siam Orchid** (30 Rodick St., Bar Harbor, 207/288-9669, www.siamorchidrestaurant.net, 11am-11pm daily) gets the locals' nod, although it's a bit pricey. House specials run $14-20; curries and noodle dishes, such as pad thai, are $12-17. There are plenty of choices for vegetarians. Siam Orchid serves beer and wine only.

Sharing the same building is **Gringo's** (30 Rodick St., Bar Harbor, 207/288-2326, 11am-10pm daily), a Mexican hole-in-the-wall specializing in take-out burritos, wraps, homemade salsas, and smoothies, with almost everything—margaritas and beer included—less than $8. For a real kick, don't miss the jalapeño brownies.

For "American fine dining with Latin flair," head to ★ **Havana** (318 Main St., Bar Harbor, 207/288-2822, www.havanamaine.com, 5pm-10pm daily May-Nov., call for off-season hours, entrées $22-35), where the innovative Cuban-esque menu changes frequently to take advantage of what's locally available. Inside, bright orange walls and white tablecloths set a tone that's equally festive and accomplished. Out back, a wood-fired grill and open-air bar offer a tapas menu. Also part of Havana is **Parrilla** (from 3pm Sun.-Thurs., from 4pm Fri.-Sat. ($8-33), a street-side outdoor bar with Argentinian-style wood-fired grill serving a selection of small and large plates.

Fine Dining

Five miles south of Bar Harbor, in the village of Otter Creek, which itself is in the town of Mount Desert, is the inauspicious-looking **Burning Tree** (Rte. 3, Otter Creek, 207/288-9331, 5pm-10pm Wed.-Mon. late June-early Oct., closed Mon. after Labor Day, $19-30), which is anything but nondescript inside. Chef-owners Allison Martin and Elmer Beal Jr. have created one of Mount Desert Island's better restaurants, but it can get quite noisy when busy, which it usually is. Reservations are essential in summer. Specialties are imaginative seafood entrées and vegetarian dishes. The homemade breads and desserts are delicious. At the height of summer, service can be a bit rushed and the kitchen runs out of popular entrées. Solution: Plan to eat early; it's worth it.

Stewman's Lobster Pound

Lobster

Nearly every restaurant in town serves some form of lobster (my top choice for a lobster roll is the Side Street Café).

Dine inside or on the dock at **Stewman's Lobster Pound** (35 West St., 207/288-0346, www.stewmanslobsterpound.com, 11am-10pm daily), where the menu ranges from burgers to lobster.

Although it lacks the oceanfront location, **West Street Café** (76 West St., Bar Harbor, 207/288-5242, www.weststreetcafe.com, 11am-9pm daily) is a fine spot for a lobster dinner at a fair price. There are other items on the menu, but the reason to go here is for the lobster (market price). A kids' menu is available. Go before 6pm for early-bird specials.

INFORMATION AND SERVICES

The **Bar Harbor Chamber of Commerce** (1201 Bar Harbor Rd./Rte. 3, Trenton, 207/288-5103 or 888/540-9990, www.bar-harbormaine.com) is open daily in summer,

Monday-Friday the rest of the year. Late May-mid-October, the chamber operates a downtown branch (corner of Main St. and Cottage St.).

Once you're on Mount Desert Island, if you manage to bestir yourself early enough to catch sunrise on the summit of Cadillac Mountain (you won't be alone—it's a popular activity), stop in at the chamber of commerce office later and request an official membership card for the **Cadillac Mountain Sunrise Club** (they'll take your word for it).

Downtown Bar Harbor has **public restrooms** in Agamont Park (West St. and Main St.), in the Harbor Place complex at the town pier, in the municipal building (the fire and police station, 37 Firefly Ln., across from the Village Green), and on the School Street side of the athletic field (School St. and Park St.), where there is RV parking. There are also restrooms at the Mount Desert Island Hospital (10 Wayman Ln.).

Libraries

Jesup Memorial Library (34 Mt. Desert St., Bar Harbor, 207/288-4245, www.jesup.lib.

me.us) is open year-round. The library holds its annual book sale on the third Saturday in August. Next door is **Second Hand Prose,** a bookstore with sales benefiting the library.

GETTING THERE AND AROUND

Bar Harbor is 12 miles from Hancock County-Bar Harbor Airport in Trenton via Route 3 West; about 20 miles or about 30-45 minutes, depending upon traffic, via Route 3 from Ellsworth; about 45 miles or 75 minutes via Routes 1A and 3 from Bangor; and about 275 miles or five hours via Routes 195 and 3 from Boston. It's about 12 miles or 20 minutes via Routes 233 and 198 or 20 miles/35 minutes via Route 3 to Northeast Harbor.

Make it easy on yourself, help improve the air quality, and reduce stress levels by leaving your car at your lodging (or if day-tripping, at the Bar Harbor Chamber of Commerce on Rte. 3 in Trenton) and taking the Island Explorer bus.

RVs are not allowed to park near the town pier; designated RV parking is alongside the athletic field, on Lower Main and Park Streets, about eight blocks from the center of town.

Northeast and Seal Harbors

Ever since the late 19th century, the upper crust from Philadelphia has been summering in and around Northeast Harbor. Sure, they also show up in other parts of Maine, but it's hard not to notice the preponderance of Pennsylvania license plates surrounding Northeast Harbor's elegant "cottages" during mid-July-mid-August. In the last decade or so, growing numbers from Washington DC, New York, and Texas have joined the Pennsylvania plates.

Actually, even though Northeast Harbor is a well-known name with special cachet, it isn't even an official township; it's a zip-coded village within the town of Mount Desert (pop. 2,053), which collects the breathtaking

property taxes and doles out the municipal services.

The attractive boutiques in Northeast Harbor's small downtown area cater to a casually posh clientele, and the well-protected harbor attracts a tony crowd of yachties. For their convenience, a palm-size annual directory, *The Redbook,* discreetly lists owners' summer residences and winter addresses—but no phone numbers.

Except for two spectacular public gardens and two specialized museums, not much here is geared to budget-sensitive visitors—but there's no charge for admiring the spectacular scenery.

Although all of Mount Desert Island is

seasonal, Northeast Harbor is especially so, and it has a tiny and decreasing year-round population. Many businesses don't open until early July and close in early September.

SIGHTS
★ Somes Sound

As you head toward Northeast Harbor on Route 198 from the northern end of Mount Desert Island, you'll begin seeing cliff-lined Somes Sound, on your right. The glacier-sculpted fjard (not as deep or as steeply walled as a fjord) juts five miles into the interior of Mount Desert Island from its mouth between Northeast Harbor and Southwest Harbor. Watch for the right-hand turn for Sargent Drive (no RVs allowed), and follow the lovely, granite-lined route along the east side of the sound. Halfway along, a marker explains the geology of this spectacular natural inlet. There aren't many pullouts en route, and traffic can be fairly thick in midsummer, but don't miss it. **Suminsby Park,** located off Sargent Drive, 400 feet from Route 3, is a fine place for a picnic. The park has rocky shore access, a hand-carry boat launch, picnic tables, grills, and a pit toilet. An ideal way to appreciate Somes Sound is from the water—sign up for an excursion out of Northeast Harbor or Southwest Harbor.

★ Asticou and Thuya Gardens

If you have the slightest interest in gardens, allow time for Northeast Harbor's two marvelous public gardens. Both are operated by the nonprofit Mount Desert Land and Garden Preserve (207/276-3727, www.gardenpreserve. org).

ASTICOU AZALEA GARDEN

One of Maine's best spring showcases is the **Asticou Azalea Garden** (Rte. 198 at Peabody Dr./Rte. 3, sunrise-sunset daily May 1-Oct. 31, $5 donation), a 2.3-acre pocket where about 70 varieties of azaleas, rhododendrons, and laurels—many from the classic Reef Point garden of famed landscape designer Beatrix Farrand—burst into bloom. When Charles K. Savage, beloved former innkeeper of the Asticou Inn, learned the Reef Point garden was being undone in 1956, he went into high gear to find funding and managed to rescue the azaleas and provide them with the gorgeous setting they have today, across the road and around the corner from the inn. Serenity is the key, with a Japanese sand garden that is mesmerizing in any

the sand garden at the Japanese-inspired Asticou Azalea Garden

season, stone lanterns, granite outcrops, pink gravel paths, and a tranquil pond. Try to visit early in the season and early in the morning to savor the effect. Blossoming occurs May-August, but the prime time for azaleas is roughly mid-May-mid-June.

The garden is on Route 198, at the northern edge of Northeast Harbor, immediately north of the junction with Peabody Drive (Rte. 3). Watch for a tiny sign on the left, if you're coming from the north, that marks access to the parking area. A small box suggests a $5 donation, and another box contains a garden guide ($2). Pets are not allowed in the garden. Take Island Explorer Route 5/Jordan Pond or Route 6/Brown Mountain and request a stop.

The Asticou Stream Trail, a lovely meander through fields and woods and down to the shoreline, connects the garden to the town. Look for a small signpost just north of the Asticou Inn and across from the Route 3 entrance to the garden.

THUYA GARDEN

Behind a carved wooden gate on a forested hillside not far from Asticou lies an enchanted garden also designed by Charles K. Savage and inspired by Beatrix Farrand. Special features of **Thuya Garden** (Peabody Dr./Rte. 3, 7am-7pm daily, $5 donation) are perennial borders and sculpted shrubbery. On a misty summer day, when few visitors appear, the colors are brilliant. Adjacent to the garden is **Thuya Lodge** (207/276-5130, 10am-4:30pm daily late June-Labor Day), former summer cottage of Joseph Curtis, donor of this awesome municipal park. The lodge has an extensive botanical library and quiet rooms for reading. A collection box next to the front gate requests a $5 donation per adult. To reach Thuya Garden, continue south on Route 3 beyond Asticou Azalea Garden and watch for the Asticou Terraces parking area (no RVs; 2-hour limit) on the right. Cross the road and climb the Asticou Terraces Trail (0.4 mile) to the garden. Allow time to hang out at the three lookouts en route. Alternately, drive 0.2 mile beyond the Route 3 parking area and watch for a minuscule Thuya Garden sign on the left. Go 0.5 mile up the steep, narrow, and curving driveway to the parking area (but walking up reaps higher rewards). Or, take Island Explorer Route 5/Jordan Pond and request a stop.

It's possible to connect Asticou and Thuya Gardens by hiking the moderately difficult (lots of exposed roots) **Eliot Mountain Trail.** From Asticou Garden, the Asticou Trail road

Thuya Garden

across from the Asticou Inn provides access to the trail; it's a private road, but foot traffic has a right of way. Allow about 90 minutes for the hike between the two gardens. Near the summit, glimpses of Northeast Harbor tease through the trees. You can return via the Asticou Terraces Trail (be sure to visit the lookouts) to Route 3, then a sidewalk to Asticou Garden, about a 10-minute walk, or simply flag down the Island Explorer bus. If you visit Thuya first, open the back gate, where you'll see a sign marking the trail.

Abby Aldrich Rockefeller Garden

The private **Abby Aldrich Rockefeller Garden** (207/276-3330 in season, www.rock-gardenmaine.wordpress.com, free), located in Northeast Harbor, was created in 1921, when the Rockefellers turned to renowned garden designer Beatrix Farrand to create a garden using treasures they'd brought back from Asia. The enclosed garden is a knockout, accented with secret passages, a sunken garden, English floral beds, Korean tombstone figures, a moon gate, and even yellow roof tiles from Beijing. It's open usually one day a week late July-early September, and numbers are limited, so reservations are vital; check the website for current details. A garden guide with map is provided, but you're free to explore at your own pace.

Petite Plaisance

On Northeast Harbor's quiet South Shore Road, **Petite Plaisance** (35 South Shore Rd., Northeast Harbor, 207/276-3940, www.petiteplaisanceconservationfund.org, Tues.-Sat. June 15-Aug. 31, donation) is a special-interest museum commemorating noted Belgian-born author and college professor Marguerite Yourcenar (pen name of Marguerite de Crayencour), the first woman elected to the prestigious Académie Française. From 1950 to 1987, Petite Plaisance was her home, and it's hard to believe she's no longer here; her intriguing possessions and presence fill the two-story house, of particular interest

to Yourcenar devotees. In 2014 the French Ministry of Culture added Petite Plaisance to its registry of illustrious houses. Free hour-long tours of the 1st floor are given, by advance appointment only. Tours are offered in French or English, depending on visitors' preferences; French-speaking visitors often make pilgrimages here. No children under 12 are allowed. Call at least a day ahead, between 9am and 4pm, to schedule an appointment. Yourcenar admirers should request directions to Brookside Cemetery in Somesville, seven miles away, where she is buried. Tours are free, but donations are much appreciated.

Great Harbor Maritime Museum

Annual exhibits focusing on the maritime heritage of the Mount Desert Island area are held in the small, eclectic **Great Harbor Maritime Museum** (124 Main St., Northeast Harbor, 207/276-5262, 10am-5pm Tues.-Sat. late June-Labor Day, donation), housed in the old village fire station and municipal building. ("Great Harbor" refers to the Somes Sound area—Northeast, Southwest, and Seal Harbors, as well as the Cranberry Isles.) Yachting, coastal trade, and fishing receive special emphasis. Look for the canvas rowing canoe, built in Veazie, Maine, between 1917 and 1920; it's the only one of its kind known to exist today.

RECREATION

Hardy folks can test the cold Atlantic waters at the small saltwater beach at the head of the harbor at **Seal Harbor Beach** (Island Explorer Route 5/Jordan Pond).

Hiking

LONG POND CARRIAGE ROAD TRAIL
Distance: 3.4 miles round-trip
Duration: 1.5-2 hours
Elevation gain: Minimal
Effort: Easy
Trailhead: South end of Long Pond, west of Seal Harbor. From Bar Harbor, take the Island Explorer bus

the Great Harbor Maritime Museum

do the loop in a clockwise direction, but counterclockwise gets you near the pond right at the start. If you're using the bus, flag it down or walk back to the Seal Harbor Beach stop.

This section of the carriage roads is not open to bicyclists.

Bicycling

Island Bike Rental (102 Main St., Northeast Harbor, 207/276-5611), sharing space with Shirt Off Your Back, a laundry service tucked down a stairway next door to the National Bank of Bar Harbor, rents bikes (half-day $19, full-day $22).

Golf

The 18-hole **Northeast Harbor Golf Club** (15 Golf Club Rd., 207/276-5335, www.nehgc.com, $45 spring and fall, $85 July-early Sept.) is open to visitors. The first nine, designed by Donald Ross, opened in 1916; the second nine, designed by Herbert Strong, opened in 1925.

EXCURSION BOATS

Northeast Harbor is the starting point for a couple of boat services headed for the **Cranberry Isles;** other boats and ferries, which are slightly less expensive but have no narration, depart from Southwest Harbor. The vessels leave from the commercial floats at the end of the concrete Municipal Pier on Sea Street. Fares are provided here as a guide, but will fluctuate with fuel prices.

The 75-foot *Sea Princess* (207/276-5352, www.barharborcruises.com) carries visitors as well as an Acadia National Park naturalist on a 2.75-hour morning trip around the mouth of Somes Sound and out to Little Cranberry Island (Islesford) for a 50-minute stopover. The boat leaves Northeast Harbor at 10am daily mid-May-mid-October. A narrated afternoon trip departs at 1pm on the same route. Other trips operate, but not daily. These include a scenic 1.5-hour Somes Sound cruise and a 1.5-hour sunset cruise of Somes Sound. Fees range $23-28 adults, $18 ages 5-12, $7 under age 5. Reservations are advisable for all trips, although even that

Route 5/Jordan Pond and get off at Seal Harbor Beach. Walk west a very short distance to Little Long Pond and enter the carriage roads. Or drive from Bar Harbor either on the Park Loop Road (the two-way section) or on Route 3 via Otter Creek, and park in a small lot on the north side of Route 3 at the bottom of Little Long Pond.

This loop—part of the 12 miles of carriage roads on private land but open to the public—is easy, a "walk in the woods" kind of experience. If you do it late in the day, use insect repellent. Be forewarned that dogs are allowed off leash here, so it doubles as an unofficial dog park. The pond is officially named Long Pond, but it's known as **Little Long Pond** to distinguish it from the far larger Long Pond on the west side of the island. Head north, on the east shore of the pond, passing signpost 35 and continuing to signpost 28. Bear left toward signpost 24 and the lovely Cobblestone Bridge, then start heading west and south, meandering to signpost 32. Turn south (left) to signpost 33, where you'll bear left toward signpost 34 and back to Route 3. You can also provides no guarantee, since the cruises require a 15-passenger minimum.

The *Helen Brooks,* built in 1970, is one of two traditional Friendship sloops operated by **Downeast Friendship Sloop Charters** (Northeast Harbor Municipal Marina, 41 Harbor Dr., 207/266-5210, www.downeastfriendshipsloop.com); the other one sails out of Southwest Harbor. Private charters start at $250 for a two-hour sail, covering up to six passengers and including an appetizer and soft drinks; shared trips are $50 per person for two hours, $75 per person for three hours. A sunset sail is a lovely way to end a day.

ENTERTAINMENT

Since 1964 the **Mount Desert Festival of Chamber Music** (207/266-2550, www.mtdesertfestival.org) has presented concerts in the century-old Neighborhood House on Main Street at 8:15pm Tuesday mid-July-mid-August. Tickets ($25 general admission, $10 students) are available at the Neighborhood House box office Monday-Tuesday during the concert season or by phone reservation.

On Thursday nights, **Movies at the Marina,** a free series of family-friendly flicks, is screened at dusk on the village green.

SHOPPING

Upscale shops, galleries, and boutiques with clothing, artworks, housewares, antiques, and antiquarian books line both sides of Main Street in Northeast Harbor, making for intriguing browsing and expensive buying (but be sure to check the sale rooms of the clothing shops for bona fide bargains). The season is short, though, with some shops open only in July-August.

Galleries

You'll enter another world at **Shaw Contemporary Jewelry** (100 Main St., Northeast Harbor, 207/276-5000 or 877/276-5001, www.shawjewelry.com). Besides the spectacular silver and gold beach-stone jewelry created by Rhode Island School of Design alumnus Sam Shaw, the work of more than 100 other jewelers is exquisitely displayed. There are also sculptures, Asian art, and rotating art exhibits. It all leads back toward a lovely, light-filled garden. Prices are in the stratosphere, but appropriately so. As one well-dressed customer was overheard saying to her companion: "If I had only one jewelry store to go to in my entire life, this would be it."

Wander behind Shaw's to find **Artemis**

The *Sea Princess* cruises around the mouth of Somes Sound and out to Islesford.

Gallery (1 Old Firehouse Ln., Northeast Harbor, 207/276-3001, www.artemisgallerybh.com), showing the work of about two dozen local artists in changing exhibitions.

Lisa Hall Studio (head of Main St., Northeast Harbor, 207/276-6900, www.lisahalljewelry.com) carries Hall's jewelry.

A seasonal branch of Bar Harbor's **Island Artisans** (119 Main St., Northeast Harbor, 207/276-4045, www.islandartisans.com) carries an exceptional selection of locally made fine crafts.

For more than 25 years, **Redfield Artisans Gallery** (125 Main St., Northeast Harbor, 207/276-3609) has been selling high-end art and crafts to the area's discriminating buyers.

Next door, at **Christopher Smith Galleries** (125B Main St., Northeast Harbor, 207/276-3343, www.smithbronze.com), browse through an array of bronze wildlife sculptures and fountains. Smith was featured on the cover of *Wildlife Art* magazine in 2005.

Gifts and Clothing

The tony shops in Northeast Harbor are worth a visit and maybe even a major splurge. You'll find plenty of pink and lime green; Lilly Pulitzer is big here.

Early and late in the season, the summer crowd shops at **The Kimball Shop & Boutique** (135 Main St., Northeast Harbor, 207/276-3300, www.kimballshop.com) to stock up on wedding and Christmas gifts. It's all very tasteful.

At **Local Color** (5 Sea St., Northeast Harbor, 207/276-3332), you'll find clothing, furnishings, artwork, and more with an emphasis on green, Maine made, and Fair Trade.

Antiques and Antiquarian Books

A small but select inventory of pre-owned hardcover books lines the walls at **Wikhegan Old Books** (117 Main St., Northeast Harbor, 207/276-5079 or 207/244-7060). Specialties include nautical books, Native American lore, women's studies, poetry, and antiques.

The shop doubles as **Pine Bough,** offering a small but well-chosen selection of antiques and decorative arts.

Science and Nature

If you're traveling with children or if you have any interest in art, science, or nature, don't miss **The Naturalist's Notebook** (16 Main St., Seal Harbor, 207/801-2777, www.thenaturalistsnotebook.com), a shop and exploratorium. Owned by artist-photographer Pamelia Markwood and her *Sports Illustrated* writer/editor husband, Craig Neff, the shop has three stories full of engaging exhibits, books, and treasures. A smaller branch operates at 15 Main Street in Northeast Harbor.

ACCOMMODATIONS

Inns

For more than 100 years, the genteel **Asticou Inn** (Rte. 3, Northeast Harbor, 207/276-3344 or 800/258-3373, www.asticou.com, $255-380) has catered to the whims and weddings of Northeast Harbor's well-heeled summer rusticators. She's an elegant old gal that seems right out of a Hollywood romance movie set in the 1950s: Hardwood floors are topped with Asian and braided rugs, rooms are papered with floral or plaid wallpapers, and gauzy ruffled curtains blow in the breeze. It's all delightfully old-fashioned, and most guests would have it no other way. But it's not for everybody. The one nod to modern times is free Wi-Fi. There's no air-conditioning, no in-room phone or TV, and no soundproofing. The inn tops a lawn that slopes down to the yacht-filled harbor, and cocktails and lunch are served daily on the porch overlooking the heated pool, tennis court, and water. Accommodations are spread out between the main inn, three cottages, and four funky Topsiders, which seem inspired by the old *Jetsons* TV show. The nicest accommodations, a mix of rooms and suites, face the harbor. The inn's restaurant serves breakfast, lunch, and dinner daily. Try to plan a late-May or early-June visit; you're practically on top of the Asticou Azalea Garden, Thuya

Garden is a short walk away (or hike via the Eliot Mountain Trail), and the rates are lowest. Asticou is a popular wedding venue, so if you're looking for a quiet weekend, check the inn's event schedule before booking a room. Note: The Acadia Corp., which lost its contract to operate the Jordan Pond House in a controversial 2014 decision, is managing the inn as of 2015.

Bed-and-Breakfasts

In 1888, architect Fred Savage designed the two Shingle-style buildings that make up the three-story **Harbourside Inn** (Main St., Northeast Harbor, 207/276-3272, www.harboursideinn.com, mid-June-mid-Sept., $150-250). The Sweet family has preserved the old-fashioned feel by decorating the 11 spacious guest rooms and three suites with antiques, yet modern amenities include some kitchenettes and phones. Most rooms have working fireplaces. A continental breakfast is served. Trails to Norumbega Mountain and Upper Hadlock Pond leave from the back of the property.

The newish **Colonel's Suites** (143 Main St., Northeast Harbor, 207/288-4775, www.colonelssuites.com, $149-219), above the bakery/restaurant of the same name, provide comfortable accommodations with modern amenities. Every suite has a separate seating area, refrigerator, and flat-screen TV. Rates include a full breakfast in the restaurant.

Three miles from Northeast Harbor, in equally tony Seal Harbor, is a true bargain, the **Lighthouse Inn and Restaurant** (12 Main St./Rte. 3, Seal Harbor, 207/276-3958, www.lighthouseinnandrestaurant.com, $75-125). Sure, the three guest rooms (one small, one very large with a kitchenette) are a bit dated and dowdy, but at these prices, who cares? There's also a suite with full kitchen ($250). This is a year-round property, and in winter rates drop to $45. Downstairs is a restaurant (11am-8pm daily) with equally reasonable prices. It's a short walk to Seal Harbor Beach and the Seal Harbor entrance to the Park Loop Road.

Motels

Although it's long overdue for an overhaul—every guest room has two double beds, towels are tiny, and the decor is uninspired—you can't beat the location of the **Kimball Terrace Inn** (10 Huntington Rd., Northeast Harbor, 207/276-3383 or 800/454-6225, www.kimballterraceinn.com, $170-235). The three-story motel faces the harbor, and every guest room has a patio or private balcony (ask for a harbor-facing room). Bring binoculars for yacht-spotting. The motel has a small pool, a restaurant, and a lounge and is a short walk from Northeast Harbor's downtown. It is a popular wedding venue, so if that's a concern, ask if there are any groups in-house before you book.

FOOD

Hours listed are for peak season, early July-early September. If you're visiting at other times, call ahead, as most restaurants are open fewer days and shorter hours during slower periods.

Local Flavors

In the **Pine Tree Market** (121 Main St., Northeast Harbor, 207/276-3335), you'll find gourmet goodies, a huge wine selection, a resident butcher, fresh fish, a deli, homemade breads, pastries, sandwiches, and salads. The market offers free delivery to homes and boats.

Pop into **Milk & Honey** (3 Old Firehouse Land, Northeast Harbor, 207/276-4003, www.milkandhoneykitchen.com, 8am-4pm Tues.-Sat.) for breakfast or lunch.

Tasteful Tides (102 Main St., Northeast Harbor, 207/276-0746, www.tastefultides.com, 10am-6pm Mon.-Sat.) sells specialty foods, including Fiore olive oils, along with house-made to-go soups, salads, and entrées.

Mrs. Brown's (104 Main St., Northeast Harbor, 207/276-3329, 10am-5pm Mon.-Fri.) sells farm-fresh produce and eggs, goat cheese, baked goods, and local crafts.

Rising Tide Partners, created to help Northeast Harbor recover from its devastating

2008 Main Street fires, is building **The Creamery** (123 Main St.), an old fashioned soda fountain and café.

From June well into October, the **Northeast Harbor Farmers Market** is set up each Thursday, 9am-noon, across from the Kimball Terrace Inn on Huntington Road.

Family Favorites

The homemade doughnuts are reason enough to visit **The Colonel's Restaurant and Bakery** (143 Main St., Northeast Harbor, 207/288-4775, www.colonelsrestaurant.com, 7am-9pm daily), but tucked behind the bakery is a full-service restaurant, serving everything from burgers to prime rib, as well as the usual seafood musts ($10-20). It draws families, thanks to a kids' menu and a casual atmosphere. It can be quite boisterous inside. There's also a deck out back and a separate bar area, which often is the quietest spot with the fastest service.

The **Docksider** (14 Sea St., Northeast Harbor, 207/276-3965, 11am-9pm daily summer) is a low-key, family-friendly, unassuming hole-in-the-wall. Located just up the hill from the chamber office, it has an outside deck, no view, and a reputation that's fading. Prices are on the high side, with burgers and sandwiches beginning around $7, and more popular options in the $15-28 range. The saving grace is Morton's Moo ice cream. Early-bird specials and a 10 percent discount are offered 4:30pm-6pm. If you're smitten, buy one of the T-shirts, featuring an upright lobster announcing, "Frankly, I don't give a clam."

Casual Dining

Peabody's at the Asticou Inn (15 Peabody Dr./Rte. 3, 207/276-3344, 7:30am-10am, noon-2:30pm, and 6pm-8:30pm daily) is open to nonguests for breakfast, lunch, afternoon tea with popovers and ice cream, and dinner ($22-36). When the weather cooperates, lunch and dinner are served on the deck, with serene views over Northeast Harbor. A lighter menu is served in the lounge.

Lobster

Abel's Lobster Pound (Rte. 198, Mount Desert, 2078/276-5827, www.abelslobsterpound.com, noon-9pm) tends to be a little pricier than other island pounds, but it does have a location overlooking Somes Sound as well as indoor dining with wait service (reservations required, with seatings at 6pm, 6:30pm, 8pm, and 8:30pm) and outdoor picnic tables.

INFORMATION AND SERVICES

The harbor-front information bureau of the **Mount Desert Chamber of Commerce** (18 Harbor Rd., Northeast Harbor, 207/276-5040, www.mountdesertchamber.org) covers the villages of Somesville, Northeast Harbor, Seal Harbor, Otter Creek, Pretty Marsh, and Hall Quarry.

Public restrooms are at the end of the building housing the Great Harbor Maritime Museum (124 Main St., Northeast Harbor), in the town office on Sea Street, and at the harbor.

GETTING THERE AND AROUND

Northeast Harbor is about 12 miles or 20 minutes via Routes 233 and 198 or 20 miles/35 minutes via Route 3 from Bar Harbor. It's about 13 miles or 25 minutes to Southwest Harbor.

Northeast Harbor is served by Route 5/Jordan Pond and Route 6/Brown Mountain of the Island Explorer bus system.

Southwest Harbor and Vicinity

Southwest Harbor (pop. 1,764) is the hub of Mount Desert Island's "quiet side." In summer, its tiny downtown district is probably the busiest spot on the whole western side of the island (west of Somes Sound), but that's not saying a great deal. "Southwest" has the feel of a settled community, a year-round flavor that Bar Harbor sometimes lacks. And it competes with the best in the scenery department. The Southwest Harbor area serves as a very convenient base for exploring Acadia National Park, as well as the island's less crowded villages and offshore Swans Island, Frenchboro, and the Cranberry Isles.

The quirky nature of the island's four town boundaries creates complications in trying to categorize various island segments. Officially, the town of Southwest Harbor includes only the villages of **Manset** and **Seawall,** but nearby is the precious hamlet of **Somesville.** The Somesville National Historic District, with its distinctive arched white footbridge, is especially appealing, but traffic gets congested here along Route 102, so rather than just rubbernecking, plan to stop and walk around.

SIGHTS
★ Wendell Gilley Museum
In the center of Southwest Harbor, the **Wendell Gilley Museum** (Herrick Rd. and Rte. 102, Southwest Harbor, 207/244-7555, www.wendellgilleymuseum.org, 10am-4pm Tues.-Sat., noon-4pm Sun. June-Oct., 10am-4pm Fri.-Sun. May. and Nov.-Dec., $5 adults, $2 ages 5-12) was established in 1981 to display the life work of local woodcarver Wendell Gilley (1904-1983), a onetime plumber who had gained a national reputation for his carvings by the time of his death. The modern, energy-efficient museum houses more than 200 of his astonishingly realistic bird specimens carved over more than 50 years. Summer exhibits also feature other wildlife artists. Many days, a local artist gives woodcarving

demonstrations, and members of the local carving club often can be seen whittling away. The gift shop carries an ornithological potpourri, including books, binoculars, and carving tools. Kids over eight appreciate this more than younger ones. If you're bitten by the carving bug, workshops are available, ranging from 90-minute introductory lessons for adults and children ($25, includes kit and admission), offered most weekdays during the summer, to multiday classes on specific birds.

Somesville Historical Museum and Gardens
The tiny **Somesville Historical Museum and Gardens** (Rte. 102, Somesville, 207/276-9323, www.mdihistory.org, 1pm-4pm Tues.-Sat. June 1-late Sept., donation) is adjacent to the gently curving white bridge in Somesville, so there's a good chance you're going to stop nearby, if just for a photo. In season, the heirloom garden, filled with flowering plants and herbs of the 19th and early 20th centuries, is worth a photo or two. The one-room museum has local artifacts and memorabilia displayed in a themed exhibit that changes annually. You can purchase a walking-tour guide to Somesville in the museum. If you're especially interested in history, ask about the museum's programs, which include speakers, demonstrations, and workshops.

Charlotte Rhoades Park and Butterfly Garden
It's easy to miss the **Charlotte Rhoades Park and Butterfly Garden** (Rte. 102, Southwest Harbor, 207/244-5405, www.rhoadesbutterflygarden.org), but that would be a mistake. This tiny seaside park was donated to the town in 1973, and the butterfly garden was established in 1998 to promote conservation education. The park is seldom busy, and it's a delightful place for a picnic. A kiosk is stocked with butterfly observation

Southwest Harbor and Tremont

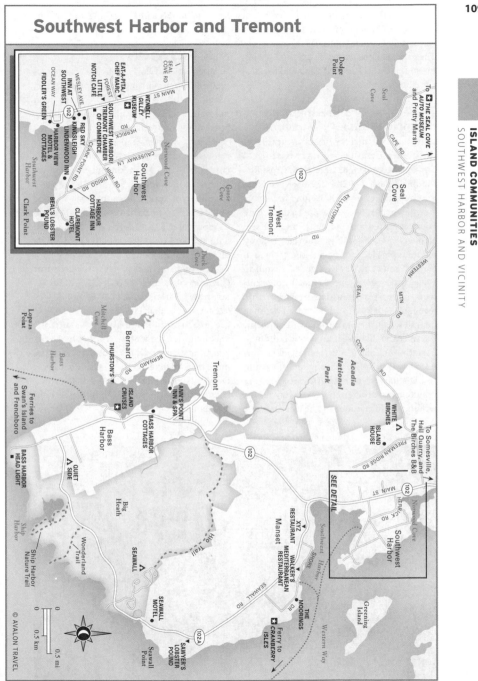

Detail inset (Southwest Harbor):

SEAL COVE RD
MAIN ST
EAT-A-PITA/CHEF MARC
CHEF MARC
INN AT SOUTHWEST
FOREST
LITTLE NOTCH CAFÉ
WESLEY AVE.
OCEAN WAY
FIDDLER'S GREEN
RED SKY
102
KINGSLEIGH
LINDENWOOD INN
HARBOR VIEW MOTEL & COTTAGES
WENDELL GILLEY MUSEUM
HERRICK RD
SOUTHWEST HARBOR/TREMONT CHAMBER OF COMMERCE
CAUSEWAY LN.
CLARK POINT RD
HIGH RD
DIRIGO RD
Southwest Harbor
HARBOUR COTTAGE INN
CLAREMONT HOTEL
BEAL'S LOBSTER POUND
Clark Point
Southwest Harbor

Main map:

Dodge Point
Seal Cove
To THE SEAL COVE AUTO MUSEUM and Pretty Marsh
CAPE RD
Seal Cove
102
KELLYTOWN RD
West Tremont
Goose Cove
Duck Cove
SEAL COVE RD
WESTERN MTN RD
Norwood Cove
Lopaus Point
Mitchell Cove
Bernard
Bass Harbor
THURSTON'S
BERNARD RD
Tremont
Acadia National Park
FREEMAN RIDGE RD
To Somesville, Hall Quarry, and The Birches B&B
ANN'S POINT INN & SPA
ISLAND CRUISES
BASS HARBOR COTTAGES
Bass Harbor
QUIET SIDE
Big Heath
WHITE BIRCHES
ISLAND HOUSE
Ferries to Swan's Island and Frenchboro
BASS HARBOR HEAD LIGHT
Wonderland Trail
SEAWALL
Ship Harbor Nature Trail
Ship Harbor
Hio Trail
SEAWALL MOTEL
Seawall Point
102A
SAWYER'S LOBSTER POUND
XYZ RESTAURANT
WALKER'S
MEDITERRANEAN RESTAURANT
Manset
SHORE DR
SEAWALL RD
THE MOORINGS
Ferry to CRANBERRY ISLES
SEE DETAIL
MAIN ST
102
HERRICK RD
Norwood Cove
Southwest Harbor
Greening Island
Western Way
Ship Harbor

0 0.5 mi
0 0.5 km

© AVALON TRAVEL

sheets, and there's usually a volunteer docent on duty on Thursday mornings. Try to time a visit with the annual butterfly release in July. The park is on the waterside of Route 102 between the Causeway Golf Club and the Seal Cove Road.

The Maine Granite Industry Historical Society Museum

Delve into the history of Maine granite at the **Maine Granite Industry Historical Society Museum** (62 Beech Hill Cross Rd., Mount Desert, 207/244-7299, www.mainegraniteindustry.org, 10am-4pm Tues.-Sun. Apr. 1-Nov. 31, winter by appt., donation). Founder and curator Steven Haynes oversees a collection comprising hundreds of tools, photographs, ledgers, books, and other artifacts related to quarry workers, blacksmiths, stone cutters, and stone carvers. Immigrants from countries including Italy, Finland, Sweden, Norway, and Portugal worked quarries in nine Maine counties, and the granite can still be seen in public buildings, including churches, courthouses, and libraries, as well as bridges throughout the country. Displays show the difference between granite from different quarries. Haynes is a wealth of information, and he loves to share his passion. He's often carving and polishing at the site.

RECREATION

Acadia National Park, of course, is the recreational focus throughout Mount Desert Island; on the island's western side, the main nonpark recreational activities are bike-, boat-, and picnic-related.

A broad swath of Acadia National Park cuts right through the center of this side of the island, and many of its hiking trails are far less congested than those elsewhere in the park. A connector trail from Southwest Harbor makes access to park trails easy. Seawall Campground, as well as the Wonderland and Ship Harbor Trails, lie within the town limits of Southwest Harbor.

At the Southwest Harbor/Tremont Chamber of Commerce office (329 Main St., Southwest Harbor, 207/244-9264 or 800/423-9264, www.acadiachamber.com), or at any of the area's stores, lodgings, and restaurants, pick up a free copy of the *Trail Map/Hiking Guide,* a very handy foldout map showing more than 20 hikes on the west side of Mount Desert Island. Trail descriptions include length, time required, and skill level (easy to strenuous).

the Somesville Historical Museum and Gardens

Bicycle Rentals

A veteran business with a first-rate reputation, **Southwest Cycle** (370 Main St., Southwest Harbor, 207/244-5856 or 800/649-5856, www.southwestcycle.com) is open all year (8:30am-5:30pm Mon.-Sat., 9:30am-4pm Sun. July-Aug., 9am-5pm Mon.-Sat., 9:30am-4pm Sun. Sept.-June). The staff will fix you up with maps and lots of good advice for three loops (10-30 miles) on the western side of Mount Desert. Rentals begin around $18 for an afternoon and $24 for a full day, with multiday discounts available. The shop also rents every imaginable accessory, from baby seats to jogging strollers.

Golf

Play a quick nine at the **Causeway Club** (Fernald Point Rd., 207/244-3780, $15 for nine holes, $20 for 18 opening-mid-June; $35/$45 mid-June-mid-Sept; $20/$25 mid-Sept.-closing), which edges the ocean. Be forewarned: It's more challenging than it looks.

Deep-Sea Fishing

Go fishing with **Vagabond Deep Sea Fishing** (Beal's Wharf, Clark Point Rd., Southwest Harbor, 207/244-5385, www.vagabondfishing.com, half-day from $59 adults, $39 ages 5-12) aboard the 43-foot *Vagabond*, and you might return with a lobster. The boat goes 8-20 miles offshore for mackerel, bluefish, codfish, and more. All equipment is included; dress warmly and come prepared with seasickness medications.

Boat Rentals and Lessons

Mansell Boat Rental Co. (135 Shore Rd., Manset, 207/244-5625, www.mansellboatrentals.com), next to Hinckley, rents sailboats and powerboats by the day or week, including a keel day-sailor for $195 per day and a 13.6-foot Boston Whaler for $175 per day. Also available are sailing lessons: $295 for a two-to three-hour sail lesson cruise for two, which includes rigging and unrigging the boat, and $100 per hour for private lessons, minimum two hours.

Half-day, full-day, and longer powerboat rentals are also available from **Manset Yacht Service** (113 Shore Rd., Manset, 207/244-4040, www.mansetyachtservice.com). Rates begin at $240 for a half-day rental of an Angler 20-footer.

Sea Kayaking

On the outskirts of Southwest Harbor's downtown is **Maine State Kayak** (254 Main St., Southwest Harbor, 207/244-9500 or 877/481-9500, www.mainestatekayak.com). Staffed with experienced, environmentally sensitive kayakers (all are Registered Maine Guides), the company offers four-hour guided trips departing at 8:30am, 10am, and 2pm along with a sunset tour, with a choice of half a dozen routes that depend on tides, visibility, and wind conditions. The rate is $48 per person, $44 in June and September. Most trips include island or beach breaks. Maximum group size is six tandems; minimum age is 12. Neophytes are welcome.

Calm-Water Paddling

Just west of Somesville (take Pretty Marsh Rd.) and across the road from Long Pond, the largest lake on Mount Desert Island, **National Park Canoe & Kayak Rental** (145 Pretty Marsh Rd./Rte. 102, Mount Desert, 207/244-5854, www.nationalparkcanoerental.com, mid-May-mid-Oct.) makes canoeing and kayaking a snap. Just rent the boat, carry it across the road to Pond's End, and launch it. Be sure to pack a picnic. Rates begin at $34 for a three-hour canoe or solo kayak rental, $37 for a tandem kayak, and $36 for a paddleboard. A do-it-yourself sunset canoe or kayak tour (5pm-sunset) is $20 per person. The late fee is $10 per half hour. Reservations are essential in July-August.

If you've brought your own canoe or kayak, launch it here at Pond's End and head off. It's four miles to the southern end of the lake. If the wind kicks up, skirt the shore; if it really kicks up from the north, don't paddle too far down the lake, because you'll have a difficult time getting back.

Another option is to launch your canoe on the quieter, cliff-lined southern end of the lake, much of which is in the park. To find the put-in, take the Seal Cove Road (on the east end of downtown Southwest Harbor). Go right on Long Cove Road to the small parking area at the end near the pumping station. You can also put in from the Long Pond Fire Road, off Route 102, in Pretty Marsh.

On a breezy day, the best paddling option is **Seal Cove Pond.** The eastern shoreline is in the park, and the best access is the Western Mountain Road boat launch, located off the Seal Cove Road. This is a gorgeous and especially tranquil pond, and it's likely you'll only share it with local wildlife.

Almost the entire west side of **Long Pond** is Acadia National Park property, so plan to picnic and swim along here; tuck into the sheltered area west of Southern Neck, a crooked finger of land that points northward from the western shore. Stay clear of private property on the east side of the lake.

EXCURSION BOATS

Southwest Harbor is the starting point for a couple of boat services headed for the Cranberry Isles. As always, rates will fluctuate with fuel prices.

Sail Acadia (Dysert's Great Harbor Marina, 11 Apple Ln., Southwest Harbor, 207/266-5210, www.downeastfriendshipsloop.com) is the umbrella for Downeast Friendship Sloop Charters and Quietside Cruises. The former sails the *Alice E.*, built in 1899 and the oldest Friendship Sloop sailing today. Private charters start at $250 for a two-hour sail, covering up to six passengers and including an appetizer and soft drinks; shared trips are $50 per person for two hours, $75 per person for three hours. The latter offers scenic Somes Sound cruises that include baiting and hauling a lobster trap and visiting a seal colony ($30 adults, $20 under age 12) aboard the *Elizabeth T,* a wooden lobster boat.

ENTERTAINMENT
Acadia Repertory Theatre

Somesville is home to the **Acadia Repertory Theatre** (Rte. 102, Somesville, 207/244-7260, www.acadiarep.com, $25 adults; $20 seniors, students, and military; $12 under age 16), which has been providing first-rate professional summer stock on the stage of Somesville's antique Masonic Hall since 1973. Classic plays by Oscar Wilde, Neil Simon, and even Molière have been

Launch a canoe or kayak from Pond's End to explore Long Pond.

staples, as has the annual Agatha Christie mystery. Performances in the 148-seat hall run at 8:15pm Tuesday-Sunday late June-late August, with 2pm matinees on the last Sunday of each play's run. Special children's plays are performed at 10:30am Wednesday and Saturday in July-August. Tickets for children's theater programs are $9 adults, $6 children.

Lecture and Concert Series

During July-August, the Claremont Hotel (22 Claremont Rd., Southwest Harbor, 207/244-5036 or 800/244-5036, www.theclaremonthotel.com) sponsors a **free weekly lecture series** at 8pm on Thursday evenings. Past topics have ranged from John Marin and Maine Modernism to Understanding Climate Change and the Climate Change Debate. It also offers a **Saturday evening concert series** ($10), with music ranging from bluegrass to classical.

EVENTS

During July-August, the Wednesday **Pie Sale** at the Somesville Union Meeting House is always a sellout. Go early; the doors open at noon, it's all over by 12:10.

In early August, the annual **Claremont Croquet Classic,** held on the grounds of the classic Claremont Hotel, is open to all ages.

In September, Smuggler's Den Campground, on Route 102 in Southwest Harbor, is home to the annual **MDI Garlic Festival,** with entertainment and opportunities to savor the stinking rose, and in October the campground hosts the annual **Oktoberfest and Food Festival** (207/244-9264 or 800/423-9264, www.acadiachamber. com), a one-day celebration with crafts, food, games, music, and about two dozen Maine microbrewers presenting about 80 different brews.

The **Acadia Night Sky Festival** (www.acadianightskyfestival.com), in late September/early October, includes lectures, movies, sky-viewing opportunities, and other activities.

SHOPPING

The best shopping locale on this side of the island is Southwest Harbor. Mind you, there aren't lots of shops, but the selection is interesting.

Fine art of the 19th and early 20th centuries is the specialty at **Clark Point Gallery** (46 Clark Point Rd., Southwest Harbor, 207/244-0920, www.clarkpointgallery.com). Most works depict Maine and Mount Desert Island.

Jewelry approaches fine art at **Aylen & Son Jewelers** (332 Main St./Rte. 102, Southwest Harbor, 207/244-7369, www.peteraylen.com). For more than 25 years, Peter and Judy Aylen have been crafting and selling jewelry in 18-karat gold and sterling silver and augmenting it with fine gemstones or intriguing beads.

Harbor Artisans (334 Main St., Southwest Harbor, no phone) is a cooperative effort operated by Maine artisans.

More than 50 coastal Maine artisans sell their crafts at **Flying Mountain Artisans** (28 Main St./Rte. 102, Southwest Harbor, 207/244-0404, www.flyingmountainartisans. homestead.com), a cooperatively owned shop with a good range of creative goods, from quilts to blown glass. Also here is a gallery showing the works of more than 20 artists. Consider stopping in after a hike on Flying Mountain.

You can stop in at the **Hinckley Ship'Store** (130 Shore Rd., Southwest Harbor, 207/244-7100 or 800/446-2553, www. hinckleyshipstore.com) and pick up books, charts, and all sorts of Hinckley-logo gear. The Hinckley Company, a name of stellar repute since the 1930s, is one of the nation's premier boatbuilders. There are no tours of the Hinckley complex, but most yachters can't resist the urge to look in at the yard.

ACCOMMODATIONS

As the Asticou Inn is to Northeast Harbor, the Claremont is to Southwest Harbor. On the other end of the lodging scale, there are several commercial campgrounds in this part of the island, plus an Acadia National Park campground. Rates listed are for peak season.

Inns

If you're pining for the "old Maine," stay at **The Claremont** (22 Claremont Rd., Southwest Harbor, 207/244-5036 or 800/244-5036, www.theclaremonthotel.com), an elegant, oceanfront grande dame dressed in mustard-yellow clapboard with a spectacular six-acre hilltop setting overlooking Somes Sound. Dating from 1884, the main building has 24 guest rooms, most of them refurbished yet pleasantly old-fashioned and neither fussy nor fancy; if you want techie frills, go elsewhere. Additional guest rooms are in the Phillips House, Rowse House, and Cole Cottage. Rates for guestrooms begin around $145 in spring and fall and rise to as high as $335 in August and include a buffet breakfast. Also on the premises are 14 cottages ($180-370). Guests have access to croquet courts, a clay tennis court, one-speed cruiser bikes, rowboats, and a library. The boathouse bar is especially popular. The most popular time here is the first week in August, during the annual Claremont Croquet Classic. Children are welcome. The hotel and dining room are open mid-June-mid-October; cottages are open late May-mid-October.

Bed-and-Breakfasts

Many of Southwest Harbor's bed-and-breakfasts are clustered downtown, along Main Street and Clark Point Road.

Set on a corner, well back from Clark Point Road, is ★ **Harbour Cottage Inn** (9 Dirigo Rd., Southwest Harbor, 207/244-5738 or 888/843-3022, www.harbourcottageinn.com, $229-290), appealingly revamped in 2002 when Javier Montesinos and Don Jalbert took over the reins. Built in 1870, it was the annex for the island's first hotel and housed the increasing numbers of rusticators who patronized this part of the island. It has evolved into a lovely bed-and-breakfast with eight guest rooms and three suites decorated in a colorful and fun cottage style. Some guest rooms have whirlpool baths and/or fireplaces, and all have TVs and Wi-Fi. Rates include a multicourse breakfast. Also part of Harbour Cottage is **Pier One,** which offers five truly waterfront suites ($1,540-1,825 weekly), including a studio cottage. All were renovated in 2009 in a comfortable cottage style; all have kitchens, TVs, and phones. Guests have private use of a 150-foot pier, and they can dock or launch canoes, kayaks, or other small boats from right outside their doors; dockage is available for

Play croquet with a view at The Claremont in Southwest Harbor.

larger boats. It's all within walking distance of downtown.

The linden-blossom fragrance can be intoxicating in summer at the **Lindenwood Inn** (118 Clark Point Rd., Southwest Harbor, 207/244-5335 or 800/307-5335, www.lindenwoodinn.com, $169-329). The inn's 15 guest rooms, split between two buildings, and poolside bungalow are decorated in a sophisticated yet comfortable style. After you hike Acadia's trails, the heated pool and hot tub are especially welcome, and after that, perhaps enjoy a drink while shooting pool or playing darts. Some guest rooms have harbor views.

Even glimpsed through the trees from the road, ★ **The Birches** (46 Fernald Point Rd., Southwest Harbor, 207/244-5182, www.thebirchesbnb.com, $199-315) is appealing. A wooded drive winds down to the large home fronting the ocean, near the mouth of Somes Sound. It's just 350 yards to the Causeway Golf Club and a short walk to the Flying Mountain trailhead and Valley Cove fire road with access to the Acadia and St. Sauveur trails. Built as a summer cottage in 1916, The Birches retains that casual summer ease, right down to the stone fireplace in the living room and the croquet court on the lawn. Guest rooms are especially large and comfortably decorated;

most have water views, and one has a sleeping porch. Innkeeper Susi Homer treats guests like family. Her breakfasts are legendary. A pet-friendly cottage also is available. Open year-round, by reservation.

In Manset, adjacent to the Hinckley Yacht complex and with jaw-dropping views down Somes Sound, is **The Moorings** (133 Shore Rd., Manset, 207/244-5523, www.mooringsinn.com, $125-225), where fourth-generation innkeeper Leslie Watson is now owner. The oceanfront complex is part motel, part cottage rental, and part old-fashioned bed-and-breakfast. Rooms are named after locally built sailing vessels. The motel-style rooms in the Lighthouse View Wing have refrigerators, microwaves, Wi-Fi, waterfront decks, and incredible views (spend the afternoon counting the Hinckley yachts). A continental breakfast is available each morning. Also on the property or nearby are cottage units ($135-245). This is an older complex, and soundproofing is minimal. Bikes, canoes, and kayaks are available for guests, so you can paddle around the harbor; Mansell Boat Rental Co. is also on the premises. Dogs are permitted with prior approval.

Built in 1884 as the Freeman Cottage, the mansard-roofed Victorian **Inn at Southwest**

The Birches bed-and-breakfast

(371 Main St./Rte. 102, Southwest Harbor, 207/244-3835, www.innatsouthwest.com, $145-200) has 13 dormers and a wraparound veranda furnished with wicker. Seven 2nd- and 3rd-floor guest rooms—named for Maine lighthouses and full of character—are decorated with a mix of contemporary and antique furnishings. Some have gas stoves or limited water views; all have Wi-Fi. Breakfast is a feast, with such treats as cheesecake crepes and eggs Florentine served indoors or on the patio. In the afternoon, cookies are available.

Across the lane is the elegant Queen Anne **Kingsleigh Inn 1904** (373 Main St., Southwest Harbor, 207/244-5302, www.kingsleighinn.com, $170-315), with eight air-conditioned rooms, some with private harbor-facing decks, on three floors; all have Wi-Fi. The best splurge is the turret suite, with a fireplace, TV, private deck, and a telescope trained on the harbor. Breakfast is an elegant, three-course affair, served on the water-view porch, weather permitting. Afternoon refreshments are served, and chocolate truffles or chocolate-raspberry rum balls and port wine are replenished daily in guest rooms.

Smack dab in the middle of town, **Penury Hall** (374 Main St., Southwest Harbor, 207/244-7102, www.penuryhall.com, $145) offers three bedrooms with private, detached bathrooms, and an unfussy, relaxed atmosphere that leans toward homestay. The living rooms are bright and cheerful and filled with games, puzzles, music, and books, and there are laundry facilities. A full breakfast is included. Penury Hall is open year-round.

Heading out toward Seawall is **The Lodgings at Southwest Harbor** (170 Seawall Rd., Southwest Harbor, 207/244-0340, www.thelodge-ings.com, $125), owned by Marge and Don Lodge, hence the name. This farmhouse-style cottage has three country-comfy guest rooms, countless books, and Wi-Fi. A full hot breakfast is included.

Motels and Cottages

Smack on the harbor and just a two-minute walk from downtown is the appropriately named **Harbor View Motel & Cottages** (11 Ocean Way, Southwest Harbor, 207/244-5031 or 800/538-6463, www.harborviewmoteland-cottages.com). The family-owned complex comprises motel rooms ($90-136/night, $560-845/week) spread out in two older, somewhat dowdy, one-story buildings and a newer, three-story structure fronting on the harbor. A meager continental breakfast is served to motel guests July 1-early September. Also on the premises are seven housekeeping cottages with kitchenettes (weekly rentals only, $775-1,225), ranging from studios to two-bedrooms. Pets are welcome in some units ($10/day or $60/week).

Directly across from the famed seawall and adjacent to the park is the **Seawall Motel** (566 Seawall Rd./Rte. 102A, Southwest Harbor, 207/244-9250 or 800/248-9250, www.seawallmotel.com, $120), a budget-friendly find. The no-surprises-but-dated two-story motel (upstairs guest rooms have the best views) has free Wi-Fi, in-room phones, cable TV, a communal microwave and fridge, a coin-op laundry, and service-oriented owners. Kids 12 and younger stay free. The location is excellent for bird-watchers. A continental breakfast is served. Also on the premises is the **Common Good Café** (207/244-3007, www.commongoodsoupkitchen.org, 7:30am-11:30am daily, donation), a nonprofit operated by the Common Good Soup Kitchen Community and serving popovers.

L. S. Robinson Co. (337 Main St., Southwest Harbor, 207/244-5563, www.lsrobinson.com) has an extensive list of cottage rentals in the area. The Southwest Harbor/Tremont Chamber of Commerce (329 Main St., Southwest Harbor, 207/244-9264 or 800/423-9264, www.acadiachamber.com) also keeps a helpful listing of privately owned homes and cottages available for rent.

Camping

Acadia National Park's Seawall Campground is on this side of the island.

On the eastern edge of Somesville, just off Route 198, at the head of Somes Sound, the Craighead family's **Mount Desert Campground** (516 Somes Sound Dr./Rte. 198, Somesville, 207/244-3710, www.mountdesertcampground.com) is especially centrally located for visiting Bar Harbor, Acadia, and the whole western side of Mount Desert Island. The campground has 152 wooded tent sites, about 45 on the water, spread out on 58 acres. Reservations are essential in midsummer—one-week minimum for waterfront sites, three days for off-water sites in July-August. (Campers book a year ahead for waterfront sites here.) This deservedly popular and low-key campground gets high marks for maintenance, noise control, and convenient tent platforms. Another plus is The Gathering Place, where campers can relax, play games, use free Wi-Fi, and purchase coffee and fresh-baked treats or ice cream. Summer rates are $40-60 per night for two adults and two children younger than 18. Electrical hookups are $2 per night. No pets are allowed July-early September, and no trailers over 20 feet are permitted. Kayak, canoe, and standup paddleboard rentals are available.

Built on the site of an old quarry, on a hillside descending to rocky frontage on Somes Sound, **Somes Sound View Campground** (86 Hall Quarry Rd., Mount Desert, 207/244-3890, off-season 207/244-7452, www.ssvc.info, late May-mid-Oct., $30-60) is among the smallest campgrounds on the island, with fewer than 60 sites, all geared to tents and vans. Rustic camping cabins are $70 per night. Facilities include hot showers (if you're camping on the lowest levels, it's a good hike up to the bathhouse), a heated pool, a boat launch, kayak, canoe, and paddleboat rentals, and a fishing dock. All sites have a faucet, fire pit, and picnic table. You can swim in the sound from a rocky beach. Leashed pets are allowed. It's two miles south and east of Somesville and a mile east of Route 102.

The Worcester family's **Smuggler's Den Campground** (Rte. 102, Southwest Harbor, 207/244-3944, www.smugglersdencampground.com, $34-59) is a midsized, pet-friendly campground between Echo Lake and

downtown Southwest Harbor. It's also the site of the annual Oktoberfest. Trails access back roads to Echo Lake (1.25 miles) and Long Pond (1 mile) as well as 25 miles of Acadia National Park trails. Big-rig sites are grouped in the top third, pop-ups and small campers are in the middle third, and tenting sites are in the lower third and in the woods rimming the large recreation field. Also available are cabins ($575 camping, $1,100 with kitchen and bath, per week). Facilities include Wi-Fi, a heated pool and kiddie pool, a four-acre recreation field with horseshoe pit, half-court basketball, and lawn games, a laundry, free hot showers, lobster and ice cream sales, and entertainment.

FOOD

Restaurant days and hours change frequently, so always call ahead to confirm.

Local Flavors

Lots of goodies for picnics can be found at **Sawyer's Market** (344 Main St., Southwest Harbor, 207/244-3315, 7:30am-8:30pm daily); for wine, cheese, and gourmet goodies, head across the street to **Sawyer's Specialties** (353 Main St., Southwest Harbor, 207/244-3317, open daily).

Here's a breakfast you can feel good about. **Common Good Café** (566 Seawall Rd./Rte. 102A, Southwest Harbor, 207/244-3007, www.commongoodsoupkitchen.org, 7:30am-11:30am daily, donation) offers a self-serve buffet comprising hot popovers, slow-simmered steel-cut oatmeal, tea, and coffee, along with accompaniments including maple syrup and plain and flavored butters in a rustic but comfy space with big windows overlooking the rugged granite shores and a freshwater pond in the Seawall section of Acadia National Park. The volunteer-run program is a fundraiser by the Common Good Soup Kitchen Community, which distributes free soup to shut-ins, offers a winter community meal, and stocks a winter community-clothing program, among other things. Be as generous as you can in your donation; remember just one popover with tea is about $12 at the Jordan Pond House; here you can eat as many as you like. That said, no one monitors it, and if you're on a tight budget, just give what you can. Every penny is appreciated. You might also consider picking up a package of the popover mix.

Good chowders, sandwiches, fried clams, lobster rolls, and even pizza are served at the cozy **Quietside Cafe** (360 Main St., Southwest Harbor, 207/244-9444, 11am-10pm Mon.-Sat., 11am-8pm Sun., $6-18). Do save room for Frances's sky-high homemade blueberry and key lime pies.

Pick up a scrumptious triple-berry, strawberry rhubarb, or blueberry pie from Mary Musson's **Island Bound Treats** (302 Main St., Southwest Harbor, 207/266-3253).

JayDub's (19 Clark Point Rd., Southwest Harbor, 207/244-5055, 11am-9pm Mon.-Sat., $8-15) is a casual spot with a full bar that makes excellent sandwiches, burgers, pizzas, soups, and desserts mostly from scratch.

Good food, good coffee, and good wine mix with a Mediterranean-influenced menu at **Sips** (4 Clark Point Rd., Southwest Harbor, 207/244-4550, www.sipsmdi.com, 7am-9pm daily), a congenial place. Small- and large-plate and tapas-style choices range $8-28; the risottos are especially good. A children's menu is available. On Thursday nights during the summer season, there usually is live music.

Treat yourself to lunch overlooking Somes Sound at the **Boat House** at the Claremont Hotel (22 Claremont Rd., Southwest Harbor, 207/244-5036 or 800/244-5036, noon-2pm daily July-Aug., $7-18). It's also a popular spot for cocktails, served 5:30pm-9pm, when you can watch the sun set behind Cadillac Mountain.

Yes, the cookies and bars that Maureen McDonald bakes at **Manset Little Farm** (281 Rte. 102A, Manset, 207/244-7013) are pricey at $4 each, but they're big and scratch-made, and after one bite, you'll be wishing you'd purchased more.

College of the Atlantic students run **Beech Hill Farm** (171 Beech Hill Rd., Mount Desert,

207/244-5204, 9am-4pm Tues.-Sat.), a five-acre farm certified organic by the Maine Organic Farmers and Gardeners Association. Also here are acres of heirloom apple trees and 65 acres of forestland. Visit the farm stand for fresh produce as well as other organic or natural foods such as cheeses and baked goods.

Tanya's Off the Grid Foods (246 Main St., Southwest Harbor, 207/244-0777, 6:30am-2pm Mon.-Fri.), a grab-and-go spot on the edge of town, is a local favorite for breakfast and lunch fare with a creative, fresh, and healthful touch.

The island's best craft beer selection can be found at the **Liquor Locker** (11 Seal Cove Rd., Southwest Harbor, 207/244-3788).

International Fare

Craving a taste of Mexico? **XYZ Restaurant** (80 Seawall Rd./Rte. 102A, Manset, 207/244-5221, www.xyzmaine.com, entrées $26) specializes in the flavors of interior Mexico: Xalapa, Yucatán, and Zacatecas (hence "XYZ"). The most popular dish is *cochinita*—citrus-marinated pork rubbed with achiote paste, worthy of its reputation. For dessert, try the XYZ pie. Dine inside or on the porch. The food is great, but it's pricey and served with a dose of attitude. Hours vary, often by the week, so call for the current schedule.

From the outside, it doesn't look like much, but locals know you can count on **DeMuro's Top of the Hill** (Rte. 102, Southwest Harbor, 207/244-0033, www.topofthehilldining.com, 5pm-close daily, $10-28) for a good meal at a fair price. The Italian-influenced menu has something in all price ranges, and includes vegetarian fare as well as lobster. Twilight specials ($12-14) are served 5pm-6pm. The Lobster Palooza special (around $30) includes chowder, steamed mussels, boiled lobster, potato, vegetable, and dessert. Nightly wine specials are around $15 per bottle.

Casual Dining

By day, **Eat-a-Pita** (326 Main St., Southwest Harbor, 207/244-4344, www.eatapitasouthwestharbor.com, 8am-4pm daily) is a casual, order-at-the-counter restaurant serving breakfast and lunch. At night it morphs into **Cafe 2,** a full-service restaurant (5pm-9pm Tues.-Sun., $9-26). The dining room, furnished with old oak tables and chairs, has a funky, artsy 'tude; there's also patio seating outside and an outdoor bar (think pink flamingos). Start the day with a Greek or Acapulco omelet. Lunch emphasizes delicious pita sandwiches, burgers, paninis, and salads (call in advance for takeout); dinner choices include salads, light meals, a half-dozen pastas, and entrées. This is my usual go-to for to-go sandwiches to enjoy while hiking in the park.

Some of the island's most creative sandwiches and pizza toppings emerge from **Little Notch Cafe** (340 Main St., Southwest Harbor, 207/244-3357, 7:30am-8:30pm daily, $8-16), next to the library in Southwest Harbor's downtown. Also available are Little Notch Bakery's famed breads, a couple of pasta choices, and homemade soups, stews, and chowders.

Earning high praise for its internationally accented fare, good service, harbor views, and specialty cocktails is ★ **Fiddlers' Green** (411 Main St., Southwest Harbor, 207/244-9416, www.fiddlersgreenrestaurant.com, 5:30pm-10pm Tues.-Sun.). House specialties, such as Asian vegetable hot pot, trout livorese, and farm-to-table roast pig, range $16-38, but you can also make a meal of small plates, soups, sandwiches, and salads.

Fine Dining

The dreamy views from **Xanthus** (22 Claremont Rd., Southwest Harbor, 207/244-5036 or 800/244-5036, 6pm-9pm daily), at the Claremont Hotel, descend over the lawns and croquet courts, boathouse, and dock to the water backed by mountains. It's truly a special place for an elegant meal complemented by an old-fashioned grace. Jackets are not required, but men won't feel out of place wearing one. Entrées range $24-30; a three-course fixed-price dinner is $30. Dining-room reservations are advised in midsummer.

Red sky at night, diners delight: Gold walls, artwork, wood floors, and a giant hearth set a chic tone for ★ **Red Sky** (14 Clark Point Rd., Southwest Harbor, 207/244-0476, www.redskyrestaurant.com, 5:30pm-9pm daily, entrées $22-35), one of the island's tonier restaurants. Owners James and Elizabeth Geffen Lindquist's creative fare emphasizes fresh seafood, hand-cut meats, and local organic produce; there's always a vegetarian choice. For smaller appetites, it's easy to make a meal from the appetizers and salads. The restaurant is open Valentine's Day-New Year's Eve.

Lobster

Eat, drink, and be messy is the slogan at **Beal's Lobster Pier** (182 Clark Point Rd., Southwest Harbor, 207/244-3202, www.bealslobster.com, 11am-9pm daily), which only serves lobster that comes from boats unloading at the pier. Go for the lobster, but if you're traveling with landlubbers, there are burgers, fried fish, salads, sandwiches, and even veggie burgers on the menu.

Vintage burger-joint-style takeout meets lobster shack at **Sawyer's Lobster Pound** (465 Seawall Rd./Rte. 102A, Southwest Harbor, 207/244-8021, 4:30pm-8:30pm Mon., 11am-8:30pm Tues.-Sun.), an order-at-the-window, eat-on-picnic-tables spot that earns raves for its lobster and lobster rolls. It's owned by a lobsterman, so the seafood is fresh and the prices are relatively low.

INFORMATION AND SERVICES

The **Southwest Harbor/Tremont Chamber of Commerce** (329 Main St., Southwest Harbor, 207/244-9264 or 800/423-9264, www.acadiachamber.com) stocks brochures, maps, menus, and other local info.

Check out **Southwest Harbor Public Library** (338 Main St., Southwest Harbor, 207/244-7065, www.swhplibrary.org).

In downtown Southwest Harbor, **public restrooms** are at the southern end of the parking lot behind the Main Street park and near the fire station. Across Main Street,

Harbor House also has a restroom, and there are portable toilets at the town docks.

GETTING THERE AND AROUND

Southwest Harbor is about 13 miles or 25 minutes via Routes 198 and 102 from Northeast Harbor. It's about 14 miles or 25 minutes to Bar Harbor and about 3 miles via Route 102 to Tremont.

Southwest Harbor is serviced by Route 7/Southwest Harbor of the Island Explorer bus system.

Tremont: Bass Harbor, Bernard, and Seal Cove

The "quiet side" of the island becomes even quieter as you round the southwestern edge into Tremont (pop. 1,563), which includes the villages of Bernard; Bass Harbor, home of Bass Harbor Head Light and ferry services to offshore islands; and Seal Cove. Tremont occupies the southwesternmost corner of Mount Desert Island. It's about as far as you can get from Bar Harbor, but the free Island Explorer bus service's Route 7/Southwest Harbor comes through here regularly.

Be sure to visit these small villages. Views are fabulous, the pace is slow, and you'll feel as if you've stumbled upon "the real Maine."

SIGHTS

Country Store Museum

Stepping inside the former general store that's now headquarters for the **Tremont Historical Society** (Shore Rd., Bass Harbor, 207/244-9753, www.tremontmainehistory.us, 1pm-4pm Mon., Wed., Fri. July-mid-Oct.) is like stepping into the 1800s. Displays highlight the local heritage. If you're lucky, seventh-generation islander Muriel Davidson might be on duty and regale you with stories about her aunt, author Ruth Moore. You can buy copies of Moore's books here—good reads all. The museum is across from the Seafood Ketch.

★ The Seal Cove Auto Museum

The late Richard C. Paine Jr.'s Brass Era (late 19th to early 20th centuries) car collection, one of the largest in the country, is nicely displayed and identified in the **Seal Cove Auto Museum** (1414 Tremont Rd./Rte. 102, Seal Cove, 207/244-9242, www.sealcoveautomuseum.org, 10am-5pm daily May 1-Oct. 31, $6 adults, $5 seniors and teens, $2 ages 5-12). All vehicles are in as-found condition; this ranges from fresh-from-the-barn to meticulously restored. It's easy for kids of any age to spend an hour here, reminiscing or fantasizing. Among the highlights are a 1913 Peugeot with mahogany skiff body; a 1915 F.R.P., the only one still in existence; an original 1903 Ford Model A, the first car commercially produced by the Ford Motor Co.; and a 1909 Ford Model T "Tin Lizzie," from the first year of production. The oldest car in the collection is an 1899 DeDion-Bouton, one of the earliest cars produced in the world. The museum is about six miles southwest of Somesville. Or, if you're coming from Southwest Harbor, take Route 102 north to Seal Cove Road (partly unpaved) west to the other side of Route 102 (it makes a giant loop) and go north about 1.5 miles. This is not on the Island Explorer route.

Harding Wharf Lighthouse

Drive to the end of the road, and you can't miss the faux lighthouse Harding Wharf. The attached fishing shack was built in 1891 by the Murphy family, who lived in the house, now called Centennial House, across the road. They sold it to Charles Harding in 1927, and it remained in the family until Charles's brother Clarence sold it to Nancy and Irving Silverman in 1981. Later that year, the Silverman's attached their colorful collection of 29 historical wooden lobster buoys to the seaward side of the shack. The lighthouse is now a wedding chapel. Visitors are welcome to take photos for private use, but commercial use requires a permit.

RECREATION
Sea Kayaking

If you have your own boat, consider putting in at either the park's Pretty Marsh picnic area, off Route 102 in Pretty Marsh, or at the public boat launch at the end of Bartlett's Landing Road, off Indian Point Road near the Route 102 end. From either put-in, you can paddle around privately owned Bartlett Island. For a longer trip, head north along the shoreline past Black and Green Islands, both privately owned, to Alley Island, which is open for day access.

EXCURSION BOATS
★ Island Cruises

High praise goes to **Island Cruises** (Little Island Marine, Shore Rd., Bass Harbor, 207/244-5785, www.bassharborcruises.com), owned and operated by Captains Kim Strauss and his son Eli, for its narrated 3.5-hour lunch cruise to Frenchboro. The 49-passenger *R. L. Gott,* which Kim built, departs at 11am daily during the summer. Kim has been navigating these waters for more than 55 years, and his experience shows not only in his boat handling but also in his narration. Expect to pick up lots of local heritage and lore about once-thriving and now abandoned granite-quarrying and fishing communities, the sardine industry, and lobstering; and to see seals, cormorants, guillemots, and often eagles. The trip allows enough time on Frenchboro for a picnic (or lunch at the summertime deli on the dock) and a short village stroll, then a return through the sprinkling of islands along the 8.3-mile route. Kim also hauls a few traps and explains lobstering. He earns major points for maneuvering the boat so that passengers on both sides get an up-close view of key sights.

It's an excellent, enthralling tour for all ages. Round-trip cost is $30 adults, $15 children 11 and younger. Make reservations; if the weather looks iffy, call ahead to confirm. Most of the trip is in sheltered water, but rough seas can put the kibosh on it. Island Cruises also does a two-hour **afternoon nature cruise** among the islands that covers the same topics but spends a bit more time at seal ledges and other spots ($25 adults, $15 children). On either trip, don't forget to bring binoculars. You'll find the Island Cruises dock by following signs to the Swans Island ferry and turning right at the sign shortly before the state ferry dock.

SHOPPING

It's fun to poke around **Ravenswood** (McMullen Ave., Bass Harbor, 207/669-4287), a musty shop filled with old books, nautical gifts, model ship kits, and marvelous birds carved on-site.

Linda Fernandez Handknits (Main St., Bernard, 207/244-7224) has beautiful hand-knit sweaters, mittens, hats, socks, Christmas stockings, and embroidered pillowcases, all crafted by the talented and extended Fernandez family. The lobster sweaters for kids are especially cute.

Potters Lisbeth Faulkner and Ed Davis can often be seen working in their studio at **Seal Cove Pottery & Gallery** (Kelleytown Rd., Seal Cove, 207/244-3602, www.sealcovepottery.com). In addition to their functional hand-thrown or hand-built pottery, they exhibit Davis's paintings as well as crafts by other island artisans.

ACCOMMODATIONS
Inns and Cottages

When price is no object and you really want pampering, check into ★ **Ann's Point Inn** (79 Anns Point Rd., Bass Harbor, 207/244-9595, www.annspointinn.com, $325-350), on private waterfront at the tip of Ann's Point. Each of four guest rooms has a king bed covered in luxurious linens, a gas fireplace, and all the amenities you might expect, including robes and slippers, in-room TVs and DVD players, phones, Wi-Fi, CD players, and air-conditioning. The guest rooms are huge, and all have ocean views. If that's not enough, there's an indoor pool, a hot tub, and a sauna, plus afternoon hors d'oeuvres and evening sweets. Even better, the inn's green and sustainable practices include solar-powered electricity and hot water and garden-fresh fare at breakfast. All this is on two acres with 690 feet of shorefront, from which you can watch eagles soar and lobster boats at work.

On a low rung of the luxury scale but also on the water is **Bass Harbor Cottages and Country Inn** (95 Harbor Dr./Rte. 102A, Bass Harbor, 207/244-3460, www.bassharborcottages.com). All accommodations are housekeeping; there's no maid service. The sturdy white home has three air-conditioned guest rooms ($135-180), some with fireplaces, kitchens, or TVs. Breakfast is not served. Also on the premises are a number of cottages and suites with a wide range of amenities ($1,600-2,800 weekly). The two-bedroom Carriage House has a fireplace, a sauna, a full kitchen, a TV, a deck, and a balcony; the two-bedroom Pine Cottage has a fireplace, a full kitchen, a TV, and a screened porch. All the Boat House Suites have a full kitchen, a TV, and a deck; some have a fireplace or a balcony. During spring and fall, nightly rates may be available. A staircase descends to a rocky beach.

Simple guest rooms, nice views, and an included continental breakfast draw guests to the **Bass Harbor Inn** (28 Shore Rd., Bass Harbor, 207/244-5157, www.bassharborinn.com, $90-135), a restored 1870 home with three guest rooms and a studio with a kitchenette. You can walk to local restaurants, the ferry dock, and the museum.

Camping

Acadia National Park's Seawall Campground is on this side of the island.

A budget-friendly option is the nicely wooded **Quietside Campground and Cabins** (397 Tremont Rd./Rte. 102, Tremont, 207/244-5992, www.quietsidecampground.

com, Memorial Day-Labor Day), with 37 sites accommodating tents ($22, platforms provided) and small RVs ($26) up to 28 feet, some with water and 30-amp electricity. It also has log camping cabins ($65-80) with heat, electricity, and a small refrigerator but no plumbing, and rustic cabins ($63) with a propane lantern, a gas grill, and a screened porch. There are two bathhouses with free hot showers, one with a coin-op laundry. Quiet, well-behaved pets are allowed for $1 per night. The campground is off the beaten track, but the tenting sites are very private, and the location ensures quiet.

Just a 10-minute walk from Bass Harbor Head Light is **Bass Harbor Campground** (342 Harbor Dr./Rte. 102A, Bass Harbor, 207/244-5857 or 800/327-5857, www.bassharbor.com), owned and operated by the Carsey family. The campground has RV sites ($35-50) with electricity, water, sewer, and cable TV as well as plenty of wooded tent sites ($30-40), some with platforms. Hot showers and Wi-Fi are included. There's a heated pool, a playground, and a self-service coin-op laundry. Also on-site are one- and two-room camping cabins ($475-575 weekly), without baths but with electricity, a small refrigerator, and an outdoor gas grill; bring your own sheets, towels, blankets, dishes, and cooking utensils. Quiet, leashed, well-behaved pets are welcome, but there is no tolerance for barking or other offenses.

FOOD

As always, call to confirm hours, especially when traveling early or late in the season.

If you have a penchant for puns—or can tune them out—head for the family-run **Seafood Ketch Restaurant** (McMullin Ave., Bass Harbor, 207/244-7463, www.seafoodketch.com, 11am-9pm daily). The corny humor begins with "Please, no fishing from dining room windows or the deck" and "What foods these morsels be," and goes up (or down, depending on your perspective) from there. But there's nothing corny about the seafood roll, an interesting change from the usual lobster or crab roll. There are a few "landlubber delights," but mostly the menu has fresh seafood dishes—including the baked lobster-seafood casserole, a recipe requested by *Gourmet* magazine. Most entrées run $19-24, a bit pricey given the informality and service, but sandwiches and lighter fare are available. Sunday omelets are the specialty, served 11am-2pm along with the full menu. This is a prime family spot, with a kids' menu, where the best tables are on the flagstone patio overlooking Bass Harbor (bring bug repellent). Follow signs for the Swans Island ferry terminal.

Right next door is **Rich's Take-Out** (49 Shore Rd., Bass Harbor, 207/244-0492, 11am-8pm daily), where you can feast on everything from burgers to lobster while savoring the views from the elevated deck hanging over the harbor.

Few restaurants have as idyllic a setting as ★ **Thurston's Lobster Pound** (9 Thurston Rd., Bernard, 207/244-7600, www.thurstonslobster.com, 11am-8:30pm daily, market rates), which overlooks lobster boat-filled Bass Harbor. The screened dining room practically sits in the water. Family-oriented Thurston's also has chowders, sandwiches, and terrific desserts. Read the directions at the entrance and order before you find a table on one of two levels. In 2014, Thurston's added a full bar, with a huge stone hearth, deck, and roll-up walls that allow as much or as little of the weather in as necessary. It's an extremely popular place to relax with a drink overlooking the sigh-worthy harbor.

INFORMATION AND SERVICES

There's a **public restroom** at the Swans Island ferry terminal.

GETTING THERE AND AROUND

Tremont is about 3 miles via Route 102 or 8 miles via Route 102A from Southwest Harbor. It's about 17 miles or 30 minutes to Bar Harbor.

Tremont and Bass Harbor are on Route 7/Southwest Harbor of the Island Explorer bus system.

Thurston's Lobster Pound overlooks working wharves and a boat-filled harbor.

Islands Near Mount Desert

Four ferry-serviced islands offshore of Mount Desert Island are ideal for day trips: Swans Island, Frenchboro, and Islesford and Great Cranberry, two neighboring Cranberry Isles that can be hopscotched in one day using the passenger ferry service.

Only 15 of Maine's offshore islands still support year-round populations, and these are four of them. An island day trip removes you from the region's hustle-bustle, limited as that may be, and allows you the opportunity to meet the folks who summer or live and work here year-round. You'll escape crowds and encounter little, if any, traffic, and experience a taste of island life. These islands aren't for those who need commercial distractions. Although there are some worthy sights, the allure of an island is the overall experience: hobnobbing with locals and summerfolk on the ferry, wandering quiet roads, and perhaps a shorefront picnic.

Getting to an island, or two, is easy, but it does take some planning. Most commercial boats and mail boats for the Cranberries depart from Northeast Harbor, although one line originates in Southwest Harbor. All carry bikes but no cars; the state car ferry for Swans Island departs from Bass Harbor, south of Southwest Harbor and part of the town of Tremont. The Maine State Ferry Service also operates the ferry to Long Island (referred to as Frenchboro, the name of the village on the island) from Bass Harbor, but for day trips the schedule requires careful planning.

★ CRANBERRY ISLES

The Cranberry Isles (pop. 141), south of Northeast and Seal Harbors, comprise **Great Cranberry, Little Cranberry** (called Islesford), **Sutton, Baker,** and **Bear Islands.** Islesford and Baker include property belonging to Acadia National Park.

Two commercial passenger ferries, one from Northeast Harbor and the other from Southwest Harbor, to-and-fro between their home ports, stopping at Great Cranberry and Isleford twice on every trip. You can visit one or both on one ticket. The schedule, along with a shuttle service on Great Cranberry, makes it easy to visit both in one day. Bring a bike to explore the narrow, mostly level roads, or simply wander on foot, but remember to respect private property. Unless you've asked for and received permission, do not cut across private land to reach the shore.

The Cranberry name has been attributed to 18th-century loyalist governor Francis Bernard, who received these islands along with all of Mount Desert Island as a king's grant in 1762. Cranberry bogs, now long gone, on the two largest islands evidently caught his attention. Permanent European settlers were here in the 1760s, and there was even steamboat service by the 1820s.

Lobstering and other marine businesses are the commercial mainstays, boosted in summer by the various visitor-related pursuits. Artists and writers come for a week, a month, or longer.

Note: There are no inns on either island, only rental houses. Plan ahead for meals, as food options are limited on Islesford on days the restaurant is closed.

Great Cranberry

Largest of the islands is Great Cranberry, with a year-round population of about 50 that swells to around 300 in the summer. You can easily explore this island's highlights in a couple of hours. The Main Road extends the length of the island, about two miles, with a few pleasant viewpoints along the way. It's an easy walk or bicycle ride, with some gentle hills and very little traffic; do follow the rules of the road, though. There's also a volunteer-operated shuttle service that makes touring the island easy. If you bring your dog, it must be kept leashed.

Day Trip to Frenchboro, Long Island

Since Maine has more Long Islands than anyone cares to count, most of them have other labels for easy identification. Here's a case in point—a Long Island known universally as Frenchboro, the name of the village that wraps around Lunts Harbor. With a year-round population hovering around 50, Frenchboro has had ferry service only since 1960. Since then, the island has acquired phone service, electricity, and satellite TV, but don't expect to notice much of that when you get here. One of only 15 Maine coastal islands that still support a year-round population, Frenchboro is a very quiet place, where islanders live as islanders always have—making a living from the sea and being proud of it.

In 1999, when roughly half of the island (914 acres, including 5.5 miles of shorefront) went up for sale by a private owner, an incredible fundraising effort collected nearly $3 million, allowing purchase of the land in 2000 by the Maine Coast Heritage Trust. Since then, thanks to a gift from David Rockefeller, it's expanded to include Richmond Head, adding 192 acres and three miles of shoreline. Visitors now have more than 10 miles of hiking trails; take heed, most are rustic and unmarked. Some of the funding has been put toward restoration of the village's church and one-room schoolhouse; islanders and visitors will still have full access to all the acreage, and interested developers will have to look elsewhere. Frenchboro is the subject of *Hauling by Hand*, a fascinating, well-researched "biography" published in 1999 by eighth-generation islander Dean Lunt.

Frenchboro is a delightful day trip. A good way to get a sense of the place is to take the 3.5-hour lunch cruise run by Captain Kim Strauss of **Island Cruises** (Little Island Marine, Shore Rd., Bass Harbor, 207/244-5785, www.bassharborcruises.com). For an even longer day trip to Frenchboro, plan to take the passenger ferry *R. L. Gott* during her weekly run for the Maine State Ferry Service. Each Friday early April-late October, the *R. L. Gott* departs Bass Harbor at 8am, arriving in Frenchboro at 9am. The return trip to Bass Harbor is at 6pm, allowing nine hours on the island. The **Maine State Ferry Service** (207/244-3254, daily recorded info 800/491-4883, www.exploremaine.org) uses the ferry *Captain Henry Lee,* the same vessel used on the Swans Island route, for service to Frenchboro on Wednesday, Thursday, and Sunday. On some days, the schedule allows five hours on the island, but the days and times are limited, so it's best to check the current schedule online.

When you go, take a picnic with you, or stop at **Lunt's Dockside Deli** (207/334-2902, www. luntlobsters.com, 11am-7:30pm), open only in July-August. It's a very casual establishment—order at the window, grab a picnic table, and wait for your name to be called. Lobster rolls and fish chowder are the specialties, but there are plenty of other choices, including sandwiches, hot dogs, and even vegetable wraps. Of course, you can get lobster too. Prices are low, the view is wonderful, and you might even get to watch lobsters being unloaded from a boat.

The **Frenchboro Historical Society Museum** (207/334-2924, www.frenchboro.lib. me.us/, free), just up from the dock, has interesting old tools, other local artifacts, and a small gift shop. It's usually open afternoons Memorial Day-Labor Day. The island has a network of easy and not-so-easy maintained trails through the woods and along the shore; some can be squishy, and some are along boulder-strewn beachfront. The trails are rustic, and most are unmarked, so proceed carefully. In the center of the island is a beaver pond. (You'll get a sketchy map on the boat, but you can also get one at the historical society.)

There's a restroom above the Dockside Deli and two others near the museum.

Every year since 1961, on the second Saturday of August, Frenchboro hosts its annual **Lobster Festival** (www.frenchboro-dinner.org/), a midday meal comprising lobster, chicken salad, hot dogs, coleslaw, homemade pies, and more, served rain or shine, with proceeds benefiting a local cause. Islanders and hundreds of visitors gather in the village for the occasion. The Maine State Ferry makes a special run that day.

The seven-passenger **Cranberry Explorer** (207/812-6712), a golf-cart shuttle service operated by volunteers with the Great Cranberry Island Historical Society, departs the Town Dock every half hour 9am-6pm late June-early September for a narrated trip to the island's end and back, with scheduled and flag stops en route. The service is free, but donations are appreciated.

It's about a 15-minute walk on the Main Road to **Cranberry House,** home to the **Preble-Marr Historical Museum** (207/244-7800, www.gcihs.org, 10am-4pm daily mid-June-mid-Oct., free), **Hitty's Café** (207/244-7845), an arts center, and free Wi-Fi. The volunteer-operated museum is a pleasure to visit, with well-informed staffers who radiate enthusiasm. One museum exhibit commemorates *Hitty, Her First Hundred Years,* the 1930 Newbery Medal-winning novel about a doll by Rachel Field, a onetime island summer resident. (Her home, not open to the public, was the Preble House, on the right between the ferry dock and the museum, with lilac bushes in front and a large pine in the right rear corner). The arts center presents movies, lectures, concerts, workshops, and other activities and events. The take-out café, with seating on the deck, serves sandwiches, lobster rolls, salads, and sweets. Better yet, get lunch to go and wander down the mile-long **Cranberry House Trail** cut behind the museum to Whistler Cove. The trail moseys through an evergreen forest with a green moss floor to a rock beach; bring insect repellent.

About another 0.5 mile up the road is Polly Bunker's **Whale's Rib Gift Shop** (207/244-5153), which carries jewelry by island artisan Lisa Hall as well as a nice selection of other items. Take the left after the gift shop to wander down to the **Cranberry Island Boatyard,** which repairs old boats and also builds new ones.

Pick up picnic fixings or order sandwiches, burgers, lobster rolls, or whatever else is on the day's menu at the **Cranberry General Store** (207/244-0622), home to the take-out **Seawich Café,** located adjacent to the ferry dock. There are a few tables inside and on the deck. It's a great spot to catch up on the island gossip and watching the comings and goings on the ferries.

Public restrooms are located midway between the store and the shore and at the Cranberry House.

Little Cranberry (Islesford)

The second-largest island is Little Cranberry,

Cranberry House on Great Cranberry Island

locally known as Islesford. Get a feel for the place by visiting www.islesford.com.

You'll arrive at the Town Dock, one of three adjacent docks; the others are the Fishermen's Wharf and the Islesford Dock.

Just east of the Islesford Dock is the handsome brick **Islesford Historical Museum** (207/288-3338, www.nps.gov/acad, free), operated by the National Park Service since 1948. Call or check the website for hours, as these vary every year. William Otis Sawtelle (1874-1939), a summer resident of the island, purchased the old island market in 1917. Inside he found artifacts belonging to the Hadlock family, which built the shorefront building in 1850. Among his finds were decoys, which he painted blue and placed around the property, including one over the door. That building, which now has public restrooms, became known as the Blue Duck. It's where he first displayed his expanding collection of local historical materials. In 1926 he began construction of the adjacent brick-and-slate current museum, which is now part of the national park. Inside, pieces from Sawtelle's collection are displayed along with other artifacts related to the Cranberry Isles' heritage.

On the wharf nearest the museum is **The Islesford Dock** (207/244-7494, www.

islesford.com/idcbusiid.html, 11am-3pm and 5pm-9pm Wed.-Sat., 10am-2pm and 5pm-9pm Sun. late June-Labor Day, $6-29), which hangs over the water. Prices are moderate, the food is home-cooked and creative, and the views across to Acadia's mountains are incredible. If the weather is good, eat on the small deck. Reservations are wise in midsummer. On Tuesday nights, there's live music ($7 cover), and a bar menu is served. Water taxis are available to return to Northeast Harbor after dinner, or, twice weekly, the Cranberry Cove Ferry adds evening runs at 7pm and 9pm.

Also on the dock is **Islesford Pottery** (207/244-9108, www.islesford.com/idcartmb.html), Marian Baker's summertime ceramic studio. A teacher at Maine College of Art in Portland, Marian makes particularly appealing functional pieces, and she carries the work of other potters as well. If you're lucky, she'll have a pot on the wheel. She also sells a handy map of the island ($1), with profits given to charity. Street and road signs are scarce on the island, but the map at least provides orientation.

Also sharing the wharf is **Winter's Work** (www.winterswork.com), a tiny, one-room gallery with an eclectic selection of

The Isleford Dock restaurant hangs over the island's harbor.

works—and fudge!—by primarily island and Maine artists and authors, and the **Islesford Dock Gallery,** displaying works by nearly two dozen artists in four rooms.

A five-minute walk from the waterfront will bring you to **Islesford Artists** (Mosswood Rd., www.islesfordartists.com, 10am-5pm daily July-Aug., 10am-4pm Mon.-Fri. or by appointment May-June and Sept.-Oct.), an excellent gallery specializing in local artists' depictions of local sites (lots of landscapes and seascapes, naturally). Run by Danny and Katy Fernald, the gallery is several blocks from the harbor, but there's a sign, and Marian Baker's map will get you here. Or just ask—the islanders are always helpful.

Across the street is **Aaron & Erin's** farm stand, where you can pick up premade sandwiches along with fresh veggies, cheese, and even milk.

On the same road, and also worth a looksee if it's open, is the **Islesford Historical Society History Room,** part of the library located in Neighborhood House. Also check out the garden here.

Islesford's imaginative postmaster, Joy Sprague, brought the island a bit of postal fame by initiating Maine's busiest stamps-by-mail operation in the early 1990s. Many of the other year-round island postmasters have now followed suit, aided by the Rockland-based Island Institute, which occasionally publishes an order form in *The Working Waterfront,* its monthly tabloid newspaper. The goal is to save island post offices from extinction; so far, so good.

The post office occupies one corner inside **The Islesford Market** (Main St., 207/244-7667), three short blocks up from the Town Dock. Suzie ("Soos") Krasnow holds forth here. Don't miss the white gingerbread; the recipe was created when the former island hotel ran out of molasses.

Islesford is home to internationally renowned artist, writer, poet, children's book illustrator, and humanitarian Ashley Bryan (b. 1923). The **Ashley Bryan Center** (207/244-7494, www.ashleybryancenter.org), created in 2013, aims to "preserve, celebrate, and share broadly" the artist's work through programs, exhibits, and a planned center honoring Bryan on the island. Ask locally about its status and any current programs. The island's two-room schoolhouse is named for Bryan, and his magnificent sea-glass panels, inspired by medieval stained-glass windows and comprising sea glass assembled with papier mâché in images depicting the life of Christ, can be seen inside the **Congregational Church**.

On the road behind the market is **Island Girl Seaglass,** a one-room shop in a shack filled with sea-glass jewelry and ornaments and other island souvenir delights.

And if you want to get out and explore the neighboring waters, book a 90-minute cruise with **Lobster Boat Tours** (207/244-7466, www.islesford.com, from $75). Captain Stefanie Alley, a year-round resident, hauls traps, explaining the process and the habitat. The boat carries a maximum of six passengers.

Events worth planning around include a **Cranberry Fest** (www.cranberrymusicfest. com), a festival in August, and **Plein Air Painting Workshops** in early September.

For **cottage rentals,** see www.islesford. com.

Getting There

Note: Do call to confirm current ferry schedules, as online versions aren't always accurate.

Decades-old, family-run **Beal and Bunker** (207/244-3575, www.bealandbunker.com) provides year-round mail and passenger boat service to the Cranberries from Northeast Harbor. The schedule makes it possible to do both islands in one day. The summer season, with more frequent trips, runs late June-Labor Day. The boats make a variety of stops on the three-island route (including Sutton in summer), so be patient as they make the circuit. It's a people-watching treat. If you just did a round-trip and stayed aboard, the loop would take about 1.5 hours. Round-trip tickets (covering the whole loop, including intraisland trips if you want to visit both Great Cranberry and Islesford)

The Maine Sea Coast Mission

The Maine Sea Coast Mission's *Sunbeam V* homeports in Northeast Harbor.

Remote islands and other isolated communities along Maine's rugged coastline may still have a church, but few have a full-time minister; fewer yet have a health-care provider. Yet these communities aren't entirely shut off from either preaching or medical assistance.

Since 1905, the **Maine Sea Coast Mission** (127 West St., Bar Harbor, 207/288-5097, www.seacoastmission.org), a nondenominational, nonprofit organization rooted in a Christian ministry, has offered a lifeline to these communities. The mission, based in Bar Harbor, serves nearly 2,800 people on eight different islands, including Frenchboro, the Cranberries, Swans, and Isle au Haut, as well as others living in remote coastal locations on the mainland. Its numerous much-needed services include a Christmas program; in-school, after-school, and summer school programs; emergency financial assistance; food assistance; a thrift shop; ministers for island and coastal communities; scholarships; and health services.

Many of these services are delivered via the mission's *Sunbeam V*, a 75-foot diesel boat that has no limitations on when it can travel and few on where it can travel. In winter, it even serves as an icebreaker, clearing harbors and protecting boats from ice damage. During your travels in the Acadia region, you might see the *Sunbeam V* homeported in Northeast Harbor or on its rounds.

A nurse and a minister usually travel on the ship. The minister may conduct services on the island or on the boat, which also functions as a gathering place for fellowship, meals, and meetings. The minister also reaches out to those in need, marginalized, or ill, and often helps with island funerals. Onboard telemedicine equipment enables the nurse to provide much-needed health care, including screening clinics for diabetes, cholesterol, and prostate and skin cancer; flu and pneumonia vaccines; and tetanus shots.

The mission welcomes donations and volunteers. You can make a difference.

are $28 adults, $14 ages 3-11, free under age 3. Bicycles are $7 round-trip. The off-season schedule operates early May-mid-June and early September-mid-October; the winter schedule runs mid-October-April. In winter, the boat company advises phoning ahead on what Mainers quaintly call "weather days."

The **Cranberry Cove Ferry** (upper town dock, Clark Point Rd., Southwest Harbor, 207/244-5882, cell 207/460-1981, www.downeastwindjammer.com) operates a summertime service to the Cranberries mid-May-mid-October. The ferry route begins at the upper town dock (Clark Point

Rd.) in Southwest Harbor (free parking, but be sure to park in one of the marked 8-hour slots; or take the Island Explorer), with stops in Manset and Great Cranberry before reaching Islesford an hour later and reversing the itinerary; two hours total, if you stay on the boat. (Stops at Sutton can be arranged.) In summer (mid-June-mid-Sept.) there are six daily round-trips, with two additional evening trips Wednesday-Saturday. Round-trip fares are $28 adults, $20 children, $6 bicycles.

Captain John Dwelley (207/244-5724) also operates a water-taxi service to the Cranberries. His six-passenger *Delight* makes the run from Northeast, Southwest, or Seal Harbor. Reservations are required for trips 6am-8am and 6pm-11pm. Round-trip rates range $80-110. Custom cruises are available, including excursions to Baker's Island. Consider the sunset cruise to The Islesford Dock for dinner ($110 round-trip covering up to 6 passengers).

The **Cadillac Water Taxi** (207/801-1898, from $60 one-way), a 26-foot lobster yacht operated by the Newman and Gray Boatyard on Great Cranberry, provides on-demand trips between the mainland and the Cranberries. Rates vary by time of day.

SWANS ISLAND

Six miles off Mount Desert Island lies scenic, roughly 7,000-acre Swans Island (www.swansisland.org), named after Colonel James Swan, who bought it and two dozen other islands as an investment in 1786. As with the Cranberries, fishing is the year-round way of life here, with lobstering being the primary occupation. In summer, the population practically triples with the arrival of artists, writers, and other seasonal visitors. The island has no campsites, few public restrooms, and only a handful of guest rooms. Visitors who want to spend more than a day tend to rent cottages by the week.

You'll need either a bicycle or a car to get around, as the ferry comes in the island's northeast corner and the village center is on the other. Should you choose to bring a car, it's wise to make reservations for the ferry, especially for the return trip. Bicycling is a good way to get around, but be forewarned that the roads are narrow, lacking shoulders, and hilly in spots. Hint: Pull over when the rush of cars off an incoming ferry passes.

If you can be flexible, wait for a clear day, then pack a picnic and catch the first ferry (7:30am) from Bass Harbor. At the ferry office in Bass Harbor, request a Swans Island map.

Captain John Dwelley taxis guests to the Cranberries aboard the *Delight.*

Keep an eye on your watch so you don't miss the last ferry (4:30pm) back to Bass Harbor.

Sights

Just 100 yards away from the ferry terminal is the **Swans Island Lobster & Marine Museum** (207/526-4282, by chance or by appointment, donation), a labor of love created by brothers Ted and Galen Turner. They've collected artifacts from the island's rich fishing heritage, and are full of stories and lore. Admission is free, but donations are appreciated. Delve into more of the island's history at **Swan's Island Library** (451 Atlantic Rd., 207/526-4330), which has exhibits.

Lighthouse Park/Hockamock Head Light (207/526-4025, www.burntcoatharborlight.com), officially called Burnt Coat Harbor Light, in Lighthouse Park, is on the island's west side. The distinctive square lighthouse, built in 1872 and now automated, sits on a rocky promontory overlooking Burnt Coat Harbor, Harbor Island, lobster-boat traffic, and crashing surf. Visitors can view art and history exhibits in the keeper's house and climb the light tower (call for current days and hours), and can admire the oil house and bell house from the exterior. Also on the headland are 1.8 miles of moderate, signed hiking trails, including a short ADA-accessible one, and two beaches. Views from the trails are spectacular; you can see Marshall Island, Merchant's Row, and Isle au Haut from the summit. Keep an eye out for bald eagles, as there are nine known nesting pairs on the island. Pick up a map at the information kiosk. An accessible vault toilet is available.

Recreation

Ask for directions to one of two prime island swimming spots: **Fine Sand Beach** (saltwater) or **Quarry Pond** (freshwater). Fine Sand Beach is on the west side of Toothacher Cove; you'll have to navigate about a mile of unpaved road to get there, but it's worth the trouble. Be prepared for chilly water, however. Quarry Pond is in Minturn, on the opposite side of Burnt Coat Harbor from the

lighthouse. Follow the one-way loop around, and you'll see it on your right as you're rounding the far side of the loop.

Events

A Swans Island summer highlight is the **Sweet Chariot Music Festival** (www.sweetchariotmusicfestival.com), a three-night midweek extravaganza in early August. Windjammers arrive from Camden and Rockland, enthusiasts show up on their private boats, and the island's Oddfellows Hall is standing room-only for three evenings of folk singing, storytelling, and impromptu high jinks. About 3:30pm the first two days, musicians go from boat to boat in Burnt Coat Harbor, entertaining with sea chanteys. Along the route from harbor to concert, enterprising local kids peddle lemonade, homemade brownies, and kitschy craft items. It's all very festive but definitely a "boat thing," not very convenient for anyone without water transport.

Accommodations

If you want to stay over, don't expect to find a bed on the island during the festival unless you know someone. Other times, there's **The Harbor Watch Inn** (111 Minturn Rd., 207/526-4563, www.swansisland.com, $95-120). Two of the motel's four spacious and clean guest rooms have kitchen facilities. Two have water views; all have Wi-Fi. There's also a one-bedroom apartment available ($150 in peak season).

Another possibility is the **Carter House** (207/266-0958 or 207/526-4198, $90), which overlooks the Mill Pond and out to the harbor. Breakfast is included, and guests have kitchen privileges.

Food

Dining choices are few. **TIMS The Island Market & Supply** (40 North Rd., 207/526-4043, www.tims-swans-island.com) is the place to go for everything, from morning sticky buns to pizza, and it has a seasonal lunch takeout. There are usually a few take-out shops operating on the island each summer. **Swans Island Tea Room** (235 Harbor Rd., 207/526-4900), a bakery and café in a Victorian home near the ferry dock, serves tea, coffee, baked goods, sandwiches, and local ice cream. Also near the ferry terminal is **Appy's Seafood and Takeout** (325 Atlantic Rd., 207/526-4200), locally popular for its lobster rolls, burgers, sandwiches, and fried fare.

Getting There and Around

Swans Island is a six-mile, 40-minute trip on the state-operated car ferry *Captain Henry Lee,* operated by the **Maine State Ferry Service** (207/244-3254, daily recorded info 800/491-4883, www.exploremaine.org). The ferry makes up to six round-trips a day, the first from Bass Harbor at 7:30am Monday-Saturday and at 9am Sunday, and the last from Swans Island at 4:30pm. Round-trip fares are around $17.50 adults, $8.50 ages 5-11; bikes are $16.50 adults, $9.50 children; vehicles are $49.50. Reservations are accepted only for vehicles; be in line at least 15 minutes before departure or you risk forfeiting your space.

To reach the Bass Harbor ferry terminal on Mount Desert Island, follow the distinctive blue signs, marked "Swans Island Ferry," along Routes 102 and 102A.

Southwest Cycle (370 Main St., Southwest Harbor, 207/244-5856 or 800/649-5856, www.southwestcycle.com, year-round) rents bikes by the day and week. It also has ferry schedules and Swans Island maps. For the early-morning ferry, you'll have to pick up bikes the day before; be sure to reserve them if you're doing this in July-August.

Schoodic Peninsula

Highlights

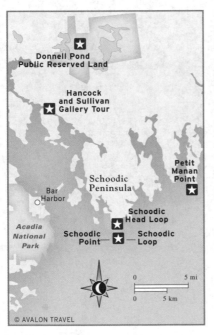

★ **Schoodic Point:** Surf crashes against slabs of pink granite on the remote tip of the Schoodic Peninsula (page 139).

★ **Schoodic Loop:** Drive around the tip of the peninsula if you must, but a better way to see it is on a bicycle (page 139).

★ **Donnell Pond Public Reserved Land:** A treasure for outdoors enthusiasts, this reserve includes mountains to hike and ponds to paddle and fish, plus sandy beaches and backwoods campsites (page 142).

★ **Petit Manan Point:** Birds, birds, birds, as well as easy hiking with great views are your rewards for visiting this part of the Maine Coastal Islands National Wildlife Refuge (page 143).

★ **Schoodic Head Loop:** Although you can drive almost to the summit, it's far more rewarding—and peaceful—to hike it (page 144).

★ **Hancock and Sullivan Gallery Tour:** Talented artists and artisans are plentiful here. Visiting their off-the-beaten-path shops and studios is a perfect way to explore the region and score some great souvenirs (page 156).

Slightly more than 2,366 of Acadia National Park's acres are on the mainland Schoodic Peninsula—the rest are all on islands, including Mount Desert. World-class scenery and the relative lack of congestion, even at the height of

summer, make Schoodic a special Acadia destination.

The Schoodic Peninsula is just one of several "fingers" of land that point seaward as part of eastern Hancock County and western Washington County. Sneak around to the eastern side of Frenchman Bay to see this region from a whole new perspective. One hour from Acadia National Park's visitors center, you'll find Acadia's mountains silhouetted against the sunset, the surf slamming onto Schoodic Point, and the peace of a calmer lifestyle. The towns and villages salting the region—Winter Harbor (pop. 516); Gouldsboro (pop. 1,737), including the not-to-be-missed villages of Birch Harbor, Corea, and Prospect Harbor; Hancock (pop. 2,394); Sullivan (pop. 1,236); and Sorrento (pop. 274)—seem suspended in time. They are quiet and rural, with lobster fishing still an economic anchor.

As with so much of Acadia's acreage on

Mount Desert Island, the Schoodic section became part of the park largely due to the deft diplomacy and perseverance of George B. Dorr. No obstacle ever seemed too daunting to Dorr. In 1928, when the owners objected to donating their land to a national park tagged with the Lafayette name (geopolitics of the time being involved), Dorr even managed to obtain congressional approval for the 1929 name change to Acadia National Park—and Schoodic was part of the deal.

This section of Acadia National Park isn't as overpowering as that on Mount Desert, but it's no less powerful. Even though it's on the mainland, it feels more remote, and the landscape has a raw edge, with too-frequent fog shrouding the stunted and scraggly spruce clinging to its pink granite shores. This may change with the addition of the Schoodic Woods Campground, slated to open in 2015 on conserved lands adjacent to the park. In addition to adding approximately 100 campsites,

---

Previous: Schoodic Point; lobster wharves on Corea's harborfront. **Above:** Lobstering is big business on the Schoodic Peninsula.

Schoodic Peninsula

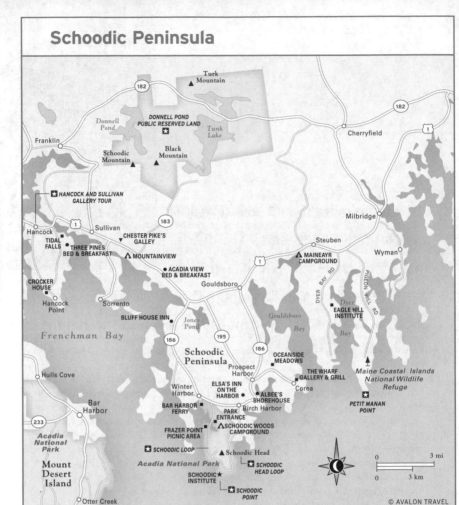

the campground will also house a day parking lot and a welcome center.

While you're this far east, explore a couple other natural treasures: the Petit Manan and Corea Heath sections of the Maine Coastal Islands National Wildlife Refuge, spectacular spots for bird-watching; and the Donnell Pond Public Reserved Land, an inland trove of lakes and peaks that lures hikers and anglers. Although beyond any traditional definition of the Acadia region, they're well worth discovering. Better yet, you can loop them together via two scenic byways, one national and one state.

PLANNING YOUR TIME

While most visitors still arrive by car or RV, the propane-powered **Island Explorer** bus service's Schoodic Route operates between late June and Labor Day and connects with ferry service from Bar Harbor. If you want to tour beyond the service routes, you'll need a car, and there's much to see. Besides the jaw-dropping scenery, the region's calling cards are outdoor recreation and shopping the artists' and artisans' studios tucked here and there.

The biggest attractions are the spectacular vignettes and vistas—of offshore lighthouses, distant mountains, close-in islands, and unchanged villages. Check out each small and large finger of land: Hancock Point, Sorrento, and Winter Harbor's Grindstone Neck. Circle the Gouldsboro Peninsula, including Prospect Harbor, and detour to Corea. Meander down the Petit Manan peninsula to the **Maine Coastal Islands National Wildlife Refuge.** If you still have enough time, head inland and follow Route 182, a designated Scenic Highway noodling between Hancock and Cherryfield, making it a point to visit the **Donnell Pond Public Reserved Land.** En route, be sure to dip in and out of at least some of the artisan's studios and galleries that dot the byways. Accomplish all this and you'll have a fine sense of place.

LOCAL TOWNS
Winter Harbor

Winter Harbor is known best as the gateway to Schoodic. It shares the area with an old-money, low-profile, Philadelphia-linked summer colony on exclusive Grindstone Neck. Only a few clues hint at the colony's presence, strung along the western side of the harbor. Winter Harbor's summer highlight is the annual Lobster Festival, the second Saturday in August. The gala daylong event includes a parade, live entertainment, games, and more crustaceans than you could ever consume.

Gouldsboro

Gouldsboro—including the not-to-be-missed villages of Birch Harbor, Corea, and Prospect Harbor—earned its own minor fame from Louise Dickinson Rich's 1958 book *The Peninsula,* a tribute to her summers on Corea's Cranberry Point, "a place that has stood still in time." Since 1958, change has crept into Corea, but not so as you'd notice. It's still the same quintessential lobstering community, perfect for photo ops.

Hancock and Sullivan

Between Ellsworth and Gouldsboro is Hancock. Venture down the ocean-side back roads and you'll discover an old-timey summer colony at Hancock Point, complete with a library, a post office, a yacht club, and tennis courts. Meander inland and you'll be rewarded with artisans' studios, especially in Sullivan. In its heyday, Sullivan was a center for shipbuilding and quarrying. It also

lobster boats anchored on the Schoodic Peninsula

has the distinction of being where two Nazi spies, William Colepaugh and Erich Gimpel, landed in the dark of a snowy November night in 1944, dropped off by the submarine *U-1230*. Their mission: sabotage the Manhattan Project. Interpretative signage at two roadside pullouts, one before the bridge and another next to Dunbar's Store, provide information on the area's heritage, flora, and fauna. Route 1 ties the region together, providing just enough glimpses and vistas of Frenchman Bay.

Sorrento

Tiny Sorrento isn't really much more than a classic summer colony, and that's all the reason you need for a leisurely drive down the peninsula. It has tennis courts, a yacht club, a nine-hole golf course edging the ocean, and a swimming pool, created in 1913 by damming a cove just above the village. If you fall for the place, try to find a copy of *Sorrento, A Well-Kept Secret,* by Catherine O'Clair Herson, published in 1995 for the town's centennial. It's filled with historical photos and stories.

Steuben

Continue northeast beyond the Schoodic Peninsula, and you'll arrive in Steuben, on the far side of Gouldsboro Bay. Not that you'll notice; frankly, there's little here to mark its presence on Route 1, and only a small village if you venture off it, although that's changing as the land is carved up by developers (the number of Land for Sale signs is frightening). Only a small sign indicates that the Petit Manan section of the Maine Coastal Islands National Wildlife Refuge awaits those who turn down Pigeon Hill Road.

Sights

SCHOODIC SECTION OF ACADIA NATIONAL PARK

The Schoodic section of Acadia National Park has an entirely different feel than the main part of the park on Mount Desert. It's much smaller, far less busy, and feels more rugged, wild, and remote. It provides fewer recreational opportunities, but it's magnificent and well worth visiting.

This section of the park is home to rare stands of jack pine and maritime shrubland communities, and it's an important breeding, nesting, and stopover for migratory songbirds.

Until recently, there was no camping in this section of the park, but a new purpose-built campground, under the National Parks reservation system, is slated to open in 2015. Private campgrounds and other lodging options are available in the area. There are also no restaurants or other food sources in the park, but you won't need to go far for a bite to eat.

To reach the park boundary from Route 1 in Gouldsboro, take Route 186 south to Winter Harbor. Continue through town, heading east, then turn right and continue to the park entrance sign, just before the bridge over Mosquito Harbor.

You can also tour the park using the free **Island Explorer** bus, which circulates around the Schoodic Loop, with stops along the way. It's an efficient and environmentally friendly way to go, and it connects with the ferry from Bar Harbor, making it possible to explore this section of the park without driving all the way around to reach it.

For years, the threat of development hung over 3,200 acres adjacent to the park, as the landowner envisioned a major eco-resort with a hotel, golf course, and perhaps 1,000 home sites. Park superintendent Sheridan Steele described the proposed development as "the biggest single threat to Acadia." Fierce opposition coupled with a slowed economy put the plans on hold. In late 2011, Schoodic makes it even more brilliant. This area is open 6am-10pm only. There are restrooms at the parking lot.

If you've brought children, keep them well back from the water; a rogue wave can sweep them off the rocks all too easily, which has happened. Picnics are great here (make sure you bring a bag for litter), and so are the tide pools at mid-tide and low tide. Birding is spectacular during spring and fall migrations.

And on the subject of birds, you'll see a sign here: Do Not Feed Gulls or Other Wildlife. Heed it—but even if you *don't* feed the gulls, they can threaten your lunch if you're having a picnic here. They'll swoop down shamelessly and snatch it away before you even realize they've spotted you. From extensive practice with unsuspecting visitors, they've become adept at thievery.

★ Schoodic Loop

The major sights of Acadia's Schoodic section lie along the six-mile one-way road that meanders counterclockwise around the tip of the Schoodic Peninsula. You'll discover official and unofficial picnic areas, hiking trailheads, offshore lighthouses, a welcome center with exhibits, and turnouts with scenic vistas. Also named the Park Loop Road, it's best referred to as the Schoodic Loop, to distinguish it from the one on Mount Desert Island. Begin at the new **Schoodic Woods Campground,** where you can pick up information and, should you choose, leave your car to explore via bicycle or the Island Explorer bus.

The first landmark is **Frazer Point Picnic Area,** with lovely vistas, picnic tables, and wheelchair-accessible restrooms. Other spots are fine for picnics, but this is the only official one. The area takes its name from Thomas Frazer, a free African American and the first recorded nonnative resident of Winter Harbor, who operated a saltworks here and was listed in the 1790 census. If you've brought bikes, leave your car here and do a counterclockwise 12.2-mile loop through the park and back to your car via Birch Harbor and Route 186. It's a fine day trip. Or, if there's

Surf crashes on the pink granite shores of Schoodic Point.

Woods LLC purchased the lands and worked with the Maine Coast Heritage Trust and the National Park Service on a conservation easement covering the southern 1,400-acre parcel. Beginning in 2015, visitors will find a new and much-needed campground on the Schoodic Peninsula, a day-use parking area, hiking trails, and nonmotorized multiuse paths that eliminate the need to pedal on Route 186 to complete the Schoodic loop on a bicycle.

★ Schoodic Point

The highlight of this part of the park is Schoodic Point, with vistas that seemingly stretch all the way to Spain. The point is at the end of a two-way spur off the Schoodic Loop Road. Although crowds gather at the height of summer, especially when the surf is raging, the tiered parking lot, amazingly, seldom fills up. Check local newspapers for the time of high tide and try to arrive here then; the word *awesome* is overused, but it certainly describes Schoodic Point's surf performance on the rugged pink granite. The setting sun

Lighthouses

The best known of the Acadia region's coastal beacons is **Bass Harbor Head Light,** part of Acadia National Park. Perched high on a promontory overlooking the entrance to Bass Harbor, it flashes a distinctive red beacon, automated since 1974. To visit the light, take Route 102 to the bottom (southern end) of Mount Desert Island, then take Route 102A and watch for signs. The setting is spectacular, and the grounds are accessible during daylight hours. The house is government property, occupied by the Southwest Harbor Coast Guard commander. Be sure to descend the stairs toward the shore and view the 26-foot tower upward from below.

Roughly from north to south (strictly speaking, though, it's east to west), here are the other still-operating lighthouses in the Acadia region. All are automated; most are accessible only by boat. None of the light towers are accessible to the public. Four lights in this area—Winter Harbor, Blue Hill, Dyce's Head, and Pumpkin Island—are no longer used as navigational beacons, although their towers still stand.

On a clear day, you can spot **Petit Manan Light** from the tip of Petit Manan Point, on the mainland Petit Manan section of the Maine Coastal Islands National Wildlife Refuge. Built in 1817 and rebuilt in 1855, it rises 119 feet from its base. It's located 3.5 miles offshore, directly south of Milbridge. Some excursion boats cruise by the island, which is also home to puffins.

Prospect Harbor Light, established in 1850, rebuilt in 1891, and automated in 1951, sits on the tip of Prospect Point. It can be viewed across the harbor from Route 186, or you can drive to the gate for a closer look.

Clearly visible (on a clear day, that is) from Acadia's Park Loop Road, **Egg Rock Light** was built in 1875 on bleak, barren Egg Rock, protecting the entrance to Frenchman Bay. The squat, square keeper's house, topped by a square light tower, resembles no other Maine lighthouse. The light, now under the aegis of the Maine Coastal Islands National Wildlife Refuge, was automated in 1976.

The Cranberry Isles mail boat out of Northeast Harbor passes dramatically located **Bear Island Light** on its daily rounds. Located on Acadia National Park land at the entrance to Northeast Harbor, the light tower and its keeper's house are privately leased in exchange for upkeep. There's no public access to the island. The automated light has been a privately maintained navigational aid since 1989. The present tower was built in 1889.

Baker Island Light, built in 1828 during John Quincy Adams's presidency and rebuilt in 1855, is accessible only by boat, and then via a boardwalk. The brick tower rises 43 feet. Most of the 123-acre island, one of the five Cranberry Isles, is part of Acadia National Park. Charles W. Eliot, president of Harvard University 1869-1909 and one of the prime movers behind the establishment of the park, shone a small spotlight on Baker Island when he published a sympathetic short mem-

room in the rack for your bike, skip Route 186 and pedal only the park loop.

From the picnic area, the road becomes one-way. Unlike the Park Loop Road on Mount Desert Island, no parking is allowed in the right lane. There are periodic pullouts, but not many cars can squeeze in. Despite the fact that this is far from the busiest section of Acadia, it can still be frustrating not to be able to find a space in the summer months. The best advice is to stay in the area and do this loop early in the morning or later in the afternoon. The late September-early October foliage is gorgeous, but traffic does increase

then. While you're driving, if you see a viewpoint you like with room to pull off, stop; it's a long way around to return.

From this side of Frenchman Bay, the views of Mount Desert Island's summits are gorgeous, rising beyond islands sprinkled here and there.

Drive 1.5 miles from the picnic area to **Raven's Head,** an unmarked, Thunder Hole-type cliff with sheer drops to the churning surf below and fabulous views. There are no fences, and the cliffs are eroded, so it's not a good place for little ones. The trail is unsigned, but there's a small pullout on the left oir of a 19th-century Baker Island farmer and fisherman. Entitled *John Gilley, One of the Forgotten Millions,* and reprinted in 1989 by Bar Harbor's Acadia Press, it's a must-read—a poignant story of a hardscrabble pioneering life.

Eleven miles out to sea from Bar Harbor, **Great Duck Island Light** stands on a 12-acre parcel owned by the College of the Atlantic in Bar Harbor. As the solar-powered Alice Eno Biological Station, it serves as a year-round site for the college's ecology researchers. The rest of the island is owned by The Nature Conservancy, which has estimated that Great Duck sustains about 20 percent of the state's nesting seabirds. In 2002, some 1,000 pairs of herring gulls nested here; others include Leach's storm petrels, black-backed gulls, and black guillemots. The 42-foot granite-and-brick light tower, built in 1890, was automated in 1986. The light is visible only from private boats, and there's no island access.

The College of the Atlantic also conducts research on the minuscule, barren, remote island surrounding **Mount Desert Rock Light,** built in 1847. The college's Allied Whale program's Edward McBlair Marine Research Station is based in the keeper's house and monitors the movements of finback and humpback whales. The tower rises 68 feet; the automated light is solar-powered. Mount Desert Rock is also an automated National Oceanic and Atmospheric Administration weather station, cited daily in marine weather reports. There's no public access to the island, but whale-watching boats out of Bar Harbor frequently head this way.

Built in 1872, **Burnt Coat Harbor Light,** also called Hockamock Head Light, with a distinctive square white tower, protects the entrance to Burnt Coat Harbor on Swans Island, accessible via the Maine State Ferry Service from Bass Harbor on Mount Desert Island. The town-owned light is about five miles from the ferry landing, so a bike comes in handy. Bring a picnic and enjoy it on the lighthouse grounds, with a fabulous view.

Isle au Haut Light, also known as Robinson Point Light, built in 1907, overlooks the Isle au Haut Thoroughfare. Access to the island is only by ferry or private boat. The tower itself, not open to the public, is owned by the town of Isle au Haut; the keeper's house is an inn, open to guests.

Looking rather lonely without a keeper's house, **Mark Island Light,** also known as Deer Island Thoroughfare Light, was built in 1857; the light keeper's house burned in 1959. All that remain are the 25-foot square tower and a tiny attached shed. Deer Isle's Island Heritage Trust owns the island, which is accessible only by boat—but not during seabird nesting season (Apr.-Aug.).

Another light station without a keeper's house (it was intentionally burned down in 1963) is **Eagle Island Light,** in East Penobscot Bay, west of the Deer Isle village of Sunset. Built in 1858, it has a 30-foot granite tower. Plans are in the works to deactivate the light. Access is only by boat.

side of the road opposite it. Be extremely careful here, stay on the path (the environment is very fragile and erosion is a major problem), and stay well away from the cliff's edge.

At 2.2 miles past the picnic area, watch for a narrow, unpaved road on the left, across from an open beach vista. It winds for one mile (keep left at the fork) up to a tiny parking circle, from which you can follow the trail (signposted Schoodic Trails) to the open ledges on 440-foot **Schoodic Head.** From the circle, there's already a glimpse of the view, but it gets much better. If you bear right at the fork, you'll come to a grassy parking area with access to the Alder Trail (over to the Blueberry Hill parking lot) and the Schoodic Head Trail.

Continue on the Schoodic Loop Road and hang a right onto a short, two-way spur to **Schoodic Point.** On your right is the **Schoodic Institute** campus (207/288-1310, www.sercinstitute.org), on the site of a former top-secret U.S. Navy base that became part of the park in 2002. At the entrance is a small info center (with ADA-accessible restroom), staffed by volunteers and park rangers. Continue up the road to the restored **Rockefeller Hall,** which opened in 2013 as a welcome center. Inside are exhibits highlighting Schoodic's ecology and history, the former Navy base's radio and cryptologic operations, and current research programs. The Schoodic Institute also offers ranger-led activities, lectures by researchers or nationally known experts addressing environmental topics related to the park and its surroundings, and other programs and events. Check the online calendar for current opportunities.

After touring SERC, continue out to **Schoodic Point,** the highlight of the drive, with surf crashing onto big slabs of pink granite. Be extremely cautious here; chances of rescue are slim if a rogue wave sweeps someone offshore.

From Schoodic Point, return to the Loop Road. Look to the right and you'll see Little Moose Island, which can be accessed at low tide. Be careful, though, not to get stranded here—ask at the info center for safe crossing times. Continue about one mile past the Schoodic Point/Loop Road intersection to the **Blueberry Hill** parking area, a moorlike setting where the low growth allows almost 180-degree views of the bay and islands. There are a few trails in this area—all eventually converging on **Schoodic Head,** the highest point on the peninsula. (Don't confuse this with Schoodic Mountain, which is

well north of here.) Across and up the road a bit is the trailhead for the 180-foot-high **Anvil headland.**

As you continue along this stretch of road, keep your eyes peeled for eagles, which frequently soar here. There's a nest on the northern end of Rolling Island; you can see it with binoculars from some of the roadside pullouts.

From Blueberry Hill, continue 1.2 miles to a pullout for the East Trail, the shortest and most direct route to Schoodic Head. From here, it's about another mile to the park exit, in Wonsqueak Harbor. It's another two miles to the intersection with Route 186 in Birch Harbor.

★ DONNELL POND PUBLIC RESERVED LAND

More than 14,000 acres have been preserved for public access in Donnell Pond Public Reserved Land, a huge area of mountain lakes and forest north and east of Sullivan that is managed by the **Maine Bureau of Parks and Lands** (207/827-1818, www.parksandlands.com). Developers had their eyes on this gorgeous real estate in the 1980s, but preservationists fortunately rallied to the cause.

Get out of your car for close-up views of spruce-topped pink granite cliffs along the Schoodic Loop.

Outright purchase of 7,316 acres, in the Spring River Lake area, came through the farsighted Land for Maine's Future program. Now the reserve includes five peaks taller than 900 feet, a 1,940-acre wetland, and 35 miles of freshwater shoreline, making it especially rich in sightings for bird-watchers. Hikers can climb Schoodic, Black, Caribou, and Tunk Mountains for expansive views taking in Frenchman Bay and Mount Desert Island; paddlers and anglers have Donnell Pond, Tunk Lake, Spring River Lake, Long Pond, Round Pond, and Little Pond, among others. Route 182, an official Scenic Highway, snakes through the Donnell Pond preserve. Hunting is permitted, so take special care during hunting season.

★ PETIT MANAN POINT

Restoring and managing colonies of nesting seabirds is the focus of the **Maine Coastal Islands National Wildlife Refuge,** which spans 250 coastal miles and comprises 55 offshore islands and four mainland parcels totaling more than 8,200 acres spread out in five refuges. Occupying a 2,195-acre peninsula in Steuben with 10 miles of rocky shoreline and three offshore islands is the refuge's outstandingly scenic **Petit Manan Point Division** (Pigeon Hill Rd., Steuben, 207/546-2124, www.fws.gov/refuge/maine_coastal_islands, sunrise-sunset daily year-round). The remote location means it sees only about 15,000 visitors per year, and most

of those are likely birders, as more than 300 different bird species have been sighted here. Among the other natural highlights are stands of jack pine, coastal raised peat lands, blueberry barrens, freshwater and saltwater marshes, granite shores, and cobble beaches. When asking directions locally, you'll hear it called "'tit Manan." Note: There is no visitors center.

The moderately easy, four-mile round-trip Birch Point Trail and the bit more difficult, 1.8-mile round-trip Hollingsworth Trail loop provide splendid views and opportunities to spot wildlife along the shore and in the fields, forests, and marshlands. The Hollingsworth Trail, leading to the shoreline, is the best. This is foggy territory, but on clear days you can see the 123-foot lighthouse on Petit Manan Island, 2.5 miles offshore (for a closer look at the puffin colony there, book a trip on an excursion boat from Milbridge). The Birch Point Trail heads through blueberry fields to Dyer Bay and loops by the waterfront, with much of the trail passing through woods. Family-friendly interpretive signage explains flora and fauna along the route.

From Route 1, on the east side of Steuben, take Pigeon Hill Road. Six miles down is the first parking lot, for the Birch Point Trail; another 0.5 mile takes you to the parking area for the Hollingsworth Trail; space is limited. If you arrive in August, help yourself to blueberries. Cross-country skiing is permitted in winter.

Recreation

DOWN EAST SUNRISE TRAIL

Hike, mountain bike, snowshoe, cross-country ski, or ride an ATV, snowmobile, or horse on the Down East Sunrise Trail (www.sunrisetrail.org). The gravel-surfaced trail, a joint effort by the Maine Department of Transportation and Maine Department of Conservation, stretches 85 miles along a

rehabilitated discontinued railroad bed between Washington Junction, in Hancock, and Ayers Junction, south of Calais. Maps, available to download from the website, show trailheads, highlights, and parking lots along the route. The 30-mile section between Washington Junction and Cherryfield roughly follows the Down East coastline of the Schoodic region. Additional access points include Franklin and Sullivan; see the map for details and directions.

The seven-mile Franklin Crossing to Tunk Lake Road section edges Schoodic Bog and the southwest corner of the Donnell Pond Public Reserved Land and offers fine views of Schoodic Mountain. There's limited parking on both ends: the Franklin Crossing intersection with Route 182 and the Tunk Lake Road intersection on Route 183.

HIKING
★ Schoodic Head Loop

Distance: 2.7 miles round-trip
Duration: varies with route; 1.5-2 hours
Elevation gain: 440 feet
Effort: Moderate, some steep sections
Trailhead: Blueberry Hill parking area, Schoodic Loop

The Schoodic Head Loop comprises three connecting trails, and it can be hiked in either direction. If time is tight, choose just one trail to hike. The clockwise route begins with the easiest terrain and ends with a downhill scramble over a steep and rocky hillside. As one ranger noted, it's tough on the knees, and you have to be very careful with your footing in this direction. If you hike it counterclockwise, beginning with the Anvil Trail, you'll get the toughest terrain out of the way first.

You can access the loop at various points, but the most parking is at the Blueberry Hill parking area. The easy one-mile Alder Trail departs from just south of the parking lot entrance and connects through the woods and some marshy areas to the unmarked Ranger Cabin Road; head left for about 50 yards and watch for the Schoodic Head trail marker.

The moderate Schoodic Head trail climbs for 0.7 mile, beginning in the woods and emerging onto ledgy terrain as it nears the summit. The views are expansive and well worth any effort.

The one-mile Anvil Trail descends over moderate terrain with a few steep sections. A highlight here is the Anvil promontory, a rocky knoll. Whichever way you choose to hike, be extremely careful on the Anvil Trail,

as the terrain is rugged, with lots of roots and loose rocks.

A fourth trail, the 0.6-mile East Trail, descends from the summit and emerges on the Schoodic Loop Road about one mile beyond the Blueberry Hill parking area. This is the shortest and most direct route to the summit and can be hiked independently or looped in with the other trails.

You can also access this loop from the unmarked Ranger Cabin Road, bearing right at the fork.

Donnell Pond Public Reserved Land

Why would a guidebook focused on Acadia send you inland for hiking? Views! The rewards for hiking these peaks are open ledge summits delivering panoramic views over island-studded Frenchman Bay, the rounded peaks of Mount Desert Island, and the Down East coastline. The hiking isn't easy here, but it isn't technical, and the options are varied. The interconnecting trail system takes in Schoodic Mountain, Black Mountain, and Caribou Mountain on Donnell Pond Public Reserved Land.

SCHOODIC MOUNTAIN

Distance: 2.8 miles round-trip
Duration: 2 hours
Elevation gain: 800 feet
Effort: Moderately difficult
Trailhead: Schoodic Beach Parking Area, off Route 183, Franklin

Follow the Schoodic Mountain Loop clockwise, heading west first. To make a day of it, pack a picnic and take a swimsuit (and don't forget a camera and binoculars for the summit views). On a brilliantly clear day, you'll see Baxter State Park's Katahdin, the peaks of Acadia National Park, and the ocean beyond. And in late July-early August, blueberries are abundant on the summit. For such rewards, this is a popular hike, so don't expect to be alone, especially on fall weekends when the foliage colors are spectacular.

Trailheads can be accessed by either boat

or vehicle. To reach the vehicle-access trailhead for Schoodic Mountain from Route 1 in East Sullivan, drive 4.5 miles northeast on Route 183 (Tunk Lake Rd.). Cross the Down East Sunrise Trail, a former railroad bed, and turn left at the Donnell Pond sign onto the gravel Schoodic Beach Road. Go about 0.25 mile, then bear left at the fork, continuing 2.3 miles to the Schoodic Beach Parking Area and trailhead for Schoodic Mountain, Black Mountain, and Caribou Mountain, and a trail to Schoodic Beach.

BLACK MOUNTAIN CLIFFS LOOP

Distance: 2.9 miles
Duration: 2 hours
Elevation gain: 800 feet
Effort: Moderately difficult
Trailhead: Schoodic Beach Parking Area, off Route 183, Franklin

This trail accesses the western side of Black Mountain. The reward for your efforts might be a refreshing swim in Donnell Pond, so come prepared. Pass through the parking lot boulder barricade, follow the beach access trail, and look for the trailhead on the right. The trail rises 1.2 miles to a junction. Bear left and continue across the cliffs before descending to the beach for an additional 1.3 miles.

It's a 0.5-mile return along the beach to the parking area. To link into the Caribou Loop Trail, go straight at the junction and continue 0.6 mile to the Black Mountain summit, with 360-degree views from its open summit.

Follow the directions for the Schoodic Mountain Trail to the Schoodic Beach Parking Area trailhead.

BIG CHIEF TRAIL

Distance: 2.6 miles
Duration: 2 hours
Elevation gain: 800 feet
Effort: Moderately difficult
Trailhead: Black Mountain Rd., off Route 183, Franklin

The ascent begins easily enough, then climbs steadily for 0.6 mile through the woods on Donnell Pond Public Reserved Land, easing off a bit before reaching bald ledges. Continue to the true summit by taking the 1.4-mile loop trail around Wizard Pond (which may seem more like Wizard Puddle). Views take in the forested lands and nearby lakes and peaks, and they extend out to Acadia's peaks. You can piggyback this hike with Schoodic Mountain, using that trailhead as a base for both climbs. Another possibility is to add Caribou Mountain. That loop exceeds seven

Schoodic Mountain, in the Donnell Pond Public Reserved Land, rises above Flanders Pond.

miles, making a full day of hiking. The Cliffs Loop departs from the Schoodic Beach parking lot.

Follow the directions for the Schoodic Mountain Trail to the Schoodic Beach Parking lot, but keep right at the fork for Black Mountain Road at the split and continue 2.2 miles to the parking area. The trailhead is just beyond and across the road.

CARIBOU LOOP TRAIL

Distance: minimum 7 miles round-trip
Duration: 6-8 hours
Elevation gain: 900 feet
Effort: Difficult to strenuous
Trailhead: Off Route 182, T10 SD, an unorganized township east of Franklin

When you're ready for an all-day hike, consider this backcountry beauty connecting Black and Caribou Mountains. The loop itself is 6.1 miles, but accessing it from the trailhead adds another 0.9 mile each way on the Caribou Mountain Trail. You can also create your own distance, as this loop links to the Schoodic Mountain and Big Chief trailheads.

Find the trailhead on the Dynamite Brook Road, approximately 0.5 mile off Route 182.

TUNK MOUNTAIN

Distance: approximately 4.4 miles round-trip
Duration: 4 hours
Elevation gain: 900 feet
Effort: Difficult to strenuous
Trailhead: Off Route 182, T10 SD, an unorganized township east of Franklin

A new parking area with a restroom was created in 2011 to provide access to Tunk Mountain, a locally popular hike that takes in several remote ponds en route to the bald summit. The trail progresses approximately 1.5 miles to open ledges with expansive views south over inland mountains toward Frenchman Bay. Approximately 0.5 mile from the trailhead, the Hidden Ponds Trail forms a one-mile loop passing Salmon and Little Long Ponds before returning to the main trail. Not far beyond the junction with the Hidden Pond Trail, the Tunk Mountain Trail becomes

steep, with stone steps and a set of iron rungs in one spot to assist hikers. If the weather is marginal, stick to the lower trail. Another 0.2 mile of trail atop the mountain ridge leads to an overlook on Nature Conservancy property with views to the north of sprawling forests and the Narraguagus River watershed. Be sure to take plenty of water and pack a lunch or energy snacks.

PARKS AND PRESERVES
Frenchman Bay Conservancy

The very active **Frenchman Bay Conservancy** (FBC, 207/422-2328, www. frenchmanbay.org) manages a number of small preserves dotting the region, and most have at least one trail providing access. The Conservancy publishes the free *Short Hikes* map, available locally, which provides directions to seven of these.

TIDAL FALLS PRESERVE

FBC's four-acre **Tidal Falls Preserve** (off Eastside Rd., Hancock) overlooks Frenchman Bay's only reversing falls (roiling water when the tide turns). There's no longer a lobster pound, but there are still picnic tables on the lawn overlooking the falls and ledges where seals often slumber. It's an idyllic spot. A summer concert series takes place here on Mondays during the summer, and usually Fisherman's Inn Restaurant, in Winter Harbor, operates a food cart selling hot dogs and lobster rolls. No dogs are permitted.

NORTHERN COREA HEATH TRAIL

In 2008, FBC purchased 600 acres of land known as the Corea Heath, and volunteers began cutting trails that summer. *Heath* is a local word for peat land or bog, and this one is a rare coastal plateau bog, distinguished because it rises above the surrounding landscape. It's a spectacular property, with divergent ecosystems including bogs, ledges, and mixed-wood forest. Natural features include pitcher plants, sphagnum mosses, rare vascular plants, and jack pines. It's a fabulous place for bird-watching too, and the preserve borders a section of the Maine Coastal Islands National Wildlife Refuge. A 1-mile trail loops through the preserve. Check with the Conservancy or stop into **Chapter Two** (611 Corea Rd., Corea, 207/963-7269, www.chaptertwocorea.com) for more info. Trail access is signed on the Corea Road, 1.9 miles from the Route 195 intersection.

BAKER HILL AND LONG LEDGES

These two adjoining preserves are laced with 5.4 miles of trails. If you only have an hour or so and want big rewards for minimal effort, hoof it up Baker Hill. Stick to the main trail for the quickest trip. Trails pass through fir trees and over ledges before a short ascent to an overlook with views over Frenchman Bay. If you have time to linger, the Boundary Trail connects to two of eight trails on Long Ledges, making it possible to loop through. Highlights in this preserve include the overgrown ruins of an old granite quarry, a small pond, and vernal pools. To find the Baker Hill parking lot from Route 1, take Punkinville Road, northeast of Route 200 in Sullivan. The parking area is on the left, 200 yards north of Route 1; continue on to find the Long Ledges parking lot and trailhead. The trails on Long Ledges are more clearly marked and mapped.

Maine Coastal Islands National Wildlife Reserve

In addition to the Petit Manan Point Division, the Petit Manan National Wildlife Refuge also encompasses the 623-acre Gouldsboro Bay Division; the 1,028-acre Sawyer's Marsh Division, in Milbridge; and the 431-acre Corea Heath Division, home to one of Maine's most significant peat lands. These two trails are in the Corea Heath Division.

SOUTHERN COREA HEATH TRAIL

Here's a welcome find for anyone with mobility issues or pushing a stroller. The Southern Corea Heath Trail is an easy, 0.4-mile round-trip, wheelchair-accessible gravel trail to an observation platform with a panoramic view of the coastal plateau bog, also known as a peat land or heath. From the intersection with Route 186 in Prospect Harbor, follow Route 195, the Corea Road, 2.6 miles to the refuge parking area on the right.

SALT MARSH TRAIL

Observe waterfowl, shorebirds, and eagles on this moderate, 1.6-mile round-trip hike through conifers to two observation platforms overlooking a salt marsh. From Route 1, take the Chicken Mill Pond Road to Fletcher Wood

the Northern Corea Heath Trail

Road and go 0.2 mile, continuing straight 0.1 mile when the main road veers right.

Pigeon Hill

It doesn't require too much effort to hike Pigeon Hill and reap views taking in Cadillac Mountain, Petit Manan Light, and the island-studded Bold Coast from its 317-foot summit, the highest point on Washington County's coastline. Since acquiring this 172-acre preserve, **Downeast Coastal Conservancy** (207/255-4500, www.downeastcoastalconservancy.org) has been enhancing the original trail and adding new ones. It now has 1.6 miles of linked trails to the summit ledges; the shortest route, 0.8 mile round-trip, ascends steeply but swiftly. For the best views on the descent, take the Summit Loop and Silver Mine Trails; the latter passes an abandoned silver mine (not much to see but a pile of rocks). The trailhead is on the western side of Pigeon Hill Road, 4.5 miles south of Route 1. If you continue on the road, you'll end up at the Petit Manan Point Division of the Maine Coastal Islands National Wildlife Refuge.

BICYCLING

The Maine Department of Transportation has mapped and provides info on area bicycle routes. These include the Schoodic Peninsula, with 10-, 12-, and 24-mile loops, and the Downeast Route-East Coast Greenway Trail, a 140-mile trail stretching from Ellsworth to Calais. PDF maps with tour details are available at www.exploremaine.org, or you can pick up a copy of *Explore Maine by Bike: 33 Loop Bicycle Tours* at any of the Maine visitors centers. Do be extremely careful pedaling in this region because, as in much of Maine, shoulders are few and traffic moves swiftly.

The best choices for cycling are the **Schoodic Loop** and the quiet roads of **Grindstone Neck and Corea.** The Down East Sunrise Trail (www.sunrisetrail.org) is also open to bicyclists.

If you have a bike, try to pedal the **Schoodic Loop Road** early or late in the day—especially if you're doing a family outing, when everyone tends to cluster together. It's a lovely bike route, but the shoulders on this peninsula are soft and sandy and not great for bikes—so you'll see Share the Road with Bicycles signs along the way. Keep to the right and use the road, not the shoulders. Leave your car at the Schoodic Woods Campground and do a counterclockwise loop through the park using the new nonmotorized paths to complete it without venturing

the Southern Corea Heath Trail

To reach the boat-launching area for Donnell Pond from Route 1 in Sullivan, take Route 200 north to Route 182. Turn right and go about 1.5 miles to a right turn just before Swan Brook. Turn and go not quite two miles to the put-in; the road is poor in spots but adequate for a regular vehicle. The Narrows, where you'll put in, is lined with summer cottages ("camps" in the Maine vernacular); keep paddling east to the more open part of the lake. Continue on Route 182 to find the boat launches for Tunk Lake and Spring River Lake (hand-carry only). Canoeists and kayakers can access Tunk Stream from Spring River Lake.

Also accessed from Route 182 is Flanders Pond, 2.9 miles off Route 1 on the Flanders Pond Road. It's a beautiful pond, with islands and mountain views. The public park has a parking area and an offshore float, as the pond is also a local swimming spot.

Well off the beaten path is **Dyer Harbor** in Steuben. Take Dyer Bay Road off Route 1, then go left on Pinkham Bay Bridge Road. Just before the bridge is a boat launch for small craft. It's a fine spot to launch a kayak for a coastal paddle in relatively protected waters.

Bicycling is a great way to loop around the Schoodic section of Acadia National Park.

onto Route 186. If arriving by ferry, take the Island Explorer bus to the campground and begin there, after picking up info at the welcome center. It's a fine day trip.

SeaScape Kayaking (207/963-5806, www.seascapekayaking.com) rents bicycles for $15 per day. It's relocating to Winter Harbor for 2015, near the park access road; call for details.

PADDLING

Experienced sea kayakers can explore the coastline throughout this region. Canoeists can paddle the placid waters of Jones Pond on the Schoodic Peninsula. In Donnell Pond Public Reserved Land, the major water bodies are **Donnell Pond** (big enough by most gauges to be called a lake) along with **Tunk Lake, Spring River Lake,** and **Long Pond;** all are accessible for boats (even, alas, powerboats). In early August, Round Mountain, rising a few hundred feet from Long Pond's eastern shore, is a great spot for gathering blueberries and huckleberries.

Outfitters and Trips

Paddle around the waters of Schoodic or Flanders Bay with **SeaScape Kayaking** (207/963-5806, www.seascapekayaking.com). Guided three-hour tours are $50 per person, including fortification: a bottle of water, trail mix, and a homemade blueberry snack. Canoe rental for lake usage is $45 for 24 hours; kayaks are $45 double, $35 single.

Antonio Blasi, a Registered Maine Sea Kayak and Recreational Guide, leads guided tours of Frenchman and Taunton Bays and hiking and camping expeditions through **Hancock Point Kayak Tours** (58 Point Rd., Hancock, 207/422-6854, www.hancockpointkayak.com). A three-hour paddle, including all equipment, safety and paddling demonstrations, and an island break, is $45 per person; $35 for two hours without the break. Overnight kayak camping trips are

$150 per person. Antonio also leads overnight backpacking trips for $125 per person, and cross-country skiing and snowshoe tours are available in winter.

If you prefer to do it yourself, rent a canoe or kayak from **Water's Edge Canoe & Kayak Rentals** (222 Franklin Rd., Franklin, 207/460-6350). Canoe rentals are $25 for one day, $65 for three days, or $125 per week; single kayaks are $30, $80, or $150; double kayaks are $40, $100, or $200. Although the location is at the water's edge on Hog Bay, it's tidal, so it's advisable to take the craft elsewhere; delivery is possible. Credit cards are not accepted.

FISHING

It's no surprise that the Donnell Pond Public Reserved Land is a favorite among anglers. Landlocked salmon can be found in Donnell Pond, Tunk Lake, and Spring River Lake. Lake trout (togue) are fished in Tunk Lake. For brown trout, cast your line in Long Pond.

Open-water season in Hancock County and adjacent Washington County is April 1-September 30, but after August 16, you must use artificial lures in brooks, rivers, and streams. Check with local wardens for information regarding catch limits and other regulations for specific bodies of water, or call the **Maine Department of Fish and Wildlife** (207/288-8000, www.state.me.us/ifw). A copy of the rules and regulations for Hancock County can be downloaded from the website.

Maine residents younger than 16 and nonresidents younger than 12 do not need licenses. Freshwater fishing licenses can be purchased at many stores and most town offices. Nonresident freshwater licenses for ages 16 and older are $64 for the season, $11 for one day (24 hours), $23 for three days (72 hours), $43 for seven days, and $47 for 15 days. Licenses for children ages 12-15 are $16. A Maine saltwater recreational fishing registration is required for anyone over the age of 16 and can be done at no extra charge when purchasing a freshwater license. It is required to have your license with you when fishing, whether in fresh- or saltwater.

SWIMMING

The best freshwater swimming in the area is at **Jones Beach** (sunrise-sunset daily), a community-owned recreation area on Jones Pond in West Gouldsboro. Here you'll find restrooms, a nice playground, picnic facilities, a boat launch, a swim area with a float, and a small beach. The beach is located at the end of Recreation Road, off Route 195, which is 0.3 mile south of Route 1. No unleashed pets are permitted.

Two beach areas on Donnell Pond are also popular for swimming, **Schoodic Beach** and **Redman's Beach,** and both have picnic tables, fire rings, and pit toilets. It's a 0.5-mile hike to Schoodic Beach from the parking lot. Redman's Beach is only accessible by boat. Other pocket beaches are also accessible by boat or via roadside pullouts.

A sand beach on a remote freshwater pond is the reward for a 0.25-mile hike into the Frenchman Bay Conservancy's **Little Tunk Pond Preserve.** From Route 1 in Sullivan, take Route 183 about five miles, then look for the parking area on the left. Just east of that is the **Spring River Lake Beach Day Use Area,** with parking and toilets.

GOLF

Play the nine-hole **Grindstone Neck Golf Course** (Grindstone Ave., Winter Harbor, 207/963-7760, www.grindstonegolf.com, May-Oct., $25 for 9 holes and $40 for 18 Mon.-Fri.; $30/$45 weekends; $15 twilight) just for the dynamite scenery or for a glimpse of this exclusive late 19th-century summer enclave. Established in 1891, the public course attracts a tony crowd; 150-yard markers are cute little birdhouses. Tee times usually aren't needed, but call to make sure.

EXCURSION BOATS

If you want to see this part of the coast from the sea, especially Petit Manan lighthouse and its puffin colony, you have to venture up to Milbridge. Although not truly part of the Acadia region by any definition, it's the closest port with lighthouse-sighting, bird-watching,

Puffins

The chickadee is the Maine state bird, and the bald eagle is our national emblem, but probably the best-loved bird along the Maine coast is the Atlantic puffin *(Fratercula arctica)*, a member of the auk (Alcidae) family. Photographs show an imposing-looking creature with a quizzical mien; amazingly, this larger-than-life seabird is only about 12 inches long. Black-backed and white-chested, the puffin has bright orange legs, "clown makeup" eyes, and a distinctive, rather outlandish red-and-yellow beak. Its diet is fish and shellfish.

Almost nonexistent in this part of the world as recently as the 1970s, the puffin (or "sea parrot") has recovered dramatically thanks to the unstinting efforts of Cornell University ornithologist Stephen Kress and his Project Puffin. Starting with an orphan colony of two on remote Matinicus Rock, Kress painstakingly transferred nearly 1,000 puffin chicks (also known fondly as "pufflings") from Newfoundland and used artificial nests and decoys to entice the birds to adapt to and re-produce on Eastern Egg Rock in Muscongus Bay.

In 1981, thanks to the assistance and persistence of hundreds of interns and volunteers, and despite predation by great black-backed gulls, puffins finally were fledged on Eastern Egg, and the rest, as they say, is history. Within 20 years, more than three dozen puffin pairs were nesting on Eastern Egg Rock, and still more had established nests on other islands in the area. Kress's methods have received international attention, and his proven techniques have been used to reintroduce bird populations in remote parts of the globe. In 2001, *Down East* magazine singled out Kress to receive its prestigious annual Environmental Award.

HOW AND WHERE TO SEE PUFFINS

Puffin-watching, like whale-watching, involves heading offshore (although you might get lucky and spot them at the tip of the Petit Manan Point Division of the Maine Coastal Islands National Wildlife Refuge), so be prepared with warm clothing, rubber-soled shoes, a hat, sunscreen, binoculars, and if you're motion-sensitive, appropriate medication. Although cruises depart from Bar Harbor on Mount Desert Island, if you're willing to venture a bit farther afield, you'll find three companies offering puffin-watching cruises.

Closest are **Robertson Sea Tours and Adventures** (207/546-3883, cell 207/461-7439, www.robertsonseatours.com, May 15-Oct. 1) in Milbridge, whose three-hour tour ($70 adults, $55 under age 13, $200 boat minimum) heads to Petit Manan Island; you view the birds from aboard the boat. Also departing from Milbridge and cruising to Petit Manan is **Downeast Coastal Cruises** (207/546-7720, cell 207/598-7740, www.downeastcoastalcruises.com), with 2.5- to 3-hour cruises for $65 adults, $45 children, with a $175 boat minimum.

Naturalist and skilled skipper Andy Patterson of Cutler-based **Bold Coast Charters** (207/259-4484, www.boldcoast.com) provides daily up-close-and-personal opportunities to view puffins on Machias Seal Island, home of the state's largest puffin colony. The *Barbara Frost* cruises to the island from late May-mid-August, departing at about 7am daily and costing about $120 per person. Weather permitting, you'll be allowed to disembark on the 20-acre island and spy on the roughly 3,000 puffins who call it their summer home.

ADOPT-A-PUFFIN PROGRAM

Stephen Kress's Project Puffin has devised a clever way to enlist supporters via the Adopt-a-Puffin program. For a $100 annual donation, you'll receive a certificate of adoption and a biography about your adoptee. How's that for a special gift for the bird lover in your life? For information, visit www.projectpuffin.org.

or scenic nature cruises. Alternatively, you can take the passenger ferry to Bar Harbor, which docks less than a block away from the whale-watching boats, but be sure not to miss the last return ferry. Note: Fares will vary with fuel prices.

Robertson Sea Tours and Adventures

Captain Jaime Robertson's **Robertson Sea Tours and Adventures** (Milbridge Marina, Fickett's Point Rd., 207/483-6110 or 207/461-7439, www.robertsonseatours.com, May 15-Oct. 1) offers 2-4-hour cruises ($60-85 adults, $45-65 children) from the Milbridge Marina aboard the *Mairi Leigh*, a classic Maine lobster boat. Options include puffins and seabirds, an island lobster bake, and a family-pleasing

Maine-themed cruise highlighting lobstering, history, and sealife. A minimum rate for the boat may apply. Captain Robertson also offers a 4-5-hour **whale-watching cruise** aboard the six-passenger, 33-foot *Elisabeth Rose or the 28-foot Kandi Leigh* ($95 adults, $75 age 11 and younger, $360 boat minimum).

Downeast Coastal Cruises

Captain Harry "Buzzy" Shinn's **Downeast Coastal Cruises** (207/546-7720, cell 207/598-7740, www.downeastcoastalcruises.com) depart from the Milbridge Landing aboard the comfortable *Alyce K.* for island cruises, lighthouse cruises, puffin cruises, lobster cruises (complete with a meal), sunset cruises, and charters. Cruises last 1.5-3.5 hours and cost $45-75 adults, $35-65 children; boat minimums apply.

Entertainment and Events

PIERRE MONTEUX SCHOOL

The **Pierre Monteux School for Conductors and Orchestra Musicians** (42 Melody Ln., Hancock, 207/460-0313, www.monteuxschool.org), a prestigious summer program founded in 1943, has achieved international renown for training dozens of national and international classical musicians. It presents two well-attended concert series late June-July. The Wednesday series (7:30pm, $12 adults, $5 students) features chamber music; the Sunday concerts (5pm, $20 adults, $5 students) feature symphonies. An annual free children's concert, followed by an "instrument petting zoo," usually is held on a Monday in early-mid-July. All concerts are held in the school's Forest Studio on Old Track Road, which is just off Route 1 across from the Ironbound restaurant.

SCHOODIC ARTS FOR ALL

Concerts, art classes, coffeehouses, workshops, and related activities are presented

year-round by the energetic **Schoodic Arts for All** (207/963-2569, www.schoodicarts.org), a volunteer organization. Many activities are held at historic Hammond Hall in downtown Winter Harbor. A summer series presents monthly concerts on a Friday evening May-October.

The **Schoodic Arts Festival** takes place over two weeks in early August and is jam-packed with daily workshops and nightly performances for all ages. Call for a schedule, and register early for any program that you don't want to miss.

MONDAY MUSIC AT TIDAL FALLS

On Monday evenings in July-August, weather permitting, the **Frenchman Bay Conservancy** (207/422-2328, www.french-manbay.org) presents a concert series at its Tidal Falls Preserve. Pack a picnic supper or purchase lobster rolls or hot dogs from the Fisherman's Inn cart. Music might include jazz, steel pan drums, ukuleles, or an orchestra.

INNSTITUTE FOR THE ARTS AND SCIENCES

Seeking to add more vibrancy and diversity to the peninsula's entertainment offerings and to indulge their own interests in music and the sciences, the owners of Oceanside Meadows Inn created the **Innstitute for the Arts and Sciences** (Rte. 195/Corea Rd., Prospect Harbor, 207/963-5557, www.oceaninn.com), which presents a series of Thursday-night events late June-late September, with a break during the Schoodic Arts Festival. The wide-ranging calendar includes lectures and concerts as well as art shows. Some are free; others are $10-12 in advance or $12-15 at the door.

SCHOODIC INSTITUTE

The **Schoodic Institute** (207/288-1310, www.schoodicinstitute.org), at Schoodic Point, offers lectures, usually by researchers or nationally known experts, addressing environmental topics related to the park and its surroundings. It also offers other programs and events, including ranger-led activities. Check the online calendar for current opportunities.

EAGLE HILL SUMMER LECTURES

The **Eagle Hill Institute** (59 Eagle Hill Rd., Steuben, 207/546-2821, www.eaglehill.us) presents advanced natural history seminars and scientific illustration workshops and publishes peer-reviewed scientific journals. It also sponsors various opportunities to meet and mingle with scientists and others. If you're especially interested in natural history and the arts, the institute offers longer programs

as well. The institute is located four miles off Route 1. Take Dyer Bay Road off Route 1, bearing left at the fork on Mogador Road, for a total of 3.6 miles, then left on Schooner Point Road, then right on Eagle Hill Road. Programs take place in the Dining Hall lecture room.

Public **lectures,** by recognized experts on often fascinating topics, are offered two or three times each week. Subjects have included Maine Poets and the Natural World: A Different Lens; the Existential Problem of the Whale in the Sagas of the Vikings; Maine's Best Edible Mushrooms; Foraging and Cooking Tips across the Season; and Songbird Superhighway: Understanding Migration in the Gulf of Maine.

WINTER HARBOR LOBSTER FESTIVAL

Winter Harbor's biggest wingding is the annual Lobster Festival, on the second Saturday in August. The gala daylong event includes a parade, live entertainment, lobster boat races (a serious competition, with 13 classes determined by size and power), a crafts fair, games, and lots and lots of crustaceans. For more information, visit www.acadia-schoodic.org.

WILD MOUNTAIN MAN

Ray Murphy began wielding his dad's chainsaw to create sculptures in 1952. Since then, the **Wild Mountain Man** (742 Route 1, Hancock, 207/565-3377, www.thewildmountainman.com) has crafted more than 50,000 pieces. He shows his works at a roadside gallery and demonstrates his art form (7pm daily, $10 pp).

Educating for the Future

The Schoodic section of Acadia National Park is well on the way to becoming a world-class center for the study of science and nature, thanks to a history of benefactors dating back to the early 19th century. Maine native and Wall Street tycoon John G. Moore once owned most of Schoodic Point. In 1927, George Dorr persuaded Moore's heirs to donate the land to the Hancock County Trustees of Public Reservations, with the stipulation that the land be used as a public park and for the "promotion of biological and other scientific research." Seven years later, more than 2,000 acres of the peninsula were donated to Acadia National Park.

The timing was perfect. John D. Rockefeller Jr. was working with the National Park Service to construct the Park Loop Road on Mount Desert Island. The U.S. Naval Radio Station on Otter Point was in the way, so Rockefeller, working with Dorr, helped the National Park Service work with the U.S. Navy to relocate the station to Schoodic Point. Six buildings were constructed. Most noteworthy is Rockefeller Hall, a French Norman Revival-style mansion designed by New York architect Grosvenor Atterbury, who used a similar design for the park's carriage road gatehouses on Mount Desert Island.

In 1935, the U.S. Naval Radio Station at Schoodic Point was commissioned, and by the late 20th century, the 100-acre campus comprised more than 35 buildings and was home to 350 Navy employees. When the station closed in 2002, the land was returned to the park for use as a research and education center.

It took ten years and millions of dollars to transform the former Navy base. The campus now offers housing and meals for individual researchers, groups, and conferences, classrooms, laboratories, and a modern 124-seat auditorium, all in the inspirational setting of Schoodic Point. A renovated Rockefeller Hall, listed on the National Register of Historic Places, now serves as Schoodic's welcome center, with exhibits highlighting Schoodic's ecology and history, the former navy base's radio and cryptologic operations, and current research programs. Credit for the renovations goes to local benefactor Edith Robb Dixon, who donated $1 million in the name of her late husband, Fitz Eugene Dixon Jr.

Schoodic Institute at Acadia National Park (207/288-1310, www.schoodicinstitute. org) is the nonprofit that partners with Acadia to manage the campus and advance science and

Shopping

The Schoodic Peninsula region is a hotbed of artists and artisans, with studios and galleries dotting the byways and back roads. It's easy to while away a day browsing and buying. Hours and days of operation vary and are often subject to whim; it's best to call ahead if you really want to visit a gallery. Begin by picking up copies of the *Artist Studio Tour Map*, which details and provides directions to about a dozen galleries in the Hancock area, and the *Schoodic Peninsula* brochure, which notes galleries and shops on the peninsula. Both are free and widely available.

SCHOODIC PENINSULA
Arts, Antiques, Gifts, and Books

To find these shops, loop down to Winter Harbor, then back up on Route 186, with a side venture to Corea and a short trip up Route 1 in Gouldsboro.

An old post office is the location for **Lee Fusion Art Glass** (679 S. Gouldsboro Rd./ Rte. 196, Gouldsboro, 207/963-7280, www. leefusionartglass.com). Although Rod Lee has died, his works live on, thanks to Wayne Tucker and Sheldon R. Bickford, who purchased the business after training with

Rockefeller Hall

education throughout the park and the region. Schoodic Institute connects education with research, while managers at Acadia National Park rely on the research to restore Acadia's ecosystems and improve their resiliency in the face of rapid environmental changes.

The Schoodic Institute offers education and research programs aimed not only at scientists and researchers but also at students and teachers. The institute also hosts Acadia National Park's artist-in-residence program and works with the park to present programs, lectures, special events, and ranger-led activities; check the online calendar for current offerings. Among these are "bio blitzes," in which teams of specialists and volunteers research the park's flora and fauna in minute detail. In 2013-2014, a two-year blitz focused on beetles found more than 100 species never previously identified in the park.

Lee. The fused-glass tableware is created by taking two pieces of window glass and firing them on terra-cotta or bisque molds at 1,500°F. What makes the end result so appealing are the colors and the patterns—crocheted doilies or stencils—impressed into the glass. The almost magical results are beautiful and delicate-looking, yet functional.

In the village center is **Artisans & Antiques** (357 Main St., Winter Harbor, 207/963-2400), a 15-member group shop with a nice mix of craftwork and treasures.

Winter Harbor Antiques and Works of Hand (424-426 Main St., Winter Harbor, 207/963-2547) is a double treat: Antiques fill one building, and a well-chosen selection of distinctive works by local craftspeople

and artists fills the other. It's across from Hammond Hall and set behind colorful, well-tended gardens.

Barbara Noel makes most of the sea-glass jewelry, mobiles, and other creations at **Harbor Treasures** (358 and 368 Main St., Winter Harbor, 207/963-7086).

Works by contemporary Maine artists, including noted painters and sculptors, are shown in rotating shows at **Littlefield Gallery** (145 Main St., Winter Harbor, 207/963-6005, www.littlefieldgallery.com). Works are displayed both in a purpose-built gallery and in the house.

Prospect Harbor Soap Co. (4 Duck Pond Rd. at Rte. 186, Winter Harbor, 207/963-7598, www.prospectharborsoapco.com) maintains an outlet where you can purchase lotions, handmade soaps, and other skin-care products.

The folk-art funk begins on the exterior of the **Salty Dog Gallery/Hurdy Gurdy Man Antiques** (173 Main St., Prospect Harbor, 207/963-7575), a twofold find. The lower level is filled with fun folk-art vintage goods. Upstairs, owner Dean Kotula displays his fine art: documentary-style photographic prints.

Visiting the **U.S. Bells Foundry & Watering Cove Pottery** (56 W. Bay Rd./Rte. 186, Prospect Harbor, 207/963-7184, www.usbells.com) is a treat for the ears, as browsers try out the many varieties of cast bronze bells made in the adjacent foundry by Richard Fisher. If you're lucky, he may have time to explain the process—particularly intriguing for children, and a distraction from their instinctive urge to test every bell in the shop. The store also carries quilts by Dick's wife, Cindy, and wood-fired stoneware and porcelain by their daughter-in-law Liza Fisher, as well as works by other area artisans. U.S. Bells is 0.25 mile up the hill from Prospect Harbor's post office.

Here's a nifty place: **Chapter Two** (611 Corea Rd., Corea, 207/963-7269, www.chaptertwocorea.com) is home to Spurling House Gallery, Corea Rug Hooking Company, and Accumulated Books Gallery. Spread out in three buildings is a nice selection of used and antiquarian books, fine crafts, and hand-hooked rugs. Yarn, rug-hooking supplies, and lessons are available.

Down the first dirt lane after the Corea Post Office is the **Corea Wharf Gallery** (13 Gibbs Ln., Corea, 207/963-2633, www.coreawharfgallery.com). Inside a humble wharf-top fishing shack are displayed historic photographs of Corea, taken in the 1940s-1960s by Louise Z. Young, born in Corea in 1919. She was a friend of painter Marsden Hartley, and took many candid photographs of him around the area. Young also worked with noted photographer Berenice Abbott. Also here are artifacts from Corea's history, especially ones connected to fishing. The gallery doubles as

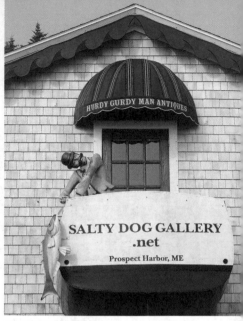

Salty Dog Gallery blends antiques and curiosities with fine art photography.

a food stand selling lobster, lobster rolls, hot dogs, and ice cream.

General Store

You can find just about anything at the **Winter Harbor 5 & 10** (349 Main St., Winter Harbor, 207/963-7927, www.winterharbor5and10.com). It's the genuine article, an old-fashioned five-and-dime that's somehow still surviving in the age of Walmart.

HANCOCK AND SULLIVAN

★ Hancock and Sullivan Gallery Tour

From Route 1 take Eastside Road, just before the Hancock-Sullivan Bridge, and drive 1.6 miles south to the Wray family's **Gull Rock Pottery** (103 Gull Rock Rd., Hancock, 207/422-3990, www.gullrockpottery.com). Torj and Kurt Wray created this gallery, which daughter-in-law Akemi now runs. She's continued crafting their wheel-thrown, hand-painted, dishwasher-safe pottery decorated with cobalt blue and white Japanese-style motifs, but has added some of her own designs. Complementing the indoor gallery is an outdoor, oceanfront sculpture gallery with views to Mount Desert Island.

Cross the Hancock-Sullivan Bridge, then take your first left off Route 1 onto Taunton Drive to find the next four galleries, beginning with Dan Farrenkopf's and Phid Lawless's **Lunaform** (66 Cedar Ln., Sullivan, 207/422-0923, www.lunaform.com), set amid beautifully landscaped grounds surrounding an old quarry. At first glance, it appears that many of the wonderfully aesthetic garden ornaments created here are hand-turned pottery, when in fact they're hand-turned steel-reinforced concrete. Take the first right off Taunton Drive onto Track Road, proceed 0.5 mile, then turn left onto Cedar Lane.

Return to Taunton Drive and take the next right onto Quarry Road, then left on Whales Back Drive, a rough dirt lane, to find granite sculptor Obadiah Bourne Buell's **Stone Designs Studio and Granite Garden Gallery** (124 Whales Back Rd., Sullivan, 207/422-3111, www.stonedesignsmaine.com). Bourne displays his home accents and garden features in a self-serve gallery adjacent to a quarry and in the surrounding gardens. This really is a magical spot, and if you time it right, you might be able to see the sculptor at work.

Continue north on Taunton Road as it changes its name to South Bay Road. Bet you can't keep from smiling at the whimsical animal sculptures and fun furniture of talented sculptor-painter Philip Barter. His work is the cornerstone of the eclectic **Barter Gallery** (South Bay Rd., Sullivan, 207/422-3190, www.bartergallery.com). But there's more: Barter's wife and seven children, especially son Matt, along with son-in-law Brian Emerson, have put their considerable skills to work producing hooked and braided rugs, jewelry, and paintings as well as wood sculptures. The gallery is 2.5 miles off Route 1.

Continue on South Bay Road (note that it becomes dirt for a roughly 0.5-mile section) and turn left, heading north, when it meets Route 200/Hog Bay Road. Almost immediately on your left is Charles and Susanne Grosjean's **Hog Bay Pottery** (245 Hog Bay Rd./Rte. 200, Franklin, 207/565-2282), in operation since 1974. Inside the casual, laid-back showroom are Charles's functional, nature-themed pottery and Susanne's stunning hand-woven wool rugs. Pottery seconds are often available.

Next, head south on Route 200/Bert Gray Road. Handwoven textiles are the specialty at **Moosetrack Studio** (388 Bert Gray Rd./Rte. 200, Sullivan, 207/422-9017, www.moosetrackhandweaving.com), where the selections range from handwoven area rugs to shawls of merino wool and silk. Camilla Stege has been weaving since 1969, and her exquisite work reflects her experience and expertise. The gallery is 1.8 miles north of Route 1.

Continue south. Just before the intersection with U.S. 1 is a double hit. Artist Paul Breeden, best known for the remarkable illustrations, calligraphy, and maps he's done for *National Geographic,* Time-Life Books, and other national and international publications, displays and sells his paintings at the **Spring Woods Gallery and Willowbrook Garden** (19 Willowbrook Ln., Sullivan, 207/422-3007, www.springwoodsgallery.com or www.willowbrookgarden.com). Also filling the handsome modern gallery space are paintings by Ann Breeden. Be sure to allow time to meander through the shady sculpture garden, where there's even a playhouse for kids.

STEUBEN

Arthur Smith (Rogers Point Rd., Steuben, 207/546-3462) is the real thing when it comes to chainsaw carvings. He's an extremely talented folk artist who looks at a piece of wood and sees an animal in it. His carvings of great blue herons, eagles, wolves, porcupines, flamingos, and other creatures are incredibly detailed, and his wife, Marie, paints them in lifelike colors. Don't expect a fancy studio; much of the work can be viewed roadside.

Also in Steuben, but on the other end of the spectrum, is **Ray Carbone** (460 Pigeon Hill Rd., Steuben, 207/546-2170, www.raycarbonesculptor.com), whose masterful wood, stone, and bronze sculptures and fine furniture are definitely worth stopping to see and perhaps buy. Don't miss the granite sculptures and birdbaths in the garden.

Accommodations

There are no lodgings in the Schoodic section of the park, but within 15 minutes are pleasant inns and bed-and-breakfasts. A park campground is opening in 2015.

INNS AND BED-AND-BREAKFASTS
Schoodic Peninsula

Overlooking the Gouldsboro Peninsula's only sandy saltwater beach, ★ **Oceanside Meadows Inn** (Rte. 195/Corea Rd., Prospect Harbor, 207/963-5557, www.oceaninn.com, May-mid-Oct., $149-209) is an eco-conscious retreat on 200 acres with organic gardens, wildlife habitat, and walking trails. Fourteen guest rooms are split between the 1860s captain's house and the 1820 Shaw farmhouse next door. Rooms have a comfy, old-fashioned, shabby-chic decor. Note that there are no TVs or air-conditioning, and many of the bathrooms are tiny. Breakfast is a multicourse vegetarian event, usually featuring herbs and flowers from the inn's gardens. The husband-and-wife team Ben Walter and Sonja Sundaram, assisted by a loyal staff, seem to have thought of everything—hot drinks available all day, a guest fridge, beach toys, even detailed guides to the property's trails and habitats (great for entertaining kids). As if all that weren't enough, Sonja and Ben have totally restored the 1820 timber-frame barn out back—creating the **Oceanside Meadows Innstitute for the Arts and Sciences.** Local art hangs on the walls, and the 125-seat barn has a full schedule of concerts and lectures June-September on natural history, Native American traditions, and more, usually on Thursday nights. Some are free, some require tickets; all require reservations.

Oceanside Meadows is six miles off Route 1. There are no nearby restaurants, so expect to head out for lunch or dinner.

Watch lobster boats unload their catch at the dock opposite ★ **Elsa's Inn on the Harbor** (179 Main St., Prospect Harbor, 207/963-7571, www.elsasinn.com, $120-165). Jeffrey and Cynthia Alley, along with their daughter Megan and her husband, Glenn Moshier, have turned the home of Jeff's mother, Elsa, into a warm and welcoming inn. The family roots in the area go back more than 10 generations, so you're guaranteed to receive solid information on where to go and what to do. Every room has an ocean view, and Megan pampers guests with sumptuous linens, down duvets, terry robes, Wi-Fi, and a hearty hot breakfast. After a day exploring, settle into a rocker on the veranda and gaze over the boat-filled harbor out to Prospect Harbor Light. And afterward? Well, perhaps a lobster bake. With advance notice, Jeff will bring over some fresh lobster, and Megan will prepare a complete lobster dinner—corn on the cob, coleslaw, homemade rolls, and a seasonal dessert, all for about $25 per person, depending on market rates. Minimums apply, but if you're interested, ask Megan to see if other guests are too. It's open year-round.

Off the beaten path is Bob Travers and Barry Canner's **Black Duck Inn on Corea Harbor** (Crowley Island Rd., Corea, 207/963-2689, www.blackduck.com, May-mid-Oct., $140-200), literally the end of the line on the Gouldsboro Peninsula. Set on 12 acres in this timeless fishing village, the bed-and-breakfast has four handsomely decorated guest rooms and plenty of common space. Across the way, perched on the harbor's edge, are two little seasonal cottages, one rented by the day with a three-night minimum and one by the week. The inn and Corea are geared to wanderers, readers, and anyone seeking serenity. Rocky outcrops dot the property, and a nature trail meanders to a millpond; in early August, the blueberries are ready. If the fog socks in the area, the large parlor has comfortable chairs and loads of books.

Something of a categorical anomaly, the **Bluff House Inn** (57 Bluff House Rd., Gouldsboro, 207/963-7805, www.bluffinn. com, year-round, $95-175) is part motel, part hotel, part bed-and-breakfast. The 1980s building overlooks Frenchman Bay. Verandas wrap around the 1st and 2nd floors, so bring binoculars for sighting ospreys and bald eagles. Pine walls and flooring give a lodge feeling to the open 1st floor. Settle by one of the fireplaces or grab a seat by the window. Breakfast is continental buffet, usually with one hot entrée. The eight 2nd-floor rooms are decorated "country" fashion, with quilts on the very comfortable beds. (In hot weather, request a corner room.) Pet-friendly rooms are available for $15 per stay.

Just off the peninsula, and set well back from Route 1, **Acadia View Bed and Breakfast** (175 Rte. 1, Gouldsboro,

866/963-7457, www.acadiaview.com, $145-175) tops a bluff with views across Frenchman Bay to the peaks of Mount Desert and a path down to the shorefront. Pat and Jim Close built the oceanfront house as a bed-and-breakfast that opened in 2005. It's filled with antique treasures from the Closes' former life in Connecticut. Each of the four guest rooms has a private deck. The Route 1 location is convenient to everything. It's open year-round.

Hancock and Sullivan

Although **Ironbound** (1513 U.S. 1, Hancock, 207/422-3395 www.ironboundinn.com, $150-175), a five-room country inn located above the restaurant of the same name, is right on Route 1, when you're on the garden-view balconies, or on the lawn out back, you're oblivious to the traffic whizzing by. Rooms are bright and airy and have Wi-Fi, Bose Wave radios, and air-conditioning, but no TV. Continental breakfast, including bagels with Sullivan Harbor Farms smoked salmon, is included. Guests have use of a comfy sitting area downstairs, adjacent to the restaurant. The inn adjoins Crabtree Neck Conservation Trust lands, laced with trails and a pond.

Follow Hancock Point Road 4.8 miles

Elsa's Inn on the Harbor overlooks working wharves in Prospect Harbor.

south of Route 1 to the three-story, gray-blue **Crocker House Country Inn** (967 Point Rd., Hancock, 207/422-6806, www.crockerhouse. com, $125-165), Rich and Liz Malaby's antidote to Bar Harbor's summer traffic. Built as a summer hotel in 1884, the inn underwent rehabbing a century later, but it retains a delightfully old-fashioned air despite now offering Wi-Fi and having air-conditioning. Breakfast is included. A few bicycles are available; clay tennis courts are nearby. If you're arriving by boat, request a mooring. The inn's dining room, open nightly for dinner in season, is a draw in itself. Some rooms are pet-friendly.

Sustainable living is the focus of Karen and Ed Curtis's peaceful ★ **Three Pines Bed and Breakfast** (274 East Side Rd., Hancock, 207/460-7595, www.threepines-bandb.com, year-round, $100-125), fronting on Sullivan Harbor, just below the Reversing Falls. Their quiet, off-the-grid, 40-acre oceanfront organic farm faces Sullivan Harbor and is home to rare-breed chickens and sheep, ducks, and a llama, as well as a large organic garden, berry bushes, an orchard, and greenhouses. Photovoltaic cells provide electricity, and appliances are primarily propane powered; satellite technology operates the phone, TV, and Wi-Fi systems. Two inviting guest rooms have private entrances and water views. A full vegetarian breakfast (with fresh eggs from the farm) is served. Bicycles and a canoe are available. You can walk or pedal along an abandoned railway line down to the point, and you can launch a canoe or kayak from the back—or is it the front?—yard. Children are welcome; pets are a possibility.

Machias native Dottie Mace operated a bed-and-breakfast in Virginia before returning to Maine to open **Taunton River Bed & Breakfast** (19 Taunton Dr., Sullivan, 207/422-2070, www.tauntonriverbandb.com, $115-125) in a 19th-century farmhouse with river views. Rooms are carefully decorated; they're warm and inviting, formal without being stuffy. Two of the three guest rooms share a bath. A full breakfast and Wi-Fi are included in the rates. It would be easy to spend the day just sitting on the porch swing, but it's an easy pedal or drive to local art galleries. The inn is just a stone's throw off Route 1, so traffic might bother the noise sensitive.

About 12 miles east of Ellsworth is the oceanfront **Island View Inn** (12 Miramar Ave., Sullivan, 207/422-3031, www.islandviewinn.net, $155-175); its name is the height of understatement. Out front are the peaks of Mount Desert across Frenchman Bay. Four of the six rooms, all with decks, capture the view from this updated 1889 summer home that evokes the easy elegance of days gone by. Many of the furnishings are original. The inn has a private beach, but the water is terminally chilly. A full breakfast is included.

MOTELS AND COTTAGES
Schoodic Peninsula

Roger and Pearl Barto, whose family roots in this region go back five generations, have four rental accommodations on their Henry Cove oceanfront property, ★ **Main Stay Cottages** (66 Sargent St., Winter Harbor, 207/963-2601, www.mainstaycottages-rvpark. com, $90-125). Most unusual is the small, one-bedroom Boat House, which has stood since the 1880s. It hangs over the harbor, with views to Mark Island Light, and you can hear the water gurgling below at high tide (but it is cramped, be forewarned). Other options include a very comfortable efficiency cottage, a one-bedroom cottage, a 2nd-floor suite with a private entrance, and a four-bedroom house ($250/night). All have big decks and fabulous views over the lobster boat-filled harbor; watch for the eagles that frequently soar overhead. Main Stay is on the Island Explorer bus route and just a short walk from where the Bar Harbor Ferry docks.

Simple and rustic, but charming in a sweet old-fashioned way, **Albee's Shorehouse Cottages** (Rte. 186, Prospect Harbor, 207/963-2336 or 800/963-2336, www. theshorehouse.com, May-mid-Oct., $92-141) is a cluster of 10 vintage cottages decorated with braided rugs, fresh flowers, and other homey touches. They're spaced out along the shoreline and in on the lawns amid gorgeous gardens and mature shade trees. Two things make this place special: the waterfront location—and it's truly waterfront; many of the cottages are just a couple of feet from the high-tide mark—and the management. Owner Richard Rieth goes out of his way to make guests feel welcome. If you're staying a week, pick up lobsters and say what time you want dinner, and they'll be cooked and delivered to your cottage. He's slowly fixing up the cottages, but these will never be fancy; if you're fussy, go elsewhere. In peak season, preference is given to Saturday-Saturday rentals, but shorter stays are often available. Wi-Fi is available throughout, and dogs are welcome. No credit cards.

Hancock and Sullivan

The views to Mount Desert are dreamy from **Edgewater Cabins** (25 Benvenuto Ave., Sullivan, 207/422-6414 May 15-Oct. 15, 603/472-8644 rest of year, www.edgewatercabins.com, $595-995/week), a colony of seven housekeeping cottages on a spit of land jutting into Frenchman Bay. The well-tended four-acre property has both sunrise and sunset water views, big trees for shade, and lawns rolling to the shorefront. Stays of at least three nights ($95-175/night) are possible, when there's availability.

Every accommodation at **Flander's Bay Cabins** (22 Harbor View Dr./U.S. 1, Sullivan, 207/422-6408, www.flandersbay.com) has views to Cadillac Mountain over Flanders Bay, and some are truly waterfront. The rustic one- and two-bedroom cabins ($525-695 weekly) have kitchens. Fancier is a pet-friendly, three-bedroom chalet ($995 weekly). Best is the shorefront four-bedroom house ($1,895 weekly). There's on-site access for kayaks and canoes as well as fishing and swimming. This property is adjacent to and run by the same family as Mountainview Campground.

CAMPING
Winter Harbor

The new **Schoodic Woods Campground** is expected to open in 2015 on an approximately 1,400-acre property over which Acadia National Park holds a conservation easement. It's sited about a mile south of Route 186, north of the Frazer Point Picnic Area. The facility has been designed and constructed to meet National Park Service standards, and Acadia National Park will operate the campground. Plans call for about 100 sites,

Albee's Shorehouse Cottages are simple and rustic.

including 12 remote walk-in sites, 34 RV sites with water and electricity, 50 tenting sites, and two group sites; a welcome center; and an amphitheater with National Park Service programming. Hiking trails will connect to Schoodic Head, and nonmotorized multiuse paths will link the east and west sides of the peninsula. As of 2016, reservations will be available through the National Park Service reservation system (877/444-6777 or 518/885-3639 international, www.recreation.gov, credit or debit card required); prior to then (the campground is slated to open in July 2015), consult the park (207/288-3338, www.nps.gov/acad) for information regarding rates and reservations.

The Bartos, owners of **Main Stay Cottages** (66 Sargent St., Winter Harbor, 207/963-2601, www.mainstaycottages-rvpark.com, $50), have added a 10-site campground overlooking Henry Cove. It's designed for self-contained RVs, as there are no restrooms or showers on-site; sewer, water, electric, and Wi-Fi are available.

Sullivan

Sites at **Mountainview Campground** (22 Harbor View Dr./Rte. 1, Sullivan, 207/422-6408, www.flandersbay.com, May-Oct.,

$26-40) are spread throughout an oceanfront field, so there's not a lot of privacy. The best sites edge the Frenchman Bay shorefront and are reserved for tents and small campers using 20-amp service. Other sites can accommodate full hookups with 30-50-amp service. Hot showers are free, and if you stay six days, your seventh day is free.

Donnell Pond Public Reserved Land

A handful of authorized primitive campsites can be found on **Tunk Lake** (southwestern corner) and **Donnell Pond** (at Schoodic Beach and Redman's Beach), all accessible on foot or by boat. Each has a table, a fire ring, and a nearby pit toilet. Many of the sites are on the lakefront. All are first-come, first-served with no fees or permits required; they are snapped up quickly on midsummer weekends. You can camp elsewhere within this public land, except in day-use areas, but fires are not permitted at unofficial sites.

Steuben

Since 1958 the Ayr family has welcomed campers at its quiet, well-off-the-beaten-path property on Joy Cove. With a convenient location 15 minutes from Petit Manan

campsite on the shores of Donnell Pond

National Wildlife Refuge and 20 minutes from Schoodic Point, **Mainayr Campground** (321 Village Rd., Steuben, 207/542-2690, www.mainayr.com, late May-mid-Oct., $30-33) has 35 tenting and RV sites, five with full hookups. Also on the premises are a playground, a laundry, a beach for tidal swimming, clamming flats, a grassy launch area for kayaks and canoes, a camp store, berries for picking, and fresh lobsters.

Food

There's no food in the park's Schoodic section, so if you're planning a picnic, you'll need to stock up along the way—in Winter Harbor or Prospect Harbor—if you haven't done so earlier. Nor are there a lot of restaurant options on the Schoodic Peninsula itself. You won't go hungry, but a little advance planning can go a long way.

Make a point to attend one of the many **public suppers** held throughout the summer in this area and in so many other rural corners of Maine. Typically benefiting a worthy cause, these usually feature beans or spaghetti or the serendipity of potluck. Everyone saves room for the homemade pies. Notices of such suppers are usually posted on public bulletin boards in country stores and in libraries, on signs in front of churches, and at other places that people gather. Local newspapers also often detail such events.

LOCAL FLAVORS
Schoodic Peninsula
Pick up veggies, meats, eggs, cheeses, and handcrafted fiber products as well as jams, preserves, and baked goods at the **Winter Harbor Farmers Market** (parking lot, corner of Newman St. and Rte. 186, Winter Harbor, 9am-noon Tues. late June-early Sept.).

J.M. Gerrish Café & Ice Cream Parlour (352 Main St., Winter Harbor, 7am-2:30pm) has had its ups and downs, but locals are confident that the century-old store is now back in local and reliable hands. It's open for breakfast and lunch, and has a classic ice cream counter along with a small penny candy section.

J.M. Gerrish Café & Ice Cream Parlour

Two Sisters Café & Deli (Corner Rtes. 186 & 195, Prospect Harbor, 207/963-2000, 11am-8pm daily) is the latest incarnation of this local go-to for pizza, subs, and fried foods.

Stock up on gourmet goodies at **Grindstone Neck of Maine** (311 Newman St./Rte. 186, Winter Harbor, 207/963-7347 or 866/831-8734, www.grindstoneneck.com), just north of downtown Winter Harbor, which earns high marks for its smoked salmon, shellfish, spreads and pâtés, and smoked cheeses, all made without preservatives or artificial ingredients. Also available are fresh fish, wine, and frozen foods for campers.

At 150-acre certified-organic **Darthia Farm** (51 Darthia Farm Rd., Gouldsboro, 207/963-7771, www.darthiafarm.com), check out Hattie's Shed for Cindy's outstanding ikat weavings and work by half a dozen other craftspeople. The **Farm Store** (8am-5pm Mon.-Fri., 8am-noon Sat. June-Sept.) sells fresh produce as well as herbal salves and vinegars, hand-spun hand-dyed yarn, and other products. Sleigh rides are available in the fall and winter.

German and Italian presses, Portuguese corks, and Maine fruit all contribute to the creation of Bob and Kathe Bartlett's award-winning dinner and dessert wines at **Bartlett Maine Estate Winery** (175 Chicken Mill Pond Rd., Gouldsboro, 207/546-2408, www.bartlettwinery.com, 10am-5pm Mon.-Sat. June-Oct., or by appointment), just north of the Schoodic Peninsula. Founded in 1982, the winery produces more than 20,000 gallons annually in a handsome wood-and-stone building designed by the Bartletts. Not ones to rest on their many laurels, in 2008 the Bartletts introduced grape wines, and more recently, the **Spirits of Maine Distillery.** There are no tours, but you're welcome to sample for a small tasting fee. Reserve wines and others of limited vintage are sold only on-site. A sculpture garden patio makes a nice spot to relax. Bartlett's is 0.5 mile south of Route 1 in Gouldsboro.

Hancock, Sullivan, and Franklin

Defying its name, **Sullivan Harbor Smokehouse** (U.S. 1, Hancock, 207/422-3735 or 800/422-4014, www.sullivanharbor-farm.com) has moved to spacious, modern new digs in Hancock. Big interior windows allow visitors to see into the production facility and watch the action.

Have a hankering for Korean? Sonye Carroll and family serve *bi-bim-bahp, boul-koh-kee,* barbecued ribs, and kimchee, along with burgers and dogs, homemade doughnuts, and Gifford's ice cream at **YU Takeout** (674 Rte. 1, Hancock, 207/667-0711, www.yutake-out.com).

Hikers, especially, frequent **Maple Knoll Pizza** (138 Blackwoods Rd./Rte. 182, Franklin, 207/565-2068), a hole-in-the-wall on the edge of in-town Franklin serving pizzas, subs, calzones, and sandwiches using family recipes rooted in the old country.

Take Route 182 to Route 200 (Eastbrook Rd.) and go 1.6 miles to family-operated **Shalom Orchard Organic Winery** (158 Eastbrook Rd., Franklin, 207/565-2312, www.shalomorchard.com). The certified-organic farm is well off the beaten path but worth a visit for its organic fruit and wines as well as for its yarns, pelts, fleece, and especially the views of Frenchman Bay from the hilltop.

FAMILY FAVORITES
Schoodic Peninsula

The best place for grub and gossip in Winter Harbor is **Chase's Restaurant** (193 Main St., Winter Harbor, 207/963-7171, 7am-8pm daily, 7am-2pm Sun.), a seasoned no-frills booth-and-counter operation.

Shoot pool, play darts or horseshoes, watch the game on TV, sip a cold drink, and savor a burger at the family-friendly **The Pickled Wrinkle** (9 E. Schoodic Dr., at the intersection with Rte. 186, Birch Harbor, 207/963-7916, from 11am daily). Don't be fooled by the humble appearance, new owners here know their way around the kitchen and opt for local and organic whenever possible. That said, the overall atmosphere is more bar than restaurant. Dine early, especially if accompanied by children. There's often live music.

Hancock and Sullivan

Don't be put off by "Wilbur," the lobster sculpture outside **Ruth & Wimpy's Kitchen** (792 Rte. 1, Hancock, 207/422-3723, www.ruthandwimpys.com, 11am-9pm Mon.-Sat.); you'll probably see a crowd as well. This family-fare standby serves hefty sandwiches, lobster prepared 30 ways, pizza, pasta, and steak. Prices begin around $3.25 for a cheeseburger and climb to about $30 for a twin lobster shore dinner. Antique license plates and collections of miniature cars and trucks accent the interior. It's five miles east of Ellsworth, close to the Hancock Point turnoff.

Good food served by friendly folks is what pulls the locals into ★ **Chester Pike's Galley** (2336 U.S. 1, Sullivan, 207/422-8200, 6am-2pm Tues.-Thurs. and Sat., 6am-2pm and 4:30pm-8:30pm Fri., 7am-2pm Sun., $6-15). The prices are low, and the portions are big. If you're on a diet, don't even *look* at the glass case filled with fresh-baked pies, cakes, and cookies. Go early if you want to snag one of the homemade doughnuts (and order dessert first). It's also open Friday nights for a fish fry with free seconds.

Tracey's Seafood (2719 Rte. 1, Sullivan, 207/422-9072) doesn't look like much from the road, but don't be fooled. The Tracey family harvests the clams and catches the lobsters, shucks and picks, and dishes out ultra-fresh lobster, chowders, and fried seafood. There's a takeout window and picnic tables on the lawn as well as a dining room with waitress service. Portions are big, prices are low—$4 burgers, two-fer lobster rolls (usually around $12-14, but I've seen them as low as $10), and weekend fish fries and clam fries with free seconds for $10.95. Don't miss the homemade pies. For inside dining, BYOB.

CASUAL DINING
Schoodic Peninsula
Ask about **Bunker's Wharf**, located

overlooking Wonsqueak Harbor on the two-way section of East Schoodic Drive. It closed in 2014, but locals are hopeful it will reopen.

The Fisherman's Inn (7 Newman St./ Rte. 186, Winter Harbor, 207/963-5585, 4:30pm-9pm daily late May-mid-Oct.) has been an institution in these parts since 1947. Kathy Johnson runs the front of the house; her husband, Carl, is the chef. He's also the brain behind Grindstone Neck of Maine, the smoked-seafood operation just up the road, and diners are welcomed with a sample of smoked-salmon spread and a cheese spread. That's followed up with Carl's focaccia bread and the house dipping sauce, a tasty blend of Romano cheese, fresh garlic, roasted red pepper, and parsley with olive oil. And that all comes before any appetizers. Seafood is the specialty here, and there's a good chance that the guy at the neighboring booth caught your lobster or fish. Asian influences are evident too. Entrées range $18-30, and some dishes can top that given seasonal market rates, but it's easy to make a meal from starters. If you're on a tight budget, aim for an early dinner. Early-bird specials, served 4:30pm-5:30pm, are around $14. Carl's daughter-in-law Nui operates a food cart out front, serving meat-packed lobster rolls and gourmet hot dogs for lunch (11am-3pm).

Hancock

In 2013, chef Mike Poirier and baker Alice Letcher opened **The Salt Box** (1161 Rte. 1, 207/422-9900, www.saltboxmaine.com, 5pm-9:30pm Thurs.-Sat., 9am-1pm Sun., $25-27), in a log building set back from the road, and they quickly earned a following. The decor is gently rustic, the food is sophisticated yet approachable and focused on fresh seasonal ingredients, and the service is excellent. Reservations are advised.

Ironbound (1513 U.S. 1, 207/422-3395, www.ironboundinn.com, from 5pm daily mid-June-mid-Oct., $12-33), opened in 2014 by the owners of Sullivan Harbor Farm, welcomes guests with a menu that ranges from sandwiches and burgers to duck breast and rib eye steak. A huge brick hearth adorned with copper pots anchors one end of the main dining room. The atmosphere is casual, with wood floors and undressed tables. The fare complements the setting, with ingredients sourced locally whenever possible. The adjacent bar, The Hop, is popular with locals, who come for the Attitude Adjustment Hour 5pm-6pm, when local oysters are featured.

Steuben

Long before farm-to-table became mainstream, Jessie King and Alva Lowe had earned a reputation for garden-fresh fare at **Kitchen Garden Restaurant** (35 Village Rd., 207/546-4269, www.thekitchengarden-restaurant.com, $17-30, no credit cards), based in their 1860s Cape-style home. When they closed in 2003, locals mourned, but in 2011 the talented duo reopened it, again drawing from their gardens as well as local, mostly organic sources to create authentic Jamaican fare, such as jerk chicken and curried goat, as well as worldly flavored seafood and vegetarian entrées. Reservations are required, and guests are requested to order their meals in advance. Bring your own wine or beer ($5 bottle fee); call for current days of operation.

When the popular Le Domain closed its doors, Chef Christopher Meyell opened ★ **Christopher's at Eagle Hill** (59 Eagle Hill Rd., 207/546-1219, www.eaglehill.us/christophers, 5pm-8pm Tues.-Sat., 10am-1pm Sun., $15-32), bringing his French American fusion fare to this remote fine-dining restaurant in a woodland setting at the Eagle Hill Institute. You might begin with a duck confit salad or foie gras and move on to entrées such as beef tenderloin, vegan meatballs, or ahi tuna. Pair dinner with attending an Eagle Hill lecture.

FINE DINING
Hancock

The unpretentious dining rooms at the ★ **Crocker House Country Inn** (967 Point Rd., Hancock Point, 207/422-6806, www.crockerhouse.com, 5:30pm-9pm daily May 1-Oct. 31, 5:30pm-8:30pm Fri.-Sun. Apr. and Nov.-Dec., entrées $25-33) provide a setting for well-prepared continental fare with flair, crafted from fresh and local ingredients; reservations are essential as this is one of the area's most consistent and popular dining spots. On Friday nights, a jazz trio provides background music.

One of the more dependable dining experiences in the area is **Chipper's** (1239 U.S. 1, 207/422-8238, www.chippersrestaurant.com, 5pm-9pm Wed.-Sun.). Owner Chipper Butterwick opened his popular restaurant in 1995 and expanded the simple cape-style building in 2010, adding a pub. The restaurant's wide-ranging menu includes rack of lamb and even chateaubriand, but the emphasis is on seafood; the crab cakes earn rave reviews. Meals include a sampling of tasty haddock chowder and a salad, but save room for the homemade ice cream for dessert. Entrées are in the $17-33 range, but some appetizer-salad combos provide budget options, and burgers and subs are available in the pub.

LOBSTER
Corea

You'd be hard-pressed to find a better place to enjoy a lobster than the ★ **Wharf Gallery & Grill** (13 Gibbs Ln., Corea, 207/963-2633, www.coreawharfgallery.com), an eat-on-the-wharf food stand overlooking dreamy, lobster boat-filled Corea Harbor. The menu includes lobster rolls, lobster grilled cheese (trust me, try it), crab claws, hot dogs, sausages, and ice cream.

Information and Services

ACADIA NATIONAL PARK

Information about Acadia National Park on the Schoodic Peninsula is available at the welcome center at the **Schoodic Woods Campground** (opening summer 2015) and **Rockefeller Hall** on the Schoodic Institute campus, both on the Schoodic Loop. On Mount Desert Island, info is available at the park's **Hulls Cove Visitors Center** and at the **Thompson Island Information Center,** at the head of the island.

To plan ahead, see the Acadia website (www.nps.gov/acad), where you can download a Schoodic map. To see the Island Explorer bus schedule for Schoodic as well as all of Mount Desert Island, visit www.exploreacadia.com. The Bar Harbor Ferry schedule is at www.barharborferry.com.

REGIONAL INFORMATION

For advance information about eastern Hancock County, contact the **Schoodic Peninsula Chamber of Commerce** (207/963-7658, www.acadia-schoodic.org). Another source for advance information is **Downeast & Acadia Regional Tourism** (207/546-3600 or 888/665-3278, www. downeastacadia.com). Also covering the area is the **Ellsworth Area Chamber of Commerce** (207/667-5584, www.ellsworthchamber.org).

To plan ahead, see the Acadia website (www.nps.gov/acad), where you can download a Schoodic map.

For information on the National and Maine Scenic Byways in this region, visit www.byways.org or www.exploremaine.org/byways.

LIBRARIES

Check out **Dorcas Library** (Rte. 186, Prospect Harbor, 207/963-4027, www.dorcas.lib.me.us) or **Winter Harbor Public Library** (18 Chapel Ln., Winter Harbor, 207/963-7556, www.winterharbor.lib.me.us), in the 1888 beach-stone and fieldstone Channing Chapel.

The inviting octagonal **Hancock Point Library** (Hancock Point Rd., Hancock Point, 207/422-6400, summer only) was formed in

Find out what's happening in Hancock at the Hancock Point Library.

SCHOODIC PENINSULA
INFORMATION AND SERVICES

Scenic Byways and Trails

The Schoodic region boasts not one but two designated scenic byways: the **Schoodic National Scenic Byway,** which wraps around the peninsula, and the **Black Woods Scenic Byway,** an inland blue highway cutting through the Donnell Pond Public Reserved Land. If time permits, drive at least one of these routes. Ideally you'd do both, because the scenery differs greatly. Best idea yet: Connect the two via Route 1, creating a loop that includes lakes and forests, mountains and fields, ocean and rocky coast. If you have only one day to explore this region, this route takes in the best of it. In early to mid-October, when the fall foliage is at its peak colors, the vistas are especially stunning.

The 29-mile Schoodic National Scenic Byway stretches from Sullivan on Route 1 to Gouldsboro and then south on Route 186 and around the Schoodic Peninsula, ending in Prospect Harbor. A detailed guide is available at www.schoodicbyway.org. Other information is available at www. byways.org. There is interpretive signage, explaining sights and history, along the route.

The 12.5-mile Black Woods Scenic Byway meanders along Route 182 inland of Route 1, from Franklin to Cherryfield, edging lakes and passing through small villages. You'll find access to trailheads and boat launches at Donnell Pond and Tunk Lake. Although Cherryfield is beyond' the Schoodic region, it's a beautiful town to visit, filled with stately Victorian homes. It's also the self-proclaimed wild blueberry capital of the world. Maps and information are available at www. blackwoodsbyway.org.

Also running through the Acadia region is the **Downeast Fisheries Trail** (www.downeas-tfisheriestrail.org), which follows Maine's coastline from Penobscot Bay to Cobscook Bay. The mapped trail comprises 45 sites celebrating Maine's maritime heritage and marine resources. Marked sites, including roughly two dozen in the Acadia region, allow you to delve into Maine's fishing and maritime heritage by visiting fish hatcheries, aquaculture facilities, active fishing harbors, processing plants, working wharves and piers, and related historic sites. You can request a printed copy of the map by calling 207/581-1435.

1899. More than a library, it's a center for village activities. Check the bulletin boards by the entrance to find out what's happening when.

GETTING THERE AND AROUND

Winter Harbor is about 25 miles via Routes 1 and 186 from Ellsworth. It's about 20 miles or 30 minutes to Milbridge, on the Down East Coast.

Although you can get here by passenger ferry from Bar Harbor or bus from Ellsworth, you'll need a car to explore beyond the part of the Schoodic Peninsula that's served by the Island Explorer bus.

Car

To reach the Schoodic region from Ellsworth, continue north on Route 1 from where it splits with Route 3. Stay on Route 1 for about 16 miles, through Hancock and Sullivan, until you reach Gouldsboro. From Route 1 in Gouldsboro, the park entrance is eight miles. Take Route 186 south to Winter Harbor. Continue through town, heading east, then turn right onto Moore Road and continue to the park entrance sign, just before the stone-lined causeway over Mosquito Harbor.

To reach the park boundary from Bar Harbor, take Route 3 north to the head of Mount Desert Island, then across Mount Desert Narrows to Trenton. The usual route is to continue to a congested intersection at the edge of Ellsworth, where you'll pick up Route 1 north (turn right) and continue as above. But you can avoid some of the traffic congestion on Route 3 in Trenton by ducking east via Route 204 toward Lamoine and its state park, and then back up to Route 1 via the Mud Creek Road.

Passenger Ferry

Although Winter Harbor is roughly 43 miles or 1.15 hours from Bar Harbor by car, it's only about 7 miles by water.

The seasonal passenger-only **Bar Harbor Ferry** (207/288-2984, www.barharborferry.com, round-trip $32 adults, $22 children, $7 bicycle) operates at least four times daily mid-June-late September between Bar Harbor and Winter Harbor, and coordinates with the free **Island Explorer** (www.exploreacadia.com) bus's summertime Schoodic route, Route 8.

Since the ferry's summer schedule is coordinated with the Island Explorer bus's summertime Schoodic route, you can board the ferry in Bar Harbor, pick up the bus at the dock in Winter Harbor, and be shuttled along the Schoodic Loop. Stop where you like for a picnic or a hike, and then board a later bus. Take the last bus back to the ferry and return to Bar Harbor. It makes for a super car-free excursion.

A ferry alternative is **Winter Harbor Water Taxi & Tours** (207/963-7007, www.winterharborwatertaxiandtours.com). Captain Wes Shaw will squire you around Schoodic's waters or over to Bar Harbor for $75 per hour, covering up to six passengers.

Bus

The free **Island Explorer** (www.exploreacadia.com), Route 8, covers the lower part of the peninsula, from Winter Harbor through Prospect Harbor, late June-August. The bus circulates roughly once an hour, with a schedule that coordinates with the ferry.

A passenger ferry connects Winter Harbor with Bar Harbor.

Blue Hill Peninsula

The Blue Hill Peninsula, once dubbed "The Fertile Crescent," is unique. Few other Maine locales harbor such a high concentration of artisans, musicians, and on-their-feet retirees juxtaposed with topflight wooden-boat builders, lobstermen, and umpteenth-generation Mainers. Perhaps surprisingly, the mix seems to work.

The peninsula dangles into Penobscot Bay, anchored by the towns of Bucksport to the west and Ellsworth to the east and tethered via bridge to Deer Isle at its tip. It comprises several enclaves with markedly distinctive personalities—artsy Blue Hill, historic Castine, quiet Orland, boaty Brooklin, rural Brooksville, and sedate Sedgwick— all stitched together by a network of narrow, winding country highways and byways. Thanks to the mapmaker-challenging coastline and a handful of freshwater ponds and rivers, there's a view of water around nearly every bend.

You can watch the sun set from atop Blue Hill Mountain; tour the home of the fascinating Jonathan Fisher; stroll through the village of Castine, charming verging on precious, whose streets are lined with dowager-like homes; visit *WoodenBoat* magazine's world headquarters in tiny Brooklin, the self-proclaimed wooden boat-building capital of the world; and browse top-notch studios and galleries salted throughout the peninsula. Mosey over to Cape Rosier, which is—if possible—even more off the beaten path, and visit the homestead of back-to-the-landers Helen and Scott Nearing, and the nearby Four Season Farm, where organic guru Eliot Coleman sets the trend, and hike the underutilized trails of the Holbrook Island Sanctuary. Venture a bit inland of Route 1 and you'll find lovely lakes for paddling and swimming and another hill to hike.

After weaving your way down the Blue Hill Peninsula and crossing the soaring pray-as-you-go bridge to Little Deer Isle, you've entered the realm of island living. Sure, bridges and causeways connect the points, but the farther down you drive, the

---

Previous: Castine's harbor; early morning low tide in Blue Hill. **Above:** local oysters ready to be sampled at Dennett's Wharf.

Highlights

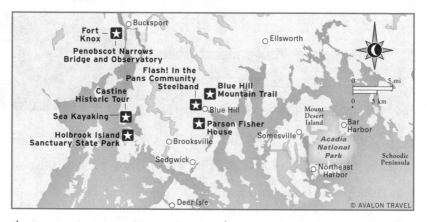

© AVALON TRAVEL

★ **Fort Knox:** A good restoration, frequent events, and secret passages make this late 19th-century fort one of Maine's best (page 174).

★ **Penobscot Narrows Bridge and Observatory:** On a clear day, the views from the 447-foot-high tower, one of only three bridge observatories in the world, extend from Mount Katahdin to Cadillac Mountain (page 175).

★ **Parson Fisher House:** More than just another historic house, the Parson Fisher House is a remarkable testimony to one man's ingenuity (page 179).

★ **Blue Hill Mountain Trail:** It's a relatively easy hike for fabulous 360-degree views from the summit of Blue Hill Mountain (page 181).

★ **Holbrook Island Sanctuary State Park:** Varied hiking trails and great birding are the rewards for finding this off-the-beaten-path preserve (page 188).

★ **Flash! In the Pans Community Steelband:** Close your eyes and you might think you're on a Caribbean island when you hear this phenomenal steel-pan band (page 190).

★ **Castine Historic Tour:** A turbulent history detailed on signs throughout town makes Castine an irresistible place to tour on foot or by bike (page 197).

★ **Sea Kayaking:** Hook up with "Kayak Karen" in Castine for a tour (page 198).

Blue Hill Peninsula

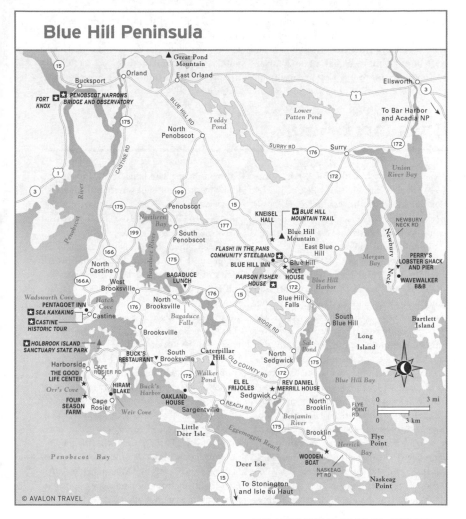

more removed from civilization you'll feel. The pace slows; the population dwindles. Fishing and lobstering are the mainstays; lobster boats rest near many homes, and trap fences edge properties. If your ultimate destination is the section of Acadia National Park on Isle au Haut, the drive down Deer Isle to Stonington serves to help disconnect you from the mainland. To reach the park's acreage on Isle au Haut, you'll board the Isle au Haut ferryboat for the trip down Merchant Row to the island.

PLANNING YOUR TIME

To truly enjoy this region, you'll want to spend at least 3-4 days here, perhaps splitting your lodging between two or three locations. The region is designed for leisurely exploring; you won't be able to zip from one location to another. Traveling along the winding roads, discovering galleries and country stores, and lodging at traditional inns are all part of the experience.

Arts fans will want to concentrate their efforts in Blue Hill, Deer Isle, and Stonington.

Outdoor-oriented folks should consider Deer Isle, Stonington, or Castine as a base for sea kayaking or exploring the area preserves. For architecture and history buffs, Castine is a must.

No visit to this region is complete without at least a cruise by—if not a visit to—Isle au Haut, an offshore island that's home to a remote section of Acadia National Park. Allow at least a few hours for a ride on the mail boat, but if you can afford the time, spend a full day hiking the park's trails. Don't forget to pack food and water.

Bucksport Area

It's a stretch to consider Bucksport (pop. 4,924) part of the Blue Hill Peninsula, let alone include it in the Acadia region, but it is the gateway to it all, and the area has some sights worth a look-see and reasonably priced accommodations and campsites.

The new Penobscot Narrows Bridge provides an elegant entry to Bucksport, a longtime rough-and-ready river port and papermaking town that's slowly gentrifying. Bucksport is no upstart. Native Americans first gravitated to these Penobscot River shores in summer, finding a rich source of salmon for food and grasses for basket making. In 1763 the area was officially settled by Colonel Jonathan Buck, a Massachusetts Bay Colony surveyor who modestly named it "Buckstown" and organized a booming shipping business here. His remains are interred in a local cemetery, where his tombstone bears the distinct outline of a woman's leg; this is allegedly the result of a curse by a witch Buck ordered executed, but in fact it's probably a flaw in the granite. Most townsfolk prefer not to discuss the matter, but the myth refuses to die—and it has immortalized a man whose name might otherwise have been consigned to musty history books. The monument is across Route 1 from the Hannaford supermarket, on the corner of Hinks Street. Papermaking came to Bucksport in 1930, and the huge mill on the riverfront closed in 2014. The riverfront walkway provides great views of Fort Knox.

Just south of Bucksport, at the bend in the Penobscot River, Verona Island (pop. 544) is best known as the mile-long link between Prospect and Bucksport. Prospect is home to the Penobscot Narrows Bridge and Observatory and Fort Knox, guarding the mouth of the Penobscot River. Just before you cross the bridge from Verona to Bucksport, hang a left, then a quick right to a small municipal park with a boat launch and broad views of Bucksport Harbor (and the paper mill). Admiral Robert Peary's Arctic exploration vessel, the *Roosevelt,* was built on this site in 1905 and used in his final 1908 expedition to the North Pole. A scale model can be viewed in the Buck Memorial Library.

Route 1 east of Bucksport leads to Orland (pop. 2,225), whose idyllic setting on the banks of the Narramissic River makes it a magnet for shutterbugs. It's also the site of a unique service organization called H.O.M.E. (Homeworkers Organized for More Employment). East Orland (officially part of Orland) claims the Craig Brook National Fish Hatchery and Great Pond Mountain (you can't miss it, jutting from the landscape on the left as you drive east on Route 1).

SIGHTS
★ Fort Knox
Looming over Bucksport Harbor, the *other* **Fort Knox** (Rte. 174, Prospect, 207/469-7719, www.fortknox.maineguide.com, 9am-sunset May 1-Oct. 31, $4.50 nonresident adults, $3 Maine residents, $1 ages 5-11) is a 125-acre state historic site just off U.S. 1. Named for Major General Henry Knox, George Washington's first secretary of war, the sprawling granite fort was begun in 1844. Built to protect the upper Penobscot

River from attack, it was never finished and never saw battle. Still, it was, as guide Kathy Williamson said, "very well thought out and planned, and that may have been its best defense." Begin your visit at the Visitor and Education Center, operated by the Friends of Fort Knox, a nonprofit group that has partnered with the state to preserve and interpret the fort. Guided tours are sometimes available. The fort's distinguishing features include two complete Rodman cannons. Wear rubberized shoes and bring a flashlight to explore the underground passages; you can set the kids loose. The fort hosts Civil War reenactments several times each summer as well as a Medieval Tournament, a paranormal-psychic fair, and other events (check the website). The Halloween Fright at the Fort is a ghoulish event for the brave. The grounds are accessible all year. Bring a picnic; views over the river to Bucksport are fabulous.

★ Penobscot Narrows Bridge and Observatory

On a clear day, do not miss the **Penobscot Narrows Bridge and Observatory** (9am-5pm daily late May-June and Sept.-Nov. 1, 9am-6pm daily July-Aug., $7 nonresident adults, $5 Maine resident adults, $3 ages 5-11,

includes fort admission), accessible via Fort Knox. The three-deck observatory caps the bridge's 447-foot-high west tower, with the observatory's top floor top sited at 420 feet above the Penobscot River. It's one of only three such structures in the world and the only one in the United States. You'll zip up in an elevator, and when the doors open, you're facing a wall of glass—it's a bit of a shocker, and downright terrifying for anyone with a serious fear of heights. Ascend two more flights (an elevator is available) and you're in the glass-walled observatory; the views on a clear day extend from Mount Katahdin to Mount Desert Island. Even when it's hazy, it's still a neat experience.

Alamo Theatre

Phoenixlike, the 1916 **Alamo Theatre** (85 Main St., Bucksport, 207/469-0924 or 800/639-1636, event line 207/469-6910, www.alamotheatre.org, 9am-4pm Mon.-Fri. year-round) has been digitally retrofitted for a new life. It shows not only contemporary films but also indie and local ones. Before each feature, it screens archival shorts about New England produced or revived by the unique **Northeast Historic Film,** which is headquartered here. NHF has more than 12 million feet of film

An observatory caps one of the towers of the Penobscot Narrows Bridge.

in its archives, including rarities. Celebrities ranging from Ken Burns to Oprah Winfry have requested footage for projects. Stop in, survey the restoration, visit the displays (donation requested), and browse the Alamo Theatre Store for antique postcards, T-shirts, toys, and reasonably priced videos on ice harvesting, lumberjacks, maple sugaring, and other traditional New England topics.

H.O.M.E.

Adjacent to the flashing light on Route 1 in Orland, **H.O.M.E.** (207/469-7961, www.home-coop.net) is tough to categorize. Linked with the international Emmaus Movement founded by a French priest, H.O.M.E. (Homeworkers Organized for More Employment) was started in 1970 by Lucy Poulin, still the guiding force, and two nuns at a nearby convent. The quasi-religious organization shelters refugees and the homeless, operates a soup kitchen and a car-repair service, runs a day-care center, and teaches work skills in a variety of hands-on cooperative programs. Seventy percent of its income comes from sales of crafts, produce, and services. At the Route 1 store (Rte. 1 and Upper Falls Rd., 9am-4:30pm daily), you can buy handmade quilts, organic produce, maple syrup, and jams—and support a worthwhile effort. You can also tour the craft workshops on the property. For information about volunteering time in the workshops, store, or learning center, check the website.

Bucksport Waterfront Walkway

Stroll the one-mile paved walkway from the Bucksport-Verona Bridge to Webber Docks. Along the way are historical markers, picnic tables, a gazebo, restrooms, and expansive views of the harbor and Fort Knox.

RECREATION
Hiking
GREAT POND MOUNTAIN TRAIL

Distance: 2.2 miles round-trip
Duration: 2 hours
Elevation gain: 500 feet

Effort: Easy to moderate
Trailhead: 0.9 mile north of Craig Brook National Fish Hatchery on Don Fish Rd., East Orland

Great Pond Mountain's biggest asset is its 1,038-foot summit, with 360-degree views and lots of space for panoramic picnics. On a clear day, Baxter State Park's Katahdin is visible from Great Pond Mountain's north side. In autumn, watch for migrating hawks. Access to the mountain is via gated private property beginning about one mile north of the hatchery parking area. Roadside parking is available near the trailhead, but during fall foliage season, you may need to park at the hatchery. Pick up a brochure from the box at the trailhead, stay on the trail, and respect the surrounding private property. The mountain is part of the 4,300-acre Great Pond Mountain Wildlands, maintained by the **Great Pond Mountain Conservation Trust** (207/469-7190, www.greatpondtrust.org). For a longer hike, access the Great Pond Mountain Trail via the Dead River Trail and Connector, a moderately difficult multiuse gravel trail, for a total distance of seven miles.

Great Pond Mountain Wildlands

Encompassing two parcels of land and roughly 4,300 acres, the Great Pond Mountain Wildlands is a jewel. Acquired by the **Great Pond Mountain Conservation Trust** (207/469-7190, www.greatpondtrust.org) in 2005 after a decade of negotiation, the Wildlands is divided into two areas. The larger parcel totals 3,420 acres and surrounds Hothole Valley, including Hothole Brook, prized for its trout, and shoreline on Hothole Pond. The smaller 875-acre tract includes two miles of frontage on the Dead River (not to be confused with the Dead River of rafting fame in northwestern Maine) and reaches up Great Pond Mountain and down to the ominously named Hellbottom Swamp. The land is rich with wildlife: black bears, moose, bobcats, and deer, to name just a few species, plus with the pond, swamp, and river, it's ideal for bird-watching. With 14 miles of woods roads lacing the land, it's prime territory for walking, mountain biking, and snowshoeing, and the waterways invite fishing and paddling. Avoid the area during hunting season. Snowmobiling is permitted; ATVs are banned. Access to the Dead River tract is from the Craig Brook National Fish Hatchery; follow Don Fish Road to the Dead River Gate and Dead River Trail. The South Gate to Hothole Pond Tract is on Route 1 just southwest of Route 176. There's a parking lot at the gate, or when it's open, you can drive in along Valley Road about 2.5 miles to another parking area.

Craig Brook National Fish Hatchery

For a day of hiking, picnicking, swimming, canoeing, and a bit of natural history, pack a lunch and head for 135-acre **Craig Brook National Fish Hatchery** (306 Hatchery Rd., East Orland, 207/469-6701), on Alamoosook Lake. Turn off Route 1 six miles east of Bucksport and continue 1.4 miles north to the parking area. The **visitors center** (8:30am-3:30pm Mon.-Fri., 8am-3:30pm Sat.-Sun. summer, free) offers interactive displays on Atlantic salmon (don't miss the downstairs viewing area), maps, and a restroom. The grounds are accessible 6am-sunset daily year-round. Established in 1889, the U.S. Fish and Wildlife Service hatchery raises sea-run Atlantic salmon for stocking six Maine rivers. The birch-lined shorefront has picnic tables, a boat-launching ramp, an Atlantic salmon display pool, additional parking, and a spectacular cross-lake view. Watch for eagles, ospreys, and loons. Also on the premises is the small **Atlantic Salmon Heritage Museum,** housed in a circa-1896 ice house and operated by the Friends of Craig Brook (call the hatchery for current hours). Inside are salmon and fly-fishing artifacts and memorabilia.

Canoeing

If you've brought a canoe, **Silver Lake,** just two miles north of downtown Bucksport, is a beautiful place for a paddle. There's no development along its shores, and the birding

is excellent. Swimming is not allowed and is punishable by a $500 fine; this is Bucksport's reservoir. To get to the public launch, take Route 15 north of U.S. 1 after crossing the Bucksport-Verona Bridge. Go 0.5 mile and turn right onto McDonald Road, which becomes Silver Lake Road, and follow it 2.1 miles to the launch site.

Golf

Bucksport Golf Club (Duck Cove Rd./Rte. 46, Bucksport, 207/469-7612, mid-Apr.-Sept.), 1.5 miles north of U.S. 1, prides itself on having Maine's longest nine-hole course. Greens fees are moderate; facilities include a pro shop, a snack bar, a driving range, and carts.

SHOPPING

Locals come just as much for the coffee and conversation as the selection of new and used reads at **BookStacks** (71 Main St., Bucksport, 207/469-8992). You'll find a smattering of antiques and curiosity shops dotting Route 1. Just south of Route 1 is **Wild Blueberry Patch Gift Shop** (Allen's Wild Maine Blueberries, Rte. 15, Orland, 207/469-7060), a tiny blue cottage next to the Allen family's blueberry processing building. Stop in for fresh, canned, frozen, or dried wild Maine blueberries and all manner of blueberry merchandise, from baking mixes to T-shirts.

ACCOMMODATIONS
Inns and Bed-and-Breakfasts

Location, location, location: If only the six simple guest rooms at the old-timey **Alamoosook Lakeside Inn** (off Route 1, Orland, 207/469-6393 or 866/459-6393, www.alamoosooklakesideinn.com, year-round, $139) actually overlooked the lake, it would be the perfect rustic lakeside lodge. The property is gorgeous, and the location is well suited for exploring the area. All guest rooms, decorated in country style, have windows and doors opening onto a long, enclosed sunporch overlooking the lake (so if the curtains are open, other guests passing by can see into the room). The upside: The lodge has 1,300 feet of lakefront and is great for wildlife-watching and fishing, especially for bass, trout, salmon, and pickerel, and guests may use the inn's canoes and kayaks. Paddle across the lake to the fish hatchery for a hike up Great Pond Mountain. If the weather doesn't cooperate, retreat to the basement rec room, with games, a fireplace, a library, and even a kitchenette. A full breakfast is served, and Wi-Fi is included. Do note, the inn often hosts events.

In downtown Bucksport, the **Fort Knox Inn** (64 Main St., Bucksport, 207/469-3113, www.fortknoxparkinn.com, $130-150) is a four-story motel right at the harbor's edge. It's a bit tired, but the 40 guest rooms have phones, air-conditioning, free Wi-Fi, and cable TV. Be sure to request a water view, preferably on an upper floor, or you'll be facing a parking lot.

Bliss! Escape everything at **Williams Pond Lodge Bed and Breakfast** (327 Williams Pond Rd., Bucksport, 207/460-6064, www.williamspondlodge.com, $120-155), a secluded, solar-powered, eco-conscious, off-the-grid retreat on 20 wooded acres with 3,000 feet of frontage on spring-fed Williams Pond. Three guest rooms are decorated in cozy lodge style. Rates include a full breakfast and snacks. Wi-Fi is provided. Canoes and kayaks are provided for guests. Access is via a long dirt road through the woods, something to keep in mind when arriving after dark.

Motels

On the edge of downtown and set back from Route 1, **The Bucksport Motor Inn** (70 Rte. 1, Bucksport, 207/469-3111 or 800/626-9734, www.bucksportmotorinn.com, late May-late Sept., $89-109) is a family-owned, vintage 1956 motel that's being updated; be sure to ask for one of the renovated rooms. Perks include Wi-Fi, TV, air-conditioning, refrigerators, and microwaves. Some rooms are dog-friendly ($15).

Camping

The rivers, lakes, and ponds between Bucksport and Ellsworth make the area especially appealing for camping, and sites tend to be cheaper than in the Bar Harbor area. Six miles east of Bucksport, on the shores of 10-mile-long Toddy Pond, which reaches 100 feet in depth in some places, is **Balsam Cove Campground** (286 Back Ridge Rd., East Orland, 207/469-7771 or 800/469-7771, www.balsamcove.com, late May-late Sept., $29-50), which leans toward bigger RVs. Facilities on the 50 acres include 60 wooded waterfront or water-view tent and RV sites, a one-room rental cabin ($75), on-site rental trailers ($95), a dump station, a store, laundry, free showers and Wi-Fi, boat rentals, and freshwater swimming. Dogs are welcome on camping sites for $2 per day. During July-August, especially on weekends, reservations are wise.

FOOD

MacLeod's (Main St., Bucksport, 207/469-3963, 11:30am-9pm Tues.-Fri., 4pm-9pm Sat.-Mon., $10-20) is Bucksport's most popular and enduring restaurant. Some tables in the pleasant dining room have glimpses of the river and Fort Knox. The wide-ranging menu has choices for all tastes and budgets. Reservations are wise for Saturday nights.

Carrier's Mainely Lobster (corner Rtes. 1 and 46, 207/469-1011, www.carriersmainelylobster.com, 11am-9pm daily) doesn't look like much, but it's owned by a fishing family and is the best local spot for lobster or fried seafood. The large lobster roll is filled with the meat from about two of the tasty crustaceans. There's an indoor dining room out back as well as picnic tables. For cheap eats, the lunch specials, served 11am-3pm, are all less than $3.

Roughly 100 yards up the road is another local fave that's stood the test of time. **Crosby's Drive-In and Dairy Bar** (30 Rte. 46, Bucksport, 207/469-3640, www.crosbysdrivein.com, 10:30am-8pm daily) has been dishing out burgers, dogs, fried seafood, and ice cream since 1938. Thursday night is Cruise Night.

INFORMATION AND SERVICES

The best source for local info is the **Bucksport Bay Area Chamber of Commerce** (207/469-6818, www.bucksport-chamber.org).

In Bucksport, **public restrooms** next to the town dock (behind the Bucksport Historical Society) are open spring-fall. Restrooms are open year-round in the Gateway gas station (at the Route 1 traffic light next to the Bucksport bridge) and in the Bucksport Municipal Office (Main St., Mon.-Fri.).

GETTING THERE AND AROUND

Bucksport is about 20 miles or 35 minutes via Route 15 from Bangor. It's about 17 miles or 25 minutes via Routes 1 and 15 to Blue Hill, about 22 miles or 30 minutes via Route 1 to Ellsworth, and about 18 miles or 30 minutes via Routes 175 and 166 to Castine.

Blue Hill

Twelve miles south of Route 1 is the hub of the peninsula, Blue Hill (pop. 2,686), exuding charm from its handsome old homes to its waterfront setting to the shops, restaurants, and galleries that boost its appeal.

Eons back, Native American summer folk gave the name Awanadjo ("small, hazy mountain") to the mini-mountain that looms over the town and draws the eye for miles around. The first permanent settlers arrived in the late 18th century, after the French and Indian War, and established mills and shipyards. More than 100 ships were built here between Blue Hill's incorporation in 1789 and 1882—bringing prosperity to the entire peninsula.

Critical to the town's early expansion was its first clergyman, Jonathan Fisher, a remarkable fellow who has been likened to Leonardo da Vinci. In 1803, Fisher founded Blue Hill Academy (predecessor of today's George Stevens Academy), then built his home (now a museum), and eventually left an immense legacy of inventions, paintings, engravings, and poetry.

Throughout the 19th century and into the 20th, Blue Hill's granite industry boomed, reaching its peak in the 1880s. Scratch the Brooklyn Bridge and the New York Stock Exchange and you'll find granite from Blue Hill's quarries. Around 1879, the discovery of gold and silver brought a flurry of interest, but little came of it. Copper was also found here, but quantities of it, too, were limited.

At the height of industrial prosperity, tourism took hold, attracting steamboat-borne summer boarders. Many succumbed to the scenery, bought land, and built waterfront summer homes. Thank these summer folk and their offspring for the fact that music has long been a big deal in Blue Hill. The Kneisel Hall Chamber Music School, established in the late 19th century, continues to rank high among the nation's summer music colonies. New York City's Blue Hill Troupe, devoted to Gilbert and Sullivan operettas, was named for the longtime summer home of the troupe's founders.

SIGHTS
★ Parson Fisher House

Named for a brilliant Renaissance man who arrived in Blue Hill in 1794, the **Parson Fisher House** (44 Mines Rd./Rte. 15/176, 207/374-2459, www.jonathanfisherhouse.org, 1pm-4pm Wed.-Sat. early July-late Aug., 1pm-4pm Fri.-Sat. to mid-Oct., $5) immerses visitors in period furnishings and Jonathan Fisher lore. And Fisher's feats are breathtaking: He was a Harvard-educated preacher who also managed to be an accomplished painter, poet, mathematician, naturalist, linguist, inventor, cabinetmaker, farmer, architect, and printmaker. In his spare time, he fathered nine children. Fisher also pitched in to help build the yellow house on Tenney Hill, which served as the Congregational church parsonage. Now it contains intriguing items created by Fisher, memorabilia that volunteer tour guides delight in explaining, including a camera obscura. Don't miss it.

Historic Houses

A few of Blue Hill's elegant houses have been converted to museums, inns, restaurants, and even some offices and shops, so you can see them from the inside out. To appreciate the private residences, you'll want to walk, bike, or drive around town.

In downtown Blue Hill, a few steps off Main Street, stands the **Holt House** (3 Water St., www.bluehillhistory.org, 1pm-4pm Tues. and Fri., 11am-2pm Sat. July-mid-Sept., $3 adults, free under age 13), home of the Blue Hill Historical Society. Built in 1815 by Jeremiah Holt, the Federal-style building contains restored stenciling, period decor, and masses of memorabilia contributed by local residents. In the carriage house are even more goodies, including old tools, a sleigh, carriages, and more.

Walk or drive up Union Street (Rte. 177),

past George Stevens Academy, and wander **The Old Cemetery,** established in 1794. If gnarled trees and ancient headstones intrigue you, there aren't many good-size Maine cemeteries older than this one.

Bagaduce Music Lending Library

At the foot of Greene's Hill in Blue Hill is one of Maine's more unusual institutions, the **Bagaduce Music Lending Library** (3 Music Library Ln./Rte. 172, 207/374-5454, www.bagaducemusic.org, 10am-4pm Mon.-Fri. or by appointment), where you can borrow from a collection of more than 250,000 titles. Somehow this seems appropriate for a community that's a magnet for music lovers. Annual membership is $20 ($10 for students); fees range $1-4 per piece.

Scenic Routes

Parker Point Road (turn off Rte. 15 at the Blue Hill Public Library) takes you from Blue Hill to Blue Hill Falls the back way, with vistas en route toward Acadia National Park. For other serene views, drive the length of **Newbury Neck** in nearby Surry, or head west on Route 15/176 toward Sedgwick, Brooksville, and beyond.

the Parson Fisher House

RECREATION
Hiking
★ BLUE HILL MOUNTAIN TRAIL

Distance: 2 miles round-trip
Duration: 1.5-2 hours
Elevation gain: 500 feet
Effort: Easy to moderate
Trailhead: Mountain Road, off Route 15 (Pleasant St., Blue Hill)

"Mountain" seems a fancy label for a 943-footer, yet Blue Hill Mountain stands alone, visible from Camden and even beyond. On a clear day, head for the summit and take in the wraparound view encompassing Penobscot Bay, the hills of Mount Desert, and the Camden Hills. In mid-June the lupines along the way are breathtaking; in fall the colors are spectacular—with reddened blueberry barrens added to the variegated foliage. Go early in the day; it's a popular, easy-to-moderate hike. Allow about 1.5 hours for the Osgood Trail, a two-mile round-trip from the Mountain Road trailhead. For a bit more challenge, take the Hayes Trail and the Connector Trail to the Osgood Trail.

The newer Becton Trail, departing from the Turkey Farm Road trailhead, passes through softwood forest en route to meeting the Osgood Trail. Connecting the Osgood and Becton Trails to the Hayes Trail is the Tower Service Trail.

Take Route 15 (Pleasant St.) to Mountain Road. Turn right and go 0.8 mile to the trailhead (on the left) and the small parking area (on the right). You can also walk (uphill) the mile from the village.

Parks and Preserves
BLUE HILL HERITAGE TRUST

Blue Hill Heritage Trust (285 Mountain Rd., 207/374-5118, www.bluehillheritagetrust.org, 8am-5pm Mon.-Fri.) works hard at preserving the region's landscape. Trail maps for all sites can be downloaded from the website. It also presents a Walks and Talks series, with offerings such as a mushroom walk and talk, a full-moon hike up Blue Hill Mountain, and farm tours. Many include talks by knowledgeable folks on complementary topics.

BLUE HILL TOWN PARK

At the end of Water Street is a small park with a terrific view, along with a small pebble beach, picnic tables, a portable toilet, and a playground.

BLUE HILL FALLS

A favorite spot for experienced kayakers and canoeists is Blue Hill Falls, which churns with white water when the tide turns. Check for times of high and low tide. Roadside parking is illegal, but the law is too often ignored. The Route 175 bridge is narrow, and cars often stop suddenly as they come over the hill, so be particularly cautious here.

Unless you own a boat or know a member of the Kollegewidgwok Yacht Club in East Blue Hill (207/374-5581, www.kollegewidgwokyc.com), there's no sailing out of Blue Hill. If you're trailing a boat, use the public boat launch down on the harbor. *Kollegewidgwok,* incidentally, is a Penobscot Indian word meaning "blue hill on shining green water."

Outfitters

The Activity Shop (61 Ellsworth Rd., 207/374-3600, www.theactivityshop.com) rents bicycles for $65 per week and Old Town canoes and kayaks beginning at $25 per day, including delivery within a reasonable area.

ENTERTAINMENT AND EVENTS

Variety and serendipity are the keys here. Check local calendar listings and tune in to **radio station WERU** (89.9 and 102.9 FM, www.weru.org), the peninsula's own community radio; there might be announcements of concerts by local resident pianist Paul Sullivan or the Bagaduce Chorale, or maybe a contra dance. **George Stevens Academy** has a free Tuesday evening lecture series in July-August.

The October **Foliage Food & Wine Festival** has workshops, lectures, music, and plentiful dining opportunities.

Live Music and Theater

Since 1922, chamber-music students have been spending summers perfecting their skills and demonstrating their prowess at the **Kneisel Hall Chamber Music School** (Pleasant St./Rte. 15, 207/374-2811, www.kneisel.org). Faculty concerts run Friday evenings and Sunday afternoons late June-late August. The concert schedule is published in the spring, and reserved-seating tickets ($30 inside, $20 on the porch outside, nonrefundable) can be ordered online or by phone. Other opportunities to hear the students and faculty exist, including young-artist concerts, children's concerts, open rehearsals, and more. Kneisel Hall is about 0.5 mile from the center of town.

The Blue Hill Congregational Church is the site for the **Vanderkay Summer Music Series** (207/374-2891), whose offerings range from choral music from the Middle Ages to bluegrass. Suggested donation is $20.

Chamber music continues in winter thanks to the volunteer **Blue Hill Concert Association** (207/326-4666, www.bluehillconcertassociation.org), which presents five concerts January-March at the Congregational church. Recommended donation is $30.

Blue Hill Bach (207/590-2677, www.bluehillbach.org) was formed in 2011 to present Baroque music, and does so with its summer Bach Festival.

The **New Surry Theatre** (918 Union St., Blue Hill, 207/200-4720) stages musicals and classics each summer.

Home to the former Surry Opera Company, the Surry Concert Barn is being revitalized by **Surry Arts: At The Barn** (8 Cross Rd., Surry, 207/669-9216, surryartsatthebarn.com), which presents concerts and films.

Lectures

The **Marine Environmental Research Institute Center for Marine Studies** (55 Main St., 207/374-2135, www.meriresearch.org) sponsors an evening lecture series, which tackles subjects such as The State of Blue Hill Bay: A 10-Year Window on a Changing Ecosystem.

Events

On Labor Day weekend, the **Blue Hill Fair** (Blue Hill Fairgrounds, Rte. 172, 207/374-9976) is one of the state's best agricultural fairs.

The **Foliage, Food & Wine Festival** takes place in October.

SHOPPING

Blue Hill Books (26 Pleasant St./Rte. 15, 207/374-5632, www.bluehillbooks.com) is a wonderful independent bookstore that organizes an "authors series" during the summer.

The **Blue Hill Wine Shop** (138 Main St., 207/374-2161), tucked into a converted horse barn, carries more than 1,000 wines, plus teas, coffees, breads, and cheeses. Monthly wine tastings (usually 2:30pm-6pm last Sat. of the month) are always an adventure.

ACCOMMODATIONS
Inns and Bed-and-Breakfasts

If you're trying to imagine a classic country inn, ★ **The Blue Hill Inn** (Union St./Rte. 177, 207/374-2844 or 800/826-7415, www.bluehillinn.com, mid-May-late Oct., $190-250) would be it. Sarah Pebworth graciously welcomes guests to her antiques-filled inn, open since 1840 and located steps from Main Street's shops and restaurants. Ten air-conditioned guest rooms and a suite have real chandeliers, four-poster beds, down comforters, fancy linens, and braided and Oriental rugs; three have wood-burning fireplaces. Rear rooms overlook the extensive cutting garden, with chairs and a hammock. A three-course breakfast is served in the elegant dining room (also available to nonguests, $16), where special chef dinners are occasionally served. Afternoon refreshments with sweets appear in the living room daily, and superb hors d'oeuvres are served 6pm-7pm in two elegant parlors or the garden. Also available are two year-round, pet-friendly suites with

Gallery Hopping in Blue Hill

Perhaps it's Blue Hill's location near the renowned Haystack Mountain School of Crafts. Perhaps it's the way the light plays off the rolling countryside and onto the twisting coastline. Perhaps it's the inspirational landscape. Whatever the reason, numerous artists and artisans call Blue Hill home, and top-notch galleries are abundant. Here's a sampling tour.

One mile north of downtown, **Rackliffe Pottery** (132 Ellsworth Rd./Rte. 172, Blue Hill, 207/374-2297, www.rackliffepottery.com), in its fourth generation of family ownership and noted for its vivid blue wares, has been producing lead-free pottery from clay sourced on the property since 1969.

Smack downtown, don't miss **Jud Hartmann** (79 Main St. at Rte. 15, Blue Hill, 207/374-9917, www.judhartmanngallery.com). The spacious, well-lighted gallery carries Hartmann's limited-edition bronze sculptures of the woodland Native Americans of the Northeast. Hartmann often can be seen working on his next model in the gallery—a real treat. He's a wealth of information about his subjects, and he loves sharing the mesmerizing stories he's uncovered during his meticulous research.

The **Liros Gallery** (14 Parker Point Rd., Blue Hill, 207/374-5370 or 800/287-5370, www.lirosgallery.com) has been dealing in Russian icons since the mid-1960s. Prices are high, but the icons are fascinating. The gallery also carries Currier & Ives prints, antique maps, and 19th-century British and American paintings. Just up the street is the **Cynthia Winings Gallery** (24 Parker Point Rd., Blue Hill, 917/204-4001, www.cynthiawiningsgallery.com), which shows contemporary works by local artists. From here it's a short walk to **Blue Hill Bay Gallery** (Main St., Blue Hill, 207/374-5773, www.bluehillbaygallery.com), which represents contemporary artists in various media.

Also on Main Street are two other fun, artsy gallery-shops. **Handworks Gallery** (48 Main St., Blue Hill, 207/374-5613, www.handworksgallery.org) sells a range of fun, funky, utilitarian, and fine-art crafts, including jewelry, furniture, rugs, wall hangings, and clothing, by more than 50 Maine artists and craftspeople. Browse **North Country Textiles** (Main St., Blue Hill, 207/374-2715, www.northcountrytextiles.com) for fine handwoven throws, rugs, clothing, and table linens as well as other fine crafts.

About two miles from downtown is another don't-miss: **Mark Bell Pottery** (289 Rte. 15, Blue Hill, 207/374-5881, www.markbellpottery.com), in a tiny building signaled only by a small roadside sign, is the home of exquisite, award-winning porcelain by the eponymous potter. It's easy to understand why his wares have been displayed at the Smithsonian Institution's Craft Show as well as at other juried shows across the country. The delicacy of each vase, bowl, or piece is astonishing, and the glazes are gorgeous. Twice each summer he has kiln openings—must-go events for collectors and fans.

Outside of Blue Hill, but just a few miles from Bell's studio, is **Clay Forms** (189 Rope Ferry Rd., Sedgwick, 207/359-2320, www.clayformspottery.com), where Melody Lewis-Kane displays her handmade functional and decorative porcelain pottery. To find it, follow Route 15 to the T intersection with Route 176 and cross it, continuing straight onto Rope Ferry Road. Follow it to the bottom of the hill, then take the road marked Private and continue to the sixth driveway on the right. Drive slowly—the road is narrow and winding. It's wise to call first.

cooking facilities in the elegant Cape House ($290-320).

What's old is new at **Barncastle** (125 South St., 207/374-2330, www.barn-castle.com, $145-195), a late 19th-century Shingle-style cottage that's listed on the National Register of Historic Places. It opens to a two-story foyer with a split stairway and balcony.

Rooms and suites open off the balcony. All are spacious, minimally decorated, and offer contemporary accents, including flat-screen TVs, Wi-Fi, a fridge, and a microwave. Rates include a continental breakfast. The downstairs tavern serves pizza, salads, and sandwiches; noise can be a factor.

The ★ **Wavewalker Bed and Breakfast**

(28 Wavewalker Ln., Surry, 207/667-5767, www.wavewalkerbedandbreakfast.com, $165-225) has a jaw-dropping location near the tip of Newbury Neck. It sits on 20 private acres with 1,000 feet of shorefront as well as woods and blueberry fields. The newly built inn is smack on the oceanfront, with views across the water to Mount Desert Island. Four spacious guest rooms have wowser views as well as Wi-Fi, DIRECTV, and a DVD player; some have fireplaces and/or oversized whirlpool tubs. The 1st-floor room is a good choice for those with mobility problems. Guests also have use of a living room, sunroom, and oceanfront deck. A full, hot breakfast is served. Kayaks are available. A separate two-bedroom-plus-loft cottage rents for $900-1,700 per week.

Seasonal Rentals

Weekly or longer rentals can pay off if you have a large family or are planning a group vacation. The Blue Hill Peninsula has lots of rental cottages, camps, and houses, but the trick is to plan well ahead. This is a popular area in summer, and many renters sign up for the following year before they leave town. For information, contact Sandy Douvarjo of **Peninsula Property Rentals** (15 Main St., Blue Hill, 207/374-2428, www.peninsulapropertyrentals.com).

The Blue Hill Inn has been welcoming guests since 1840.

FOOD
Local Flavors

Picnic fare and pizza are available at **Merrill & Hinckley** (11 Union St., 207/374-2821, 6am-9pm Mon.-Fri., 7am-9pm Sat., 8am-8pm Sun.), a quirky, 150-year-old family-owned grocery and general store.

Craving chocolate? **Black Dinah Chocolatiers** (5 Main St., 207/374-5621, www.blackdinahchocolatiers.com) has a mainland home, sharing space with Fairwinds Florist. Here you'll find the Isle au Haut confectioner's freshly made to-die-for chocolates, ice cream, and sorbet, as well as a coffee/tea/hot chocolate bar. Don't miss the Art Box, a vending machine with $10 works by 10 local artists—perfect gift for someone back home, perhaps?

The **Blue Hill Co-op and Cafe** (4 Ellsworth Rd./Rte. 172, 207/374-2165, bluehill.coop, 7am-8pm daily) sells organic and natural foods. Breakfast items, sandwiches, salads, and soups—many with ethnic flavors—are available in the café.

Local gardeners, farmers, and craftspeople peddle their wares at the **Blue Hill Farmers Market** (9am-11am Sat. late May-mid-Oct.). It's a particularly enduring market, well worth a visit. Demonstrations by area chefs and artists are often on the agenda. Late May-late August the Saturday market is at the Blue Hill Fairgrounds, then it moves to the Blue Hill Congregational Church.

Eat in or pick up sandwiches, salads, soups, and baked goods to go at **The Mill Stream Deli, Bakery & BBQ** (58 Main St., 207/374-1049, 8am-4pm Tues.-Sat., 8am-3pm Sun.).

Every Thursday morning, the **Northern Bay Market** (177 Southern Bay Rd.,/Rte. 175, 207/326-8606) sells Toni Staples's homemade

For scrumptious chocolates and ice cream, dip into Black Dinah Chocolatiers.

com, 3pm-8pm Sun.-Thurs., 3pm-9pm Fri.-Sat., entrées $8-20), serving a creative selection of wood-fired pizzas in three sizes as well as sandwiches, subs, panini, calzones, and salads in a lovely Shingle-style cottage. There are vegetarian options. Expect to wait for a table; this is one popular spot.

Fine Dining

For a lovely dinner by candlelight, make reservations at ★ **Arborvine** (33 Upper Tenney Hill/Main St., 207/374-2119, www.arborvine.com, 5:30pm-9pm Wed.-Sun., entrées $28-35), a conscientiously renovated, two-century-old Cape-style house with four dining areas, each with a different feel and understated decor. Chef-owner John Hikade and his wife, Beth, prepare classic entrées such as crispy roasted duckling and roasted rack of lamb. Their mantra has been fresh and local for more than 30 years.

Seafood

For lobster, fried fish, and the area's best lobster roll, head to **The Fish Net** (163 Main St., 207/374-5240, 11am-8pm daily), an inexpensive, mostly take-out joint on the eastern end of town.

It's not easy to find ★ **Perry's Lobster Shack and Pier** (1076 Newbury Neck Rd., Surry, 207/667-1955, 10am-7pm daily), but for a classic lobster-shack experience, make the effort. The traditional Maine lobster shack is about five miles down Newbury Neck, just after the Causeway Place beach. Expect lobster, lobster and crab rolls, corn, chips, mussels, and clams. From the pier-top picnic tables, you're overlooking the water with Mount Desert Island as a backdrop.

With a full bar, indoor and outdoor seating, and a boatyard location, the **Boatyard Grill** (13 E. Blue Hill Rd., 207/374-3533, from 3pm Tues.-Sat., from $8) attracts the sailing crowd, who appreciate its laid-back, Caribbean-esque style. The menu ranges from burgers to lobster.

cake and yeast-raised doughnuts. Go early, or risk being disappointed; the market opens at 6am.

Blue Hill's first microbrewery, **Deep Water Brew Pub** (33 Tenney Hill Rd., 207/374-2441, www.deepwaterbrewing.com, 5:30pm-9pm Wed.-Sun.) serves pub-style fare such as ribs, burgers, and tacos ($9-14). Ask about tours of the brewery, located in a beautifully renovated, historic barn behind the pub.

Family Favorites

Marlintini's Grill (83 Mines St./Rte. 15, 207/374-2500, www.marlintinisgrill.com, from 11am daily, $8-22) is half sports bar and half restaurant. You can sit in either, but the bar side can get raucous. Best bet: the screened-in porch. The menu includes soups, salads, burgers, fried seafood, rib eye, and nightly home-style specials; there's a kids' menu too. The portions are big, the service is good, and the food is decent.

Just south of town is **Barncastle** (125 South St., 207/374-2300, www.barn-castle.

INFORMATION AND SERVICES

The **Blue Hill Peninsula Chamber of Commerce** (207/374-3242, www.bluehill-peninsula.org) is the best source for information on Blue Hill and the surrounding area.

At the **Blue Hill Public Library** (5 Parker Point Rd., Blue Hill, 207/374-5515, www.bluehill.lib.me.us), ask to see the suit of armor, which *may* have belonged to Magellan. The library sponsors a summer lecture series.

Public restrooms are in the Blue Hill Town Hall (Main St.), Blue Hill Public Library (Main St.), and Blue Hill Memorial Hospital (Water St.).

GETTING THERE AND AROUND

Blue Hill is about 17 miles or 25 minutes via Routes 1 and 15 from Bucksport. It's about 14 miles or 20 minutes via Route 172 to Ellsworth, about 8 miles or 15 minutes via Route 15 to Brooksville, and about 20 miles or 35 minutes via Routes 15, 175, 199, and 166 to Castine.

Brooklin, Brooksville, and Sedgwick

I'm going to let you in on a secret, a part of Maine that seems right out of a time warp, a place with general stores and family farms, a place where family roots go back generations and summer rusticators have returned for decades. Nestled near the bottom of the Blue Hill Peninsula and surrounded by Castine, Blue Hill, and Deer Isle, this often-missed area offers superb hiking, kayaking, and sailing, plus historic homes and unique shops, studios, lodgings, and personalities.

The best-known town is **Brooklin** (pop. 824), thanks to two magazines: *The New Yorker* and *WoodenBoat*. Wordsmiths extraordinaire E. B. and Katharine White "dropped out" to Brooklin in the 1930s and forever afterward dispatched their splendid material for *The New Yorker* from here. (The Whites' former home, a handsome colonial not open to the public, is on Route 175 in North Brooklin, 6.5 miles from the Blue Hill Falls bridge.) In 1977, *WoodenBoat* magazine moved its headquarters to Brooklin, where its 60-acre shore-side estate attracts builders and dreamers from all over the globe.

Nearby **Brooksville** (pop. 934) drew the late Helen and Scott Nearing, whose book *Living the Good Life* made them role models for back-to-the-landers. Their compound now verges on must-see status. **Buck's Harbor,** a

section of Brooksville, is the setting for *One Morning in Maine,* one of Robert McCloskey's beloved children's books.

Incorporated in 1789, the oldest of the three towns is **Sedgwick** (pop. 1,196), which once included all of Brooklin and part of Brooksville. Now wedged between Brooklin and Brooksville, it includes the hamlet of Sargentville, the Caterpillar Hill scenic overlook, and a well-preserved complex of historic buildings. The influx of pilgrims—many of them artists bent on capturing the spirit that has proved so enticing to creative types—continues in this area.

SIGHTS
WoodenBoat Publications

On Naskeag Point Road, 1.2 miles from Route 175 in downtown Brooklin, a small sign marks the turn to the world headquarters of *WoodenBoat* (Naskeag Point Rd., Brooklin, 207/359-4651, www.woodenboat.com). Buy magazines, books, clothing, and all manner of nautical merchandise at the handsome store, stroll the grounds, or sign up for one of the dozens of one- and two-week spring, summer, and fall courses in seamanship, navigation, boatbuilding, sail making, marine carving, and more; tuition varies by course and duration. Special courses are geared to kids, women, pros, and all-thumbs neophytes; the camaraderie is legendary, and so is the cuisine. School visiting hours are 8am-5pm Monday-Saturday June-October.

Historical Sights

Now used as the museum and headquarters of the Sedgwick-Brooklin Historical Society, the 1795 **Reverend Daniel Merrill House** (Rte. 172, Sedgwick, 2pm-4pm Sun. July-Aug. donation) was the parsonage for Sedgwick's first permanent minister. Inside the house are period furnishings, old photos, toys, and tools; a few steps away are a restored 1874 schoolhouse, an 1821 cattle pound (for corralling wandering bovines), and a hearse barn. Pick up a brochure during open hours and guide yourself around the buildings and grounds. The **Sedgwick Historic District,** crowning Town House Hill, comprises the Merrill House and its outbuildings, plus the imposing 1794 Town House and the 23-acre Rural Cemetery (the oldest headstone dates from 1798) across Route 172.

The **Brooksville Historical Society Museum** (150 Coastal Rd./Rte. 176, Brooksville, www.brooksvillehistoricalsociety.org, 1pm-4pm Wed. and Sun. July-Aug.) houses a collection of nautical doodads, farming implements, blacksmith tools, and quilts in a converted boathouse. The museum is restoring a local farmhouse for more exhibits.

The Good Life Center

Forest Farm, home of the late Helen and Scott Nearing, is now the site of **The Good Life Center** (372 Harborside Rd., Harborside, 207/326-8211, www.goodlife.org). Advocates of simple living and authors of 10 books on the subject, the Nearings created a trust to perpetuate their farm and philosophy. Resident stewards lead tours (usually 1pm-5pm Thurs.-Mon. mid-June-early Sept., Sat.-Sun. early Sept.-mid-Oct., $5 donation). Ask about the schedule for the traditional Monday-night meetings (7pm), featuring free programs by gardeners, philosophers, musicians, and other guest speakers. Occasional work parties,

workshops, and conferences are also on the docket. The farm is on Harborside Road, just before it turns to dirt. From Route 176 in Brooksville, take Cape Rosier Road and go eight miles, passing Holbrook Islands Sanctuary. At the Grange Hall, turn right and follow the road 1.9 miles to the end. Turn left onto Harborside Road and continue 1.8 miles to Forest Farm, across from Orrs Cove.

Four Season Farm

About a mile beyond the Nearings' place is **Four Season Farm** (609 Weir Cove Rd., Harborside, 207/326-4455, www.fourseasonfarm.com, 1pm-5pm Mon.-Sat. June-Sept.), the lush organic farm owned and operated by internationally renowned gardeners Eliot Coleman and Barbara Damrosch. Both have written numerous books and articles and starred in TV gardening shows. Coleman is a driving force behind the use of the word *authentic* to mean "beyond organic," demonstrating a commitment to food that is local, fresh, ripe, clean, safe, and nourishing. He's successfully pioneered a "winter harvest," developing environmentally sound and economically viable systems for extending fresh vegetable production October-May in cold-weather climates. Visitors are welcome to drive in and around the farm, but no produce is sold here in summer.

Scenic Routes

No one seems to know how **Caterpillar Hill** got its name, but its reputation comes from a panoramic vista of water, hills, and blueberry barrens—with a couple of convenient picnic tables where you can stop for lunch, photos, or a ringside view of sunset and fall foliage. From the 350-foot elevation, the views take in Walker Pond, Eggemoggin Reach, Deer Isle, Swans Island, and even the Camden Hills. The signposted rest area is on Route 175/15, between Brooksville and Sargentville; watch out for the blind curve when you pull off the road. If you want to explore on foot, the one-mile Cooper Farm Trail loops through the blueberry barrens and woods. From the scenic overlook, walk down to and out Cooper Farm Road to the trailhead.

Between Sargentville and Sedgwick, Route 175 offers nonstop views of Eggemoggin Reach, with shore access to the Benjamin River just before you reach Sedgwick village.

Two other scenic routes are **Naskeag Point** in Brooklin and **Cape Rosier,** the westernmost arm of the town of Brooksville. Naskeag Point Road begins off Route 175 in "downtown" Brooklin, heads down the peninsula for 3.7 miles past the entrance to *WoodenBoat* Publications, and ends at a small shingle beach (limited parking) on Eggemoggin Reach. Here you'll find picnic tables, a boat launch, a seasonal toilet, and a marker commemorating the 1778 Battle of Naskeag, when British sailors came ashore from the sloop *Gage,* burned several buildings, and were run off by a ragtag band of local settlers. Cape Rosier's roads are poorly marked, perhaps deliberately, so keep your DeLorme atlas handy. The Cape Rosier loop takes in Holbrook Island Sanctuary, Goose Falls, the hamlet of Harborside, and plenty of water and island views. Note that some roads are unpaved, but they usually are well maintained.

RECREATION
★ Holbrook Island Sanctuary State Park

In the early 1970s, foresighted benefactor Anita Harris donated to the state 1,230 acres in Brooksville that would become the **Holbrook Island Sanctuary** (207/326-4012, www.parksandlands.com, free). From Route 176, between West Brooksville and South Brooksville, head west on Cape Rosier Road, following brown-and-white signs for the sanctuary. Trail maps and bird checklists are available in boxes at trailheads or at park headquarters. The easy Backshore Trail (about 30 minutes) starts here, or go back a mile and climb the steepish trail to **Backwoods Mountain** for the best vistas. Other attractions include shorefront picnic tables and grills, four old cemeteries, super bird-watching during spring and fall migrations, a pebble beach, and a stone beach. Leashed pets are allowed, but no bikes are allowed on the trails, and camping is not permitted. The park is officially open May 15-October 15, but the access road and parking areas are plowed in winter for cross-country skiers.

Swimming

A small, relatively little-known beach is

Easy-on-the-eyes scenery and solitude are Cape Rosier's calling cards.

E. B. White: Some Writer

Every child since the mid-1940s has heard of E. B. White—author of the memorable *Stuart Little, Charlotte's Web,* and *Trumpet of the Swan*—and every college kid for decades has been reminded to consult his copy of *The Elements of Style.* But how many realize that White and his wife, Katharine, were living not in the big city but in the hamlet of North Brooklin, Maine? It was Brooklin that inspired Charlotte and Wilbur and Stuart, and it was Brooklin where the Whites lived very full, creative lives.

Abandoning their desks at *The New Yorker* in 1938, Elwyn Brooks White and Katharine S. White bought an idyllic saltwater farm on the Blue Hill Peninsula and moved here with their young son, Joel, who became a noted naval architect and yacht builder in Brooklin before his untimely death in 1997. Andy (as E. B. had been dubbed since his college days at Cornell) produced 20 books, countless essays and letters to editors, and hundreds (maybe thousands?) of "newsbreaks"—those wry clipping-and-commentary items sprinkled through each issue of *The New Yorker.* Katharine continued wielding her pencil as the magazine's standout children's-book editor, donating many of her review copies to Brooklin's Friends Memorial Library, one of her favorite causes. (The library also has two original Garth Williams drawings from *Stuart Little,* courtesy of E. B., and a lovely garden dedicated to the Whites.) Katharine's book, *Onward and Upward in the Garden,* a collection of her *New Yorker* gardening pieces, was published in 1979, two years after her death.

Later in life, E. B. sagely addressed the young readers of his three award-winning children's books:

Are my stories true, you ask? No, they are imaginary tales, containing fantastic characters and events. In real life, a family doesn't have a child who looks like a mouse; in real life, a spider doesn't spin words in her web. In real life, a swan doesn't blow a trumpet. But real life is only one kind of life—there is also the life of the imagination. And although my stories are imaginary, I like to think that there is some truth in them, too—truth about the way people and animals feel and think and act.

E. B. White died on October 1, 1985, at the age of 86. He and Katharine and Joel left large footprints on this earth, but perhaps nowhere more so than in Brooklin.

BLUE HILL PENINSULA
BROOKLIN, BROOKSVILLE, AND SEDGWICK

Brooklin's **Pooduck Beach.** From the Brooklin General Store (Rte. 175), take Naskeag Point Road about 0.5 mile, watching for the Pooduck Road sign on the right. Turn right and drive to the end; parking is very limited. You can also launch a sea kayak here into Eggemoggin Reach.

Bicycling

Bicycling in this area is for confident, experienced cyclists. The roads are particularly narrow and winding, with poor shoulders. Best bets for casual pedal pushers are the **Naskeag scenic route** or around **Cape Rosier,** where traffic is light.

Boating

Buck's Harbor Marine (on the dock, South

Brooksville, 207/326-8839, www.bucksharbor.com) offers morning, afternoon, and evening excursions aboard sailboats and powerboats. Each lasts up to two hours and costs $65 per person. Minimum party size is four (max is six), but the marina will try to match you with another party if your group is smaller. Buck's Harbor charters bareboat sail and power yachts to qualified skippers; rates begin at $180 per day ($1,200/week).

Picnicking

You can take a picnic to the **Bagaduce Ferry Landing,** in West Brooksville off Route 176, where there are picnic tables and cross-river vistas toward Castine. Another good spot is **Holbrook Island Sanctuary State Park** on Cape Rosier.

ENTERTAINMENT AND EVENTS

★ Flash! In the Pans Community Steelband

If you're a fan of steelband music, the **Flash! In the Pans Community Steelband** (207/374-2172, www.flashinthepans.org) usually performs somewhere on the peninsula 7:30pm-9pm Monday mid-June-early September. Local papers carry the summer schedule for the nearly three-dozen-member band, which deserves its devoted following. Admission is usually a small donation to benefit a local cause.

Eggemoggin Reach Regatta

Wooden boats are big attractions hereabouts, so when a huge fleet sails in for the **Eggemoggin Reach Regatta** (usually the first Sat. in Aug., but the schedule can change), crowds gather. Don't miss the parade of wooden boats. The best locale for watching the regatta itself is on or near the bridge to Deer Isle or near the Eggemoggin Landing grounds on Little Deer Isle. For details, see www.erregatta.com.

SHOPPING

Most of these businesses are small, owner-operated shops, which means they're often catch-as-catch-can.

Antiques

When you need a slate sink, a claw-foot tub, brass fixtures, or a Palladian window, **Architectural Antiquities** (52 Indian Point Ln., Harborside, 207/326-4938, www.archantiquities.com), on Cape Rosier, is just the ticket—a restorer's delight. Prices are reasonable for what you get, and they'll ship your purchases. It's open all year by appointment; ask for directions when you call. Antiques dating from the Federal period through the turn of the 20th century are the specialties at **Sedgwick Antiques** (775 N. Sedgwick Rd./Rte. 172, Sedgwick, 207/359-8834). Early furniture, handmade furniture, and a full range of country accessories and antiques can be found at **Thomas Hinchcliffe Antiques** (26 Cradle Knolls Ln., off Rte. 176, West Sedgwick, 207/326-9411). Painted country furniture, decoys, and unusual nautical items are specialties at Peg and Olney Grindall's **Old Cove Antiques** (106 Caterpillar Rd./Rte. 15, Sargentville, 207/359-2031 or 207/359-8585),

Pushcart Press bills itself as the world's smallest bookstore.

a weathered-gray shop across from the Eggemoggin Country Store.

Artists' and Artisans' Galleries

Small studio-galleries pepper Route 175 (Reach Rd.) in Sedgwick and Brooklin; most are marked only by small signs, so watch carefully. Here are a few to watch for: First up is **Eggemoggin Textile Studio** (off Rte. 175/ Reach Rd., Sedgwick, 207/359-5083, www. chrisleithstudio.com), where the incredibly gifted Christine Leith weaves scarves, wraps, hangings, and pillows with hand-dyed silk and wool; the colors are magnificent. You might catch her at work on the big loom in her studio shop, a real treat.

Just down the road is **Mermaid Woolens** (Reach Rd., Sedgwick, 207/359-2747, www. mermaidwoolens.com), source of Elizabeth Coakley's wildly colorful hand knits—vests, socks, and sweaters. They're pricey but worth every nickel.

Continue over to Brooklin, where Virginia G. Sarsfield handcrafts paper products, including custom lampshades, calligraphy papers, books, and lamps, at **Handmade Papers** (113 Reach Rd., Brooklin, 207/359-8345, www.handmadepapersonline.com).

Just a short hop up the Naskeag Point Road, find **Tilia Gallery** (10 Mountain Ash Rd., Brooklin, 781-799-4091, www.tiliagallery.com), a former stable that now houses fine arts, crafts, estate jewelry, antiques, and clothing.

It's worth the mosey out Flye Point to find **Flye Point Sculpture & Art Gallery** (436 Flye Point Rd., Brooklin, 207/610-0350), where Peter Stremlau displays fine works in varied media by Maine-based and Maine-inspired artists. Wander through gardens and woodlands accented with sculptures. More sculptures, as well as paintings and accordion books, are inside the gallery. The waterfront location is spectacular.

Wine, Books, and Gifts

Three varieties of English-style hard cider are specialties at **The Sow's Ear Winery** (Rte. 176 at Herrick Rd., Brooksville, 207/326-4649, no credit cards), a minuscule operation in a funky two-story shingled shack. Winemaker Tom Hoey also produces sulfite-free blueberry, chokecherry, and rhubarb wines; he'll let you sample it all. Ask to see his cellar, where everything happens. Lining the walls in the tiny tasting room/shop are books, also for sale, that concentrate on architecture and history, with specialty areas highlighting Gothic arches and Russian history, but including plenty of other esoteric topics.

Betsy's Sunflower (12 Reach Rd., 207/359-5030), in Brooklin village, is a browser's delight filled with garden and kitchen must-haves and books. Her motto: "It has to be affordable, useful, and fun."

Don't miss the "world's smallest bookstore," Bill Henderson's **Pushcart Press Bookstore** (Rte. 172, Sedgwick, 207/359-2427), behind Sedgwick Antiques. It's a trove of literary fiction both used (paperbacks $2, hardbacks $5) and new, including editions of the *Pushcart Prize: Best of the Small Presses* annual series. Sales help support Pushcart fellowships.

Nautical books, T-shirts, gifts, food (including fresh lobsters and key lime pie), and boat gear line the walls and shelves of the shop at **Buck's Harbor Marine** (on the dock, South Brooksville, 207/326-8839, www.bucksharbor.com).

ACCOMMODATIONS
Bed-and-Breakfast

Best known for its restaurant and pub, **The Brooklin Inn** (Rte. 175, Brooklin, 207/359-2777, www.brooklininn.com, $105-125 with breakfast; add $10 for a 1-night stay) also has five country-style bedrooms; two share a bath. It's open year-round and often offers packages including meals; ask.

Cottage Colonies

The two operations in this category feel much like informal family compounds—where you quickly become an adoptee. These are extremely popular spots, where successive generations of hosts have catered to successive generations of visitors, and reservations are usually essential for July-August. Many guests book for the following year before they leave. We're not talking fancy; the cottages are old-shoe rustic, of varying sizes and decor. Most have cooking facilities; one colony includes breakfast and dinner in July-August. Both have hiking trails, playgrounds, rowboats, and East Penobscot Bay on the doorstep.

The fourth generation manages the **Hiram Blake Camp** (220 Weir Cove Rd., Harborside, 207/326-4951, www.hiram-blake.com, Memorial Day-late Sept., no credit cards), but other generations pitch in and help with gardening, lobstering, maintenance, and kibitzing. Thirteen cottages and a duplex line the shore of this 100-acre property, which has been in family hands since before the Revolutionary War. The camp itself dates from 1916. Don't bother bringing reading material: The dining room has ingenious ceiling niches lined with countless books. Guests also have the use of rowboats, and kayak rentals are available. Home-cooked breakfasts and dinners are served family-style; lobster is always available at an additional charge. Much of the fare is grown in the expansive gardens.

Other facilities include a dock, a recreation room, a pebble beach, and an outdoor chapel. There's a one-week minimum (beginning Sat. or Sun.) in July-August, when cottages go for $1,100-3,500 per week (including breakfast, dinner, and linens). Off-season rates (no meals or linens, but cottages have cooking facilities) are $650-1,100 per week. The best chances for getting a reservation are in June and September. Dogs are welcome.

Sally Littlefield is the hostess at ★ **Oakland House Seaside Resort** (435 Herrick Rd., Brooksville, 207/359-8521, www.oaklandhouse.com). Much of this rolling, wooded land, fronting on Eggemoggin Reach, was part of the original king's grant to her late husband Jim's ancestors, way back in 1765. Jim was the eighth generation on the property; the ninth generation occasionally helps out. Ten one- and two-bedroom nicely furnished and well-equipped cottages are tucked along the shoreline or in the trees. All but one have ocean views; five have kitchenettes, and four have full kitchens. One is pet-friendly ($10/night). Weekly rates begin around $900, varying with month and by cottage; nightly rates begin around $145. Other pluses are trails threading through the woods and providing access to viewpoints and a pocket beach. Open

cottage at Oakland House Seaside Resort

mic nights are held weekly in the barn recreation room during the summer.

Camping

With 730 feet of waterfront on Eggemoggin Reach and 16 wooded acres, **Oceanfront Camping @ Reach Knolls** (666 Reach Rd., Brooklin, 207/359-5555, www.reachknolls.com, $25-30, no credit cards) is a no-frills campground with 32 wooded sites. The camp office building has free Wi-Fi, free showers, and potable water; there is no water at the sites. The campground can accommodate RVs up to 35 feet in length, and electricity is available. There are privies and a dump station. A path leads to the pebbly beach, where you can launch a kayak.

FOOD

Local Flavors

The **Brooklin General Store** (1 Reach Rd., junction of Rte. 175 and Naskeag Point Rd., Brooklin, 207/359-8817), vintage 1872, carries groceries, beer and wine, newspapers, takeout sandwiches, and local chatter.

Wine, cheese, espresso, ice cream, and chocolate—what's not to like about **Sandy's Provisions** (123 Reach Rd., Brooklin,

207/359-8008, www.sandysprovisions.com), which also serves breakfast and lunch.

The **Millbrook Company** bakery and restaurant (160 Snow's Cove Rd./Rte. 15, Sedgwick, 207/359-8344, www.millbrookcompany.com, 7:30am-2pm and 5pm-8pm Thurs.-Sat., 7:30am-2pm Sun.-Mon.) is a good bet for reasonably priced meals made from scratch using primarily local ingredients.

Lunch is the specialty at **Buck's Harbor Market** (Rte. 176, South Brooksville, 207/326-8683), a low-key, marginally gentrified general store popular with yachties in summer. Pick up sandwiches, cheeses, breads, and treats for a Holbrook Island adventure.

You often can find **Tinder Hearth's** (1452 Coastal Rd., Brooksville, 207/326-8381, http://tinderhearth.com) organic, wood-fired, European-style breads and croissants in local shops and at farmers markets, but you can buy it right at the bakery on Tuesday and Friday. In addition, purchase thin-crust pizzas on Wednesday, Friday, and Saturday evenings 5pm-8pm. It's on the western side of Route 176 north of the Cape Rosier Road. It's not well marked, so keep an eye out for the Open sign.

In North Brooksville, where Route 175/176 crosses the Bagaduce River, stands the **Bagaduce Lunch** (11am-7pm Thurs.-Tues,

El El Frijoles serves Mexican with a Maine accent.

11am-3pm Wed.), a take-out shack named an "American Classic" by the James Beard Foundation in 2008. Owners Judy and Mike Astbury buy local fish and clams. Check the tide calendar and go when the tide is changing; order a clam roll or a hamburger, settle in at a picnic table, and watch the reversing falls. If you're lucky, you might sight an eagle, osprey, or seal. The food is so-so, but the setting is tops.

International Fare

★ El El Frijoles (41 Caterpillar Rd./Rte. 15, Sargentville, 207/359-2486, www.elelfrijoles. com, 11am-8pm Wed.-Sun., $5-16)—that's *L. L. Beans* to you gringos—gets raves for its made-from-scratch California-style empanadas, burritos, and tacos, many of which have a Maine accent. Try the spicy lobster burritos or a daily special, such as ranchero shrimp tacos or crab quesadillas. Dine in the screen house or on picnic tables on the lawn; there's a play area for children.

Casual Dining

Behind the Buck's Harbor Market is ★ Buck's Restaurant (6 Cornfield Hill Rd., Brooksville, 207/326-8688, 5:30pm-8:30pm Mon.-Sat., $22-28), where guests dine at white-clothed tables inside or on a screened porch. Chef Jonathan Chase's menu reflects what's locally available and changes frequently. Possibilities include grilled marinated swordfish or pan-seared duck breast. Service is excellent.

What's not organic is local, and what's not local is organic at The Brooklin Inn (Rte. 175, Brooklin, 207/359-2777, www.brooklininn.com, 5:30pm-9pm daily, $12-28). The upstairs restaurant is old-school genteel. A children's menu is available. In addition to à la carte selections, a three-course fixed-price menu usually is offered daily for about $25. Downstairs, the less formal Irish pub (5:30pm-10pm daily) serves burgers, Guinness stew, and pizza in addition to the upstairs menu. On Friday night, it's all the fresh-baked haddock you can eat for $15 in the pub, or $16 in the dining room.

INFORMATION AND SERVICES

The best source of information about the region is the Blue Hill Peninsula Chamber of Commerce (207/374-2281, www.bluehillpeninsula.org).

Local Penobscot Bay Press (www.penobscotbaypress.com), which publishes a collection of local newspapers, also maintains an excellent website, with listings for area businesses as well as articles highlighting area happenings.

The public libraries in this area are small and welcoming, but hours are limited. Most have Wi-Fi and restrooms. Friends Memorial Library (Rte. 175, Brooklin, 207/359-2276) has a lovely Circle of Friends Garden, with benches and a brick patio. It's dedicated to the memory of longtime Brooklin residents E. B. and Katharine White. Also check out Free Public Library (1 Town House Rd./Rte. 176, Brooksville, 207/326-4560) and Sedgwick Village Library (Main St., Sedgwick, 207/359-2177).

GETTING THERE AND AROUND

Brooksville is about eight miles or 15 minutes via Route 15 from Castine. It's about 11 miles or 25 minutes to Deer Isle Village.

Castine

Castine (pop. 1,366) is a gem—a serene New England village with a tumultuous past. It tips a cape, surrounded by water on three sides, including the entrance to the Penobscot River, which made it a strategic defense point. Once beset by geopolitical squabbles, saluting the flags of three different nations (France, Britain, and Holland), its only crises now are local political skirmishes. This is an unusual community, a National Register of Historic Places enclave that many people never find. The town celebrated its bicentennial in 1996. Today a major presence is Maine Maritime Academy, yet Castine remains the quietest college town imaginable. Students in search of a party school won't find it here; naval engineering is serious business.

What visitors discover is a year-round community with a busy waterfront, an easy-to-conquer layout, wooded trails on the outskirts of town, an astonishing collection of splendid Georgian and Federalist architecture, and water views nearly every which way you turn. If you're staying in Blue Hill or even Bar Harbor, spend a day here. Or book a room in one of the town's lovely inns, and use Castine as a base for exploring here and beyond. Either way, you won't regret it.

HISTORY

Originally known as Fort Pentagöet, Castine received its current name courtesy of Jean-Vincent d'Abbadie, Baron de St-Castin. A young French nobleman manqué who married a Wabanaki princess named Pidiwamiska, d'Abbadie ran the town in the second half of the 17th century and eventually returned to France.

A century later, in 1779, occupying British troops and their reinforcements scared off potential American seaborne attackers (including Col. Paul Revere), who turned tail up the Penobscot River and ended up scuttling their more than 40-vessel fleet—a humiliation known as the Penobscot Expedition and still regarded as one of the worst naval defeats for the United States.

When the boundaries for Maine were finally set in 1820, with the St. Croix River marking the east rather than the Penobscot

BLUE HILL PENINSULA
CASTINE

Castine's downtown tumbles to the waterfront.

Maine Maritime Academy

When in port, it's possible to tour Maine Maritime Academy's training vessel *State of Maine*.

The state's only merchant-marine college—one of only seven in the nation—occupies 35 acres in the middle of Castine. Founded in 1941, the academy awards undergraduate and graduate degrees in such areas as marine engineering, ocean studies, and marina management, preparing a student body of about 850 men and women for careers as ship captains, naval architects, and marine engineers.

The academy owns a fleet of 60 vessels, including the historic gaff-rigged research schooner *Bowdoin*, flagship of Arctic explorer Admiral Donald MacMillan, and the 499-foot training vessel *State of Maine*, berthed down the hill at the waterfront. In 1996-1997, the *State of Maine*, formerly the U.S. Navy hydrographic survey ship *Tanner*, underwent a $12 million conversion for use by the academy. It is still subject to deployment, and in 2005 the school quickly had to find alternate beds for students using the ship as a dormitory when it was called into service in support of rescue and rebuilding efforts after Hurricane Katrina in New Orleans. Midshipmen conduct free 30-minute tours of the vessel on weekdays in summer (mid-July-late Aug.). The schedule is posted at the dock, or call 207/326-4311 to check; photo ID is required.

Weekday tours of the campus can be arranged through the admissions office (207/326-2206 or 800/227-8465 outside Maine, www.mainemaritime.edu). Campus highlights include the three-story Nutting Memorial Library, in Platz Hall; the Henry A. Scheel Room, a cozy oasis in Leavitt Hall containing memorabilia from late naval architect Henry Scheel and his wife, Jeanne; and the well-stocked bookstore (Curtis Hall, 207/326-9333).

River, the last British Loyalists departed, some floating their homes north to St. Andrews in New Brunswick, Canada, where they can still be seen today. For a while, peace and prosperity became the bywords for Castine—with lively commerce in fish and salt—but it all collapsed during the California gold rush and the Civil War trade embargo, leaving the town down on its luck.

Of the many historical landmarks scattered around town, one of the most intriguing must be the sign on "Wind Mill Hill," at the junction of Route 166 and State Street:

On Hatch's Hill there stands a mill. Old Higgins he doth tend it. And every time he grinds a grist, he has to stop and mend it.

In smaller print, just below the rhyme, comes the drama:

Here two British soldiers were shot for desertion.

Castine has quite a history indeed.

SIGHTS
★ Castine Historic Tour

To appreciate Castine fully, you need to arm yourself with the Castine Merchants Association's visitors brochure-map (all businesses and lodgings in town have copies) and follow the numbers on bike or on foot. With no stops, walking the route takes less than an hour, but you'll want to read dozens of historical plaques, peek into public buildings, shoot some photos, and perhaps even do some shopping.

Highlights of the tour include the late 18th-century **John Perkins House,** moved to Perkins Street from Court Street in 1969 and restored with period furnishings. It's open in July-August for guided tours on the hour (2pm-5pm Sun. and Wed., $5).

Next door, **The Wilson Museum** (107 Perkins St., 207/326-8545, www.wilsonmuseum.org, 10am-5pm Mon.-Fri., 2pm-5pm Sat.-Sun. late May-late Sept., free), founded in 1921, contains an intriguingly eclectic two-story collection of prehistoric artifacts, ship models, dioramas, baskets, tools, and minerals assembled over a lifetime by John Howard Wilson, a geologist-anthropologist who first visited Castine in 1891 (and died in 1936). Among the exhibits are Balinese masks, ancient oil lamps, cuneiform tablets, Zulu artifacts, pre-Inca pottery, and assorted local finds.

Open the same days and hours as the Perkins House are the **Blacksmith Shop,** where a smith does demonstrations, and the **Hearse House,** containing Castine's 19th-century winter and summer funeral vehicles. Both have free admission.

At the end of Battle Avenue stands the 19th-century **Dyce's Head Lighthouse,** no longer operating; the keeper's house is owned by the town. Alongside it is a public path (signposted; pass at your own risk) leading via a wooden staircase to a tiny patch of rocky shoreline and the beacon that has replaced the lighthouse.

The highest point in town is **Fort George,** site of a 1779 British fortification. Nowadays, little remains except grassy earthworks, but there are interpretive displays and picnic tables.

Main Street, descending toward the water, is a feast for historic architecture fans. Artist Fitz Hugh Lane and author Mary

The historic John Perkins House is open for tours.

McCarthy once lived in elegant houses along the elm-lined street (neither building is open to the public). On Court Street between Main and Green Streets stands turn-of-the-20th-century **Emerson Hall,** site of Castine's municipal offices. Since Castine has no official information booth, you may need to duck in here (it's open weekdays) for answers to questions.

Across Court Street, **Witherle Memorial Library,** a handsome early 19th-century building on the site of the 18th-century town jail, looks out on the Town Common. Also facing the Common are the Adams and Abbott Schools, the former still an elementary school. The **Abbott School** (17 School St., 10am-4pm Tues.-Sat., 1pm-4pm Sun. July-early Sept., reduced schedule spring and fall, donation), built in 1859, has been carefully restored for use as a museum and headquarters for the **Castine Historical Society** (207/326-4118, www.castinehistoricalsociety.org). The big draws at the volunteer-run museum are the permanent Penobscot Expedition of 1779 exhibition and the 24-foot-long Bicentennial Quilt, assembled for Castine's 200th anniversary in 1996. The historical society, founded in 1966, organizes lectures, exhibits, and special events (some free) in various places around town.

On the outskirts of town, across the narrow neck between Wadsworth Cove and Hatch's Cove, stretches a rather overgrown canal (signposted British Canal) scooped out by the occupying British during the War of 1812. Effectively severing land access to the town of Castine, the Brits thus raised havoc, collected local revenues for eight months, then departed for Halifax with enough funds to establish Dalhousie College, now Dalhousie University. Wear waterproof boots to walk the canal route; the best time to go is at low tide.

If a waterfront picnic sounds appealing, settle in on the grassy earthworks along the harbor-front at **Fort Madison,** site of an 1808 garrison (then Fort Porter) near the corner of Perkins and Madockawando Streets. The views from here are fabulous, and it's

accessible all year. A set of stairs leads down to the rocky waterfront.

RECREATION

Witherle Woods

The 185-acre **Witherle Woods,** owned by Maine Coast Heritage Trust (www.mcht.org), is a popular walking area with a 4.2-mile maze of trails and old woods roads leading to the water. Many Revolutionary War-era relics have been found here; if you see any, do not remove them. Access to the preserve is via a dirt road off Battle Avenue, between the water district property (at the end of the wire fence) and the Manor's exit driveway, and diagonally across from La Tour Street. You can download a map from the website.

★ Sea Kayaking

Right near Dennett's Wharf is **Castine Kayak Adventures** (17 Sea St., Castine, 207/866-3506, www.castinekayak.com), spearheaded by Maine Guide Karen Francoeur. All skill levels are accommodated; "Kayak Karen," as she's known locally, is particularly adept with beginners, delivering wise advice from beginning to end. Three-hour half-day trips are $55; six-hour full-day tours are around $105 and include lunch. Two-hour sunset tours are $45; the sunrise tour includes a light breakfast for $55. Friday and Saturday nights, there are special two-hour phosphorescence tours under the stars (weather permitting) for $55 per person. Longer trips are available for $150 per day. If you have your own boat, call Karen; she knows these waters. She offers instruction for all levels as well as a Maine Sea Kayak Guide course. Karen also rents bikes for $20 per day.

Swimming

Backshore Beach, a crescent of sand and gravel on Wadsworth Cove Road (turn off Battle Ave. at the Castine Golf Club), is a favorite saltwater swimming spot, with views across the bay to Stockton Springs. Be forewarned, though, that ocean swimming in this part of Maine is not for the timid. The best time to try it is on the incoming tide, after the sun has had time to heat up the mud. At mid- to high tide, it's also the best place to put in a sea kayak.

Golf

The nine-hole **Castine Golf Club** (200 Battle Ave., 207/326-8844, www.castinegolf-club.com) dates to 1897, when the first tee required a drive from a 30-step-high mound. Willie Park Jr. redesigned it in 1921.

Boat Excursions

Glide over Penobscot Bay aboard the handsome and quite comfortable wooden motor-sailer *Guildive* (207/701-1421, www.guildivecruises.com), constructed in 1934 and captained by Kate Kana and Zander Parker. Two-hour sails, departing up to three times daily from Dennett's Wharf, cost $40; sunset sails, which include a light appetizer, are $45.

ENTERTAINMENT AND EVENTS

Possibilities for live music include **Dennett's Wharf** (15 Sea St., Castine, 207/326-9045, www.dennettswharf.net), where some performances require a ticket, and **Danny Murphy's Pub** (on the wharf, tucked underneath the bank and facing the parking area and harbor).

The **Castine Town Band** often performs free concerts on the Common, and **Waterfront Wednesdays** feature live music 6pm-8pm on the town dock; check www.castine.me.us for schedules.

The Wilson Museum (107 Perkins St., Castine, 207/326-8545, www.wilsonmuseum.org) frequently schedules concerts, lectures, and demonstrations.

The **Trinitarian Church** often brings in high-caliber musical entertainment.

Castine sponsors the intellectual side of the late July/early August Wooden Boat Regatta; the **Castine Yacht Club** brings in a who's who of big-name sail-related designer and racers for this annual lecture series. Other events include on-the-dock boat tours and limited sailing opportunities.

Another source of intellectual stimulation is the **Castine Library,** which presents lectures and other programs.

Gardening fans should ask about **Kitchen and Garden Tours,** which take place every few years.

Watch artists paint and then view the

Kayaking provides a different perspective on Castine's harbor.

finished works during the July **Plein Air Festival.**

SHOPPING

Clustered downtown along Castine's Main Street are **Gallery B** (5 Main St., 213/839-0851, www.gallerybgallery.com) showing fine art and crafts; **Lucky Hill** (15 Main St., 207/326-1066), a combination gallery and home-goods boutique; **Compass Rose Bookstore** (3 Main St., 207/326-8526) and **Castine Handwovens** (Main St.), where Elise Earl handspins yarns and handweaves textiles on historic looms. Down on the town wharf, **SaraSara's** (1 Main St., 207/326-4442) carries a fun selection of clothing and accessories for women.

Oil paintings by local artists Joshua and Susan Adam are on view at **Adam Gallery** (140 Battle Ave., 207/326-8272).

ACCOMMODATIONS
Inns

Castine is not the place to come if you require in-room phones, air-conditioning, or fancy bathrooms. The pace is relaxed, and the accommodations reflect the easy elegance of a bygone era.

The three-story Queen Anne-style

★ **Pentagöet Inn** (26 Main St., Castine, 207/326-8616 or 800/845-1701, www.pentagoet.com, May-late Oct., $135-295) is the perfect Maine summer inn, right down to the lace curtains billowing in the breeze, the soft floral wallpapers, and the intriguing curiosities that accent but don't clutter the guest rooms. Congenial innkeepers Jack Burke, previously with the U.S. Foreign Service, and Julie Van de Graaf, a pastry chef, took over the century-old inn in 2000 and have given it new life, upgrading rooms and furnishing them with Victorian antiques, adding handsome gardens, and carving out a niche as a dining destination. Their enthusiasm for the area is contagious. The inn's 16 guest rooms are spread between the main house (with Wi-Fi service) and the adjoining 1791 Federal-style Perkins House (newly renovated, with marble baths, Wi-Fi, and in-room TVs; pet-friendly). A hot buffet breakfast, afternoon refreshments, and evening hors d'oeuvres are provided. Jack holds court in the pub (chock-full of vintage photos and prints as well as exotic antiques), advising guests on activities and opportunities. Borrow one of the inn's bikes and explore around town or simply walk—the Main Street location is convenient to

the Queen Anne-style Pentagöet Inn

everything Castine offers. Better yet, just sit on the wraparound porch and take it all in.

In 2010, a group of local residents purchased the venerable **Castine Inn** (41 Main St., Castine, 207/326-4365, www.castineinn.com, $135-235), with 19 2nd- and 3rd-floor guest rooms and suites; some have water views. Public space includes a formal living room as well as a wraparound porch overlooking the gardens. Wi-Fi is available in public areas, as is a TV. Breakfast ($10 guests, $12 public) is served in the dining room, which features a wraparound mural of Castine.

Rental Properties

Several Castine real estate agents have listings for summer cottage rentals; start with **Saltmeadow Properties** (7 Main St., Castine, 207/326-9116, www.saltmeadowproperties.com).

FOOD
Local Flavors

The **Castine Farmers Market** takes place on the Town Common 9am-11:30am Thursday.

The Breeze (Town Dock, 207/326-9200, 10am-8pm daily), a waterfront take-out stand, serves good basics such as homemade doughnuts, burgers, fried clams, and ice cream, but it also dishes out some intriguing specials, such as Korean teriyaki chicken, Hawaiian beef tenderloin, and Thai curry chicken, for less than $10. You can't beat the location or the view.

Castine Variety (5 Main St., 207/326-9920, 6:30am-8pm daily), The Breeze's sister operation, operates out of a restored former general store. Luscious baked goods fill the counter, and there are tables, although everything is available to go. The menu may range from eggs Benedict to Hawaiian corned beef hash for breakfast; pizzas, burgers, wraps, and fried seafood for lunch or dinner.

Your best bet for late-night eats is **Danny Murphy's Pub** (2 Sea St., on the wharf, tucked underneath the bank facing the parking area and harbor, 207/326-1004, 11am-1am daily), a sports bar, with video games, a pool table, and frequent live entertainment. The pizza gets high marks.

On a warm summer day, it's hard to find a better place to while away a few hours than **Dennett's Wharf** (15 Sea St., 207/326-9045, www.dennettswharf.net, 11am-11pm

Dennett's Wharf hangs over Castine Harbor and is a good spot for a brew and a burger.

daily May-mid-Oct., $10-30), and that's likely what you'll do here, as service can be slow. Next to the Town Dock, it's a colorful barn of a place with an outside deck and front-row windjammer-watching seats in summer. The best advice is to keep your order simple.

MarKels (26 Water St., Castine, 207/326-9510, www.markelsbakehouse.com, 7am-3pm daily), a higgledy-piggledy eatery of three rooms and a deck at the end of an alleyway tucked between Main and Water Streets, is a delicious find for breakfast, lunch, or sweets. Stop here for coffee, cold juices, pastries, interesting snacks and salads, homemade soups, specials, and delicious sandwiches.

Casual Dining

Jazz music plays softly and dinner is by candlelight at the ★ **Pentagöet** (26 Main St., Castine, 207/326-8616 or 800/845-1701, www.pentagoet.com, from 6pm Tues.-Sat., entrées $18-29). In fine weather you can dine on the porch. Choices vary from roasted *loup de mer* to slow-cooked lamb shank, or simply make a meal of bistro plates, such as lamb lollipops and crab cakes and a salad. Don't miss the lobster bouillabaisse or the chocolate *budino,* a scrumptious warm Italian pudding that melts in your mouth (a must for chocoholics). On Tuesday nights, there's live jazz on the porch during dinner.

INFORMATION AND SERVICES

Castine has no local information office, but all businesses and lodgings in town have copies of the Castine Merchants Association's visitors brochure-map. For additional information, go to the **Castine Town Office** (Emerson Hall, 67 Court St., 207/326-4502, www.castine.me.us, 8am-3:30pm Mon.-Fri.).

Check out **Witherle Memorial Library** (41 School St., Castine, 207/326-4375, www.witherle.lib.me.us). Also accessible to the public is the Nutting Memorial Library, in Platz Hall on the Maine Maritime Academy campus.

Find **public restrooms** by the dock, at the foot of Main Street.

GETTING THERE AND AROUND

Castine is about 16 miles or 25 minutes via Routes 1 175 and 166 from Bucksport. It's about 20 miles or 35 minutes via Routes 166, 199, and 175 from Blue Hill.

Deer Isle and
Isle au Haut

Highlights

© AVALON TRAVEL

★ Haystack Mountain School of Crafts:
This internationally renowned crafts school with

an award-winning architectural design is located in a stunning setting (page 208).

★ Nervous Nellie's: Sculptor Peter Beerits's ever-expanding whimsical world captivates all ages, and it's free (page 208).

★ Arts and Crafts Galleries: Given Haystack's presence and the inspiring scenery, it's no surprise to find dozens of fabulously talented artisans on Deer Isle (page 211).

★ Edgar Tennis Preserve: Serene views and pleasant places to picnic are reasons enough to hike the easy trails here (page 213).

★ Barred Island Preserve: Bring binoculars to sight nesting eagles on the island (page 213).

★ Sea Kayaking: Paddle between the plentiful islands off Stonington and into hidden coves (page 214).

★ Guided Island Tours: Captain Walter Reed knows these waters and is an expert on the flora and fauna (page 216).

★ Acadia National Park: Isle au Haut's limited access makes this remote section of the park truly special. It's unlikely you'll have to share the trails—or the views—with more than a few other people (page 222).

A fter weaving your way down the Blue Hill Peninsula and crossing the soaring pray-as-you-go bridge to Little Deer Isle, you've entered the realm of island living. Sure, bridges and causeways connect the points, but the farther

down you drive, the more removed from civilization you'll feel. The pace slows; the population dwindles. Fishing and lobstering are the mainstays; lobster boats rest near many homes, and trap fences edge properties. If your ultimate destination is the section of Acadia National Park on Isle au Haut, the drive down Deer Isle to Stonington serves to help disconnect you from the mainland. To reach the park's acreage on Isle au Haut, you'll board the Isle au Haut ferryboat for the trip down Merchant Row to the island. In summer, you can go directly to the park's Duck Harbor Landing; in other months, it's a hike through the woods.

Deer Isle and Isle au Haut are inexorably linked yet distinctly separate and very different. Both seduce visitors with their rugged independence and undeveloped landscapes. Deer Isle's main town of Stonington is a metropolis compared to Isle au Haut, with a population of about 1,200 versus fewer than

50. The sidewalks roll up relatively early in Stonington, but there's not much even in the way of pavement on Isle au Haut. Deer Isle has stepped tentatively into the 21st century; Isle au Haut remains pretty much in the 20th—and the early 20th at that. Let it be said, though, that electricity came to Isle au Haut in 1970; telephone service soon followed—although cellular service is spotty at best—and Internet access is available near the village.

Deer Isle is a colony of artists and artisans in equal parts due to the inspiring scenery and the inspirational Haystack Mountain School of Crafts. Top-notch galleries and working studios are found throughout the island. It's also home to numerous small preserves, ideal for easy hiking and bird-watching, and its bevy of nearby islands beckon sea kayakers.

While dreamers and summer rusticators are plentiful, Stonington is first and foremost a working waterfront dominated by lobster and fishing boats and the remnants of

Previous: Isle au Haut; Robinson Point Light. **Above:** Peter Beerits's whimsical sculptures at Nervous Nellie's.

once-active granite quarrying operations. It's also the jumping-off point for trips to Isle au Haut, an offshore gem that has gained fame thanks to author Linda Greenlaw.

The biggest attraction on Isle au Haut is a remote section of Acadia National Park that's raw and rugged, beautiful, even breathtaking in parts. It's not as dramatic as the Mount Desert Island section, but it seduces visitors with its simplicity, peacefulness, and lack of cars. On the trails that hug the granite shoreline and climb the forested hills, perhaps more than in any other section of the park, you can truly feel removed from civilization.

PLANNING YOUR TIME

If you're coming to this region specifically to visit Acadia National Park on Isle au Haut, plan your visit to time with the Isle au Haut Company's boat service directly to the park

(early June-mid-Sept.); otherwise it's nearly a 10-mile round-trip from the Town Dock to Duck Harbor and back. The park boat is first come, first served, so it's wise to be in line well before your intended departure. The park limits visitors to only 128 people, including campers, each day, although there's no real way to enforce that. Reservations for the park's primitive campground open in early April, and slots go quickly. Deer Isle and Little Deer Isle are primarily fishing communities with seasonal tourism centered primarily on touring galleries, sea kayaking, hiking the preserves, soaking in the small Maine town vibe, and savoring the island-dotted vistas. July and August are the busiest months—although the region is well off the usual tourist trail—with September being a lovely month to visit, although businesses have fewer open hours and some galleries close.

Deer Isle

"Deer Isle is like Avalon," wrote John Steinbeck in *Travels with Charley*. "It must disappear when you are not there." Deer Isle, the name of both the island and its midpoint town, has been romancing authors and artisans for decades, but it is unmistakably real to the quarry workers and fishermen who've been here for centuries. These longtimers are a sturdy lot, as even Steinbeck recognized: "I would hate to try to force them to do anything they didn't want to do."

Early 18th-century maps show no name for the island, but by the late 1800s nearly 100 families lived here, supporting themselves first by farming, then by fishing. In 1789, when Deer Isle was incorporated, 80 local sailing vessels were scouring the Gulf of Maine in pursuit of mackerel and cod, and Deer Isle men were circling the globe as yachting skippers and merchant seamen. At the same time, in the once-quiet village of Green's Landing (now called Stonington), the shipbuilding and granite industries boomed, spurring

development, prosperity, and the kinds of rough high jinks typical of commercial ports the world over.

Green's Landing became the "big city" for an international crowd of quarry workers carving out the terrain on Deer Isle and nearby Crotch Island, source of high-quality granite for Boston's Museum of Fine Arts, the Smithsonian Institution, a humongous fountain for John D. Rockefeller's New York estate, and less showy projects all along the eastern seaboard. The heyday is long past, but the industry did extend into the 20th century, including a contract for the pink granite at President John F. Kennedy's Arlington National Cemetery gravesite. Today, Crotch Island is the site of Maine's only operating island granite quarry.

Measuring about nine miles north to south (plus another three miles for Little Deer Isle), the island of Deer Isle today has a handful of hamlets (including **Sunshine, Sunset, Mountainville,** and **Oceanville**) and two

Deer Isle

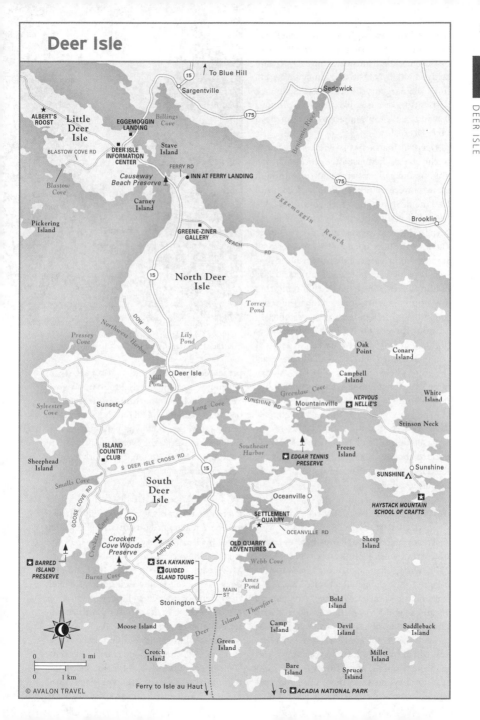

To Blue Hill

15

Sargentville

Sedgwick

175

ALBERT'S ROOST

Little Deer Isle

EGGEMOGGIN LANDING

Billings Cove

Benjamin River

BLASTOW COVE RD

DEER ISLE INFORMATION CENTER

Stave Island

FERRY RD

175

Blastow Cove

Causeway Beach Preserve

INN AT FERRY LANDING

Carney Island

Pickering Island

GREENE-ZINER GALLERY

Eggemoggin Reach

Brooklin

REACH RD

15

North Deer Isle

Torrey Pond

Northwest Harbor

DOW RD

Lily Pond

Oak Point

Conary Island

Pressey Cove

Mill Pond

Deer Isle

Campbell Island

White Island

Sylvester Cove

Sunset

Long Cove

Greenlaw Cove

SUNSHINE RD

Mountainville

NERVOUS NELLIE'S

Stinson Neck

ISLAND COUNTRY CLUB

Southeast Harbor

EDGAR TENNIS PRESERVE

Freese Island

Sunshine

Sheephead Island

S DEER ISLE CROSS RD

15

SUNSHINE

Smalls Cove

GOOSE COVE RD

South Deer Isle

15A

Oceanville

HAYSTACK MOUNTAIN SCHOOL OF CRAFTS

Crockett Cove Woods Preserve

AIRPORT RD

SETTLEMENT QUARRY

OCEANVILLE RD

Sheep Island

BARRED ISLAND PRESERVE

Burnt Cove

SEA KAYAKING

GUIDED ISLAND TOURS

OLD QUARRY ADVENTURES

Webb Cove

Ames Pond

MAIN ST

Stonington

Deer Island Thorofare

Bold Island

0   1 mi

0   1 km

Moose Island

Crotch Island

Green Island

Camp Island

Devil Island

Saddleback Island

Millet Island

Bare Island

Spruce Island

© AVALON TRAVEL

Ferry to Isle au Haut

To ACADIA NATIONAL PARK

towns—**Stonington** (pop. 1,043) and **Deer Isle** (pop. 1,975). Road access is via Route 15 on the Blue Hill Peninsula. A huge suspension bridge, built in 1939 over Eggemoggin Reach, links the Sargentville section of Sedgwick with Little Deer Isle; from there, a sinuous 0.4-mile causeway connects to the northern tip of Deer Isle.

Deer Isle is an artisans' enclave, anchored by the Haystack Mountain School of Crafts. Studios and galleries are plentiful, although many require noodling along back roads to find them. Stonington, a rough-and-tumble fishing port with an idyllic setting, is slowly being gentrified as more and more galleries and upscale shops open for the summer each season. Long-empty downtown buildings have recently been purchased, and locals are holding their collective breath hoping that any improvements don't change the town too much (although most visitors could do without the car racing on Main Street at night). Already, real estate prices and accompanying taxes have escalated way past the point where many a local fisherman can hope to purchase, and in some cases maintain, a home.

Architect Edward Larrabee Barnes designed the Haystack Mountain School of Crafts on Deer Isle.

SIGHTS

Sightseeing on Deer Isle means exploring back roads, browsing the galleries, walking the trails, hanging out on the docks, and soaking in the ambience.

★ Haystack Mountain School of Crafts

The renowned **Haystack Mountain School of Crafts** (Sunshine Rd., Deer Isle, 207/348-2306, www.haystack-mtn.org) in Sunshine is open to the public on a limited basis, but if it fits into your schedule, go. Anyone can visit the school store and dining room or walk down the central stairs to the water; to see more of the campus, take a tour (1pm Wed., $5), which includes a video, viewing works on display, and the opportunity to visit some studios. Beyond that, there are slide programs, lectures, demonstrations, and concerts presented by faculty and visiting artists on varying weeknights early June-late August. Perhaps the best opportunities are the End-of-Session auctions, held on Thursday nights every 2-3 weeks, when you can tour the studios for free before the evening auction. It's a great opportunity to buy craftwork at often very reasonable prices.

★ Nervous Nellie's

Part museum, part gallery, part jelly kitchen, and part tearoom: **Nervous Nellie's** (600 Sunshine Rd., Deer Isle, 800/777-6845, www.nervousnellies.com, free) is all that and more. Most visitors come to purchase the hand-produced jams and jellies and, perhaps, watch them being made. Once here, they discover sculptor Peter Beerits's "natural history museum of the imagination." Beerits, who has an MFA in sculpture, has built a fantasy world that's rooted in his boyhood and complements *The Nervous Nellie Story,* his comic-book-format illustrated series. "Ten years ago, I was primarily an artist who exhibited works in galleries. Now I'm primarily a museum curator," he says.

The buildings, fields, gardens, and woods are filled with interactive scenes and whimsical wood and metal sculptures Beerits has created from the flotsam and jetsam of everyday island life—farming implements, household furnishings, and industrial whatnots—what Beerits calls "good junk from the dump." Take a closer look at that dragon frolicking in the meadow. Its tail and legs are culled from four pianos, the scales are backhoe teeth, the claws are roof-ladder hooks, the neck is a potato harvester, and the head is a radar dish.

There's an interactive Western Town complete with a hotel, a Chinese laundry, a jail, a fortune-teller, a sheriff's office, blacksmith shop, and the Silver Dollar Saloon. Inside the saloon, Wild Bill Hickok is playing his last hand of cards, his back to a gunman sneaking through the back door. "Hickok made the mistake one time of sitting with his back to a door, not the wall," Beerits says, adding that the hand he holds, two aces and two eights, is now known as a dead man's hand in poker. It's that kind of detail that adds a touch of reality to the scenes, and it's the opportunity to grab a seat at the table that engages visitors and keeps the cameras clicking. The West fades

into the Mississippi Delta, where blues music draws visitors into Red's Lounge, where a pianist and guitarist crank out the blues, while a couple flirts in a corner booth.

Beerits moved the original Hardy's Store here. Like a living-history museum, it provides a glimpse into island life decades ago. No detail is overlooked, from the red hot dogs and buns in the steamer to the pickled eggs on the counter, from Neville Hardy at the register to the women seated out front eyeing the gas pump. As in every exhibit, fans have left notes, often illustrated, sharing their thoughts and impressions.

Many visitors take in these sights and then settle into the café for a snack, not realizing that there's more to see. In the woods behind, King Arthur's knights in shining armor, some larger than life, guard and inhabit the Grail Castle. A feast is in progress, and the Grail maidens are parading through the hall bearing holy objects.

You can easily spend an hour here, and there's no admission; wander freely. Beerits will gladly explain his creations, if he's free. The property is also home to **Nervous Nellie's Jams and Jellies,** known for outstanding, creative condiments. You can peek into the kitchen to see the jams being made.

Nervous Nellie's is the creation of sculptor Peter Beerits, who has filled the property with his works.

Getting Crafty

Internationally famed artisans—sculptors and papermakers, weavers and jewelers, potters and printmakers—become the faculty each summer for the unique **Haystack Mountain School of Crafts** (207/348-2306, www.haystack-mtn.org). Founded in 1950 by Mary Beasom Bishop (1885-1972) and a group of talented Maine artisans as a studio research and study program, Haystack has grown into one of the top craft schools in the country, and its campus is listed on the National Register of Historic Places.

Under the direction of beloved former director Francis Merritt, the school opened its first campus near Haystack Mountain, in Montville, Maine, in 1951. Ten years later, when the state unveiled plans to build a new highway (Rte. 3) that would bisect that campus, the school relocated to its present 40-acre oceanfront location at the end of the Sunshine Road in Deer Isle. It was a good move.

You would be hard-pressed to find a more artistically stimulating and architecturally stunning environment. Architect Edward Larrabee Barnes's award-winning campus perfectly complements its dramatic setting. The angular, cedar-shingled buildings are connected via walkways, teaching decks, and a central staircase that cascades like a waterfall down the wooded hillside to the rocky coast below. The visual impression is one of spruce and ledge, glass and wood, islands and water.

One thing that makes Haystack work is its diverse student body. Students of all abilities, from beginners through advanced professionals, come from around the globe for the 2-3-week summer sessions, taking weekday classes and enjoying round-the-clock studio access to follow their creative muses. In a recent year, students ranged in age from 18 to 75 and represented professions from retired teacher to physicist. What brings them all here, said former director Stuart Kestenbaum, is the "direct making experience." That experience draws not only those who make but also those who collect. For a collector of fine craft, he says, taking a class is a "great way to get insight into the making process; it gives a different relationship with the craft being collected." Each session also includes a range of craft. These may include blacksmithing, drawing, metals, wood, beads, clay, fiber, printmaking, glass, weaving, mixed media, paper, and baskets.

The best time to come is 9am-5pm daily May-early October, when the shop operates the casual **Mountainville Cafe,** serving tea, coffee, and delicious scones—with, of course, delicious Nervous Nellie's products; sampling is encouraged. Stock up, because they're sold in only a few shops. Also sold is a small, well-chosen selection of Maine products. Really, trust me, you must visit this place.

Historic Houses and Museums

There's more to the 1830 **Salome Sellers House** (416 Sunset Rd./Rte. 15A, Sunset Village, 207/348-6400, www.dis-historicalsociety.org, 1pm-4pm Wed., Thurs., Fri., mid-June-mid-Sept., donation) than first meets the eye. A repository of local memorabilia, archives, and intriguing artifacts, it's also the headquarters of the **Deer Isle-Stonington Historical Society.** Sellers, matriarch of

an island family, was a direct descendant of *Mayflower* settlers. She lived to be 108, a lifetime spanning 1800-1908, earning the record for oldest recorded Maine resident. The house contains Sellers's furnishings, and in a small exhibit space in the rear is a fine exhibit of baskets made by Maine Native Americans. Behind the house are the archives, heritage gardens, and an exhibit hall filled with nautical artifacts. Bringing all this to life are enthusiastic volunteer guides, many of them island natives. They love to provide tidbits about various items; seafarers' logs and ship models are particularly intriguing, and don't miss the 1920s peapod, the original lobster boat on the island. The house is just north of the Island Country Club and across from Eaton's Plumbing. Hours vary season to season; call for current schedule.

Close to the Stonington waterfront, the

Deer Isle Granite Museum (51 Main St., Stonington, 207/367-6331, www.deerisle-granitemuseum.org, 9am-5pm Sat.-Tues. and Thurs. July-Aug.) was established to commemorate the centennial of the quarrying business hereabouts. The best feature of the small museum is a 15-foot-long working model of Crotch Island, center of the industry, as it appeared at the turn of the 20th century. Flatcars roll, boats glide, and derricks move—it all looks very real. Donations are welcome.

Another downtown Stonington attraction is a Lilliputian complex known as the **Miniature Village.** Beginning in 1947, the late Everett Knowlton created a dozen and a half replicas of local buildings and displayed them on granite blocks in his yard. Since his death, they've been restored and put on display each summer in town—along with a donation box to support the upkeep. The village is set up on East Main Street (Rte. 15), below Hoy Gallery.

Pumpkin Island Light

A fine view of Pumpkin Island Light can be had from the cul de sac at the end of the Eggemoggin Road on Little Deer Isle. If heading south on Route 15, bear right at the information booth after crossing the bridge and continue to the end.

Penobscot East Resource Center

The purpose of the **Penobscot East Resource Center** (13 Atlantic Ave., Stonington, 207/367-2708, www.penobscoteast.org, 10am-4pm Mon.-Fri.) is "to energize and facilitate responsible community-based fishery management, collaborative marine science, and sustainable economic development to benefit the fishermen and the communities of Penobscot Bay and the Eastern Gulf of Maine." Bravo to that! At the center are educational displays and interactive exhibits, including a touch tank, highlighting Maine fisheries and the Gulf of Maine ecosystem.

One of the driving forces behind the venture is Ted Ames, who won a $500,000 MacArthur Fellowship "genius grant" in 2005.

★ ARTS AND CRAFTS GALLERIES

Thanks to the presence and influence of Haystack Mountain School of Crafts, super-talented artists and artisans lurk in every corner of the island. Most galleries are tucked away on back roads, so watch for roadside signs. Many have studios open to the public where you can watch the artists at work. **Deer Isle Galleries and Studios** (deerislegalleriesandstudios.com) usually present monthly art openings; check the site for details. Here is a sampling of galleries.

Little Deer Isle

Alfred's Roost (360 Eggemoggin Rd., 207/348-6699) is a fun gallery and working glass studio in an old schoolhouse. Ask Dusty Eagen to share mascot Alfred Peabody's life story.

Deer Isle

The **Greene-Ziner Gallery** (73 Reach Rd., 207/348-2601, www.melissagreene.com) is a double treat. Melissa Greene turns out incredible painted and incised pottery—she's represented in the Smithsonian's Renwick Gallery—and Eric Ziner works magic in metal sculpture and furnishings. Your budget may not allow for one of Melissa's pots (in the four-digit range), but I guarantee you'll covet them. The gallery also displays the work of several other local artists.

The **Hutton Gallery** (89 N. Deer Isle Rd./ Rte. 15, 207/348-6171, www.huttongallery.com) offers a nice range of fine art and craft work, including prints, jewelry, paintings, basketry, glass, and fiber art.

The **Frederica Marshall Gallery** (81 N. Deer Isle Rd., 207/348-2782, www.fredericamarshall.com) is a multifaceted find. Marshall is a master brush painter who delights in explaining Japanese sumi-e work and demonstrating the brushes that vary from a cat's whisker to four horsetails in size. She also has a classroom and offers workshops ranging from two hours to four days in length. Her husband, Herman Kidder, operates **Kidder Forge** on the same property. His knives forged from old tools are available in the gallery.

One of the island's premier galleries is Elena Kubler's **The Turtle Gallery** (61 N. Deer Isle Rd./Rte. 15, 207/348-9977, www. turtlegallery.com), in a handsome space formerly known as the Old Centennial House Barn (owned by the late Haystack director Francis Merritt) and the adjacent farmhouse. Group and solo shows of contemporary paintings, prints, and crafts are hung upstairs and down in the barn; works by gallery artists are in the farmhouse; and there's usually sculpture in the gardens both in front and in back. It's just north of Deer Isle Village, across from the Shakespeare School.

The **Dowstudio Gallery** (19 Dow Rd., 207/348-6498, www.dowstudiodeerisle.com) shows pottery, metalwork, jewelry, prints, and drawings by Ellen Wieske, Carole Ann Fer, and other artists and artisans.

In the village, **Deer Isle Artists Association** (5 Main St., 207/348-2330, www. deerisleartists.com) features two-week exhibits of paintings, prints, drawings, and photos by member artists.

Also downtown is **Gallery Mozelle** (4 Main St., 207/348-2787, www.gallerymozelle. com), showing works in varied media, including jewelry, clay, fibers, and glass.

Just a bit south is **John Wilkinson Sculpture** (41 Church St., 207/348-2363, www.sculptor1.com), open by chance or appointment. Wilkinson works in concrete, wood, and plaster.

Detour down Sunshine Road to view sculptor **Peter Beerits Sculpture at Nervous Nellie's** (600 Sunshine Rd., 800/777-6845, www.nervousnellies.com), a world of whimsy that will entertain all ages, and if the timing works, catch the Wednesday tour at Haystack.

STONINGTON

Cabinetmaker Geoffrey Warner features his work at **Geoffrey Warner Studio** (431 N. Main St., 207/367-6555, www.geoffreywarnerstudio.com). Warner mixes classic techniques with contemporary styles and Eastern, nature-based, and arts and crafts accents to create some unusual and rather striking pieces. He also crafts the budget-friendly ergonomic Owl stool as well as offers kits and workshops.

Bright and airy **Isalos Fine Art** (26 Main St., 207/367-2700, www.isalosfineart.com) shows the work of local artists in rotating shows.

The **Watson Gallery** (68 Main St., 207/367-2900, www.gwatsongallery.com) is a fine-art gallery representing a number of top-notch painters and printmakers. Occasionally it hosts live performances.

More paintings, many in bold, bright colors, can be found at Jill Hoy's **Hoy Gallery** (80 Main St., 207/367-2368, www.jillhoy.com).

On the other end of Main Street, **Marlinespike Chandlery** (58 W. Main St., 207/348-2521, www.marlinespike.com) specializes in rope work, both practical and fancy.

A bit off the beaten path but worth seeking out is the **Siri Beckman Studio** (115 Airport Rd., 207/367-5037, www.siribeckman.com), Beckman's home studio-gallery featuring her woodcuts, prints, and watercolors.

RECREATION
Parks and Preserves

Foresighted benefactors have managed to set aside precious acreage for respectful public use on Deer Isle. The Nature Conservancy (207/729-5181, www.nature.org) owns two properties: **Crockett Cove Woods Preserve** and **Barred Island Preserve.** The conscientious steward of other local properties is the **Island Heritage Trust** (420 Sunset Rd., Sunset, 207/348-2455, www.islandheritagetrust.org, 8am-4pm Mon.-Fri.). At the office you can pick up notecards, photos, T-shirts, and helpful maps and information on hiking trails and nature preserves. Proceeds benefit the Island Heritage Trust's efforts; donations are appreciated.

SETTLEMENT QUARRY

One of the easiest, shortest walks in the area leads to an impressive vista. From the parking lot on Oceanville Road, just under 1 mile off Route 15, marked by a carved granite sign, it's about five minutes to the top of the old quarry, where the viewing platform (aka the "throne room") takes in the panorama—all the way to the Camden Hills on a good day. In early August, wild raspberries are an additional enticement. Three short loop trails lead into the surrounding woods from here. A map is available in the trailhead box.

★ EDGAR TENNIS PRESERVE

The 145-acre **Tennis Preserve** (sunrise-sunset daily), off Sunshine Road, has very limited parking, so don't try to squeeze in if there isn't room; schedule your visit for another hour or day. But do go, and bring at least a snack if not a full picnic to enjoy on one of the convenient rocky outcroppings (be sure to carry out what you carry in). Allow at least 90 minutes to enjoy the walking trails, one of which skirts Pickering Cove, providing sigh-producing views. Another trail leads to an old cemetery. Parts of the trails can be wet, so wear appropriate footwear. Bring binoculars for bird-watching. To find the preserve, take Sunshine Road 2.5 miles to Tennis Road, and follow it to the preserve.

SHORE ACRES PRESERVE

The 38-acre preserve, a gift in 2000 from Judy Hill to the Island Heritage Trust, comprises old farmland, woodlands, clam flats, a salt marsh, and granite shorefront. Three walking trails connect in a 1.5-mile loop, with the Shore Trail section edging Greenlaw Cove. As you walk along the waterfront, look for the islands of Mount Desert rising in the distance and seals basking on offshore ledges. Do not walk across the salt marsh, and try to avoid stepping on beach plants. To find the preserve, take Sunshine Road 1.2 miles and then bear

left at the fork onto Greenlaw District Road. The preserve's parking area is just shy of one mile down the road. Park only in the parking area, not on the paved road.

CROCKETT COVE WOODS PRESERVE

Donated to The Nature Conservancy by benevolent, eco-conscious local artist Emily Muir, 98-acre **Crockett Cove Woods Preserve** (sunrise-sunset daily year-round) is Deer Isle's natural gem—a coastal fog forest laden with lichens and mosses. Four interlinked walking trails cover the whole preserve, starting with a short nature trail. Pick up the helpful map-brochure at the registration box. Wear rubberized shoes or boots, and respect adjacent private property. From Deer Isle Village, take Route 15A to Sunset Village. Go 2.5 miles to Whitman Road, and then to Fire Lane 88.

★ BARRED ISLAND PRESERVE

Owned by The Nature Conservancy but managed by the Island Heritage Trust, Barred Island Preserve was donated by Carolyn Olmsted, grandniece of noted landscape architect Frederick Law Olmsted, who summered nearby. A former owner of adjacent Goose Cove Lodge donated an additional 48 acres of maritime boreal fog forest. A single walking trail, one mile long, leads from the parking lot to the point. At low tide, and when eagles aren't nesting, you can continue out to Barred Island. Another trail skirts the shoreline of Goose Cove, before retreating inland and rejoining with the main trail. From a high point on the main trail, you can see more than a dozen islands, many of which are protected from development, as well as Saddleback Ledge Light, 14 miles distant. To get to the preserve, follow Route 15A to Goose Cove Road, and then continue to the parking area on the right. If it's full, return another day.

HOLT MILL POND PRESERVE

The Stonington Conservation Commission administers this town-owned preserve, where more than 47 bird species have been identified (bring binoculars). It comprises four habitats: upland spruce forest, lowland spruce-mixed forest, freshwater marsh, and saltwater marsh. A self-guided nature trail is accessible off Airport Road (off Rte. 15 at the intersection with Lily's Café). Look for the Nature Trail sign just beyond the medical center. The detailed self-guided trail brochure, available at the trailhead registration kiosk, is illustrated with drawings by noted artist Siri Beckman.

AMES POND

Ames Pond is neither park nor preserve, but it might as well be. On a back road close to Stonington, it's a mandatory stop in July-August, when the pond wears a blanket of pink and white water lilies. From downtown Stonington, take Indian Point Road just under one mile east to the pond.

CAUSEWAY BEACH AND SCOTT'S LANDING

If you're itching to dip your toes in the water, stop by Causeway Beach along the causeway linking Little Deer Isle to Deer Isle. It's popular for swimming and is also a significant habitat for birds and other wildlife. On the other side of Route 15 is Scott's Landing, with more than 20 acres of fields, trails, and shorefront.

ED WOODSUM PRESERVE AT MARSHALL ISLAND

The Maine Coast Heritage Trust (www.mcht.org) owns 985-acre **Marshall Island,** the largest undeveloped island on the eastern seaboard. Since acquiring it in 2003, the trust has added 10 miles of hiking trails. After exploring, picnic on Sand Cove beach on the southeastern shore. **Old Quarry Ocean Adventures** (Stonington, 207/367-8977, www.oldquarry.com) offers full-day trips on select dates for $50 per person. Or charter a trip aboard Captain Steve Johnson's *Bert & I* (207/460-8679). Johnson will transport you to Marshall on weekends for about $140 per person round-trip plus $35 per person for each additional person or hour. Primitive camping

is available by **reservation** (207/729-7366) at designated sites; fires require a **permit** (207/827-1800).

Guided Walks

The **Island Heritage Trust** (402 Sunset Rd., Sunset, 207/348-2455, www.islandheritagetrust.org), along with the Stonington and Deer Isle Conservation Commissions, sponsors a Walks and Talks series. Guided walks cover topics such as "Bird Calls for Beginners," "Salt Marsh Ecology," and "Butterflies, Bees, and Biodiversity." Call for information and reservations.

★ Sea Kayaking

The waters around Deer Isle, with lots of islets and protected coves, are extremely popular for sea kayaking, especially off Stonington.

If you sign up with the **Maine Island Trail Association** (207/761-8225, www.mita.org, $45/year), you'll receive a handy manual that steers you to more than a dozen islands in the Deer Isle archipelago where you can camp, hike, and picnic—eco-sensitively, please. Boat traffic can be a bit heavy at the height of summer, so to best appreciate the tranquility of this area, try this in September after the Labor Day holiday. Nights can be cool, but days are likely to be brilliant. Remember that this is a working harbor.

The six-mile paddle from Stonington to Isle au Haut is best left to experienced paddlers, especially since fishing folks refer to kayakers as "speed bumps."

For equipment rentals or guided trips, **Old Quarry Ocean Adventures** (Stonington, 207/367-8977, www.oldquarry.com) is especially helpful and provides many services for kayakers. Old Quarry is off Oceanville Road, less than one mile from Route 15, just before you reach the Settlement Quarry preserve. It's well signposted.

Swimming

The island's only major freshwater swimming hole is the **Lily Pond,** northeast of Deer Isle Village. Just north of the Shakespeare School,

The Maine Island Trail

In the early 1980s, a "trail" of coastal Maine islands was only the germ of an idea. By the end of the millennium, the **Maine Island Trail Association** (MITA) counted some 4,000 members dedicated to conscientious (i.e., low- or no-impact) recreational use of more than 200 public and private islands and coastal sites along 375 miles of Maine coastline from the New Hampshire border to Machias Bay. Access to the trail is only by private boat, and the best choice is a sea kayak, to navigate shallow or rock-strewn coves.

The trail's publicly owned islands—supervised by the state Bureau of Public Lands—are open to anyone; the private islands are restricted to MITA members, who pay $45 individual or $65 family per year for the privilege (and, it's important to add, the responsibility). With the fee comes the **Maine Island Trail Guidebook,** providing directions and information for each of the islands, full MITA Smartphone App access, a biannual newsletter, and local discounts. With membership comes the expectation of care and concern. "Low impact" means different things to different people, so MITA experienced acute growing pains when enthusiasm began leading to "tent sprawl."

To cope with and reverse the overuse, MITA has created an "adopt-an-island" program, in which volunteers become stewards for specific islands and keep track of their use and condition. MITA members are urged to pick up trash, use tent platforms where they exist, and continue elsewhere if an island has reached its assigned capacity (stipulated on a shoreline sign and/or in the guidebook).

Membership information is available from the **Maine Island Trail Association** (207/761-8225, www.mita.org).

turn into the Deer Run Apartments complex. Park and take the path to the pond, which has a shallow area for small children.

Golf and Tennis

About two miles south of Deer Isle Village, watch for the large sign on the left for the **Island Country Club** (Rte. 15A, Sunset, 207/348-2379, early June-late Sept.), a nine-hole public golf course that has been here since 1928. Also at the club are three Har-Tru tennis courts. The club's cheeseburgers and salads are among the island's best bargain lunches.

Outfitters and Guided Trips

The biggest operation is **Old Quarry Ocean Adventures** (Stonington, 207/367-8977, www.oldquarry.com), with a broad range of outdoor adventure choices. Bill Baker's ever-expanding enterprise rents canoes, kayaks, sailboats, bikes, moorings, platform tent sites, and cabins. Bicycle rentals are $22 per day or $110 per week. Sea-kayak rentals are $70 per day for a single, $85 for a tandem. Half-day rates (based on a 4-hour rental) are $50 and $64, respectively. Overnight 24-hour rental is available for a 10 percent surcharge. Other options include canoes, rowboats, and sailboats; check the website for details. For all boat rentals, you must demonstrate competency in the vessel. They'll deliver and pick up anywhere on the island for a fee of $30 each way. All-day guided sea-kayaking tours are $130 per person; half-day is $65 per person. Plenty of other options are available, including sunset tours and family trips.

A Registered Maine Guide leads overnight kayaking camping trips on nearby islands. Rates, for kayak rental and guide, begin around $300 per adult for one night, with a three-person minimum; add meals for $8 per person. If you're bringing your own kayak, you can park your car ($7/night up to 2 nights, $6/night for 3 or more nights) and launch from here ($5/boat for launching); they'll take your trash and any trash you find. Old Quarry is off the Oceanville Road, less than a mile from

Route 15, just before you reach the Settlement Quarry preserve. It's well signposted.

EXCURSION BOATS
Isle au Haut Boat Company

The *Miss Lizzie* departs at 2pm Monday-Saturday mid-June-late August from the **Isle au Haut Boat Company** (Seabreeze Ave., Stonington, 207/367-5193 or 207/367-6516, www.isleauhaut.com) dock in Stonington for a narrated 1.25-hour Lobster Fishing Scenic Cruise, during which the crew hauls a string of lobster traps. Cost is $22 adults, $9.50 under age 12. Special puffin and lighthouse cruises are offered on a limited basis. Another option is to cruise over and back to Isle au Haut without stepping foot off the boat ($22 adults). Reservations are advisable, especially in July-August. Dockside parking is around $10, or find a spot in town and save the surcharge.

★ Guided Island Tours

Captain Walter Reed's **Guided Island Tours** (207/348-6789, www.guidedislandtours.com, no credit cards) aboard the *Gael* are custom designed for a maximum of four passengers. Walt is a Registered Maine Guide and professional biologist who also is a steward for Mark Island Lighthouse and several uninhabited islands in the area. He provides in-depth perspective and the local scoop. The cost is $35 per person for the first hour plus $25 per person for each additional hour; kids under 12 are half price. Reservations are required; box lunches are available for an additional fee.

Old Quarry Ocean Adventures

Yet another aspect of the **Old Quarry Ocean Adventures** (Stonington, 207/367-8977, www.oldquarry.com) empire are sightseeing tours on the *Nigh Duck*. The three-hour trips, one in the morning (9am-noon) and one in the afternoon (1pm-4pm), are $40 adults and $30 under age 12. Both highlight the natural history of the area as Captain Bill navigates the boat through the archipelago. Lobster traps are hauled on both trips (but not on Sunday); the morning trip visits Isle au Haut. The afternoon excursion features an island swimming break in a freshwater quarry. Also available is a 1.5-hour sunset cruise, departing half an hour before sunset, for $38 adults and $30 under age 12. And if that's not enough, Old Quarry also offers puffin-watching, lighthouse, and island cruises, with rates beginning at $65 adults, $45 children. Of course, if none of this floats your boat, you can also arrange for a custom charter for $200 per hour.

Sea kayakers favor Deer Isle's craggy coastline.

the *Miss Lizzie*

Stonington's National Historic Landmark, the 1912 **Opera House** (207/367-2788, www. operahousearts.org), is home to Opera House Arts, which hosts films, plays, lectures, concerts, family programs, and workshops year-round.

Bird-watchers flock to Deer Isle in mid-May for the annual **Wings, Waves & Woods Weekend** (www.deerisle.com).

Mid-June, when lupines in various shades of pink and purple seem to be blooming everywhere, brings the **Lupine Festival** (www. deerisle.com), a weekend event that includes art openings and shows, boat rides, a private garden tour, and entertainment ranging from a contra dance to movies.

Early July-September is the season for **First Friday,** an open-house night held on the first Friday evening of each month, with demonstrations, music, and refreshments sponsored by the Stonington Galleries (www.stonington-galleries.com).

Mid-July brings the **Stonington Lobsterboat Races** (207/348-2804), very popular competitions held in the harbor, with lots of possible vantage points. Stonington is one of the major locales in the lobster-boat race circuit.

The **Peninsula Potters Studio Tour and Sale** (www.peninsulapotters.com) is held in October, when more than a dozen potters from Blue Hill to Stonington welcome visitors.

Want to meet locals and learn more about the area? **Island Heritage Trust** (www. islandheritagetrust.org) sponsors a series of walks, talks, and tours late May-mid-September. For information and reservations, call 207/348-2455.

SHOPPING

The greatest concentration of shops is in Stonington, where galleries, clothing boutiques, and eclectic shops line Main Street.

In "downtown" Deer Isle Village, Candy and Jim Eaton have taken over **The Periwinkle** (8 Main St., Deer Isle,

Old Quarry also offers a number of special trips in conjunction with Island Heritage Trust. Most are noted on Old Quarry's website, but for reservations or more info, call 207/348-2455.

Sunset Bay Co.

Cruise through East Penobscot Bay aboard the mail boat *Katherine* (207/701-9316, $24 adults, $12 under age 12), which departs the Deer Isle Yacht Club at 9am Mon.-Sat., for a two-hour excursion taking in Eagle, Butter, Barred, and Great Spruce Head Islands.

Bert & I Charters

Former Stonington harbormaster Captain Steve Johnson and his wife, first mate Roberta, enjoy sharing Stonington Harbor's highlights aboard the *Bert & I* (207/360-8679 or 207/367-2991). Harbor, lighthouse, seal-watching, and sunset tours range 1-2 hours. Ask about his drop-off service to Green Island, where you can spend a few hours exploring, picnicking, and swimming in a freshwater quarry.

207/348-2256) from Neva Beck. They're continuing the shop's quirky yet fun inventory: a mix of books, handcrafts, and niceties.

Just beyond the Opera House, **Dockside Books & Gifts** (62 W. Main St., Stonington, 207/367-2652) carries just what its name promises, with a specialty in marine and Maine books. The rustic two-room shop has spectacular harbor views.

Shoppers need to be cautious going into **The Dry Dock** (24 Main St., Stonington, 207/367-5528), where the merchandise instantly sells itself. Imported women's clothing from Nigerian, Tibetan, and Indian cottage industries; unique jewelry; and unusual notecards are just some of the options in one large room and a smaller back room.

ACCOMMODATIONS
Inns and Bed-and-Breakfasts
Pilgrim's Inn (20 Main St., Deer Isle, 207/348-6615, www.pilgrimsinn.com, early May-mid-Oct., $149-259) comprises a beautifully restored colonial building with 12 rooms and three newer cottages overlooking the peaceful Mill Pond. The inn, on the National Register of Historic Places, began life in 1793 as a boardinghouse named The Ark. Rates include a full breakfast, snacks,

and Wi-Fi. The Whale's Rib Tavern serves dinner.

★ **The Inn on the Harbor** (45 Main St., Stonington, 207/367-2420 or 800/942-2420, www.innontheharbor.com, $150-240) is exactly as its name proclaims—its expansive deck hangs right over the harbor. Although recently updated, the 1880s complex still has an air of unpretentiousness. Most of the 14 guest rooms and suites, each named after a windjammer, have fantastic harbor views and private or shared decks where you can keep an eye on lobster boats, small ferries, windjammers, and pleasure craft; binoculars are provided. All have a small fridge, Wi-Fi, and flat-screen TV and DVD. Street-side rooms can be noisy at night. Rates include a continental buffet breakfast. An espresso bar is open 11am-4:30pm daily. Nearby are antiques, gift, and crafts shops; guest moorings are available. The inn is open all year, but call ahead in the off-season, when rates are lower.

Eggemoggin Reach is almost on the doorstep at **The Inn at Ferry Landing** (77 Old Ferry Rd., Deer Isle, 207/348-7760, www.ferrylanding.com, $130-185), overlooking the abandoned Sargentville-Deer Isle ferry wharf. The view is wide open from the inn's great room, where guests gather to read, play

Stonington's Opera House is an umistakable landmark when viewed from sea.

games, talk, and watch passing windjammers. Professional musician Gerald Wheeler has installed two grand pianos in the room; it's a treat when he plays. His wife, Jean, is the hospitable innkeeper, managing three water-view guest rooms and a suite. A harpsichord and a great view are big pluses in the suite. The Mooring, an annex that sleeps five, is rented by the week ($1,200 without breakfast). The inn is open year-round except Thanksgiving and Christmas; Wi-Fi is available throughout.

Penny's B&B (41 Main St., Stonington, 949/494-7747, www.pennys-bnb.com, $90-$150), an art-filled, shingled and turreted Victorian sited on the edge of downtown, is a laid-back, low-key spot to kick back and relax. Not a place for fussbudgets, this is more of a homestay, with three bedrooms (and an overflow single room) sharing two baths, a tiny one upstairs and a spacious one downstairs. Owner Penny Parkinson, an artist, is a great resource about the area, but don't expect handholding or even a hot breakfast—it's a simple self-serve continental available whenever you desire. Best room is the queen-bedded one opening to a huge private deck with harbor views; that's the one you want. If you're day-tripping to Isle au Haut, you can simply wake up and roll down the hill to the dock.

Motels

Right in downtown Stonington, just across the street from the harbor, is **Boyce's Motel** (44 Main St., Stonington, 207/367-2421 or 800/224-2421, www.boycesmotel.com, year-round, $70-145). Eleven units all have TVs, phones, Wi-Fi, and refrigerators; some have kitchens and living rooms, and one has two bedrooms. Across the street, Boyce's has a private harbor-front deck for its guests. Ask for rooms well back from Main Street to lessen the noise of locals cruising the street at night.

Hostel and Bunkhouse

In 2009, the rustic bordering on primitive **Deer Isle Hostel** (65 Tennis Rd., Deer Isle, 207/348-2308, www.deerislehostel.com, $25 adults, $30 pp private room, no credit cards)

opened near the Tennis Preserve. Owner Dennis Carter, a Surry, Maine, native and local stoneworker and carpenter, modeled it on The Hostel in the Forest in Brunswick, Georgia. It's completely off the grid, with a pump in the kitchen for water, an outhouse, watering-can shower, and wood-fired hot tub. Carter expects guests to work in the extensive organic gardens, using produce for shared meals prepared on a woodstove, the sole source of heat. The three-story timber-frame design is taken from a late 17th-century home in Massachusetts. Carter hand-cut the granite for the basement, and the timbers in the nail-free frame are hand-hewn from local blown-down spruce. The goal is sustainability, not profit. Communal dinners are available nightly.

Old Quarry Ocean Adventures Bunkhouse (130 Settlement Rd., Stonington, 207/367-8977, www.oldquarry.com) sleeps up to eight in three private rooms for $60-70 double; weekly rates as well as whole-building rates are available. Guests use the campground bathhouse facilities. Bring your own sleeping bag or linens, or rent them for $4.

Camping

Plan ahead if you want to camp at **Old Quarry Ocean Adventures Campground** (130 Settlement Rd., Stonington, 207/367-8977, www.oldquarry.com), with both oceanfront and secluded platform sites for tents and just three RV sites. Rates range $40-54 for two people, plus $17 for each additional adult, varying with location and hookups. Children ages 5-11 are $6. Leashed pets are permitted ($2/stay); Wi-Fi is $3 per stay. Parking is designed so that vehicles are kept away from most campsites, but you can use a garden cart to transport your equipment between your car and your site. The campground is adjacent to the Settlement Quarry preserve.

FOOD

Options for dining are few, and restaurants suffer from a lack of consistency. Patience is more than a virtue here; it's a necessity.

Local Flavors

Craving sweets? Head to **Susie Q's Sweets and Curiosities** (40 School St., Stonington, 207/367-2415, 8am-3pm Wed.-Sun.). Susan Scott bakes a fine selection of cookies and pies, offers breakfast and lunch choices (including homemade doughnuts, blueberry pancakes, and often crabmeat quiche), and also carries antiques, books, quilts, toys, and other fun items. It's a Wi-Fi hotspot.

Water's Edge Wines (6 Thurlow's Hill Rd., Stonington, 207/367-6348) sells wine, beer, baked goods, and specialty food, as well as pizzas and sandwiches.

Coffee zealots praise **44 North Coffee** (11 Church St./Rte. 15, Deer Isle, 207/348-5208, 44northcoffee.com, 8am-4pm Mon.-Fri., 8am-2pm Sat.), located upstairs in the old Deer Isle schoolhouse. Don't miss the doughnuts.

On a fine afternoon, there's no better place to hang out and sip coffee than the **Espresso Bar at the Inn on the Harbor** (45 Main St., Stonington, 800/942-2420).

Burnt Cove Market (Rte. 15, Stonington, 207/367-2681, 6am-8pm Mon.-Thurs., 6am-9pm Fri.-Sat., 7am-8pm Sun.) sells pizza, fried chicken, and sandwiches, plus beer and wine.

Although chef-owner Kyra Alex no longer operates **Lily's House** (450 Airport Rd. at Rte. 15, Stonington, 207/367-5936) as a traditional restaurant, she still offers food-themed and other special events.

The Fairway Café (442 Sunset Rd., Deer Isle, 207/348-2379, www.islandcountryclub. net, 11am-2pm daily), located at the country club, is a good bet for a reasonably priced lunch.

Fried seafood, lobsters, burgers, ice cream, and other usuals are available at **Madelyn's Drive In & Takeout** (495 N. Deer Isle Rd./Rte. 15, 207/348-9444, 11am-7pm daily), a popular family spot with picnic tables and a playground.

The Island Community Center (6 Memorial Ln., just off School St., Stonington) is the locale for the lively **Island Farmers Market** (10am-noon Fri. late May-late Sept.), with more than 50 vendors selling smoked and organic meats, fresh herbs and flowers, produce, gelato and yogurt, maple syrup, jams and jellies, fabulous breads and baked goods, chocolates, ethnic foods, crafts, and so much more. Go early; items sell out quickly.

The **Island Culinary & Ecological Center** (www.edibleisland.org), comprising area chefs, aims to create a high-level cooking school and also supports the region as a culinary destination. It offers occasional workshops and programs, as well as an annual fund-raiser featuring a five-course dinner prepared by renowned chefs.

Family Favorites

Harbor Cafe (36 Main St., Stonington, 207/367-5099, 6am-8pm Mon.-Sat., 6am-2pm Sun., $5-20) is *the* place to go for breakfast (you can eavesdrop on the local fisherfolk if you're early enough), but it's also open for lunch and dinner (especially popular on Friday night for the seafood fry, with free seconds). Food varies as does the service; best advice is to stick to the basics.

The views are top-notch from the harborfront **Fisherman's Friend Restaurant** (5 Atlantic Ave., Stonington, 207/367-2442 www. fishermansfriendrestaurant.com, from 11am daily, $10-25). The restaurant turns out decent fried food, generous portions, fresh seafood, and outstanding desserts, but it seems to have lost its soul since it moved from its old digs to this larger and more modern space. Still, where else can you get lobster prepared 18 different ways? Prices are reasonable—the Friday-night fish fry, with free seconds, is around $11.

Dine downstairs in the tavern, upstairs in the dining rooms, or outside in the gardens at **The Factory Tavern** (25 Seabreeze Ave., Stonington, 207/367-2600, www.thefactorytavern.com, 5pm-8:30pm Wed.-Sun., 10:30am-1:30pm Sat.-Sun., $12-30), located just steps from the Isle au Haut ferry terminal. The menu ranges from burgers to lobster arancini.

Casual Dining

The **Whale's Rib Tavern** (20 Main St./Sunset Rd., Deer Isle Village, 207/348-5222, 5pm-8:30pm Tues.-Sun., $18-30) is a comfy, white-tablecloth tavern with a rustic feel in the lower level of the Pilgrim's Inn. Well-prepared entrées may include seared halibut with lobster risotto, rack of lamb, and vegetarian fare.

Views! Views! Views! Gaze over lobster boats toing-and-froing around spruce-and-granite-fringed islands and out to Isle au Haut from ★ **Aragosta** (27 Main St., Stonington, 207/367-5500, www.aragostamaine.com, 5pm-9pm Mon.-Tues., 11am-2pm and 5pm-9pm Wed.-Sat., $21-30), a culinary bright spot fronting on the harbor in downtown Stonington. The emphasis is on seafood—the lobster ravioli earns raves—but Chef Devin Finigan's oft-changing menu draws from what's currently available from local farms. She also makes her own charcuterie, flavored salts, and ice cream. Lunch is served on the harbor-hugging deck, dinner in the unpretentiously elegant dining room; live music, tapas, and cocktails are featured on the deck 5pm-8pm Fri.-Sat. Reservations are wise.

INFORMATION AND SERVICES

The **Deer Isle-Stonington Chamber of Commerce** (207/348-6124, www.deerisle-maine.com) has a summer information booth on a grassy triangle on Route 15 in Little Deer Isle, 0.25 mile after crossing the bridge from Sargentville (Sedgwick).

Across from the Pilgrim's Inn is the **Chase Emerson Memorial Library** (Main St., Deer Isle Village, 207/348-2899). At the tip of the island is the **Stonington Public Library** (Main St., Stonington, 207/367-5926).

Find **public restrooms** at the Atlantic Avenue Hardware pier and the Stonington Town Hall on Main Street, Chase Emerson Library in Deer Isle Village, and behind the information booth on Little Deer Isle.

GETTING THERE AND AROUND

Deer Isle Village is about 12 miles or 25 minutes via Route 15 from Brooksville. Stonington is about six miles or 15 minutes via Route 15 from Deer Isle Village.

Isle au Haut

Eight miles off Stonington lies Isle au Haut. Approximately 3,200 acres, roughly half the island, belongs to Acadia National Park. Pronounced variously as "I'll-a-HO" or "I'LL-a-ho," the island has nearly 20 miles of hiking trails, excellent birding, and a tiny village. The 2010 census counts the population as 73, but islanders say it hovers around 50 souls. Most of those who call Isle au Haut home year-round eke out a living from the sea. Each summer, the population temporarily swells with day-trippers, campers, and cottagers—then settles back in fall to the measured pace of life on an offshore island.

Native American shell middens document 5,000 years of use. Samuel de Champlain, threading his way through this archipelago in 1604 and noting the island's prominent central ridge, named it Isle au Haut (High Island). Appropriately, the tallest peak (543 feet) is now named Mount Champlain.

First settled in 1792, then incorporated on its own in 1874, Isle au Haut earned a world record during World War I, when all residents were members of the Red Cross. Electricity came in 1970, and phone service in 1988.

More recent fame has come to the island thanks to island-based authors Linda Greenlaw, of *Perfect Storm* fame, who wrote *The Lobster Chronicles,* and more recently Kate Shaffer, of Black Dinah Chocolatiers, who shared her recipes along with island tales, in *Desserted.* Although both books piqued interest in the island, Isle au Haut remains uncrowded and well off the beaten tourist track.

Most of the southern half of the

Isle au Haut

Ferry to Stonington and Deer Isle
Burnt Island
Kimball Island
TOWN LANDING
PARK RANGER STATION
Mt Champlain
BLACK DINAH CHOCOLATIERS
Isle au Haut Thorofare
York Island
Robinson Point
THE KEEPER'S HOUSE
Isle au Haut
Harbor Trail
Moore Harbor
Bowditch Mountain
Deep Cove
Duck Harbor
ACADIA NATIONAL PARK
Little Spoon Island
Great Spoon Island
DUCK HARBOR LANDING
Long Pond
Boom Beach
Duck Harbor
DUCK HARBOR
Duck Harbor Mountain
0   1 mi
0   1 km
Head Harbor
Eastern Ear
Western Head
Eastern Head
Thunder Gulch
Western Ear
© AVALON TRAVEL

six-mile-long island belongs to Acadia National Park, thanks to the wealthy summer visitors who began arriving in the 1880s. It was their heirs who, in the 1940s, donated valuable acreage to the federal government. Today, this offshore division of the national park has a well-managed 19-mile network of trails, a few lean-tos, several miles of paved and unpaved road, a lighthouse inn, and summertime passenger-ferry service to the park entrance. The National Park Service has a no-promote policy regarding Isle au Haut; unless you ask about it, you won't be told about it.

In the island's northern half are the private residences of fishing families and summer folk, a minuscule village (including a market, chocolate shop café, gift store, takeout shack, and post office), and a five-mile stretch of paved road. The only vehicles on the island are owned by residents.

If spending the night on Isle au Haut sounds appealing (it is), you'll need to plan well ahead; it's no place for spur-of-the-moment sleepovers. (Even spontaneous day trips aren't always possible.) The best part about staying on Isle au Haut is that you'll have much more than seven hours to enjoy this idyllic island.

Folk singer Gordon Bok penned the lyrics to *The Hills of Isle au Haut:*

The winters drive you crazy
And the fishin's hard and slow
You're a damn fool if you stay
But there's no better place to go

★ ACADIA NATIONAL PARK

Mention **Acadia National Park** and most people think of Bar Harbor and Mount Desert Island, where more than two million visitors arrive each year. The Isle au Haut section of the park sees about 5,000-7,500 day-use visitors annually, with an official daily cap of 128, including a maximum of 30 camping at

Duck Harbor. The limited boat service, the remoteness of the island, and the scarcity of campsites contribute to the low count, leaving the trails and views for only a few hardy souls. According to a 2014 draft General Management Plan, Isle au Haut provides perhaps the best opportunity in the park for low density/solitude experiences. Consider it Acadia's backcountry. Park facilities are limited to a ranger station, maintenance facility, dock, and primitive campground.

Isle au Haut is rich in natural resources, with more than 700 species of plants. Three vascular plants—swarthy sedge, screwstem, and inkberry—are considered endangered or threatened in Maine, and a fourth, mountain sandwort, is listed as of special concern. The island's diverse habitats range from bogs and small wetlands to ledges.

This section of the park not only is remote, but it also offers a rare opportunity to view an undeveloped shoreline, to experience solitude amid the glory of nature, and to ponder unhindered Atlantic views.

About a third of a mile from the town landing, where the year-round mail boat and an excursion boat dock, is the **park ranger station** (207/335-5551), where you can pick up trail maps and park information—and use

this end of the island's only public toilet. (Do yourself a favor, though: Plan ahead by downloading Isle au Haut maps and information from the Acadia National Park website, www.nps.gov/acad).

RECREATION
Hiking

Hiking on Acadia National Park trails is the major recreation on Isle au Haut, and even in the densest fog, you'll see valiant hikers going for it. A loop road circles the whole island; an unpaved section goes through the park, connecting with the mostly paved nonpark section. Walking on it makes for an easy hike. Beyond the road, none of the park's 19 miles of trails could be labeled "easy"; the footing is rocky, rooty, and often squishy. The park is committed to maintaining the primitive nature of the Isle au Haut trails; they're narrower, with few man-made enhancements. But the views—of islets, distant hills, and ocean—make the effort worthwhile. Wear proper footwear and come prepared with water bottles and food; there are no stores in the park.

A park ranger meets the boat that docks in Duck Harbor and provides a brief orientation for visitors. The biggest mistake most daytrippers make is overestimating how much

local art on Isle au Haut

terrain they can cover. It's wise to confer with the ranger about plans, especially if you're not an avid and experienced hiker. Be sure to top off water bottles at the pump. There's also a composting toilet available.

DUCK HARBOR TRAIL

Distance: 7.6 miles round-trip
Duration: 4 hours
Elevation gain: Minimal
Effort: Moderate
Trailhead: Park Ranger Station, north end of the island

The most-used park trail connects the town landing with Duck Harbor. You can either use this trail or follow the island road—mostly unpaved in this stretch—to get to the campground when the summer ferry ends its Duck Harbor runs.

DUCK HARBOR MOUNTAIN TRAIL

Distance: 2.4 miles round-trip
Duration: 3-4 hours
Elevation gain: 300 feet
Effort: Strenuous
Trailhead: Western Head Road

Even though the summit is only 314 feet, this is the island's toughest trail. Still, it's worth the effort for the stunning, 360-degree views from the summit. Option: Rather than return via the trail's steep, bouldery sections, cut off at the Goat Trail and return to the trailhead that way.

WESTERN HEAD AND CLIFF TRAILS

Distance: 4 miles round-trip
Duration: 2 hours
Elevation gain: 150 feet
Effort: Moderate
Trailhead: Western Head Road

For terrific shoreline scenery, take these two trails, at the island's southwestern corner, that form a nice loop around Western Head. The route follows the coastline, ascending to ridges and cliffs and descending to rocky beaches, with some forested sections. Option: Close the loop by returning via the Western

Hike in relative solitude on Isle au Haut.

Head Road. If the tide is out (and only if it's out), you can walk across the tidal flats to the quaintly named Western Ear for views back toward the island. The Goat Trail adds another four miles (round-trip) of moderate coastline hiking east of the Cliff Trail; views are fabulous and birding is good, but if you're only here for a day, you'll need to decide whether there's time to catch the return boat. If you do have the time and the energy, you can connect from the Goat Trail to the Duck Harbor Mountain Trail.

LONG POND TRAIL

Distance: 3 miles one-way
Duration: 2 hours
Elevation gain: 150 feet
Effort: Strenuous
Trailhead: Main road, western side of the island

This difficult loop hike crosses from the west to the east side of the island and passes along a ridge paralleling Long Pond before climbing to the summit of Bowditch Mountain. Option: The trail intersects with the Median

Ridge Trail (1.6 miles of moderate terrain to where it intersects with the main road) and the Bowditch Trail.

BOWDITCH TRAIL
Distance: 4 miles round-trip
Duration: 2 hours
Elevation gain: 350 feet
Effort: Moderate
Trailhead: Off Duck Harbor Trail, 1.5 miles from the ranger station

The Bowditch Trail passes through bogs, forests, and wet ledges as it climbs to the mountain's 405-foot summit, where it connects to the Median Ridge-Long Pond Trail. Varied terrain and good views make the effort worthwhile.

WALKS AND UNMARKED HIKES
Befriend a local and ask for directions to **Seal Trap,** an easy trail to a postcard-worthy harbor on the island's west side. (The name, by the way, evolved from *Ciel Trappe,* which means Sky Trap and has nothing to do with seals). The unmarked trail crosses private property, so do ask locally whether you can hike it, and practice good trail etiquette. Another unmarked trail that's worth discovering is **Mount Champlain,** a moderate hike

up to the 543-foot summit, which provides few views as it's heavily forested. Access is on the north end of the island.

For an easy half-hour round-trip village hike with great views, ascend **Black Dina,** the small mountain behind the chocolatier of the same name. The trailhead is located off the rear corner of the café's porch. It moseys through the woods, before rising to summit ledges with views to Robinson Point Light and beyond—a fine place for a picnic. Reward your minimal efforts with ice cream or chocolates, perhaps both, at the café, afterward.

When the water is rough, **Boom Beach,** on the island's east side, is the place to be. As crashing waves roll in over the round rocks, they rumble, hence the boom. The stormier it is, the wilder this spot becomes. It's an easy five-minute walk to the stone beach from the main road (the only road) along a spruce-lined path edged with moss- and lichen-covered rocks. Bring a picnic, but don't even consider swimming here. Boom Beach is approximately 0.25 mile north of Long Pond beach; look for a grassy pullout, where there might be a few metal lobster traps.

If you're traveling counterclockwise around the island, take the first road on the right just north of Head Harbor, when the road turns

Robinson Point Light

to tar (you'll see a bright yellow house just down the road); across from the log cabin in the field, follow the mowed path to the shore, then look for a sign for **Thunder Gulch.** Follow the trail through the woods and down the middle of Eastern Head. Tension seems to build as you walk through the woods, and then the trail emerges to open ocean views. Waves roll into a cleavage in the rock before erupting in a tower of spray. One islander describes it as a Zen-like place "where all your questions will be answered."

In Duck Harbor, park rangers suggest **Eben's Head** as a great trail for those visiting with young children. It's a short loop skirting the coastline and taking in two cobble beaches that are ideal for beachcombing and splashing. An offshoot climbs a rocky knob guarding the entrance to Duck Harbor, a fine place for a picnic, but keep youngsters away from the edges. The trail is on the park map, and the ranger who meets the boat can provide directions.

Bird-Watching

Isle au Haut's offshore location makes it a popular stopover for migrating bats; shorebirds, including purple sandpipers; songbirds; and raptors, including bald eagles. It's also renowned as a wintering haven for harlequin ducks.

Bicycling

Pedaling is limited to the 12 or so miles of hilly roads: five miles paved, and seven with loose gravel and ledges. While cycling is a way to get around, frankly, the terrain is neither exciting, fun, nor view-worthy. Mountain bikes are not allowed on the park's hiking trails. You can rent a bike (about $25/day) for the island from the Isle au Haut Ferry Service or Old Quarry Ocean Adventures. It costs $22 round-trip to bring your own bike aboard the Isle au Haut ferry. Both boats carry bikes *only* to the town landing, not to Duck Harbor.

Swimming

For freshwater swimming, head for **Long Pond,** a skinny, mile-long swimming hole running north-south on the east side of the island, abutting national park land. You can bike over there, clockwise along the road, almost five miles, from the town landing. Or bum a ride from an island resident. There's a minuscule beach-like area on the southern end with a picnic table and a float. If you're here only for the day, though, there's not enough time to do this *and* get in a long hike. Opt for the hiking—or do a short hike and then go for a swim (the shallowest part is at the southern tip).

ENTERTAINMENT AND EVENTS

Although Isle au Haut is pretty much a make-your-own-fun place, summer events usually include a Fourth of July parade, which all islanders participate in, so there are few spectators, and an island talent show in August. Look also for signs at the town landing dock about themed cook-offs, which might include such gourmet items as Spam.

If visiting with young children, there are swings and a cedar climbing gym at the **Isle au Haut School,** a one-room schoolhouse for children in grades K-8. The **Revere Memorial Library** (www.revere.lib.me.us) has an excellent children's room.

SHOPPING

One doesn't go to Isle au Haut to shop, but if you want to purchase books by island authors, Maine-made jewelry and gifts, or other souvenirs, Kendra Chubbuck's **Shore Shop Gifts** (1 Main Rd., 207/335-2244, www.maineshoreshopgifts.com) is well worth a visit. The shop is in the village, just north of the Town Dock.

The **Isle au Haut General Store** (207/335-5211, www.theislandstore.net), just north of the Town Dock, stocks essentials and a few splurges.

A handful of galleries dot the village. Possibilities may include the tiny **Pretty Good Gallery,** where Jeff Burke shows his portraits, and the **Ruth Van Doren Studio,** with painting, pottery, quilts, glass, hand-made quilts, and more.

ACCOMMODATIONS
Inns

Escape to ★ **The Keeper's House** (P.O. Box 26, Lighthouse Point, Isle au Haut 04645, 207/335-2990, www.keepershouse.com, from $325), a light-station inn. Connected by boardwalk to the automated Robinson Point Light and within night sight of three other lighthouses, the inn and outlying rustic cottages reopened under new ownership in 2013. This is a truly special, all-inclusive, rustic retreat. The spacious top-floor Garret Room, tucked under the eaves—perhaps not the best choice for tall folks—has a bath across from it. The three other rooms in the main building share a bath on the 2nd floor. Although guests have access to both bathrooms, most use the one on their floor. The best view is from The Keeper's Room, overlooking the light tower and Isle au Haut Thorofare. Detached from the main house are the rustic Oil House, with a private outhouse, and The Woodshed, with two bedrooms, kitchenette, and bath. Guests relax outdoors or gather in the small living room. Rates include breakfast, lunch, and candlelight dinners as well as use

of mountain bicycles and a rowboat. Adding to the yesteryear ambience are a 1924 Model T Doctor's Coupe and a 1928 AA Ford commercial vehicle, both parked at the inn. Guests may have the opportunity to cruise aboard the inn's restored 1949 Isle au Haut lobster boat or Friendship sloop. In season, the Isle au Haut Boat Company stops at the inn's dock. BYOB and pack a light. Battery-powered electricity, no phones, no TV, no Internet, no smoking, no credit cards, no pets, no stress. Nirvana.

Camping

You'll need to get your bid in early to reserve one of the five six-person lean-tos at **Duck Harbor Campground,** open May 15-October 15. Before April 1, contact the park for a reservation request form (207/288-3338, www.nps.gov/acad). From April 1 on *(not before, or the park people will send it back to you),* return the completed form, along with a check for $25, covering camping for up to six people for a maximum of three nights May 15-October 15; only one camping visit per person is permitted during a calendar year. Competition is stiff in the height of summer, so list alternative dates. The park refunds the check if there's no space; otherwise, it's non-refundable and you'll receive a "special-use

The Keeper's House is the only overnight lodging on Isle au Haut.

permit" (*do not* forget to bring it along). There's no additional camping fee. Sites are awarded on a first-come, first-choice basis.

Unless you don't mind backpacking nearly five miles to reach the campground, try to plan your visit between mid-June and late September, when the mail boat makes a stop in Duck Harbor. It's wise to check with the **Isle au Haut Boat Company** (207/367-5193, www.isleauhaut.com) for the current ferry schedule before choosing dates for a lean-to reservation.

Note: Campers must carry all gear on/off the boat, which means navigating ramps and docks, and lean-to access is via a trail ascending through rocky and rooty terrain. The distance from boat to dock is roughly one-quarter mile.

Trash policy is carry-in/carry-out, so pack a trash bag or two with your gear. Also bring a container for carting water from the campground pump, since it's 0.3 mile from the lean-tos. It's a long walk to the general store for food—when you could be off hiking the island's trails—so bring enough to cover your stay.

The three-sided lean-tos are big enough (8-by-12 feet, 8 feet high) to hold a small (two-person) tent, so bring one along if you prefer being fully enclosed. A tarp will also do the trick. (Also bring mosquito repellent—some years, the critters show up here en masse.) No camping is permitted outside of the lean-tos, and nothing can be attached to trees. If you're even tempted by the idea of trying to sneak off and backpack into the park for an overnight, forget it. The island is small and rangers, boat captains, and locals keep track of the comings and goings; don't risk federal fines.

FOOD

Isle au Haut is pretty much a BYO place—and for the most part, that includes BYO food.

Thanks to the **Isle au Haut General Store** (207/335-5211, www.theislandstore. net), less than a five-minute walk from the town landing, you won't starve. The summer inventory includes all the makings for a great picnic. On the other hand, food probably won't be your prime interest here—Isle au Haut is as pretty as it gets.

Black Dinah Chocolatiers (207/335-5010, www.blackdinahchocolatiers.com, call or check website for current hours) is located half a mile west of the Town Landing dock. Steve and Kate Shaffer's little shop doubles as a café, serving pastries, organic coffees and

The only camping on Isle au Haut is in primitive lean-tos.

Sweet Success

Life doesn't get much sweeter than creating a successful gourmet chocolate business, and that's what Kate and Steve Shaffer have done with **Black Dinah Chocolatiers** (207/335-5010, www. blackdinahchocolatiers.com, call or check website for current hours) on Isle au Haut, half a mile west of the Town Landing dock. Kate and Steve never imagined living on a remote island off the Maine coast, but after marrying in 1999, the couple, who met in a California commune, packed their lives into a 20-foot RV and headed for the Pine Tree State. Eventually, they combined Steve's business savvy with Kate's long-standing yearning to work with chocolate and opened Black Dinah Chocolatiers, naming it for the rock formation behind their home.

It began with an honor stand. "The first summer, I would bake in the morning and put everything out on a table at the end of our road on the honor system. Every day people left more money than the value of what they were taking," Kate says. The success of the stand convinced Steve that there was a demand for Kate's pastries, but they wanted to get Kate's chocolates into people's hands too.

Steve also recognized that the island needed a communal space, and he knew that their home was one of the few in the three-mile radius with Internet access. So they put it all together and opened an Internet café. It has been a smashing success: Not only have Black Dinah chocolates gained attention in food and travel publications nationwide, but in 2011 Kate was named one of North America's top 10 chocolatiers by *Dessert Professional* magazine.

Operating a successful mail-order chocolate company on an island has its challenges. "We have limited resources," Steve says. And all deliveries are dependent on the mail boat. "It has to be clockwork. You don't get a second chance out here."

Both credit the tiny Isle au Haut community for their success. "Year-round island communities are so tenuous right now. There are only 15 left in a state that had over 300 at the turn of the last century," Kate says. "I think there's this urgency to maintaining a year-round community. Everyone is very aware of it. Each person who arrives is potential to sustaining our lives." Although production for the chocolates has moved to Greater Portland, Isle au Haut remains the company's heart and soul and the Shaffer's home.

Kate shares many of her recipes along with her thoughts on island life in her 2011 cookbook, *Desserted: Recipes and Tales from an Island Chocolatier*, as well as on her blog (http://blackdinah. wordpress.com).

teas, a few lunch-type offerings, exquisite ice cream, and, of course, decadent handmade chocolates. Eat inside or on the deck. The café has free Wi-Fi.

And then there's **The Maine Lobster Lady** (207/669-2751, www.mainelobsterlady. com), Diana Santospago's seasonal takeout serving lobster and fried clam rolls, creative sandwiches, blueberry pie, and homemade ice cream, of course.

INFORMATION AND SERVICES

Information about the section of Acadia National Park on Isle au Haut is available both online (www.nps.gov/acad) and at the ranger station (207/335-5551), about 0.3 mile from

the town landing boat dock. General information on the island is available online from **Isle au Haut Community Development Corporation** (http://isleauhaut.org) and **Isle au Haut Boat Company** (www.isleauhaut. com).

GETTING THERE AND AROUND

Until recently, unless you had your own vessel, the only access to Isle au Haut's town landing was the mail boat. That's still the only way to get there year-round, but two companies now offer transportation to and from the island. Use Isle au Haut Boat Company if your destination is the park, as it lands right at Duck Harbor twice daily during peak season and is the only commercial operation allowed to do so.

If you disembark at the town dock, it's a 4-5-mile journey via rugged road or trails to the other end of the park. If you're overnighting at The Keeper's House, you can shuttle via the mail boat's park service for an additional rate (about $7.50 each way); ask the inn to radio the captain. While it may appear as if you can easily pedal from the town dock to Duck Harbor, it requires a mountain bike and even then, you'll be walking it on many sections. A mountain bike is fine for pedaling around the town end of the island and out to Long Pond (expect hills). From there, you can hike into the park.

Private boats can anchor in Duck Harbor, but there are no moorings. Dinghies can be tied up on one side of the float, as marked.

Isle au Haut Boat Company

The **Isle au Haut Boat Company** (Seabreeze Ave., Stonington, 207/367-5193, www.isleauhaut.com) generally operates five daily trips Monday-Saturday, plus two on Sunday mid-June-early September. Other months, there are two or three trips Monday-Saturday. The best advice is to request a copy of the current schedule, covering dates, variables, fares, and extras.

Round-trips April-mid-October are $38 adults, $19.50 kids under 12 (two bags per adult, one bag per child). Round-trip surcharges include bikes ($23), kayaks/canoes ($46 minimum), and pets ($10.50). If you're considering using a bike, inquire about on-island bike rentals ($25/day). Weather seldom affects the schedule, but be aware that heavy seas could cancel a trip.

There is twice-daily ferry service, early June-mid-September, from Stonington to Duck Harbor, at the edge of Isle au Haut's Acadia National Park campground. For a day trip, the schedule allows you 6.5 hours on the island Monday-Saturday and 4.5 hours on Sunday. No boats or bikes are allowed on this route, and no dogs are allowed in the campground. A ranger boards the boat at the

The Maine Lobster Lady is a seasonal takeout on Isle au Haut.

town landing and goes along to Duck Harbor to answer questions and distribute maps. Before mid-June and after Labor Day, you'll be off-loaded at the Isle au Haut town landing, about five miles from Duck Harbor. The six-mile passage from Stonington to the Isle au Haut town landing takes 45 minutes; the trip to Duck Harbor is 1.25 hours.

Ferries depart from the Isle au Haut Boat Company dock (Seabreeze Ave., off E. Main St. in downtown Stonington). Parking, $10, usually is available next to the ferry landing. Arrive at least an hour early to get all this settled so you don't miss the boat. Better yet, spend the night on Deer Isle before heading to Isle au Haut.

Old Quarry Ocean Adventures

Also offering seasonal service to Isle au Haut is **Old Quarry Ocean Adventures** (Stonington, 207/367-8977, www.oldquarry.com), which transports passengers on the *Nigh Duck*. The boat usually leaves Old Quarry at 9am and arrives at the island's town landing at

10am, returning from the same point at 5pm. The fee is $38 round-trip for adults, $20 for children under 12. Bring your own bike for free or add an island bike rental for an additional $22. Old Quarry also offers a taxi service to Isle au Haut for $175 per hour for up to six people. Note: Old Quarry only services the town dock, not the park dock.

The Isle au Haut Boat Company ferries people to the village and, in season, Acadia's Duck Harbor.

Ellsworth and Trenton

The punch line to an old Maine joke is "Ya cahn't get they-ah from he-ah." Truth is, you can't get to Mount Desert Island without going through Ellsworth and Trenton. Indeed, when you're crawling along in traffic, it might seem

as if all roads to Mount Desert Island pass through downtown Ellsworth and its big-box strip. Truth is, most do.

While there are ways to skirt around a few of the worst traffic spots, both Ellsworth and Trenton have a few surprises that invite exploration. Historic homes, a grand theater, a delightful bird sanctuary, an inviting downtown, fun shops and galleries, and good dining options make Ellsworth worth more than a pit stop. Trenton, linked by a bridge to Mount Desert Island, is little more than a 6-7-mile strip of tourist-oriented businesses, but this stretch of road provides the first glimpses of the prize: the rounded peaks of Mount Desert Island.

Other pluses for the area include inexpensive lodging and the Bar Harbor Chamber of Commerce Information Center location on Route 3 in Trenton. If you're day-tripping to Mount Desert Island, you can leave your car here and hop aboard the free Island Explorer bus, eliminating driving and parking hassles.

PLANNING YOUR TIME

Most people pass right through Ellsworth and Trenton, never stopping to visit the handful of sights. Ellsworth is a thriving year-round community that doubles as a suburb for people employed on Mount Desert Island. It's also the Hancock county seat, the region's shopping hub, and home to the region's most traffic lights, although that's fewer than a half dozen. Don't expect to whiz through on Route 1, but unless there's a major accident or construction, it's not a major time suck. It's also the best spot to pick up necessities or even lunch before arriving on the island. Trenton is far more seasonal, but traffic often bogs down around the lone traffic light and drivers rubber-necking the views. If you want to go car free on Mount Desert Island, the Island Explorer's Route 1 bus services Trenton.

Previous: taking flight in a biplane with Scenic Flights of Acadia; Ellsworth City Hall. **Above:** a resident of Birdsacre wildlife rehabilitation center.

Look for ★ to find recommended sights, activities, dining, and lodging.

Highlights

★ **Woodlawn:** This treasure-filled Georgian mansion has gardens, carriage houses, and walking trails (page 235).

★ **Kisma Preserve:** Splurge on a behind-the-scenes tour of this preserve dedicated to conserving and protecting rescued and retired exotic animals (page 244).

★ **Flightseeing:** Get a proper introduction to Mount Desert Island by gliding with the hawks or getting a bird's-eye view from a small plane (page 244).

★ **The Great Maine Lumberjack Show:** A must for kids, this show demonstrates all the old-time logging skills (page 246).

Ellsworth and Trenton

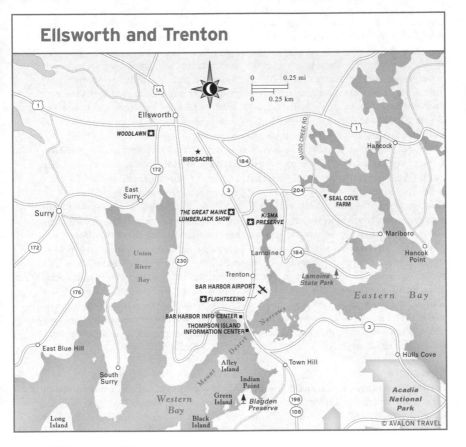

0   0.25 mi

0   0.25 km

Ellsworth

WOODLAWN

BIRDSACRE

172

East Surry

Surry

172

Union River Bay

230

176

East Blue Hill

South Surry

Western Bay

Long Island

1A

184

3

THE GREAT MAINE LUMBERJACK SHOW

KISMA PRESERVE

204

SEAL COVE FARM

Lamoine

184

Trenton

BAR HARBOR AIRPORT

FLIGHTSEEING

BAR HARBOR INFO CENTER

THOMPSON ISLAND INFORMATION CENTER

Alley Island

Green Island

Black Island

Blagden Preserve

Indian Point

MUDD CREEK RD

Hancock

1

Marlboro

Hancock Point

Lamoine State Park

Eastern Bay

Narrows

Town Hill

Hulls Cove

3

Acadia National Park

198

108

© AVALON TRAVEL

Ellsworth

Ellsworth (pop. 7,741), Hancock County's shire town, has mushroomed with the popularity of Acadia National Park, but you can still find handsome architectural remnants of the city's 19th-century lumbering heyday (which began shortly after its incorporation in 1800). Brigs, barks, and full-rigged ships—built in Ellsworth and captained by local fellows—loaded lumber here and carried it around the globe. Despite a ruinous 1855 fire that swept through downtown, the lumber trade thrived until late in the 19th century, along with factories and mills turning out shoes, bricks, boxes, and butter.

These days, Ellsworth is the region's shopping mecca. Antiques shops and small stores line Main Street, which doubles as Route 1 in the downtown section; supermarkets, strip malls, and big-box stores line Routes 1 and 3 between Ellsworth and Trenton.

SIGHTS
★ Woodlawn

Very little has changed at **Woodlawn** (Surry Rd./Rte. 172, 207/667-8671, www.woodlawnmuseum.com, 10am-5pm Tues.-Sat., 1pm-4pm Sun. June-Sept., 1pm-4pm Tues.-Sun. May and Oct., $10 adults, $3 ages 5-12, grounds free) since George Nixon Black donated his home, also known as the Black Mansion, to the town in 1928. Completed in 1828, the Georgian house is a marvel of preservation—one of Maine's best—filled with Black family antiques and artifacts. House highlights include a circular staircase, rare books and artifacts, canopied beds, a barrel organ, and lots more. After taking a self-guided audio tour, plan to picnic on the manicured grounds, and then explore two sleigh-filled barns, the Memorial Garden, and the two miles of mostly level trails in the woods up beyond the house. Consider timing a visit with one of the frequent events: There's a farmers market on Sunday, and on several Wednesday afternoons in July-August there are elegant teas ($25 pp) in the garden (or in the carriage house if it's raining), with china, silver, linens, special-blend tea, sandwiches, pastries, and live music; reservations are required. On Route 172, watch for the small sign 0.25 mile southwest of Route 1, and turn into the winding uphill driveway.

Birdsacre

En route to Bar Harbor, watch carefully on the right for the sign that marks **Birdsacre** (289 Rte. 3/High St., 207/667-8460, www.birdsacre.

com, sunrise-sunset daily, donation), a 200-acre urban sanctuary. Wander the trails in this peaceful preserve, spotting wildflowers, birds, and well-labeled shrubs and trees, and you'll have trouble believing you're surrounded by prime tourist territory. One trail, a boardwalk loop through woods behind the nature center, is accessible for wheelchairs and strollers.

At the sanctuary entrance is the 1850 **Stanwood Homestead Museum,** once owned by noted ornithologist Cordelia Stanwood. Previously open to the public, the home, with period furnishings and wildlife exhibits, was badly damaged in 2014 by arson. Restoration is planned. Birdsacre is also a wildlife rehabilitation center, so expect to see all kinds of winged creatures, especially hawks and owls, in various stages of recuperation. Some will be returned to the wild, and others remain here for educational purposes. Stop by the **nature center** (10am-4pm daily June through Sept., volunteer dependent) for even more exhibits.

Downeast Scenic Railroad

All aboard! The all-volunteer **Downeast Rail Heritage Preservation Trust** (245 Main St., 866/449-7245, www.downeastscenicrail.org)

Woodlawn is one of Maine's best-preserved Georgian houses.

has restored a 1948 diesel engine and rehabilitated the Calais Branch Line from Ellsworth to Ellsworth Falls, and then back and on to Washington Junction. Saturday-Sunday (late May-mid-Oct.) you can board the two vintage coaches, an open flatcar, or the caboose for a roughly 10-mile, 90-minute scenic excursion ($15 adults, $8 ages 3-12). Work continues on the track to Green Lake, which will allow a 24-mile round-trip. Boarding takes place behind the Maine Community Foundation (245 Main St.). If you're a train buff, ask about volunteer opportunities.

Telephone Museum

What was life like before cell phones? Find out at the **Telephone Museum** (166 Winkumpaugh Rd., 207/667-9491, www.the-telephonemuseum.org, $10 adults, $5 children), a hands-on museum with the largest collection of old-fashioned switching systems in the East. To find the museum, head 10 miles north on Route 1A toward Bangor, then go left on Winkumpaugh Road for one mile. Call for schedule.

Ellsworth Historical Society

Kids love the Old Hancock County Jail, now home to the **Ellsworth Historical Society**

Museum (40 State St., www.ellsworthme. org/ellshistory, 10am-3pm Thurs. and Sat. July-Aug., free). Built in 1886, the Queen Anne Revival building housed both the jail and the jail keeper's residence, an interesting combo. Even more interesting is that each of the cells is named, a more contemporary twist, since these refer to local accommodations. The residence is filled with the whatnots of Ellsworth's history, a hodgepodge of antiques and artifacts, with a decor reflecting the Victorian period.

Green Lake National Fish Hatchery

Approximately one million endangered Atlantic salmon smolts and fall parr are reared annually at the **Green Lake Fish Hatchery** (Rte. 180, 207/667-9531, www.fws.gov/northeast/greenlake), which is open for self-guided tours (8am-4pm daily). The facility is located about 10 minutes north of downtown. Take Route 1A north to the junction with Route 179/180, then bear left on Route 180 and look for the sign on the left.

RECREATION

Hiking

Frenchman Bay Conservancy (207/422-2328,

the Stanwood Homestead Museum at Birdsacre

www.frenchmanbay.org) oversees the 13-acre **Indian Point Preserve.** The reward for following the footpath through the woods and across bog bridges to the Union River shorefront is a lovely view of the city. To find the preserve, drive south on Water Street, cross Card Brook, and at the top of the next hill, look for Tinker Farm Way on the right. The road to the preserve's parking lot angles off to the right.

Nature trails lace **Birdsacre** (289 Rte. 3/High St., 207/667-8460, www.birdsacre.com), a 200-acre urban sanctuary with three small ponds; one is accessible for wheelchairs and strollers. Two miles of mostly level trails can also be found behind the Black House at **Woodlawn** (Surry Rd./Rte. 172, 207/667-8671, www.woodlawnmuseum.com).

Meander more than three miles of signed trails through 239 acres of woodlands to the rocky lakeshore in **Branch Lake Forest,** owned by the City of Ellsworth (207/667-2563). To find it, from downtown Ellsworth, take Route 1A 6.5 miles north to the signed access road on your left, and follow it for one mile to the parking lot.

Boat Launches

If you've brought your own boat, you can launch it into the Union River at the **Waterfront Park and Marina** on Water Street, which intersects Route 1 at the traffic light on the lower end of Main Street. Also here are picnic tables and Scoops, a homemade ice cream kiosk. Another launch is on **Graham Lake,** just above the dam, on Route 180. To find it, take Route 1A north from downtown Ellsworth, then Route 180/179 to the split, then Route 180. Look for the boat launch sign on the right, just after the dam.

ENTERTAINMENT

Ellsworth has three free summer series (www.downtownellsworth.com). The **Ellsworth Concert Band** performs Wednesday evening in the plaza outside Ellsworth City Hall (City Hall Ave.). If it rains, it's held inside City Hall. Practice begins at 6:30pm, concerts start at 8pm, and the 30-member community band even welcomes visitors with talent and instruments—just show up at practice time. **Outdoor family movies** are shown at sunset Thursday at the Knowlton Playground on State Street (donations appreciated). **Concerts** are staged at Waterfront Park at 6pm on Friday.

The carefully restored art deco **Grand Auditorium of Hancock County** (100 Main St., 207/667-9500, www.grandonline.org) is the year-round site of films, concerts, plays, and art exhibits.

SHOPPING

Ellsworth has an especially appealing downtown with a nice mix of independent shops.

Specialty Shops

Don't miss **Rooster Brother** (29 Main St./Rte. 1, 207/667-8675 or 800/866-0054, www.roosterbrother.com) for gourmet cookware, cards, and books on the main floor; coffee, tea, candy, cheeses, a huge array of exotic condiments, fresh breads, and other gourmet items on the lower level; and discounted merchandise on the 2nd floor, open seasonally. You can easily pick up all the fixings for a fancy picnic here.

John Edwards Market (158 Main St., 207/667-9377) is a twofold find: Upstairs is a natural-foods store; downstairs is the Wine Cellar Gallery, a terrific space showcasing Maine artists throughout the year.

The eclectic mix of clothing, housewares, toys, accessories, and other finds makes **The Grasshopper Shop** (124 Main St., 207/667-5816) an especially fun spot.

The Sand Castle (163 Main St., 207/667-9399) is an especially appealing store devoted to nature- and ocean-themed merchandise and artwork.

Just a block off Main Street and worth the detour is **Atlantic Art Glass** (25 Pine St., 207/664-0222), where you can watch Linda and Ken Perrin demonstrate glassblowing and buy their contemporary creations.

Brothers Dave and Don Herrington are the creative goldsmiths who design the jewelry sold at **Pyramid Studios** (10 State St., 207/667-3321, www.pyramid.ws).

Toy land, joy land! **Union River Book & Toy Co.** (100 Main St., 207/667-6604, www.unionrivertoys.com) is filled with books, toys, games, puzzles, dolls, stuffed animals, puppets, and more to keep the kiddos happy should the weather turn gloomy. Out back is Karen's Café.

Just south of downtown, at the corner of Court Street and Route 1, **Courthouse Gallery Fine Art** (6 Court St., 207/667-6611, www.courthousegallery.com) showcases works by some of Maine's top contemporary artists. Gallery owners Karin and Michael Wilkes have restored the 1834 Greek Revival courthouse, listed on the National Register of Historic Places. In addition to nine interior galleries, artwork is also shown in an adjacent historic building and in the sculpture park on the front lawn.

Antiques

The 40-plus dealers of the **Old Creamery Antique Mall** (13 Hancock St., 207/667-0522) fill 6,000 square feet on two jam-packed floors.

When the building housing **The Dream Catcher Antique and Collectibles** (107 Main St., 207/667-7886, www.dreamcatcherellsworth.com) was constructed in 1933, it first housed Harry C. Austin & Co., furniture dealers and funeral directors, an interesting combination. Now its three stories house more than 75 vendors selling everything from genuine antiques to shabby chic, estate jewelry, and Native American art.

It's hard to categorize **J&B Atlantic Company** (142 Main St./Rte. 1, 207/667-2082). It takes up a good part of the block, with room after room filled with furniture, home accessories, gifts, books, and antiques.

You're unlikely to meet a single person who has left **Big Chicken Barn Books and Antiques** (1768 Bucksport Rd./Rte. 1, 207/667-7308, www.bigchickenbarn.com) without buying something. You'll find every kind of collectible on the vast 1st floor, courtesy of more than four-dozen dealers. Climb the stairs for books, magazines, old music, and more. With free coffee, restrooms, and 21,000 square feet of floor space, this place is addictive. The Big Chicken is 11 miles east of Bucksport, 8.5 miles west of Ellsworth.

Downtown Ellsworth is lined with independently owned shops like Rooster Brother.

Discount Shopping

Forgot to pack a fleece or sweater for cool evenings? Need a rain jacket or shorts? Wish you had a beach towel or a cooler. You'll find all that and more at the outlets and discount stores hugging the Route 3 strip in Ellsworth.

The **L. L. Bean Factory Store** (150 High St./Rte. 1, 207/667-7753) carries everything from clothing to sporting equipment, but don't expect a full range of sizes or designs. That said, I've never left empty-handed.

Across the road is **Reny's Department Store** (Ellsworth Shopping Center, 185 High St./Rte. 1, 207/667-5166, www.renys.com), a Maine-based discount operation with a "you never know what you'll find" philosophy. Trust me, you'll find something.

Marden's (441 High St./Rte. 3, 207/669-6036, www.mardenssurplus.com) is another Maine "bit of this, bit of that" enterprise with the catchy slogan "I shoulda bought it when I saw it." Good advice.

Sporting Goods

For an extensive sporting-gear inventory, plus advice on outdoors activities, stop in at **Cadillac Mountain Sports** (34 High St./Rte. 1, 207/667-7819).

ACCOMMODATIONS

If all you want is a good bed in a clean room, the family-owned and operated **Sunset Motor Court** (210 Twin Hill Rd., 207/667-8390, www.sunsetmotorcourtmotel.com, $68-125), a pet-friendly tourist court facing Route 1 south of town, fits the bill. It's also well situated for exploring the Blue Hill Peninsula region. Each of the comfortably renovated, rainbow-colored, one- and two-bedroom cabins has heat, air-conditioning, a TV, a microwave, a refrigerator, and in-room coffee with prepackaged pastries. There's even a coin-op laundry. French and Polish are also spoken.

FOOD
Local Flavors

Days and hours of operation reflect peak season and are subject to change.

Order breakfast anytime at **The Riverside Café** (151 Main St., 207/667-7220, www.insideriversidecafe.com, 6am-2pm Mon.-Thurs., 6am-8pm Fri., 7am-8pm Sat., 7am-2pm Sun.). Lunch service begins at 11am. On weekend nights there's often entertainment. And the café's name? It used to be down the street, overlooking the Union River.

Less creative but no less delicious are the home-style breakfasts at **Martha's Diner**

Sunset Motor Court in Ellsworth

(Reny's Plaza, 151 High St., 207/664-2495, 6am-2pm Tues.-Fri., 6am-1pm Sat., 7am-1pm Sun., under $10), where lunch is also served 11am-2pm Tuesday-Friday. Booths are red leatherette and Formica, and the waitresses likely will call you "doll."

Downright cheap breakfasts are served all day at **Sylvia's Café** (248 State St./Rte. 1A, 207/667-7014, 5am-3pm Mon.-Sat., 6am-2pm Sun.), located in the Mini Mall strip plaza on the north side of town. A prime rib dinner is served on Friday nights.

Locals have long favored **The Maine Grind** (192 Main St., 207/667-0011, www.mainegrind.com, 7:30am-5:30pm Mon.-Wed., 7:30am-10pm Thur.-Sat., 10am-6:30pm Sun.). Go for sandwiches, grilled pizzas and flatbreads, soups, salads, and even tapas. Everything is made from scratch. You can either order at the counter and find a table or couch or dine in the restaurant section. This congenial spot, dubbed Ellsworth's Living Room, also has free Wi-Fi and live music on some evenings.

Hidden in the back of Union River Book & Toy Co. is **Karen's Café** (100 Main St., 207/412-0102, 8am-3pm Mon.-Sat.), a local secret for hearty sandwiches (gluten-free bread is available) and seafood chowder.

Big flavors come out of tiny **86 This** (2 State St., 207/610-1777, 10:30am-4:30pm Mon.-Fri., 10:30am-3pm Sat.), a wrap and burrito joint with a handful of tables. The flavors are rich, the portions are generous, and wraps are named after the owners' favorite indie bands. Get it to go and walk the half block to the picnic tables on the shady lawn of the library.

Jordan's Snack Bar (200 Down East Hwy./Rte. 1, 207/667-2174, 10:30am-7pm Sun.-Thurs., 10:30am-8pm Fri.-Sat.) has an almost cult following for its crabmeat rolls and fried clams. Wednesday Cruise-Ins, beginning at 6pm, usually feature live entertainment and draw up to 50 vintage cars.

Ice cream doesn't get much finer than that sold at ★ **Morton's Moo** (9 School St., 207/266-9671), a family-run spot with a deservedly giant reputation for homemade Italian gelato and ice cream in creative flavors. It's half a block off Main Street behind The Maine Grind.

For cheap eats, you can't beat **Rocky Point Clam Cakes** (270 High St./Rte. 3, 207/669-2526), a food truck serving Rhode Island-style clam cakes, along with chowder, New York hot dogs, hand-cut fries, and doughboys. It's usually parked just south of

The Maine Grind is dubbed Ellsworth's Living Room.

the Route 1/Route 3 split, but call if you can't find it.

The **Ellsworth Farmers Market** gets under way in the parking lot behind the Maine Community Foundation (245 Main St., 2pm-5:30pm Mon. and Thurs. mid-June-late Oct.), and in the Hancock Oil parking lot (190 Main St., 9:30am-noon Sat. mid-June-late Oct.). It features fresh produce as well as jams, pickles, maple syrup, homemade breads, and homespun yarns.

Casual Dining

Decent pub fare is served at **Finn's Irish Pub** (156 Main St., 207/667-2808, 11am-9pm Sun.-Tues., 11am-10pm Wed.-Thurs., 11am-11pm Fri.-Sat., $7-15), and there's a kids' menu too.

Meat, meat, meat is on the menu at **Mainely Meat on Maine** (193 Main St., 207/664-5239, 11am-8pm Sun.-Thurs., 11am-9pm Fri.-Sat., $9-16). There's often live entertainment, including open-mic on Wednesday.

International Fare

Mighty fine pizza is served at **Finelli Pizzeria** (12 U.S. 1, 207/664-0230, www.finellipizzeria.com, 11am-8pm Sun.-Thurs., 11am-9pm Fri.-Sat., $7-20), a homely little spot where the pizza dough and focaccia bread are made fresh daily. The specialty is New York-style thin-crust pizza, but other options include calzones, pastas, subs, and salads.

Down East meets Far East at **Shinbashi** (139 High St., 207/667-6561, www.myshinbashi.com, 11:30am-9:30pm Sun.-Thurs., 11:30am-10pm Fri.-Sat., $8-24), serving an extensive menu of Japanese, Chinese, Vietnamese, and Thai specialties, including sushi and Peking duck; there's also a children's menu.

Lobster

It's hard to say which is better—the serene views or the tasty lobster—at Brian and Jane Langley's **Union River Lobster Pot** (8 South St., 207/667-5077, www.lobsterpot.com, 4pm-9pm daily June-mid-Sept., $15-24). It's tucked behind Rooster Brother, right on the banks of the Union River. The menu includes far more than lobster, with chicken, fish, meat, and pasta dishes, and a kids' menu is available. Remember to save room for the pie, especially the blueberry.

INFORMATION AND SERVICES

It can be hard to spot the **Ellsworth Area Chamber of Commerce** (163 High St., 207/667-5584, www.ellsworthchamber.org) amid the malls and fast-food places lining High Street (Rte. 1). Watch for a small gray building topped by an Information Center sign (close to the road, on the right when heading toward Bar Harbor, just before Shaw's Plaza). **Downtown Ellsworth** (www.ellsworthdowntown.com) also has info.

Public restrooms can be found in City Hall (City Hall Ave.) in downtown Ellsworth, open 24 hours daily, seven days a week; the library (46 State St.); the chamber of commerce; and the picnic area and boat launch (Water St.).

Libraries

Don't miss a chance to visit one of the state's loveliest libraries, the **Ellsworth Public Library** (46 State St., 207/667-6363, www.ellsworth.lib.me.us), listed on the National Register of Historic Places. George Nixon Black, grandson of the builder of the Woodlawn museum, donated the Federal-style building to the city in 1897.

GETTING THERE AND AROUND

Ellsworth is about 14 miles via Route 172 from Blue Hill. It's about 20 miles or 30-45 minutes, depending upon traffic, to Bar Harbor and about 25 miles or 35 minutes via Routes 1 and 186 to Winter Harbor on the Schoodic Peninsula.

Road-wise, Ellsworth is the epicenter of Acadia. Route 1, the main thoroughfare along the coast, and Route 1A, which connects to Bangor, meet in downtown Ellsworth.

The Lobster Experience

No visit to Maine can be considered complete without the experience of a "lobstah dinnah" at a lobster wharf, pound, or shack. Keep an eye on the weather, pick a sunny day, and head out.

If you're in the area before Memorial Day or after Labor Day, the options are not as varied—many such enterprises have a short season, although more and more are staying open at least through September.

There's nowhere to eat lobster within Acadia National Park (unless you're camping and cook it yourself over a campfire), but Mount Desert Island and the surrounding region provide plenty of opportunities. Almost every restaurant, café, or bistro serves lobster in some form or other. But as you drive, bus, bike, or walk around, watch for the genuine article—the "real" lobster wharf. You want to eat outdoors, at a wooden picnic table, with a knockout view of boats and the sea. If you're camping, most lobster wharves will boil lobsters for you free or for a small fee. They'll wrap them in newspaper so they stay warm until you get back to your campsite. The best advice is to order them like pizza: Call ahead so they'll be ready when you show up for them.

At whatever place you choose, the drill is much the same, and the "dinners" are served anytime from 11am or noon onward (some places close as early as 7pm). First of all, dress very casually so you can manhandle the lobster without messing up decent clothes. If you want beer or wine, call ahead and ask if the place serves it; you may need to bring your own, since many such operations don't have beer-and-wine licenses, much less liquor licenses. In the evening, carry some insect repellent, in case mosquitoes crash the party.

A basic one-pound lobster and go-withs (coleslaw or potato salad, potato chips, and butter for dipping) should run $15-22, based on the seasonal lobster price; some shacks will include steamed clams too. Unfortunately, some places use margarine, which doesn't do lobster any favors. Don't skip dessert; many lobster pounds are known for their homemade pies.

It's not unusual to see lobster-wharf devotees carting picnic baskets with hors d'oeuvres, salads, and baguettes. I've even seen candles, champagne, tablecloths, and fresh flowers. Creativity abounds, but don't stray too far from the main attraction—the crustaceans.

Typically, you'll need to survey a chalkboard or whiteboard menu and step up to a window to order. You'll either give the person your name or get a number. A few places have staff to take your order or deliver your meal (and help you figure out how to eat it), but usually you'll head back to the window when your name or number is called. Don your plastic lobster bib and begin the attack. If you're a neophyte, watch a pro at a nearby table. Some lobster wharves have "how-to" info printed on paper placemats. If you're really concerned (you needn't be), contact the Maine Lobster Promotion Council (www.mainelobsterpromo.com), which produces a brochure with detailed instructions. Don't worry about doing it wrong; you'll eventually get what you came for, and it'll be an experience to remember.

Here are five classic lobster experiences in Maine's Acadia region:

- **Bernard (Mount Desert Island):** Thurston's Lobster Pound (Steamboat Wharf Rd., Bernard, 207/244-7600, www.thurstonslobster.com, 11am-8:30pm daily)

- **Southwest Harbor (Mount Desert Island):** Beal's Lobster Pier (182 Clark Point Rd., Southwest Harbor, 207/244-3202, 11am-sunset daily)

- **Corea (Schoodic Peninsula):** Corea Wharf & Gallery, 13 Gibbs Ln, Corea, 207/963-2633, www.coreawharfgallery.com, 11am-5pm daily)

- **Surry:** Perry's Lobster Shack and Pier (1076 Newbury Neck Rd., Surry, 207/667-1955, 10am-7pm daily)

- **Trenton:** Trenton Bridge Lobster Pound (Bar Harbor Rd./Rte. 3, Trenton, 207/667-2977, www. trentonbridgelobster.com, 11am-7:30pm Mon.-Sat.)

Route 172 connects Ellsworth to the Blue Hill Peninsula and on to Deer Isle, Stonington, and the mail boat to Isle au Haut. Route 1 continues north, providing access to the Schoodic Peninsula and a remote section of the park. And the Bar Harbor Road (Rte. 3) is something of an Achilles heel—often a summertime bottleneck as it funnels all traffic to Mount Desert Island. If you want to hit the region's highlights, by all means stay on Routes 1 and 3, but if your time is limited and your goal is maximum park time, consider these shortcuts.

If you're approaching from the south on Route 1 and your destination is Mount Desert Island, you can avoid downtown and the strip. When you cross the bridge in Ellsworth, turn right at the traffic light onto Route 230 (Water St.) and follow it about 6.5 miles, turning left onto Goose Cove Road, which rejoins Route 230. (You can stay on Route 230; it's just longer as it loops around the point.) Bear left on Route 230, then right at the T intersection with Route 3. The causeway connecting to Mount Desert Island is less than a mile away.

If your destination is the Schoodic region, at the intersection of Route 1A and Route 1 (Main St.) in downtown Ellsworth, stay on Main Street (east of the light called E. Main St.) and avoid the Route 1 strip. East Main Street morphs into Washington Junction Road and reconnects with Route 1 northeast of the Route 3 split for Mount Desert Island, avoiding the worst congestion.

Trenton

Unless you're arriving by boat, you can't get to Mount Desert Island without first going through Trenton (pop. 1,481), which straddles Route 3 from Ellsworth south. Big-box stores, restaurants, motels, amusements, and gift shops line the congested six-mile strip, and some are worth at least a nod. If you're traveling with children, count on being begged to stop. Rural Lamoine (pop. 1,602) provides a reprieve. Few discover this peninsula-tipping town, with a state park and gorgeous views over Eastern and Frenchman Bay to Mount Desert Island.

SIGHTS
★ Kisma Preserve

I can't stress this enough: **Kisma Preserve** (446 Bar Harbor Rd./Rte. 3, 207/667-3244, www.kismapreserve.org, 10am-6pm daily mid-May-late fall, basic tour $14) is not a zoo; it's a nonprofit educational facility, and everything revolves around preserving and protecting the animals, most of which are either rescues or retirees. Rules are strictly enforced—no running, loud voices, or disruptive behavior is permitted. The easiest way to view the animals is on a one-hour guided tour. Guides educate visitors about the biology of the animals, how they came to be here, and whether they'll be returned to the wild. For serious animal lovers, the preserve offers behind-the-scenes tours and close-ups; there are even options for staying in the preserve overnight. It truly is a special place, home to more than 100 exotic and not-so-exotic creatures, with an emphasis on wolves and bears. Donations are essential to Kisma's survival, and yes, it's pricey, but so is feeding and caring for these animals.

★ Flightseeing

Two businesses provide options for getting an eagle's-eye view of the area. Both are based on the Route 3 side of Hancock County/Bar Harbor Airport, just north of Mount Desert Island.

Scenic Flights of Acadia (Bar Harbor Rd./Rte. 3, 207/667-6527, www.scenicflightsofacadia.com) offers low-level flightseeing services in the Mount Desert Island region.

Kisma Preserve is a sanctuary for retired or relocated exotic animals.

$3 Maine resident adults, $1 ages 5-11) features a pebble beach and a picnic area with a spectacular view, a children's play area, and campsites. If you've brought your own boat, the park also provides a boat ramp for launching. Careful, though, the currents are strong here. Although the 55-acre park isn't officially open in winter, it's popular for cross-country skiing and snowshoeing. This is strictly do-it-yourself fun, as there are no marked trails.

Lamoine Beach and Bloomfield Park

Follow Route 184 to the end (about a mile beyond the park), and you'll arrive at **Lamoine Beach,** a town-owned sand swath with picnic tables, a boat launch, and spectacular views of Mount Desert Island. For freshwater swimming, try **Bloomfield Park** (on Bloomfield Park Rd., off Asa's Ln.), a town-owned park with picnic tables on Blunt's Pond. Both have toilets.

Thompson Island Picnic Area

Edging the ocean at Mount Desert Narrows is the **Thompson Island Picnic Area** (Rte. 3, Thompson Island, Trenton). It has picnic tables, fire grills, a water fountain, and restrooms. At low tide, you might see locals raking the mudflats for clams.

Paddling

Acadia 1 Watersports (1564 Shore Rd., Lamoine, 207/667-2963 or 888/786-0676, www.kayak1.com) rents solo sea kayaks for $40 per day or $155 per week; tandems are $54 per day or $195 per week. Delivery is free to Lamoine Beach and can be arranged throughout the Acadia region for fuel fee. Be careful if paddling the Mount Desert Narrows, as the currents can be tricky.

Golf

Try to keep your eye on the ball rather than the views at the challenging 18-hole **Bar Harbor Golf Course** (Rte. 3 and Rte. 204, 207/667-7505, www.barharborgolfcourse.

Flights range 15-75 minutes, with prices beginning around $50 per person with a two-passenger minimum.

Scenic Biplane and Glider Rides (968 Bar Harbor Rd./Rte. 3, 207/667-7627, www.acadiaairtours.com) lets you soar in silence with daily glider flights. The one- or two-passenger gliders are towed to an altitude of at least 2,500 feet and then released. An FAA-certified pilot guides the glider. Rates begin at $150 for a 15-minute flight for one or two. Or ride in a biplane: A 20-minute ride in an open-cockpit plane is $250 for two. Or for a different twist, consider experiencing a World War II-era T-6 fighter plane, with flights beginning at $275 for 15 minutes. All flights are subject to an airport fee.

RECREATION

Lamoine State Park

Lamoine State Park (23 State Park Rd./Rte. 184, Lamoine, 207/667-4778, www.parksandlands.com, day-use $4.50 nonresident adults, com). Despite the name, it's not in the island community, nor even on the island.

ENTERTAINMENT
★ The Great Maine Lumberjack Show

Ace lumberjack "Timber" Tina Scheer has been competing around the world since she was seven, and she shows her prowess at **The Great Maine Lumberjack Show** (Rte. 3, 207/667-0067, www.mainelumberjack.com, 7pm daily mid-June-early Sept., 4pm Sat. and 2pm Sun. early Sept.-mid-Oct., $12 adults, $11 over age 62, $7.50 ages 4-11). During the 75-minute "Olympics of the Forest," you'll watch two teams compete in 12 events, including ax throwing, crosscut sawing, log rolling, speed climbing, and more. Some events are open to participation. (Kids can learn some skills by appointment.) Performances are held rain or shine. Seating is under a roof, but dress for the weather if it's inclement. The ticket office opens at 6pm.

SHOPPING

Adults can browse the books, antiques, and even wine selections housed in **Country Store Antiques** (410 Rte. 3/Bar Harbor Rd., 207/667-5922), a huge red barn with 30 dealers selling a wide range of goods.

Stock up on Maine-made jams, syrups, honeys, and other specialty foods at **Maine's Own Treats** (68 Rte. 3/Bar Harbor Rd., 207/667-8888, www.mainesowntreats.com).

ACCOMMODATIONS

Most of the motels and cabin complexes along the Trenton stretch are small, family-owned operations—not fancy, but their rates are usually far lower than what you'll find on Mount Desert Island. Those in Trenton are on Route 3, so expect traffic noise; the B&Bs in Lamoine are off the beaten path. Rates reflect peak season.

The Kelley family's **Isleview Motel** (1169 Bar Harbor Rd./Rte. 3, Trenton, 207/667-5661 or 866/475-3843, www.isleviewmoteland-cottages.com, $60-90) comprises a motel, one- and two-bedroom cottages, and a few "sleep-and-go" rooms above the office, all decorated in country style. At these prices and with this location—eight miles from the park entrance, on the Island Explorer shuttle route, across from a lobster restaurant, and just 0.5 mile from the Thompson Island Picnic Area—don't go looking for fancy, but wallet-conscious travelers will be tickled with it. Although small, most guest rooms are equipped with a mini-refrigerator,

Scenic Biplane and Glider Rides offers daily glider flights.

a microwave, Wi-Fi, a coffeemaker, air-conditioning, and a TV. Outside are picnic tables and grills. Rates include breakfast pastries, juice, and coffee.

Clean, cheap, convenient, and charming describe the family-owned **Open Hearth Inn** (Bar Harbor Rd./Rte. 3, Trenton, 207/667-2930 or 800/655-0034, www.openhearthinn.com, year-round, $65-130). Choose an inn room or opt for a tourist court-style cottage or motel room, or an apartment with a kitchen. All have TVs, fridges, air-conditioning, and Wi-Fi. Also on the premises are an enclosed family hot tub and a putting green. Kids under 12 stay free, and free pickup at Bar Harbor Airport is offered during business hours. On most mornings, until they run out, homemade muffins are available in the office, along with tea and coffee. It's on the Island Explorer bus route, less than 0.25 mile from the bridge connecting Trenton to Mount Desert Island and within walking distance of four lobster restaurants.

New owners, since 2009, have been upgrading and updating the pet-friendly **Acadia Sunrise Motel** (952 Bar Harbor Rd./Rte. 3, Trenton, 207/667-8452, www.acadiasunrisemotel.com, $69-105), originally built in 1985 as a strip mall. All guest rooms have air-conditioning, cable TV, phones, refrigerators, microwaves, and coffeemakers; efficiency units have kitchenettes with stoves. Perks include an outdoor heated pool and a guest laundry. Ask for a room at the back, away from the street noise and overlooking the airport with the ocean and Acadia's mountains in the distance.

Chocoholics, take note: The **Chocolate Chip Bed & Breakfast** (720 Lamoine Beach Rd., Lamoine, 207/610-1691, www.chocolatechipbb.com, $125-155) treats guests to all kinds of chocolate treats, from muffins in the morning to cookies at night. Eric and Sue Hahn's lovingly rebuilt, early 19th-century, pond-side farmhouse has four comfy guest rooms decorated in country style, all with hardwood floors, handmade quilts, free Wi-Fi, and cable TV.

You can't beat the view from **Capt'n N Eve's Eden** (461 Lamoine Beach Rd., Lamoine, 207/667-3109, $65-75), a newer home with three bedrooms, one with private bath and two sharing onc bath, all with commanding views over fields and ocean to Mount Desert Island. Rates include a full breakfast. Smoking is permitted in limited areas. This has a bit of a homestay feel, as the living areas are shared with owner Evelyn Farrell.

cottages at the Open Hearth Inn

Camping

Here's a prize. Equally convenient to the Schoodic region and Mount Desert Island is the 55-acre, oceanfront ★ **Lamoine State Park** (23 State Park Rd./Rte. 184, Lamoine, 207/667-4778, www.parksandlands.com, day-use $4.50 nonresident adults, $3 Maine resident adults, $1 ages 5-11). Park facilities include a picnic area with a spectacular view, a boat-launch ramp, a children's play area, a treehouse, and a dumping station. Camping (mid-May-mid-Oct., $25 nonresidents, $15 Maine residents, reservations $2/night) is available at 62 sites. Most are wooded and several are oceanfront. No hookups are available (except for one site designated for the disabled), and the minimum stay in July and August is 2 nights, with a 14-night maximum. The campground has a modern bathhouse with free hot showers. Reserve online with a credit card, or call 207/624-9950 or 800/332-1501 weekdays within Maine. Leashed pets are allowed; cleanup is required.

FOOD

One of the best-known and longest-running (since 1956) lobster joints is **Trenton Bridge Lobster Pound** (Bar Harbor Rd./Rte. 3, Trenton, 207/667-2977, www. trentonbridgelobster.com, 11am-7:30pm Mon.-Sat. late May-mid-Oct.), on the right next to the bridge leading to Mount Desert Island. Watch for the "smoke signals"—steam billowing from the huge vats.

Mosey through Lamoine to **Seal Cove Farm** (202 Partridge Cove Rd./Rte. 204, Lamoine, 207/667-7127, www.maine-goatcheese.com), a working goat farm best known for its handcrafted artisan cheeses. Adjacent to the small post-and-beam farm stand is an outdoor wood-burning oven. Ten-inch handcrafted pizzas ($10) are made not only with Seal Cove's fresh goat and mixed-milk cheeses, but also with seasonal, farm-fresh produce. For dessert, don't miss the goat gelato. There's a small picnic pavilion. Human kids will get a kick out of watching the goat kids romping in the pasture.

INFORMATION AND SERVICES

The **Thompson Island Information Center** (Rte. 3, Thompson Island, 207/288-3411, 8am-6pm daily mid-May-mid-Oct.) represents the Mount Desert Island Regional Chambers of Commerce, which includes the Trenton Chamber of Commerce.

The **Ellsworth Area Chamber of**

The Chocolate Chip Bed & Breakfast is a treat for chocoholics.

Seal Cove Farm bakes pizzas made with its artisan cheeses in an outdoor oven.

Commerce (207/667-5584, www.ellsworth-chamber.org) also covers Trenton.

En route from Ellsworth on Route 3, on the right shortly before you reach Mount Desert Island, you'll see the **Bar Harbor Chamber of Commerce** (Rte. 3, 207/288-5103 or 888/540-9990, www.barharbormaine.com). You'll find all sorts of info on the island and other locations, plus restrooms, phones, and helpful staff.

GETTING THERE AND AROUND

Trenton is about 8 miles via Route 3 from Ellsworth. It's about 12 miles or 15-20 minutes, depending upon traffic, to Bar Harbor.

Route 1 of the **Island Explorer** (www.exploreacadia.com) bus system, which primarily serves Mount Desert Island with its fleet of propane-fueled fare-free vehicles, connects the Hancock County/Bar Harbor Airport in Trenton with downtown Bar Harbor. Operated by Downeast Transportation, the Island Explorer runs late June-mid-October.

Before or after visiting Mount Desert Island, if you're headed farther Down East—to Lamoine, the eastern side of Hancock County, and beyond—there's a good shortcut from Trenton. About five miles south of Ellsworth on Route 3, just north of the Kisma Preserve, turn east onto Route 20, bear left at the T intersection, then take your first right, following Route 204/Pinkhams Flats Road. Turn right onto Mud Creek Road, which wiggles through a salt marsh and eventually spits out on Route 1 just west of Franklin.

Background

The Landscape

IN THE BEGINNING

Maine is an outdoor classroom for Geology 101, a living lesson in what the glaciers did and how they did it. I tell anyone who will listen that I plan to be a geologist in my next life—and the best place for the first course is Acadia National Park.

Geologically, Maine is something of a youngster; the oldest rocks, found in the Chain of Ponds area in the western part of the state, are only 1.6 billion years old—more than two billion years younger than the world's oldest rocks.

But most significant is the great ice sheet that began to spread over Maine about 25,000 years ago, during the late Wisconsin Ice Age. As it moved south from Canada, this continental glacier scraped, gouged, pulverized, and depressed the bedrock in its path. On it continued, charging up the north faces of mountains, clipping off their tops, and moving south, leaving behind jagged cliffs on the mountains' southern faces and odd deposits of stone and clay. By about 21,000 years ago, glacial ice extended well over the Gulf of Maine, perhaps as far as the Georges Bank fishing grounds.

But all that began to change with melting, beginning about 18,000 years ago. As the glacier melted and receded, ocean water moved in, covering much of the coastal plain and working its way inland up the rivers. By 11,000 years ago, glaciers had pulled back from all but a few minor corners at the top of Maine, revealing the south coast's beaches and the intriguing geologic traits—eskers and erratics, kettle holes and moraines, even a fjard—that make Mount Desert Island and the rest of the state such a fascinating natural laboratory.

Mount Desert's Somes Sound (named after pioneer settler Abraham Somes)—a rare fjard—is just one distinctive feature on an island loaded with geologic wonders. There are pocket beaches, pink granite ledges, sea caves, pancake rocks, wild headlands, volcanic dikes, and a handful of pristine ponds and lakes. And once you've glimpsed the Bubbles—two curvaceous, oversize mounds on the edge of Jordan Pond—you'll know exactly how they earned their name.

CLIMATE

Acadia National Park fits into the National Weather Service's **coastal** category, a 20-mile-wide swath that stretches from Kittery on the New Hampshire border to Eastport on the Canadian border. In the park and its surrounding communities, the proximity of the Gulf of Maine moderates the climate, making coastal winters generally warmer and summers usually cooler than elsewhere in the state.

Average June temperatures in **Bar Harbor**, adjoining the park, range 53-76°F; July-August temperatures range 60-82°F. By December, the average range is 20-32°F.

The Seasons

Maine has four distinct seasons: summer, fall, winter, and mud. Lovers of spring weather need to look elsewhere in March, the lowest month on the popularity scale, with its mud-caked vehicles, soggy everything, irritable temperaments, tank-trap roads, and occasionally the worst snowstorm of the year.

Summer can be idyllic—with moderate temperatures, clear air, and wispy breezes—but it can also close in with fog, rain, and chills. Prevailing winds are from the southwest. Officially, summer runs June

21-September 23, but consider summer to be June, July, and August. The typical growing season is 148 days long.

A poll of Mainers might well show autumn as the favorite season—days are still warmish, nights are cool, winds are optimal for sailors, and the foliage is brilliant—particularly throughout Acadia. Fall colors usually reach their peak in the park in early October, about a week before Columbus Day. Early autumn, however, is also the height of hurricane season, the only potential flaw with this time of year.

Winter, officially December 21-March 20, means an unpredictable potpourri of weather along the park's coastline. But when the cold and snow hit this region, it's time for cross-country skiing, snowshoeing, and ice-skating. The park receives an average of 61 inches of snow over the season.

Spring, officially March 20-June 21, is the frequent butt of jokes. It's an ill-defined season that arrives much too late and departs all too quickly. Spring planting can't occur until well into May; lilacs explode in late May and disappear by mid-June. And just when you finally can enjoy being outside, blackflies stretch their wings and satisfy their hunger pangs. Along the shore, fortunately, steady breezes often keep the pesky creatures to a minimum.

Northeasters and Hurricanes

A northeaster is a counterclockwise-swirling storm that brings wild winds out of—you guessed it—the northeast. These storms can occur at any time of year, whenever the conditions brew them up. Depending on the season, the winds are accompanied by rain, sleet, snow, or all of them together.

Hurricane season officially runs June-November, but hurricanes are most active in late August-September. Some years, Maine remains out of harm's way; other years, head-on hurricanes and even glancing blows have eroded beaches, flooded roads, splintered boats, downed trees, knocked out power, and inflicted major residential and commercial damage. Winds—the greatest culprit—average 74-90 mph. A hurricane watch is announced on radio and TV about 36 hours before the hurricane hits, followed by a hurricane warning indicating that the storm is imminent. Find shelter away from plate-glass windows, and wait it out. If especially high winds are predicted, make every effort to secure yourself, your vehicle, and your possessions. Resist the urge to head for the shore to

Fog adds an element of mystery to the Acadia landscape.

watch the show; rogue waves combined with ultrahigh tides have been known to sweep away unwary onlookers. Schoodic Point, the mainland section of Acadia, is a particularly perilous location in such conditions.

Sea Smoke and Fog

Sea smoke and fog, two atmospheric phenomena resulting from opposing conditions, are only distantly related. But both can radically affect visibility and therefore be hazardous. In winter, when the ocean is at least 40°F warmer than the air, billowy sea smoke rises from the water, creating great photo ops for camera buffs but seriously dangerous conditions for mariners.

In any season, when the ocean (or lake or land) is colder than the air, fog sets in, creating nasty conditions for drivers, mariners, and pilots. Romantics, however, see it otherwise, reveling in the womb-like ambience and the muffled moans of foghorns.

Storm Warnings

The National Weather Service's official daytime signal system for wind velocity consists of a series of flags representing specific wind speeds and sea conditions. Beachgoers and anyone planning to venture out in a kayak, canoe, sailboat, or powerboat should heed these signals. The signal flags are posted on all public beaches, and warnings are announced on TV and radio weather broadcasts, as well as on cable TV's Weather Channel and the National Oceanic and Atmospheric Administration (NOAA) broadcast network.

Plants and Animals

In the course of a single day at Acadia National Park—where more than two dozen mountains meet the sea—the casual visitor can pass through a landscape that lends itself to a surprising diversity of animal and plant life. On one outing, you can explore the shoreline—barnacles encrust the rocks, and black crowberry, an arctic shrub that finds Maine's coastal climate agreeable, grows close to the ground alongside trails. On the same outing, you can wander beneath the boughs of the leafy hardwood forest that favors more southern climes, as well as the spruce-fir forest of the north. A little farther up the trail are subalpine plants more typically associated with mountain environments and neotropical songbirds providing background music.

Acadia's creatures and plants will endlessly intrigue any nature lover; the following are but a sampling of what you might encounter during a visit.

OFFSHORE

Acadia National Park is surrounded by the sea—from the rockbound Schoodic Peninsula jutting from the mainland Down East to the offshore island in Penobscot Bay that Samuel de Champlain named Isle au Haut. While the park's boundaries do not extend out to sea, the life that can be found there draws travelers and scientists alike.

The Maine coastline falls within the Gulf of Maine, a "sea within a sea" that extends from Nova Scotia to Cape Cod and out to the fishing grounds of Brown and Georges Banks. It is one of the most biologically rich environments in the world. Surface water, driven by currents off Nova Scotia, swirls in counterclockwise circles, delivering nutrients and food to the plants and animals that live there. Floating microplants, tiny shrimplike creatures, and jellyfish benefit from those nutrients and once supported huge populations of groundfish, now depleted by overfishing.

These highly productive waters lure not only fishing vessels but also sea mammals. **Whales** may rarely swim into the inshore bays and inlets bounded by Acadia, but whale-watching cruises based on Mount Desert Island ferry passengers miles offshore to the locales where whales gather. Whales fall into two groups: toothed and baleen. Toothed whales hunt individual prey, such as squid, fish, and the occasional seabird; they include porpoises and dolphins, killer whales, sperm whales, and pilot whales. Baleen whales have no teeth, so they must sift food through horny plates called baleen; they include finback whales, minke whales, humpback whales, and right whales. Any of these species may be observed in the Gulf of Maine.

Harbor porpoises, which grow to a length of six feet, can be spotted from a boat in the inshore waters around Mount Desert Island, traveling in pods as they hunt schools of herring and mackerel. The most you'll usually see of them are their gray backs and triangular dorsal fins as they perform their graceful ballet through the waves.

Of great delight to wildlife watchers is catching glimpses of **harbor seals.** While the shores of Mount Desert Island are too busy with human activity for seals to linger, they are usually spotted during nature cruises that head out to the well-known "seal ledges." Check the tide chart and book an excursion for low tide. Seals haul themselves out of the ocean at low tide to rest on the rocks and sunbathe. Naps are a necessity for harbor seals,

which have less blubber and fur to insulate them from the frigid waters of the Gulf of Maine than other seal species. Hauling out preserves energy otherwise spent heating the body, and it replenishes their blood with oxygen.

At high tide, you might see individual "puppy dog" faces bobbing among the waves as the seals forage for food. Harbor seals, sometimes called "sea dogs," almost disappeared along the coast of Maine in the early 20th century. It was believed they competed with fishermen for the much-prized lobster and other valuable catches, and they were hunted nearly into oblivion. When it became obvious that the absence of seals did not improve fish stocks, the bounty placed on them was lifted. The Marine Mammal Protection Act of 1972 made it illegal to hunt or harm any marine mammal, except by permit—happily, populations of harbor seals now have rebounded all along the coast.

Every now and then, park rangers receive reports of "abandoned" seal pups along Acadia's shore. Usually it's not a stranded youngster, but rather a pup left to rest while its mother hunts for food. If you discover a seal pup on the shore, leave it undisturbed and report the sighting to rangers.

The best time to sight seals basking on rocks and ledges is at low tide.

ALONG THE SHORE

Whether walking the shore or cruising on a boat, there is no symbol so closely associated with the coast as the ubiquitous **gull.** Several species of gulls frequent Acadia's skies, but none is more common than the herring gull. Easily dismissed as brassy sandwich thieves (which, of course, they are), herring gulls almost vanished in the 20th century as a result of hunting and egg collecting. Indeed, many seabird populations declined in the early 1900s due to the demand for feathers to adorn ladies' hats. Conservation measures have helped some of these bird species recover, including the large, gray-backed herring gull, an elegant flyer that often lobs sea urchins onto the rocky shore from aloft to crack them open for the morsels within.

Common **eider duck** females, a mottled brown, and the black-and-white males, nick-named "floating skunks," congregate in large "rafts" on the icy ocean during the winter to mate. When spring arrives, males and females separate. While the males provide no help in raising the young, the females cooperate with one another, often gathering ducklings together to protect them from predators. Adult eiders may live and breed for 20 years or more, though the mortality rate is high among the young. Present along Acadia's shore all year long, they feed on mussels, clams, and dog whelks, their powerful gizzards grinding down shells and all.

A smaller seabird regularly espied around Acadia is the **black guillemot,** also known as the "sea pigeon" and "underwater flyer" because it seems to fly through the water. Guillemots learn to swim before they learn to fly. Black-and-white with bright red feet, guillemots are cousins to puffins. They nest on rock ledges along the shore, laying pear-shaped eggs that won't roll over the edge and into the waves below.

Bald eagles and **ospreys** (also known as fish hawks) take advantage of the fishing available in Acadia's waters. Both of these majestic raptors suffered from the effects of the pesticide DDT, which washed down through waterways and into the ocean, becoming concentrated in the fish the raptors consumed. As a result, they laid thin-shelled eggs that broke easily, preventing the development of young. The banning of DDT in the United States has resulted in a strong comeback for both species and the removal of the bald eagle from the federal endangered species list. Along the coast of Maine, however, the bald eagle's return has been less triumphant than in other

Osprey build their nests atop high points, such as rocky cliffs.

parts of the country. Biologists continue to seek explanations for the lag, and the bald eagle remains on state and federal lists as a threatened species.

Boat cruises, some with park rangers aboard, depart from several Mount Desert Island harbors and offer good chances for sightings. They allow passengers to approach (but not too closely) nesting islands of eagles and ospreys. Both species create large nests of sticks from which they can command a wide view of the surrounding area. Some osprey nests have been documented as being 100 years old, and researchers have found everything from fishing tackle to swim trunks entwined in the sticks of the nests.

Look also for eagles and ospreys flying above inland areas of the park. Ospreys hunt over freshwater ponds and lakes, hovering until a fish is sighted, then plummeting from the sky into the water to grab the prey. For aerodynamic reasons, they carry the fish headfirst.

Acadia visitors often ask rangers if there are sea otters in the park. After all, there is an Otter Creek, which flows into Otter Cove, which is bounded by Otter Cliffs. At one time, Gorham Mountain was known as Peak of Otter! With all these place-names devoted to the otter, it would be logical to assume that Mount Desert Island teems with them. In fact, though, there are no sea otters along the entire eastern seaboard of the United States—perhaps the earliest European settlers mistook sea minks (now extinct) for sea otters. River otters do reside in the park, but they are reclusive and spend most of their time in freshwater environments. You might observe one during the winter frolicking on a frozen pond.

INTERTIDAL ZONE

Some of the most alien creatures on earth live where the ocean washes the rocky shoreline. The creatures of this intertidal zone are at once resilient and fragile, and always fascinating. Some of the creatures and plants live best in the upper reaches of the intertidal zone, which is doused only by the spray of waves and the occasional extra-high tide. Others, which would not survive the upper regions, thrive in the lower portions of the intertidal zone, which is almost always submerged. The rest live in rocky pockets of water in between, and all are influenced by the ebb and flow of the tide. Temperature, salinity, and the strength of crashing waves all determine where a creature will live in the intertidal zone.

As you approach the ocean's edge, the first creatures likely to come underfoot are **barnacles**—vast stretches of rock can be encrusted with them. Step gently, for walking on barnacles crushes them. Their tiny, white, volcano-shaped shells remain closed when exposed to the air, but they open to feed when submerged. Water movement encourages them to sweep the water with feathery "legs" to feed on microscopic plankton.

Despite the tough armor with which barnacles cover themselves, they are preyed on by **dog whelks** (snails), which drill through the barnacle shells with their tongues to feed on the creature within. A dog whelk can be distinguished from the common periwinkle by the elliptical opening of its shell. Periwinkles have teardrop-shaped openings.

Sea stars find blue mussels yummy. Blue mussels siphon plankton from the water and anchor themselves in place with byssus threads. Sea stars creep up on the mussels, wrap their legs around them, and pry open their shells just enough to insert their stomachs and consume the animal inside. Look for sea stars and mussels in the lower regions of tide pools.

Related to sea stars are **sea urchins**—spiky green balls most often seen as empty, spineless husks littered along the shoreline (they are frequently preyed on by gulls). If you come upon a live sea urchin, handle it with care. While their spikes are not poisonous, they are sharp. Gently roll a sea urchin over to see its mouth and the five white teeth with which it gnaws on seaweed and animal remains. (While the green sea urchins found in Acadia do not possess poisonous spines, some of their counterparts in other regions do.)

Limpets, with cone-shaped shells, are snails that rely on seaweed for food. They suction themselves to rocks, which prevents them from drying up when exposed at low tide. Do not tear limpets from rocks—doing so hurts the animal.

Many intertidal creatures depend on seaweed for protection and food. Rockweeds drape over rocks, floating with the waves, their long fronds buoyed by distinctive air bladders. Dulse (edible for people) is common along the shore, as is Irish moss, used as a thickener in ice cream, paint, and other products.

Tide Pool Tips

The best way to learn about the fascinating world that exists between the tides is to look for creatures in their own habitats, with a good field guide as a reference.

- Go at low tide—there are two low tides daily, 12 hours apart.
- Tread carefully. Shoreline rocks are slippery.
- Do not remove creatures from their habitats; doing so could harm them.
- Be aware of the ocean at all times. Sudden waves can wash the shore and sweep you to your death.

- Join a ranger-guided shoreline walk to learn more about this unique environment. Check the *Beaver Log,* Acadia's official park newspaper, for the schedule and details.

FRESHWATER LAKES AND PONDS

Known best for its rocky shoreline and mountains, Acadia National Park cradles numerous glistening lakes and ponds in its glacially carved valleys. Several lakes serve as public water supplies for surrounding communities, and swimming is prohibited in most. Echo Lake and the north end of Long Pond are excellent designated swimming areas. Freshwater fishing requires a state license for adults. Obey the posted regulations.

The voice of the northern wilderness belongs to the **common loon,** whose roots are so ancient it is the oldest bird species found in North America. During the summer months, loons are garbed in striking white-and-black plumage, which fades to gray during the winter when they migrate to the ocean's open waters. Graceful swimmers, loons are clumsy on land. Their webbed feet are set to the rear of their bodies, making them front-heavy. Land travel is a struggle. Consequently, they nest very close to the water's edge, which makes

The intertidal zone is rich in flora and fauna.

Tides

Nowhere is the adage "Time and tide wait for no one" more true than along the Maine coastline. The nation's most extreme tidal ranges occur in Maine, and they become even more dramatic as you head "Down East," toward the Canadian Maritime provinces. Every six hours or so, the tide begins either ebbing or flowing, so you'll have countless opportunities for observing tidal phenomena.

Tides govern coastal life, and everyone is a slave to the tide calendar or chart, which coastal-community newspapers diligently publish in every issue. Each issue of the free *Acadia Weekly*, available widely on the island, also contains tide info (as well as times of sunrise and sunset), as does the *Park Ranger Program* issued by the park. In tidal regions, boats tie up with extra-long lines, clammers and worm-diggers schedule their days by the tides, hikers have to plan ahead for shoreline exploring, and kayakers need to plan their routes to avoid getting stuck in the muck.

Average tidal ranges (between low tide and high tide) in the area around Acadia National Park are 10-11 feet, and extremes are 12-13 feet.

Tides, as we all learned in elementary school, are lunar phenomena, created by the gravitational pull of the moon; the tidal range depends on the lunar phase. Tides are most extreme at new and full moons—when the sun, moon, and earth are all aligned. These are **spring tides,** supposedly because the water springs upward (the term has nothing to do with the season). And tides are smallest during the moon's first and third quarters—when the sun, earth, and moon have a right-angle configuration. These are **neap tides** (*neap* comes from an Old English word meaning "scanty"). Other lunar and solar phenomena, such as the equinoxes and solstices, can also affect tidal ranges.

The best time for shoreline exploration is on a new-moon or full-moon day, when low tide exposes mussels, sea urchins, sea cucumbers, sea stars, periwinkles, hermit crabs, rockweed, and assorted nonbiodegradable trash. Rubber boots or waterproof treaded shoes are essential on the wet, slippery terrain.

Caution is also essential in tidal areas. Unless you've carefully plotted tide times and heights,

them vulnerable to such human hazards as the wakes of motorized watercraft.

The loon's mysterious ululating call can be heard echoing across lakes on most any summer evening, an eerie sound not quickly forgotten.

Evening is actually an excellent time to observe wildlife. Creatures that seem shy and reclusive by day tend to be most active at dawn and dusk (crepuscular) or at night (nocturnal). Carriage roads along Eagle Lake, Bubble Pond, and Witch Hole Pond make nighttime walking easy. (Hint: Go at dusk so your eyes adjust with the darkening sky, and keep in mind that abrupt flashlight use ruins night vision.)

Frog choruses form the backdrop to the cries of loons. In Acadia, there are eight **frog and toad** species, which tend to be most vocal during the spring mating season. Close

your eyes and listen to see if you can distinguish individual species, such as the "banjo-twanging" croak of the green frog and the "snore" of the leopard frog.

The onset of moonlight may reveal small winged creatures swooping, darting, and careening over lakes and ponds. Acadia is home to several species of **bats,** including the common little brown bat. Don't scream! Bats have no desire to get entangled in your hair. Their echolocation (radar) is so fine-tuned that it can detect a single strand of human hair. Bats are far more interested in the mosquitoes attracted to your body heat. True insect-munching machines, a single pinky-size little brown bat can eat hundreds, if not thousands, of insects in one evening.

Bandit-faced **raccoons** are also creatures of the night, and they sometimes can be found scampering alongside the shore. They are

Wait for the tide to recede before exploring tide pools left behind.

don't park a car, bike, or boat trailer on a beach; make sure your sea kayak is lashed securely to a tree or bollard; don't take a long nap on shoreline granite; and don't cross a low-tide land spit without an eye on your watch.

A perhaps apocryphal but almost believable story goes that one flatlander stormed up to a ranger at a Maine state park one bright summer morning and demanded indignantly to know why they had had the nerve to drain the water from her shorefront campsite during the night. When it comes to tides, you just have to go with the flow.

omnivorous, dining on anything from grubs, frogs, and small mammals to fish, berries, and garbage. Rabies is present in Maine, and raccoons are common carriers of the disease. Do not approach sick-acting animals (seeing them during the daytime may indicate illness), and report any strange behavior to a park ranger. When camping or picnicking, stow food items in your vehicle and dispose of scraps properly. Raccoons are opportunistic thieves that have been known to claw their way into tents to find food.

And where are the moose? The question is asked often at Acadia's visitors center, and wildlife watchers are disappointed to learn that moose, the largest member of the deer family, are rarely sighted in the park. Moose are more frequently observed in western and northern Maine, in the Moosehead Lake and Baxter State Park regions. However,

individuals are spotted from time to time on Mount Desert Island, and there may even be a small family group residing on the west side. Moose like to dine on aquatic vegetation, such as the tubers of cattails and lily pads, and they frequent marshes and lakes to escape biting flies. Bass Harbor Marsh is inviting habitat for moose, but good luck spotting one.

A prehistoric-looking creature sometimes encountered on carriage roads near ponds is the **snapping turtle.** An average adult may weigh 30 pounds or more. Keep well clear of the snapper's powerful beak, which is lightning-quick when grabbing prey; it can do real damage, such as biting off fingers. Adult snappers have no predators (except people), and they will dine on other turtles, frogs, ducklings, wading birds, and beaver kits.

By midsummer, many of Acadia's ponds are beautifully adorned with yellow water lilies and white pond lilies. Lily pads are a favorite food of **beavers,** which emerge from their lodges—large piles of sticks and mud—at dusk and dawn to feed and make necessary repairs to their dams. Beavers create their own habitat by transforming streams into ponds. They move awkwardly on land, so they adjust the water level close to their source of building materials and other favored foods: aspen and birch trees. Doing so limits their exposure to dry land and predators.

Beavers are large rodents that were trapped excessively for centuries for the fur trade. They have since made a strong comeback in Acadia—to the point that their ponds now threaten roads, trails, and other park structures. Resource managers try to keep ahead of the beavers by inserting "beaver foolers" (PVC pipes) through dams that block road culverts. This moderates pond levels and prevents damage to roads by allowing water to drain through the culvert. Sometimes the beavers, however, get ahead of the resource managers. They have been known to plug the beaver foolers with sticks and mud, or to chew through them with their strong teeth.

Amazingly adapted for life in the water, beavers are fascinating to watch. A very accessible location along the Park Loop Road, just past Bear Brook Picnic Area, is Beaver Dam Pond, featuring a few lodges, a dam, and an active beaver population. The best viewing times are dawn and dusk. In the fall the beavers are busiest, preparing food stores for the winter to come. The park often presents a beaver-watch program at that time of year, which is a great way to learn more about the habits and adaptations of the beaver.

Beavers act as a catalyst for increasing natural diversity in an area. Their ponds attract ospreys, herons, and owls; salamanders, frogs, and turtles; insects and aquatic plants; foxes, deer, muskrats, and river otters. Their ponds help maintain the water table, enrich soils, and prevent flooding.

While beavers may bring diversity to a wetland, an invader has been endangering Acadia's ponds and lakes. **Purple**

loosestrife, a showy stalked purple flower not native to North America, was introduced into gardens as an ornamental. Highly reproductive and adaptive and with no natural predators, purple loosestrife escaped the confines of gardens and has literally choked the life out of some wetlands by crowding out native plants on which many creatures depend, thus creating a monoculture. Few native species find purple loosestrife useful.

Purple loosestrife has been contained at Acadia, but it's an ongoing process. Uprooting it seems to encourage more to grow, and jostling stalks at certain times of the year disperses vast numbers of seeds, so resource managers have resorted to treating individual plants with an approved herbicide in a way that does not harm the surrounding environment.

WOODLANDS

A dark, statuesque **spruce-fir forest** dominates much of Acadia's woodlands and does well in the cooler, moist environs of Maine's coast. Red spruce trees are tall and pole-like and often cohabit with fragrant balsam fir. The spruce grows needles only at the canopy, sparing little energy for growing needles where the sun cannot reach. Because the sun barely touches the forest floor, little undergrowth emerges from the bump and swale of acidic, rust-colored needles that carpet the ground, except for more tiny, shade-loving spruce, waiting for their chance to grow tall.

The spruce-fir forest can be uncannily quiet, especially in the middle of the day. The density of the woods and the springy, needle-laden floor seem to buffer noise from without. Listen closely, however, and you may hear the cackle of ravens, the squabble of a territorial red squirrel, or the rat-a-tat of a woodpecker.

Red squirrels are energetic denizens of the spruce-fir forest, scolding innocent passersby or sitting on tree stumps scaling spruce cones and stuffing their cheeks full of seeds. Observant wildlife watchers will find their middens (heaps of cone scales) about the forest. Squirrels are especially industrious (even

It's not rare to sight deer on Mount Desert Island.

destroying numerous year-round and seasonal homes. In all, 17,000 acres burned, 10,000 of them in the park.

Researchers have studied 6,000 years of the park's fire history by pulling core samples from ponds to analyze the layers of pollen and charcoal that have settled in their bottoms over time. The charcoal indicates periods of fire, and the most significant layer of charcoal appeared in the period around 1947, indicating the intensity of the great fire.

The aftermath of the fire—the scorched mountainsides and skeletal, blackened remains of trees—must have been a devastating sight. Loggers salvaged usable timber and removed unsafe snags. Seed was ordered so replanting could begin in earnest. Soils needed to be stabilized and the landscape restored.

Then a curious thing happened the following spring: As the snow melted, green shoots began to poke up out of the soil among the sooty remains. "Pioneer plants," such as low-bush blueberry and Indian paintbrush, took over the job of stabilizing the soil. By the time the ordered seeds arrived two years later (demand had been overwhelming, for much of Maine had burned in 1947), nature was already mending the landscape without human intervention. What had been blackened showed promise and renewal in green growing things.

Over the decades since then, a mixed deciduous forest has grown up from the ashes of the fire, supplanting the dominance of the spruce-fir forest on Mount Desert Island's east side. **Birch, aspen, maple, oak,** and **beech** have embraced wide-open sunny places where shady spruce once thrived. The new growth not only added colorful splendor to the autumn landscape but also diversified the wildlife.

Populations of **white-tailed deer** benefited from all the new browse (and a lack of major predators), and by the 1960s, the island's deer herd had soared in numbers. Recent studies have shown the population to be healthy and stable—perhaps due to

comical) in autumn as they frantically prepare for the winter by stocking up on food, tearing about from branch to branch with spruce cones poking out of their mouths like big cigars.

Woodpeckers favor dead, still-standing trees, shredding the bark to get at the insects infesting the trunk. The pileated woodpecker—a large black-and-white bird with a red cap—is relatively shy, so you are more likely to encounter evidence of its passage (rectangular and oval holes in trees) than the bird itself. Other common species you might observe are the hairy and the downy woodpecker.

The face of Acadia's woodlands changed dramatically in 1947. That fall, during a period of extremely dry conditions, a fire began west of the park's present-day visitors center in Hulls Cove. Feeding on tinder-dry woods and grasses, and whipped into an inferno by gale-force winds, the fire roared across the eastern half of Mount Desert Island, miraculously skirting downtown Bar Harbor but car-deer collisions and predation from the recently arrived eastern coyote.

Coyotes crossed the Trenton Bridge and wandered onto Mount Desert Island in the 1980s. They had been expanding their territory throughout the northeast, handily picking up the slack in the food chain caused when other large predators, such as the northern gray wolf and the lynx, were hunted and trapped out of the state. While coyote sightings do occur, you are more likely to be serenaded by yipping and howling in the night. Their vocalizations warn off other coyotes, or let them keep in touch with the members of their packs.

The **snowshoe hare,** or varying hare, is a main prey species of the coyote. The large hind feet of these mammals allow them to stay aloft in the snow and speed away from predators. Camouflage also aids these fleet-footed hares—their fur turns white during the winter and brown during the summer, hence the name varying hare. Not all hares escape their predators. It is not uncommon to encounter coyote scat full of hare fur along a carriage road or trail.

Also along a carriage road or trail, you might encounter a **snake** sunning itself on a rock. Five species of snakes—including the garter snake, milk snake, and green snake—inhabit Acadia. None of these snakes are poisonous, but they will bite if provoked.

While autumn may cloak Acadia's mountainsides in bright beauty, spring and summer bring relief to Mainers weary of ice storms, shoveling, freezing temperatures, and short, dark days. Spring arrives with snowy clusters of star flowers along roadsides, and white mats of **bunchberry** flowers (dwarf members of the dogwood family) on the forest floor. Birdsong provides a musical backdrop. Twenty-one species of wood warblers migrate to Acadia from South America to nest—among them are the **American redstart, ovenbird, yellow warbler,** and **Blackburnian warbler.** At the visitors center, request a bird checklist, which names 273 species of birds that have been identified on Mount Desert Island and adjacent areas. Then join a ranger for an early-morning bird walk. Check the *Beaver Log* for details.

The fire of 1947 may have transformed a portion of Acadia's woodlands, but change is always part of a natural system. While the broad-leafed trees that grew up in the wake of the fire continue to grow and shed leaves as the cycle of nature demands, young spruce trees poke up through duff and leaf litter, waiting in the shade for their chance to dominate the landscape once again.

MOUNTAINS

A hike up one of Acadia's granite-domed mountains will allow you to gaze down at the world with a new perspective. Left behind is the confining forest—the woods, in fact, seem to shrink as you climb. On the south-facing slopes of some mountains, you'll encounter squat and gnarled pitch pines. The fire of 1947 not only was beneficial to the growth of deciduous vegetation, but it also aided in the regeneration of **pitch pines,** which rely on heat, such as that generated by an intense fire, to open their cones and disperse seeds.

Wreathing rocky outcrops and the sides of trails are such shrubs as **low-bush blueberry, sheep laurel (lambkill),** and **bayberry.** In the fall, their leaves turn blood-red. In the spring, **shadbush** softens granite mountainsides with white blossoms.

Green and gray lichens plaster exposed rocks in patterns like targets. Composed of algae and fungi, lichens were probably among the first organisms to grow in Acadia as the vast ice sheets retreated 10,000-20,000 years ago. Sensitive to air pollution and acid rain, lichens have become barometers of air quality all over the world.

On mountain summits, the trees are stunted. These are not necessarily young trees—some may be nearly 100 years old. The tough, cold, windy climate and exposed conditions of summits force plantlife to adapt to survive. Growing close to the ground to avoid fierce winds is one way in which trees have adapted to life at the summit.

Fall Foliage

The timing and quality of Maine's fall foliage owes much to the summer weather that precedes it, but the annual spectacle never disappoints. In early September, as deciduous trees ready themselves for winter, they stop producing chlorophyll, and the green begins to disappear from their leaves. Taking its place are the spectacular pigments—brilliant reds, yellows, oranges, and purples—that paint the leaves and warm the hearts of every "leaf-peeper," shopkeeper, innkeeper, and restaurateur.

The colorful display begins slowly, reaches a peak, then fades—starting in Maine's north in early-mid-September and working down to the southwest corner by mid-October. **Peak foliage** in Acadia National Park typically occurs in early-mid-October, with the last bits of color hanging on almost until the end of the month.

The fall palette is stunning, especially in Acadia. The leaves of white ash turn purple; sumac and sugar and red maples turn scarlet; mountain ash, beech, basswood, and birch trees turn various shades of yellow.

brilliant autumn foliage in Acadia

Trees put on their most magnificent show after a summer of moderate heat and rainfall. A summer of excessive heat and scant rainfall means colors will be less brilliant and disappear more quickly. Throw a September or October northeaster or hurricane into the mix, and estimates are up for grabs.

So predictions are imprecise, and you'll need to allow some schedule flexibility to take advantage of optimum color. Early September-mid-October, check the foliage section on the state Department of Conservation's website (www.mainefoliage.com) for frequently updated maps, panoramic photographs, recommended driving tours, and weekly reports on the foliage status (this is gauged by the percentage of "leaf drop" in every region of the state). Early September-early October, you can even sign up via the website for weekly email reports (Acadia straddles zones 1 and 2 in the report maps). The state's toll-free fall foliage hotline is 888/624-6345.

Fall foliage trips are extremely popular and have become more so in recent years, so lodging can be scarce. Plan ahead and make reservations; sleeping in your car can be mighty chilly at that time of year.

Other plants huddle in the shallow, gravelly soil behind solitary rocks, such as **three-toothed cinquefoil,** a member of the rose family that produces a tiny white flower in June-July, and **mountain sandwort,** which blooms in clusters June-September.

While adapted to surviving the extreme conditions of mountain summits, plants can be irreparably damaged by feet trampling off-trail or by removal of rocks to add to cairns (trail markers) or stone "art." One has only to look at the summit area of Cadillac Mountain to see the damage wrought by millions of roving feet: the missing vegetation and the eroded soils. It may take 50-100 years for some plantlife, if protected, to recover. Some endangered plant species that grow only at summits may have already disappeared from Cadillac due to trampling.

To protect mountain summits and to preserve the natural scene, follow Leave No Trace principles of staying on the trail and on durable surfaces, such as solid granite. Do not add to cairns or build rock art, a form of graffiti that not only damages plants and soils but also blemishes the scenery for other visitors.

Autumn provides a terrific opportunity to observe **raptors** of all kinds. In the fall, during their south migration, raptors take advantage of northwest winds flowing over Acadia's mountains. Eagles, red-tailed hawks, sharp-shinned hawks, goshawks, American kestrels, peregrine falcons, and others can be spotted. The peregrine, a seasonal mountain dweller, has been reintroduced to Acadia after a long absence. Late August-mid-October, join park staff for the annual Hawkwatch atop Cadillac Mountain (weather permitting) to view and identify raptors. Check the *Beaver Log* for details. In a typical year, hawk-watchers count an average of 2,500 raptors from 10 species. The most prevalent species are American kestrels and sharp-shinned hawks.

WILDLIFE-WATCHING TIPS

• Seek out wildlife at **dusk** and **dawn** when it is more active. Bring binoculars and a field guide.

• Leave Rover at home—**pets** are intruders into the natural world, and they will scare off wildlife. If leaving your dog behind is not an option, remember that in the park, pets must be restrained on a leash no longer than six feet. This is for the safety of both

the pet and wildlife, and it is courteous to other visitors.

• **Never approach wildlife,** which could become aggressive if sick or feeling threatened. Enjoy wildlife at a distance.

• **Do not feed wildlife,** not even gulls. Feeding turns wild animals into aggressive beggars that lose the ability to forage for themselves, and it often ends in their demise.

• Join walks, talks, hikes, cruises, and evening **programs** presented by park rangers to learn more about your national park and its flora and fauna. Programs are listed in the *Beaver Log,* readily available at the Hulls Cove Visitors Center, the Acadia Nature Center, and park campgrounds, as well as online (www.nps.gov/acad).

• Visit the **nature center at Sieur de Monts Spring,** where exhibits show the diversity of flora and fauna in the park and the challenges that resource managers face in protecting it.

(The Plants and Animals *section of this chapter was written by Kristen Britain, former writer and editor for Acadia National Park.)*

Environmental Issues

You've already read about some of Acadia's major environmental issues, but still others exist. Tops among these are air pollution and overcrowding. Of utmost importance is the matter of "zero impact," addressed by the Leave No Trace philosophy actively practiced at Acadia.

AIR QUALITY

In 2002, a study by the private National Parks Conservation Association revealed that Acadia National Park had the fifth-worst air quality of all the national parks; Acadia allegedly has twice as much haze as the Grand Canyon. Most scientists and

environmentalists attribute the problem primarily to smoke and haze from power plants in the Midwest and the South. New England is the end of the line, so to speak, for airborne pollutants, and it's estimated that 80 percent of Maine's pollution arrives from other regions. Maine has the highest asthma rate in the nation, rivers and lakes have high concentrations of mercury, and rainfall at Acadia is notably acidic. Maine's four federal legislators and others in the region have been especially active in their efforts to strengthen the Clean Air Act and improve conditions at Acadia and in the rest of New England.

To heighten public awareness of pollution

Leave the Rocks for the Next Glacier

Acadia's relatively small size among national parks (compared to Yosemite, say, or Yellowstone) and high volume of visitors have necessitated a very active campaign to heighten sensitivity to the park's ecosystem. While you're in Acadia, do your part to "Keep Acadia Beautiful" by adhering to principles (guidelines, really) developed by the national organization **Leave No Trace** (LNT, www.lnt.org), based in Boulder, Colorado:

· Plan ahead and prepare.

· Travel and camp on durable surfaces.

· Dispose of waste properly.

· Leave what you find.

· Minimize campfire impacts.

· Respect wildlife.

· Be considerate of other visitors.

While all seven of these are important, two are especially critical for Acadia:

· **Travel and camp on durable surfaces.** Since there is no backcountry camping in Acadia, and park rangers do their best to monitor the park's three "front-country" campgrounds (two on Mount Desert, one on Isle au Haut), the focus is on hiking and use of the trails. Stay on existing trails—paying attention to signposts, blazes, and cairns—and don't be seduced by false trails where hikers have begun to stray. Walk single file down the center of a trail to avoid trampling the sensitive vegetation alongside; slow-growing lichens are particularly fragile. Remember, plants grow by the inch and die by the foot. Every footstep can make a difference. If you must step off the trail, step onto a durable surface. Acadia's most fragile sites are the summits and ridges. Especially vulnerable is the summit of Cadillac Mountain—it's a matter of sheer numbers. Yes, walk the summit loop for its great views, but above all, stick to the trail, or at least step on solid rock.

· **Leave what you find.** That means *take no souvenirs*. Save the wildflowers for the next visitors to enjoy, and leave the tide pool creatures where you find them. Above all, don't mess with cairns, the carefully constructed stone trail markers. Resist the urge to build or unbuild or rebuild cairns along the way—in some instances, removal or addition of a single stone can threaten a cairn's stability. It's a safety issue too—a collapsed cairn becomes a missing link in the trail-marking system. Follow cairns, don't build them. As the slogan has it, "leave the rocks for the next glacier." Imagine if every one of the park's two million visitors each year removed one cobble or rock. Unfortunately, enough already have. Bar Harbor Airport screeners, under heightened security regulations, have been seeing visitors departing with beach rocks. But what to do with them? Who can say exactly where they came from? If you're planning to camp at one of the park campgrounds, purchase firewood—you'll see dozens of Firewood for Sale signs along the roads leading to the park. Stop and buy a bundle; it'll set you back just a few dollars.

Also essential—anywhere, not just in Acadia—is the carry-in, carry-out message. If you're planning a picnic, enjoy it (on a durable surface—there's plenty of granite in Acadia), then remove all evidence of it. Carry trash bags and use them.

To keep wildlife wild, *do not feed any of the park's wildlife*—a problem of increasing concern at Acadia. Animals become dependent on humans and risk being hit by cars or otherwise meeting their end.

We all love the park, but we can't love it to death.

problems, a new government-private joint program has initiated **CAMNET,** an intriguing monitoring system that provides real-time pollution and visibility monitoring. Acadia is one of the nine New England sites with cameras updating images every 15 minutes. Log on to www.hazecam.net for data on current temperature and humidity, wind speed and direction, precipitation totals, visual range, and the air-pollution level (low, medium, or high). The site also includes a selection of photos showing the variations that have occurred in the past at Acadia. In the "clear day" photo, visibility was pegged at 199 miles! Ozone alerts, according to Environmental Protection Agency standards, usually occur at Acadia a couple of times each summer. When they do, rangers put out signs to caution visitors—particularly hikers and bikers—to restrict strenuous activity.

While pollution is an Acadia issue—affecting the park, its vegetation and wildlife, and its visitors—the solution must be a national one. Stay tuned.

PARK CAPACITY

With more than two million visitors each year, Acadia and National Park Service officials are wrestling with a question: How many people are too many people? Other national parks have initiated visitor limitations, but Acadia has so far not done so. The time may come, however.

The establishment of the propane-powered Island Explorer bus service has greatly alleviated traffic (and thus also auto, SUV, and RV emissions) during the months it operates (late June-early October) and has freed up space in Acadia's parking areas, but will it encourage more visitors?

Cruise-vessel visits in Bar Harbor have multiplied exponentially in recent years. Most passengers spend at least some time in the park, but it's a minimal amount of time— often just a carriage ride or a visit to Jordan Pond House or the Cadillac summit. (Bar Harbor merchants, of course, welcome the influx.)

The heaviest use of the park occurs in July-August, with marginally less use in September, yet there are still quiet corners of the park; it's a matter of finding them. The best advice, therefore, is to visit in shoulder seasons—May-June and late September-early October. You take your chances then with weather and temperatures, but if you're flexible and adaptable, it could be the best vacation you've ever had.

History

NATIVE AMERICANS

As the great continental glacier receded out of Maine to the northwest about 11,000 years ago, some prehistoric grapevine must have alerted small bands of hunter-gatherers—fur-clad Paleo-Indians—to the scrub sprouting in the tundra, burgeoning mammal populations, and the ocean's bountiful food supply, because they came to the shore in droves—at first seasonally, then year-round. Anyone who thinks tourism is a recent phenomenon in this part of Maine need only explore the shoreline of Mount Desert Island, where cast-off oyster shells and clamshells document the migration of early Native Americans from woodlands to waterfront. "The shore" has been a summertime magnet for millennia.

Archaeological evidence from the Archaic period in Maine—roughly 8000-1000 BC— is fairly scant, but paleontologists have unearthed stone tools and weapons and small campsites attesting to a nomadic lifestyle supported by fishing and hunting, with fishing becoming more extensive as time went on. Toward the end of the tradition, during the late Archaic period, there emerged a rather anomalous Indian culture known officially as the Moorehead phase but informally called the Red Paint People; the name comes from their curious trait of using a distinctive red ocher (pulverized hematite) in burials. Dark red puddles and stone artifacts have led excavators to burial pits in Ellsworth and Hancock. Just as mysteriously as they had arrived, the Red Paint People disappeared abruptly and inexplicably around 1800 BC.

Following them almost immediately—and almost as suddenly—hunter-gatherers of the Susquehanna Tradition arrived from well to the south, moved across Maine's interior as far as the St. John River, and remained until about 1600 BC, when they too enigmatically vanished. Excavations have turned up relatively sophisticated stone tools and evidence that they cremated their dead. It was nearly 1,000 years before a major new cultural phase appeared.

The next great leap forward was marked by the advent of pottery making, introduced about 700 BC. The Ceramic period stretched to the 16th century, and cone-shaped pots (initially stamped, later incised with coiled-rope motifs) survived until the introduction of metals from Europe. During this time, at Pemetic (their name for Mount Desert Island) and on some of the offshore islands, Native American fisherfolk and their families built houses of sorts—seasonal, wigwam-style birch-bark dwellings—and spent the summers fishing, clamming, trapping, and making baskets and functional birch-bark objects.

THE EUROPEANS ARRIVE

The identity of the first Europeans to set foot in Maine is a matter of debate. Historians dispute the romantically popular notion that Norse explorers checked out this part of the New World as early as AD 1000. Even an 11th-century Norse coin found in 1961 in Brooklin, near Blue Hill, west of Mount Desert Island, was probably carried there from farther northeast.

Not until the late 15th century, the onset of the great Age of Discovery, did credible reports of the New World, including what is

now Maine, filter back to Europe's courts and universities. Thanks to innovations in naval architecture, shipbuilding, and navigation, astonishingly courageous fellows crossed the Atlantic in search of rumored treasure and new routes for reaching it.

John Cabot, sailing from England aboard the ship *Mathew,* may have been the first European to reach Maine, in 1498, but historians have never confirmed a landing site. There is no question, however, about the account of Giovanni da Verrazzano, a Florentine explorer commanding *La Dauphine* under the French flag, who reached the Maine coast in 1524. Encountering less-than-friendly Native Americans, Verrazzano did a minimum of business and sailed onward toward Nova Scotia. Four years later, he died in the West Indies. His brother's map of their landing site (probably on the Phippsburg Peninsula, near Bath) labels it "The Land of Bad People." Esteban Gómez, a Portuguese explorer sailing under the Spanish flag, followed in Verrazzano's wake in 1525, but the only outcome of his exploits was an uncounted number of captives whom he sold into slavery in Spain. A map created several years later from Gómez's descriptions seems to indicate he had at least glimpsed Mount Desert Island.

More than half a century passed before the Maine coast turned up again on European explorers' itineraries. This time, interest was fueled by reports of a Brigadoon-like area called Norumbega (or Oranbega, as one map had it), a myth that arose, gathered steam, and took on a life of its own in the decades following Verrazzano's voyage.

By the 17th century, when Europeans began arriving in more than twos and threes and getting serious about colonization, Native American agriculture was already under way, the cod fishery was thriving on offshore islands, Native Americans far to the north were hot to trade furs for European goodies, and the birch-bark canoe was the transport of choice when the Penobscots headed down Maine's rivers toward their summer sojourns on the coast.

MOUNT DESERT ISLAND "DISCOVERED"

In the early 17th century, English dominance of exploration west of the Penobscot River (roughly from present-day Bucksport down to the New Hampshire border and beyond) coincided roughly with increasing French activity east of the river—including Mount Desert Island and the nearby mainland.

In 1604, French nobleman Pierre du Gua, Sieur de Monts, bearing a vast land grant for "La Cadie" (Acadia) from King Henry IV, set out with cartographer Samuel de Champlain to map the coastline. They first reached Nova Scotia's Bay of Fundy and then sailed up the St. Croix River. Mid-river, just west of present-day Calais, a crew planted gardens and erected buildings on today's St. Croix Island while du Gua and Champlain went off exploring. The two men and their crew sailed up the Penobscot River to present-day Bangor, searching fruitlessly for Norumbega, and next "discovered" the imposing island Champlain named l'Île des Monts Déserts because of its treeless summits. Here they entered Frenchman Bay, landed at today's Otter Creek in early September, and explored inlets and bays in the vicinity before returning to St. Croix Island to face the elements with their ill-fated compatriots. Scurvy, lack of fuel and water, and a ferocious winter wiped out nearly half of the 79 men in the St. Croix settlement. In spring 1605, du Gua, Champlain, and other survivors headed southwest again, exploring the coastline all the way to Cape Cod before returning northeast and settling permanently at Nova Scotia's Port Royal (now Annapolis Royal).

Eight years later, French Jesuit missionaries en route to the Kennebec River (or, as some allege, seeking Norumbega) ended up on Mount Desert Island. With a band of about three dozen French laymen, they set about establishing the St. Sauveur mission settlement at present-day Fernald Point. Despite the welcoming presence of amiable Native Americans (led by Asticou, an eminent Penobscot sagamore), leadership squabbles led to building delays, and English marauder Samuel Argall—assigned to reclaim this territory for England—arrived in his warship *Treasurer* to find them easy prey. The colony was leveled, the settlers were set adrift in small boats, the priests were carted off to the Jamestown colony in Virginia, and Argall moved on to destroy Port Royal.

Even though England yearned to control the entire Maine coastline, her turf, realistically, remained south and west of the Penobscot River. During the 17th century, the French had expanded from their Canadian colony of Acadia. Unlike the absentee bosses who controlled the English territory, French merchants actually showed up, forming good relationships with the Native Americans and cornering the market in fishing, lumbering, and fur trading. And French Jesuit priests converted many Native Americans to Catholicism. Intermittently, overlapping Anglo-French land claims sparked messy local conflicts.

In the mid-17th century, the strategic heart of French administration and activity in Maine was Fort Pentagoet, a sturdy stone outpost built in 1635 in what is now Castine, on the peninsula west of Mount Desert Island. From Pentagoet, the French controlled coastal trade between the St. George River and Mount Desert Island and well up the Penobscot River. In 1654, England captured and occupied Pentagoet and much of French Acadia, but thanks to the 1667 Treaty of Breda, title returned to the French in 1670, and Pentagoet briefly became Acadia's capital.

A short but nasty Dutch foray against Acadia in 1674 resulted in Pentagoet's destruction ("levell'd with ye ground," by one account) and the raising of yet a third national flag over Castine.

THE REVOLUTION AND STATEHOOD

From the late 17th to the late 18th centuries, half a dozen skirmishes along the coast—often sparked by conflicts in Europe—preoccupied the Wabanaki (Native American groups), the

French, and the English. In 1759, roughly midway through the Seven Years' War, the British came out on top in Quebec, allowing Massachusetts Governor John Bernard to divvy up the acreage on Mount Desert Island. Two brave pioneers—James Richardson and Abraham Somes—arrived with their families in 1760, and today's village of Somesville marks their settlement. Even as the American Revolution consumed the colonies, Mount Desert Island maintained a relatively low profile, politically speaking, into the early 19th century. A steady stream of homesteaders, drawn by the appeal of free land, sustained their families by fishing, farming, lumbering, and shipbuilding. On March 15, 1820, the District of Maine, which included Mount Desert Island, broke from Massachusetts to become the 23rd state in the Union, with its capital in Portland (the capital moved to Augusta in 1832).

ARRIVAL OF THE "RUSTICATORS"

Around the middle of the 19th century, explorers of a different sort arrived on Mount Desert Island. Seeking dramatic landscapes rather than fertile land, painters of the acclaimed Hudson River School found more than enough inspiration for their canvases. Thomas Cole (1801-1848), founder of the group, visited Mount Desert only once, in 1844, but his onetime student Frederic Edwin Church (1826-1900) vacationed here in 1850 and became a summer resident two decades later. Once dubbed "the Michelangelo of landscape art," Church traveled widely in search of exotic settings for his grand landscapes. After his summers on Mount Desert, he spent his final days at Olana, a Persian-inspired mansion overlooking the Hudson River.

It's no coincidence that artists formed a large part of the 19th-century vanguard here: The dramatic landscape, with both bare and wooded mountains descending to the sea, still inspires those who see it. Those pioneering artists brilliantly portrayed this area, adding a few romantic touches to landscapes that

really need no enhancement. Known collectively as "rusticators," the artists and their coterie seemed content to "live like the locals" and rented basic rooms from island fisherfolk and boatbuilders. But once the word got out and painterly images began confirming the reports, the surge of visitors began—particularly after the Civil War, which had so totally preoccupied the nation. Tourist boardinghouses appeared first, then sprawling hotels—by the late 1880s, there were nearly 40 hotels on the island, luring vacationers for summer-long stays.

At about the same time, the East Coast's corporate tycoons zeroed in on Mount Desert, arriving by luxurious steam yachts and building over-the-top grand estates (quaintly called "summer cottages") along the shore north of Bar Harbor. Before long, demand exceeded acreage, and mansions also began appearing in Northeast and Southwest Harbors. Their seasonal social circuit was a catalog of rich and famous families—Rockefeller, Astor, Vanderbilt, Ford, Whitney, Schieffelin, Morgan, Carnegie, just for a start. Also part of the elegant mix were noted academics, doctors, lawyers, and even international diplomats. The "Gay Nineties" earned their name on Mount Desert Island.

BIRTH OF A NATIONAL PARK

Fortunately for Mount Desert—and, let's face it, for all of us—many of the rusticators maintained a strong sense of noblesse oblige, engaging regularly in philanthropic activity. Notable among them was George Bucknam Dorr (1853-1944), who spent more than 40 years fighting to preserve land on Mount Desert Island and ultimately earned the title "Father of Acadia."

As Dorr related in his memoir, the saga began with the establishment of the Hancock County Trustees of Public Reservations, a nonprofit corporation modeled on the Trustees of Public Reservations in Massachusetts and chartered in early 1903 "to acquire, by devise, gift or purchase, and to own, arrange, hold, maintain or improve for public use lands in Hancock County, Maine (encompassing Mount Desert Island as well as Schoodic Point), which by reason of scenic beauty, historical interest, sanitary advantage or other like reasons may become available for such purpose." President of the new corporation was Charles W. Eliot, president emeritus of Harvard. Dorr became the vice president and "executive officer," and he dedicated the rest of his life to the cause.

Dorr wrote letters, cajoled, spoke at meetings, arrived on potential donors' doorsteps, and even resorted to polite ruses as he pursued his mission. He also delved into his own pockets to subsidize land purchases. Dorr was a fund-raiser par excellence, a master of networking decades before the days of instant communications. Gradually he accumulated parcels—ponds, woodlands, summits, trails— and gradually his enthusiasm caught on. But easy it wasn't. He faced down longtime local residents, potential developers, and other challengers, and he politely but doggedly visited grand salons, corporate offices, and the halls of Congress in his quest.

In 1913, Bar Harbor taxpayers—irked by the increasing acreage being taken off the tax rolls—prevailed on their state legislator to introduce a bill to annul the corporation's charter. Dorr's effective lobbying doomed the bill, but the corporation saw trouble ahead and devised a plan on a grander scale. Again thanks to Dorr's political and social connections and intense lobbying in Washington DC, President Woodrow Wilson created the Sieur de Monts National Monument on July 8, 1916, from 5,000 acres given to the government by the Hancock County Trustees of Public Reservations. Dorr acquired the new title of Custodian of the Monument.

After the establishment of the National Park Service in August 1916, and after Sieur de Monts had received its first congressional appropriation ($10,000), Dorr forged ahead to try to convince the government to convert "his" national monument into a national park. "No" meant nothing to him. Not only

did he schmooze with members of Congress, cabinet members, helpful secretaries, and even former president Theodore Roosevelt, he also provided the pen (filled with ink) and waited in the president's outer office to be sure Wilson signed the bill. On February 26, 1919, Lafayette National Park became the first national park east of the Mississippi River; George Bucknam Dorr became its first superintendent. Ten years later, the name was changed to Acadia National Park.

THE GREAT FIRE OF 1947

Wildfires are no surprise in Maine, where woodlands often stretch to the horizon, but 1947 was unique in the history of the state and of Acadia. A rainy spring led into a dry, hot summer with almost no precipitation and then an autumn with still no rain. Wells went dry, vegetation drooped, and the inevitable occurred—a record-breaking inferno. Starting on October 17 as a small, smoldering fire at the northern end of the island, it galloped south and east, abetted by winds, and moved toward Bar Harbor and Frenchman Bay before coming under control on October 27. More than 17,000 acres burned, including more than 10,000 in Acadia National Park. Sixty-seven magnificent "cottages" were incinerated on "Millionaires' Row," along the shore north of Bar Harbor, with property damage of more than $20 million. Some of the mansions, incredibly, escaped the flames, but most of the estates were never rebuilt. Miraculously, only one person died in the fire. A few other deaths occurred from heart attacks and traffic accidents as hundreds of residents scrambled frantically to escape the island. Even the fisherfolk of nearby Lamoine and Winter Harbor pitched in, staging their own mini Dunkirk to evacuate more than 400 residents by boat.

THE PARK TODAY

If only George Dorr could see today's Acadia, covering more than 46,000 acres on Mount Desert Island, the Schoodic Peninsula mainland, and parts of Isle au Haut, Baker Island, and Little Cranberry Island. The fire changed Mount Desert's woodland profile—from the dark greens of spruce and fir to a mix of evergreen and deciduous trees, making the fall foliage even more dramatic than in Dorr's day. If ever proof were needed that one person (enlisting the help of many others) can indeed make a difference, Acadia National Park provides it.

People and Culture

Maine's population didn't top the one million mark until 1970. Forty years later, according to the 2010 census, the state had 1.3 million residents.

Despite the long-standing presence of several substantial ethnic groups, plus four Native American groups that account for about 1 percent of the population, diversity is a relatively recent phenomenon in Maine, and the population is about 95 percent Caucasian. A steady influx of refugees, beginning after the Vietnam War, forced the state to address diversity issues, and it continues to do so today. While Portland is the state's most diverse city, tiny Milbridge has a surprisingly diverse population thanks to immigrants who arrive to pick blueberries and often settle there.

POPULATION GROUPS
Natives and "People from Away"

People who weren't born in Maine aren't natives. Even people who were born here may experience close scrutiny of their credentials. In Maine, there are natives and *natives*. Every day the obituary pages describe Mainers who have barely left the houses in which they were born—even in which their grandparents were born. We're talking roots.

Along with this kind of heritage comes a whole vocabulary all its own—lingo distinctive to Maine or at least to New England. Part of the "native" picture is the matter of native produce. Hand-lettered signs sprout everywhere during the summer advertising native corn, native peas, even—believe it or not—native ice. In Maine, homegrown is well grown.

"People from away," on the other hand, are those whose families haven't lived here year-round for at least a generation. But people from away (also called "flatlanders") exist all over Maine, and they have come to stay, putting down roots of their own and altering the way the state is run, looks, and will look. You'll find flatlanders as teachers, corporate executives, artists, retirees, writers, town selectmen, and even lobstermen.

In the 19th century, arriving flatlanders were mostly "rusticators" or "summer complaints"—summer residents who lived well, often in enclaves, and never set foot in the state off-season. They did, however, pay property taxes, contribute to causes, and provide employment for local residents. Another 19th-century wave of people from away came from the bottom of the economic ladder: Irish escaping the potato famine and French Canadians fleeing poverty in Quebec. Both groups experienced subtle and overt anti-Catholicism but rather quickly assimilated into the mainstream, taking jobs in mills and factories and becoming staunch American patriots.

The late 1960s and early 1970s brought bunches of "back-to-the-landers," who scorned plumbing and electricity and adopted retro ways of life. Although a few pockets of diehards still exist, most have changed with the times and adopted contemporary mores (and conveniences).

Today, technocrats arrive from away with computers, smart phones, and other high-tech gear and "commute" via the Internet and modern electronics, although getting a cell phone signal is still a challenge in parts of the Acadia region.

Artists and Artisans: A Studio Tour

Given the inspiring scenery, it's no surprise that the Acadia region is home to dozens of immensely talented artists and artisans. Visiting them in their studios allows you to view the region through their eyes. Galleries are abundant on the Blue Hill Peninsula and Deer Isle and in the Schoodic region, and more and more artists and artisans are calling Mount Desert Island home.

MOUNT DESERT ISLAND

- Must-see Contemporary Craft: **Island Artisans** (99 Main St., Bar Harbor, 207/288-4214, www. islandartisans.com) and **Shaw Contemporary Jewelry** (100 Main St., Northeast Harbor, 207/276-5000 or 877/276-5001, www.shawjewelry.com)

- Must-see Contemporary Art: **Redfield Artisans Gallery** (125 Main St., Northeast Harbor, 207/276-3609)

- Wild about Wildlife: **Christopher Smith Galleries** (125B Main St., Northeast Harbor, 207/276-3343, www.smithbronze.com)

- Don't-miss Museum: **Wendell Gilley Museum** (Herrick Rd. and Rte. 102, Southwest Harbor, 207/244-7555, www.wendellgilleymuseum.org)

SCHOODIC REGION

- Most Talented Family: **Barter Gallery** (South Bay Rd., Sullivan, 207/422-3190, www.barter-gallery.com)

- Take It for Granite: Obadiah Bourne Buell's **Stone Designs Studio and Granite Garden Gallery** (124 Whales Back Rd., 207/422-3111, www.stonedesignsmaine.com)

- Must-see Contemporary Art: **Spring Woods Gallery and Willow Brook Garden** (40A Willowbrook Ln., Sullivan, 207/422-3007, www.springwoodsgallery.com or www.willow-brookgarden.com)

Native Americans

In Maine, the *real* natives are the Wabanaki (People of the Dawn)—the Micmac, Maliseet, Penobscot, and Passamaquoddy of the eastern woodlands. Many live in or near three reservations, near the headquarters for their governors. The Passamaquoddies are at Pleasant Point in Perry, near Eastport, and at Indian Township in Princeton, near Calais. The Penobscots are based on Indian Island in Old Town, near Bangor. Other Native American population clusters—known as "off-reservation Indians"—are the Aroostook Band of Micmacs, based in Presque Isle, and the Houlton Band of Maliseets in Littleton, near Houlton.

In 1965, Maine became the first state to establish a Department of Indian Affairs, but just five years later the Passamaquoddy and

Penobscot people initiated a 10-year-long land-claims case involving 12.5 million Maine acres—about two-thirds of the state—weaseled from their ancestors by Massachusetts in 1794. In late 1980, a landmark agreement, signed by President Jimmy Carter, awarded the tribes $80.6 million in reparations. Despite this, Native American communities still struggle to provide jobs on the reservations and to increase their overall standard of living.

One of the true Native American success stories is the revival of traditional arts as businesses. The Maine Indian Basketmakers Alliance has an active apprenticeship program, and two renowned basket makers—Mary Gabriel and Clara Keezer—have achieved National Heritage Fellowships. Several well-attended annual summer festivals—including

- Folk Art Favorite: **Arthur Smith** (Rogers Point Rd., Steuben, 207/546-3462)

- Best Sculpture and Sculptor: **Ray Carbone** (460 Pigeon Hill Rd., Steuben, 207/546-2170, www. raycarbonesculptor.com)

BLUE HILL PENINSULA

- Must-see Contemporary Art: **Cynthia Winings Gallery** (24 Parker Point Rd., Blue Hill, 917/204-4001, www.cynthiawiningsgallery.com)

- Best Sculpture and Sculptor: **Jud Hartmann** (79 Main St. at Rte. 15, Blue Hill, 207/374-9917, www.judhartmanngallery.com)

- Smithsonian-worthy Pottery: **Mark Bell Pottery** (289 Rte. 15, Blue Hill, 207/374-5881)

- Dream Weaver: Christine Leith at **Eggemoggin Textile Studio** (Rte. 175/Reach Rd., Sedgwick, 207/359-5083, www.chrisleithstudio.com)

DEER ISLE

- Just Plain Fun: **Nervous Nellie's** (600 Sunshine Rd., Deer Isle, 800/777-6845, www.nervous-nellies .com)

- Most Dynamic Duo: **Greene-Ziner Gallery** (73 Reach Rd., Deer Isle, 207/348-2601, www. melissagreene.com)

- Must-see Contemporary Art: **The Turtle Gallery** (61 N. Deer Isle Rd./Rte. 15, Deer Isle, 207/348-9977, www.turtlegallery.com)

- Furnish Your Future: **Geoffrey Warner Studio** (431 N. Main St., Stonington, 207/367-6555, www.geoffreywarnerstudio.com)

one in Bar Harbor—highlight Indian traditions and heighten awareness of Native American culture. Basket making, canoe building, and traditional dancing are all parts of the scene. The splendid Abbe Museum in Bar Harbor features Native American artifacts, interactive displays, historic photographs, and special programs. Fine craft shops also sell Native American jewelry and baskets.

LOCAL CULTURE

Mainers are an independent lot, many exhibiting the classic Yankee characteristics of dry humor, thrift, and ingenuity. Those who can trace their roots back at least a generation or two in the state and have lived here through the duration can call themselves natives; everyone else, no matter how long they've lived here, is "from away."

Mainers react to outsiders depending on how those outsiders treat them. Treat a Mainer with a condescending attitude, and you'll receive a cold shoulder at best. Treat a Mainer with respect, and you'll be welcome, perhaps even invited in to share a mug of coffee. Mainers are wary of outsiders, and often with good reason. Many outsiders move to Maine because they fall in love with its independence and rural simplicity, and then they demand that the farmer stop spreading that stinky manure on his farmlands, or insist that the town initiate garbage pickup, or build a glass-and-timber McMansion in the middle of historic white-clapboard homes.

In most of Maine, money doesn't impress folks. The truth is, that lobsterman in the old truck and the well-worn work clothes might be sitting on a small fortune, or living on it.

Perhaps nothing has caused more troubles between natives and newcomers than the rapidly increasing value of land and the taxes that go with that. For many visitors, Maine real estate is a bargain they can't resist.

If you want real insight into Maine character, listen to a CD or watch a video by one Maine master humorist, Tim Sample. As he often says, "Wait a minute; it'll sneak up on you."

THE ARTS
Fine Art

In 1850, in a watershed moment for Maine landscape painting, Hudson River School artist par excellence, Frederic Edwin Church (1826-1900), vacationed on Mount Desert Island. Influenced by the luminist tradition of such contemporaries as Fitz Hugh Lane (1804-1865), who summered in nearby Castine, Church accurately but romantically depicted the dramatic tableaux of Maine's coast and woodlands that even today attracts slews of admirers.

Another notable is John Marin (1870-1953), a cubist who painted Down East subjects, mostly around Deer Isle and Addison (Cape Split).

Fine art galleries are clustered in Blue Hill, Bar Harbor, and Northeast Harbor.

Crafts

Any survey of Maine art, however brief, must include the significant role of crafts in the state's artistic tradition. As with painters, sculptors, and writers, craftspeople have gravitated to Maine—most notably since the establishment in 1950 of the **Haystack Mountain School of Crafts.** Started in the Belfast area, the school put down roots on Deer Isle in 1960. Each summer, internationally famed artisans—sculptors, glassmakers, weavers, jewelers, potters, papermakers, and printmakers—become the faculty for the unique school, which has weekday classes and 24-hour studio access for adult students on its handsome 40-acre campus. Many Haystack students have chosen to settle in the region.

Galleries and studios pepper the Blue Hill-Deer Isle peninsula. Another craft enclave is in the Schoodic region.

Down East Literature

Maine's first big-name writer was probably the early 17th-century French explorer Samuel de Champlain (1570-1635), who scouted the Maine coast, established a colony in 1604 near present-day Calais, and lived to describe in detail his experiences.

Today, Maine's best-known author lives not on the coast but just inland in Bangor—Stephen King (born 1947), wizard of the weird. Many of his dozens of horror novels and stories are set in Maine, and several have been filmed here for the big screen. King and his wife, Tabitha, also an author, are avid fans of both education and team sports and have generously distributed their largesse among schools and teams in their hometown as well as other parts of the state.

CLASSIC WRITINGS ON THE REGION

Louise Dickinson Rich (1903-1972) entertainingly described her coastal experiences in Corea in *The Peninsula*, after first having chronicled her rugged wilderness existence in *We Took to the Woods*.

Ruth Moore (1903-1989), born on Gott's Island, near Acadia National Park, published her first book at the age of 40. Her tales, recently brought back into print, have earned her a whole new appreciative audience.

Mary Ellen Chase was a Maine native, born in Blue Hill in 1887. She became an English professor at Smith College in 1926 and wrote about 30 books, including some about the Bible as literature. She died in 1973.

A WORLD OF HER OWN

For Marguerite Yourcenar (1903-1987), Maine provided solitude and inspiration for subjects ranging far beyond the state's borders. Yourcenar was a longtime Northeast Harbor resident and the first woman elected to the prestigious Académie Française. Her house, now a shrine to her work, is open to the public by appointment in summer.

ESSAYISTS AND CRITICS, NATIVE AND TRANSPLANTED

Maine's best-known essayist was and is E. B. White (1899-1985), who bought a farm in tiny Brooklin in 1933 and continued writing for *The New Yorker. One Man's Meat,* published in 1944, is one of the best collections of his wry, perceptive writings. His legions of admirers also include two generations raised on his classic children's stories *Stuart Little, Charlotte's Web,* and *The Trumpet of the Swan.*

Writer and critic Doris Grumbach (born 1918), who settled in Sargentville, not far from Brooklin, but far from her New York ties, wrote two particularly wise works from the perspective of a Maine transplant: *Fifty Days of Solitude* and *Coming Into the End Zone.*

MAINE LIT FOR LITTLE ONES

Besides E. B. White's children's classics, *Stuart Little, Charlotte's Web,* and *The Trumpet of the Swan,* American kids were also weaned on books written and illustrated by Maine island summer resident Robert McCloskey (1914-2003), notably *Time of Wonder, One Morning in Maine,* and *Blueberries for Sal.*

Essentials

Getting There

ORIENTATION

Acadia National Park lies about three-fifths of the way up the Maine coast. The primary section, on Mount Desert Island, is located about 46 miles south of Bangor and 160 miles northeast of Portland. Here is where you'll find the park's visitors center. Although it's an island, Mount Desert is connected to the mainland by bridges and causeways, so you can arrive by car or by bus. Not so with Isle au Haut, the most remote section of the park. Isle au Haut is located off the tip of the Blue Hill-Deer Isle peninsula, southwest of Bangor, and can only be reached by boat. Access is limited, unless you have your own boat, and facilities are few. The Schoodic section of the park tips a mainland peninsula east of Bar Harbor and is easily reachable by vehicle or via passenger ferry from Bar Harbor.

There are no direct commercial flights from overseas to any of Maine's airports. The closest **international airport** is Boston's Logan Airport (BOS). **Bus service** to Portland, Bangor, and in season, Bar Harbor, is available from Logan; **train service** is available from Boston's North Station terminal to Portland and Brunswick, and both stations also are served by bus. Rental cars are available at Logan.

DRIVING ROUTES

The major highway access to Maine from the south is **I-95,** which roughly parallels the coast until Bangor. Other busy access points are **U.S. (Route) 1,** entering the state at the Kittery border with New Hampshire and exiting at the Canadian border in Fort Kent; **U.S. 302,** from North Conway, New Hampshire, entering Maine at Fryeburg; **U.S. 2,** from Gorham, New Hampshire, to Bethel; **U.S.**

201, entering Maine at the Jackman border with Quebec; and a couple of crossing points from New Brunswick into Washington County in northeastern Maine.

The maximum speed on I-95 and the Maine Turnpike is 70 mph, on some stretches 55 mph. In snow, sleet, or dense fog, the limit drops to 45 mph; only rarely does the highway close. On other highways, the speed limit is usually 55 mph in rural areas and posted in built-up areas. Published distances can be deceptive; you'll never average even 55 mph on the two-lane roads.

The Maine Department of Transportation (800/877-9171, www.state.me.us/mdot) has general road information on its website and also operates the Explore Maine site (www.exploremaine.org), which has information on all forms of transportation in Maine. For real-time information on road conditions, weather, construction, and major delays, dial 511 in Maine, 866/282-7578 from out of state, or visit www.511maine.gov. Information is available in both English and French.

If you're arriving by car, the **Maine Tourism Association** operates state visitors information centers in Calais, Fryeburg (May-Oct.), Hampden, Houlton, Kittery, and Yarmouth. These are excellent places to visit to stock up on brochures, pick up a map, ask advice, and use the restrooms.

The Interstate and the Maine Turnpike

The interstate can be a bit confusing to motorists; it's important to consult a map and pay close attention to the green directional signs to avoid heading off in the wrong direction. Between York and Augusta, I-95 is the same as

---

Previous: Island Explorer bus; Isle au Haut Boat Company.

the Maine Turnpike, a toll highway regulated by the Maine Turnpike Authority (877/682-9433, travel conditions 800/675-7453, www.maineturnpike.com). All exit numbers along I-95 reflect the distance in miles from the New Hampshire border. I-295 splits from I-95 in Portland and follows the coast to Brunswick before veering inland and rejoining I-95 in Gardiner. Exits on I-295 reflect the distance from where it splits from I-95 just south of Portland at exit 44.

Two exits off I-95 provide access to the Acadia region; for either the trip is about three hours: From exit 113 in Augusta, take Route 3 east to Belfast, which joins Route 1 north. From Bangor, take exit 182A, merging onto I-395 east to Route 1A north, which joins Routes 1 and 3 in Ellsworth. Be sure to follow signs for Ellsworth and Bar Harbor; avoid Route 1A south to Hampden and Stockton Springs.

The Maine Turnpike becomes extremely congested on summer weekends, especially summer holiday weekends. The worst times on the turnpike are 4pm-8pm Friday (northbound), 11am-2pm Saturday (southbound; most weekly cottage rentals run noon Saturday-noon Saturday), and 3pm-7pm Sunday (southbound). On three-day holiday weekends, avoid heading southbound 3pm-7pm Monday.

U.S. 1

Two lanes wide from Kittery in the south to Fort Kent at the top, U.S. (Route) 1 is the state's most congested road, particularly July-August. Mileage distances can be extremely deceptive, since it will take you much longer than anticipated to get from point A to point B. If you ask anyone about distances, chances are good that you'll receive an answer in hours rather than miles. Plan accordingly. If you're trying to make time, it's best to take I-95; if you want to see Maine, take Route 1 and lots of little offshoots. If you drive Route 1 without stops and without encountering slow-moving traffic, it's about a four-hour trip.

TRAVEL HUB: BANGOR

Airport

Bangor International Airport (BGR, 207/947-0384, www.flybangor.com) is northern and eastern coastal Maine's hub for flights arriving from Boston and points beyond. Bangor is the closest large airport to Bar Harbor, Acadia National Park on Mount Desert Island, and the park's other outposts. About 500,000 passengers move through Bangor International annually, a user-friendly facility on the outskirts of the city. Although flights tend to be pricier to Bangor than to Portland or especially Boston, there's a big convenience factor to flying in here.

Despite the "international" in the airport's name, passenger service from international destinations to Bangor tends to be limited to charter airlines, which sometimes arrive here to clear customs, refuel, and then continue on to points south and west; military flights; and alerts, in which badly behaving passengers are removed from international flights. More typically, international visitors arrive in Bangor via New York or Boston gateways. Bad weather in Portland or Boston can also create unexpected domestic and international arrivals at Bangor's less-foggy airfield.

The airport's lower level has an interactive information kiosk, where you can contact local hotels and motels for rooms and airport shuttle service.

Suggested Driving Routes

Bangor is slightly fewer than 50 miles from Bar Harbor, but you'll be traveling almost entirely on two-lane roads; in summer, figure on 1.5 hours. Drive Route 1A to Ellsworth and then Route 3 to Bar Harbor. Do not take Route 1A to Hampden, or you'll end up on the wrong side of the Penobscot River. For the Schoodic section of the park, when Route 1 and Route 3 split in Ellsworth, take Route 1 north to Gouldsboro, then head south on Route 186. For the Blue Hill Peninsula, Deer Isle, and Isle au Haut, from Ellsworth take Route 1 south to Route 172, then in Blue Hill, Route 15 south to reach Stonington and the boat to Isle au Haut.

Car Rentals

Car rentals at the airport include **Alamo** (207/947-0158 or 800/462-5266, www.alamo. com), **Avis** (207/947-8383 or 800/831-2847, www.avis.com), **Budget** (207/945-9429 or 800/527-0700, www.drivebudget.com), **Hertz** (207/942-5519 or 800/654-3131, www. hertz.com), and **National** (207/947-0158 or 800/227-7368, www.nationalcar.com).

Bus and Taxi Services

Concord Coach Lines (1039 Union St./Rte. 222, Bangor, 207/945-4000 or 800/639-3317, www.concordcoachlines.com) provides daily bus service year-round from Logan Airport in Boston to the Bangor Transportation Center via Portland. **Greyhound** (430 Coldbrook Rd., Hermon, 207/945-3000 or 800/231-2222, www.greyhound.com) offers less frequent service between Boston's South Station and Dysart's Truck Stop in Hermon, a less convenient spot just west of Bangor. Neither bus line services Bar Harbor, but both offer connections to the Bar Harbor-Bangor Shuttle.

While there are ways to connect various points in the Acadia region via regional bus services (see www.exploremaine. org), most operate only one or two buses per day and often only on a few days each week. The most convenient and reasonably priced transportation between Bangor and Bar Harbor is provided by **Bar Harbor-Bangor Shuttle** (207/479-5911, www.bar-harborbangorshuttle.com), which offers at least four round-trips daily April-November. Shuttle stops include Bangor Airport, Bangor Transportation Center, the Greyhound station, and Hollywood Casino Hotel in Bangor; the Hancock County-Bar Harbor Airport; Mike's Groceries in Ellsworth; and numerous lodging properties in Bar Harbor.

Round-the-clock **taxi service** is provided by Airport/River City Taxi (207/947-8294 or 800/997-8294), Brad's Cab (207/941-9695), and Town Taxi (207/945-5671 or 800/750-9935). Bar Harbor-based Bar Harbor Coastal Cab (207/288-1222, www.barharborcoastalcab.com) provides both local and long distance service and accepts credit cards. More companies are listed on the airport's website.

Accommodations

Bangor International Airport is approximately 45 miles from Bar Harbor. Depending on when your flight arrives, you may wish to spend the night here and begin your journey refreshed. Most of the mid-rate chains have properties here. Your choice of a hotel or motel near the Bangor Mall or the Bangor Airport may depend on your frequent-flyer memberships or where you get the best auto club deal. There are lots of options, and most offer free shuttle service to and from the airport.

Many properties book far in advance for the fourth weekend in August, when the American Folk Festival is in town and traffic can be a bear.

For early morning flights, you can't beat the convenience of the **Four Points Sheraton Hotel** (307 Godfrey Blvd., Bangor, 207/947 6721 or 800/228-4609, www.fourpointsbangorairport.com, from $155), which is linked to the terminal by a skyway. Renovated in 2009, it has a restaurant, a fitness room, an indoor pool, and free Internet access. Pets are permitted for $20 per stay.

Next to the Bangor Mall, with restaurants and a food court, is the 96-room **Country Inn at the Mall** (936 Stillwater Ave., Bangor, 207/941-0200 or 800/244-3961, www.countryinnatthemall.net, from $110), which includes a continental breakfast, free lodging for kids rooming with parents, free local calls, Wi-Fi, and HBO.

Hollywood Casino Hotel & Raceway (500 Main St., Bangor, 877/779-7771, www. hollywoodcasinobangor.com, $99-349) is the best downtown hotel, but it is a casino and you have to deal with the noise and hoopla that goes with it. That said, the 152 rooms have flat-screen TVs and free Wi-Fi. Facilities include two restaurants, a lounge, a fitness center, and the casino. The location puts all of downtown within footsteps. Airport shuttles are available.

Twelve miles southeast of Bangor and about 40 miles northwest of Bar Harbor is **The Lucerne Inn** (Bar Harbor Rd./Rte. 1A, Dedham, 207/843-5123, www.lucerneinn. com, $119-219), an updated early 19th-century stagecoach hostelry on a 10-acre hilltop overlooking Phillips Lake and the hills beyond. The fall panorama is spectacular. Despite the highway out front, noise is no problem in the rear-facing guest rooms, all with lake views, gas fireplaces, and whirlpool tubs. Outside there's a pool. Rates include a continental breakfast, and an on-site dining room serves dinner and a popular Sunday brunch. One-night packages, including dinner, are a good idea, as you're in the middle of nowhere and not likely to head out again once you get here.

Camping

On Bangor's western perimeter are two clean, well-managed campgrounds convenient to I-95 and Bangor. The emphasis is on RVs, but tent sites are available. Closest to the city is the 52-site **Paul Bunyan Campground** (1862 Union St./Rte. 222, Bangor, 207/941-1177, www.paulbunyancampground.com, mid-Apr.-Oct., from $24), about three miles northwest of I-95 on Route 222 west. Facilities at this attractive campground include a recreation hall and a huge outdoor heated pool; activities are offered most weekends in midsummer. Leashed pets are welcome (cleanup is required), and noise rules are strictly enforced.

About two miles farther out on Route 222, **Pleasant Hill Campground** (45 Mansell Rd., at Rte. 222, Hermon, 207/848-5127, www. pleasanthillcampground.com, from $24), also a Good Sam Park, has 105 sites on 60 acres. Facilities include mini golf, laundry, play areas, a rec room, a heated pool, free showers, and a small store. Pets are welcome.

Food

You'll find lots of fast food and family-friendly chains between the airport and the mall. Just south on I-95 at exit 180 is **Dysert's** (Coldbrook Rd., Hermon, 207/942-4878, www.dysarts.com, $5-16), a 24-hour trucker's destination resort with good grub. For a nicer meal, head downtown to **Fiddlehead** (84 Hammond St., Bangor, 207/942-3336, www.thefiddleheadrestaurant.com, 4pm-9pm Tues.-Fri., 5pm-10pm Sat., 5pm-9pm Sun., $16-25) or **11 Central** (11 Central St., Bangor, 207/922-5115, www.11centralbangor. com, 4pm-10pm daily, $15-30), an American bistro serving steaks, pastas, seafood, and pizzas in a casual yet stylish downtown spot with a hip vibe.

TRAVEL HUB: PORTLAND

For anyone planning to go *just* to Acadia National Park, the primary gateway typically is Bangor. But if you're visiting Acadia as part of a Maine vacation, you might well choose Portland—160-180 miles south of Bar Harbor, depending on the route—as a springboard for getting to Acadia. Another consideration: Because the airport is served by JetBlue and Southwest, prices tend to be lower.

Airport

Although it keeps expanding, **Portland International Jetport** (PWM, 207/874-8877 or 207/774-7301 automated info, www.portlandjetport.org) remains an easily navigable airport, where all flights leave from and arrive at the same building. Don't be fooled by the "international" in the airport's name; you can't even get a direct flight to Canada from here. Note that, being on the coast, the Portland airport is more subject to fog shutdowns than Bangor. Also note that Portland is the terminus of many airline routes, and the airline companies, which provide the baggage handlers and unloading equipment, give low priority to locations that don't require fast turnaround. As a result, having only carry-on luggage is a plus here. Baggage-handling offices surround the luggage carousels. Airlines are responsible for luggage, so if you have a problem, contact a representative from your airline. If you have an emergency, contact the airport manager (207/773-8462).

Trains

Amtrak's *Downeaster* (800/872-7245, www.
thedowneaster.com) makes daily round-trip
runs between Boston's North Station and
Brunswick, with stops in Wells, Saco, Old
Orchard Beach (May 1-Oct. 31), Portland,
and Freeport. From the Portland station,
Portland's Metro municipal bus service
will take you gratis to downtown Portland;
just show your Amtrak ticket stub. From
Brunswick, take the **Maine Eastern Railway**
(866/637-2457, www.maineeasternrailroad.
com), a seasonal excursion train between
Brunswick and Rockland with stops in Bath,
Newcastle, and Wiscasset.

Amtrak trains from Washington via New
York arrive in Boston at South Station, not
North Station, and there's no direct link between the two. While you can connect via the
T (Boston's subway), it's a real hassle with baggage. Instead, splurge on a taxi or take the bus
north from South Station.

There are no train connections to the
Acadia region.

Ferry

In 2014, **Nova Star Cruises** (888/216-9018
U.S., 888/762-4058 Canada, www.novastar-
cruises.com) launched a new international
cruise-car-ferry service between Ocean
Gateway Terminal in Portland, Maine, and
Yarmouth International Ferry Terminal in
Yarmouth, Nova Scotia. The 528-foot *Nova
Star* provides daily round-trip ferry service
early May-early November. The nine-hour
overnight crossing departs Portland at 8pm
EST and arrives in Yarmouth at 7am AST. The
day cruise departs Yarmouth at 9am AST and
arrives in Portland at 5pm EST. Ferry ame-
nities include restaurants, a casino, live entertainment, a theater, an art gallery, a fitness
center and spa, a children's area, and duty-free
shopping.

Suggested Driving Routes

There are several routes for driving from
Portland to Mount Desert Island. Route A follows the four-lane interstate for most of the
way, and then finishes up on two-lane roads.
Route B is half interstate, half two-lane roads.
Route C is almost all on two-lane roads—it's
also the most scenic and the slowest route.
As with most other Maine auto explorations,
it's particularly helpful to use the DeLorme
Maine Atlas and Gazetteer (www.delorme.
com, $20).

For **Route A,** depart Portland north on
I-295 and continue to just south of Augusta,
where it merges with I-95. Continue on I-95
to Bangor and take exit 182A, merging onto
I-395 east toward Holden and Ellsworth (and
Acadia). At the end of I-395, you're also at
the end of four-lane highways; it's two lanes
the rest of the way. Continue on Route 1A
to Ellsworth, then Route 3 through Trenton
to Mount Desert Island. Allow at least three
hours.

For Blue Hill, Deer Isle, and Isle au Haut,
from Ellsworth head south on Route 1 (Main
St.) through town, then take Route 172 south
to Blue Hill, and then Route 15 south to reach
Stonington and the boat to Isle au Haut.

For the Schoodic Peninsula, in Ellsworth
take Route 1 north to Gouldsboro, and then
take Route 186 south to the park.

For **Route B,** start out the same way from
Portland, on I-295 to I-95, then just north of
Augusta, take exit 113 for Route 3 east. You'll
be on two-lane roads the rest of the way. Route
1 doubles as Route 3 from Belfast to the southern end of Ellsworth. Allow at least 3.5 hours.

For the Blue Hill Peninsula, Deer Isle, and
Isle au Haut, take Route 15 south from Orland.
If your destination is Castine, take Route 175
south from Bucksport.

For the Schoodic Peninsula, stay on Route 1
to Gouldsboro, and then take Route 186.

Route C is the coastal route, where you'll
be winding through and skirting small communities the whole way. This route lends itself to (no, requires!) stops—for photos, for
exploring, for shopping, for overnights.
Stopping only for lunch and restrooms, you'll
still need to allow 4.5-6 hours from Portland
to Bar Harbor. And all bets are off on Friday
afternoons in summer, when towns such as

Wiscasset and Camden can be major bottle-necks. They're lovely towns, though—definitely worth a stop.

To take Route C from Portland, you can start off on two-lane Route 1, or you can go north on four-lane I-295 and I-95 to Brunswick, then cut over when you see the Coastal U.S. 1 sign. Follow Route 1 the rest of the way—through Bath, Wiscasset, Newcastle, Waldoboro, Thomaston, Rockland, Rockport, Camden, Belfast, Searsport, Bucksport, Orland, and the turnoffs for the Blue Hill Peninsula, and on to Ellsworth, where you'll split off onto Route 3 and head for Mount Desert Island, or stay on Route 1 to Gouldsboro and the Schoodic Peninsula.

Between Brunswick and Rockland, down each of the "fingers" east of Route 1, are even more towns and villages—Harpswell, Phippsburg, Georgetown, Boothbay Harbor, Damariscotta, Friendship, and Cushing.

Which brings us to the bottom line: You could spend *weeks* visiting Portland and making your way from there to Acadia.

Car Rentals

Car rentals at the airport include **Alamo** (207/775-0855 or 877/222-9075, www.alamo.com), **Avis** (207/874-7500 or 800/230-4898, www.avis.com), **Budget** (207/874-7500 or 800/527-0700, www.drivebudget.com), **Hertz** (207/774-4544 or 800/654-3131, www.hertz.com), and **National** (207/773-0036 or 877/222-9058, www.nationalcar.com).

Bus Services

Concord Coach Lines (800/639-3317, www.concordcoachlines.com) departs downtown Boston's South Station Transportation Center and Logan Airport for Portland almost hourly from the wee hours of the morning until late at night, making pickups at all Logan airline terminals (on the lower level). Most of the buses continue directly to Bangor; a few daily nonexpress buses continue along the coast to Searsport before turning inland to Bangor. The Portland bus terminal is the Portland Transportation Center, on Thompson Point Road just west of I-295. If you're headed for downtown Portland from the bus terminal, board the Metro city bus at the terminal and show your bus ticket to receive a free trip.

Also serving Maine but with far less frequent service is **Greyhound** (800/231-2222, www.greyhound.com).

Local Transportation

Portland airport's small size and practically downtown location are big pluses for many travelers. It's simple to get on I-95 headed north if you're heading right out. If you're planning on spending the night, you can be in downtown Portland within 10-15 minutes via taxi.

Accommodations

You'll find most of the major chain hotels in the Greater Portland area. Also here are some lovely B&Bs and excellent independent hotels and inns; see www.visitportland.com. Some offer airport shuttle service.

Right at the airport, with free shuttles, are **Embassy Suites Hotel** (1050 Westbrook St., 207/774-2200, www.embassysuites.com, from $200), with an indoor heated pool, a restaurant, free full breakfast and afternoon reception, and coin laundry, and the **Hilton Garden Inn** (145 Jetport Blvd., 207/828-1117, www.hiltongardeninn.com, from $200), with an indoor heated pool and coin laundry.

Railroad tycoon John Deering built **The Inn at St. John** (939 Congress St., 207/773-6481 or 800/636-9127, www.innatstjohn.com, $110-260) in 1897. The comfortable (if somewhat tired), moderately priced 39-room hostelry is a good choice for value-savvy travelers who aren't seeking fancy accommodations. Some rooms share baths. The inn welcomes children and pets and even has bicycle storage. Cable TV, Wi-Fi, air-conditioning, free local calls, free parking, and a meager continental breakfast are provided. Reimbursement for taxi from the airport or transportation center is available at a fixed price. Most guest rooms have private baths (some are detached); some have fridges and microwaves. The downside is the lackluster neighborhood—in the evening you'll want to drive or take a taxi when going out.

The **Portland Harbor Hotel** (468 Fore St., 207/775-9090 or 888/798-9090, www.portlandharborhotel.com, from $299) is an upscale boutique hotel built around a garden courtyard in the desirable Old Port neighborhood. Rooms are plush, with chic linens, duvets, down pillows on the beds, Wi-Fi, digital cable TV, and baths with separate soaking tubs and showers. The hotel has a cozy lounge, the restaurant has 24-hour room service, and a free local car service is available.

About 20 minutes north of Portland, the family-run **Casco Bay Inn** (107 U.S. 1, 207/865-4925 or 800/570-4970, www.cascobayinn.com, from $106) is a budget-friendly motel with spacious guest rooms and perks that include a guest Internet station, free Wi-Fi, and a continental breakfast.

Food

Named "America's Foodiest Small Town" by *Bon Appétit* magazine in 2009, downtown Portland alone has more than 100 restaurants. The city's proximity to fresh foods from both farms and the sea makes it popular with chefs, and its Italian roots and growing immigrant population mean a good variety of international dining too. Do make reservations, whenever possible, and as far in advance as you can, especially in July-August. If you're especially into the food scene, check www.portlandfoodmap.com for a breakdown by cuisine of Portland restaurants, with links to recent reviews. Here are a few favorites.

Chef Abby Harmon's **Caiola's Restaurant** (58 Pine St., 207/772-1110, www.caiolas.com, from 5:30pm Mon.-Sat., 9am-2pm Sun., entrées from $14) delivers comfort food with pizzazz in a cozy neighborhood bistro. This little gem is off most visitors' radar screens, but locals fill it nightly.

Ask around and everyone will tell you the best seafood in town is at **Street and Company** (33 Wharf St., Old Port, 207/775-0887, www.streetandcompany.net,

5pm-9:30pm Sun.-Thurs., 5pm-10pm Fri.-Sat., entrées from $18). Fresh, beautifully prepared fish is what you get, often with a Mediterranean flair. Tables are tight, and it's often noisy in the informal brick-walled rooms.

For lobster in the rough, head to **Portland Lobster Company** (180 Commercial St., 207/775-2112, www.portlandlobstercompany.com, 11am-10pm daily). There's a small inside seating area, but it's much more pleasant to sit out on the wharf and watch the excursion boats come and go. Expect to pay in the low $20 range for a one-pound lobster with fries and slaw. Other choices ($8-23) and a kids' menu are available.

Huge portions at rock-bottom prices make **Silly's** (40 Washington Ave., 207/772-0360, www.sillys.com, 11am-9pm Tues.-Fri., 9am-9pm Sat.-Sun., $8-16) an ever-popular choice among the young and budget-minded. The huge menu has lots of international flair along with veggie, vegan, gluten-free, and dairy-free options.

Vegan and vegetarian cuisine comes with an Asian accent at **Green Elephant** (608 Congress St., 207/347-3111, www.greenelephantmaine.com, 11:30am-2:30pm Tues.-Sat. and from 5pm daily, $9-14). There's not one shred of meat on the creative menu, but you won't miss it.

Plan well in advance to land a reservation at the city's nationally lauded tables: **Fore Street** (288 Fore St., Old Port, 207/775-2717, www.forestreet.biz, from 5:30pm daily, entrées from $20); **Hugo's** (88 Middle St., at Franklin St., 207/774-8538, www.hugos.net, 5:30pm-9pm Tues.-Thurs., 5:30pm-9:30pm Fri.-Sun., $13-21); **Five Fifty-Five** (555 Congress St., 207/761-0555, www.fivefiftyfive.com, from 5pm daily and 9:30am-2pm Sun., $10-32); and **Eventide Oyster Co.** (86 Middle St., 207/774-8538, www.eventideoysterco.com, 11am-midnight daily, from $25).

TRAVEL HUB: BOSTON

Boston's Logan Airport is the region's closest international airport, and due to its larger size, it often has fares that are lower than those serving Maine's airports.

Airport
General Edward Lawrence Logan International Jetport (BOS, 800/234-6426 automated info, www.massport.com) has four terminals (A, B, C, E) grouped in a horseshoe pattern. Terminal E handles most, but not all, international flights. Blue-and-white Massport On-Airport Shuttle buses connect the terminals with the Rental Car Center and the MBTA's Airport Station for the subway's Blueline: During peak midday hours: Bus 22 serves Terminals A and B; Bus 33 serves Terminals C and E. During late morning and late evening off-peak hours, Bus 55 serves all terminals. Shuttle Bus 66 serves all terminals, the subway station, and the Water Transportation Dock; Bus 11 circulates between all terminals, but doesn't go to the subway; Bus 88 serves all terminals and the parking garage. Buses usually run every 5-6 minutes. In addition, the MBTA's Silver Line SL1 bus provides transportation between all terminals and South Station, with stops en route; a free connection is offered to the Redline (which connects to North Station); fare is $2.10.

Car Rentals
Car rentals at Logan's Rental Car Center include **Advantage** (617/567-4140, www.advantage.com), **Alamo** (888/826-6893, www.alamo.com), **Avis** (617/568-6600, www.avis.com), **Budget** (617/497-3733, www.drivebudget.com), **Dollar** (866/434-2226, www.dollar.com), **Enterprise** (617-561-4488, www.enterprise.com), **Hertz** (617-568-5200, www.hertz.com), **National** (888/826-6890, www.nationalcar.com), and **zipcar** (866/494-7227, www.zipcar.com)

Bus
Concord Coach Lines (800/639-3317, www.concordcoachlines.com) departs downtown Boston's South Station Transportation Center and Logan Airport for Portland almost hourly

from the wee hours of the morning until late at night, making pickups at all Logan airline terminals (on the lower level). Most of the buses continue directly to Bangor; a few daily nonexpress buses continue along the coast to Searsport before turning inland to Bangor.

Trains
Amtrak's *Downeaster* (800/872-7245, www.thedowneaster.com) makes daily round-trip runs between Boston's North Station and Brunswick, with stops in Wells, Saco, Old Orchard Beach (May 1-Oct. 31), Portland, and Freeport. From the Portland station, Portland's Metro municipal bus service will take you gratis to downtown Portland; just show your Amtrak ticket stub. Amtrak trains from Washington via New York arrive in Boston at South Station, not North Station, and there's no direct link between the two. While you can connect via the T (Boston's subway), it's a real hassle with baggage. Instead, splurge on a taxi or take the bus north from South Station.

There are no train connections to the Acadia region.

Suggested Driving Routes
It would be interesting to know the statistics on how many people drive directly from Boston to Acadia National Park without stopping en route. I'd guess not many; perhaps mostly those who have summer homes on Mount Desert Island or nearby. The trip is around 270 miles (about five hours), and not all of the trek is on multilane highway. You can't count on averaging 60 mph when you hit the two-lane roads, especially in midsummer. Even on the 4-6-lane I-95, traffic can choke up at tollbooths. Also, you'll need bathroom breaks, snack breaks, maybe a gas fill-up—and all of Maine south of Acadia has its own attractions to lure you into detours (L.L.Bean and the Freeport outlet shops are major magnets).

But if you're determined to drive from Boston, the best route is I-95, through 18 miles of New Hampshire into Maine and directly toward Bangor (the Maine Turnpike and I-95 are the same road for some stretches). Take exit 182A for U.S. 395 and watch for signs for Route 1A to Ellsworth and then Route 3 to Bar Harbor. Do not take Route 1A to Hampden, or you'll end up on the wrong side of the Penobscot River. For the Schoodic section of the park, when Route 1 and Route 3 split in Ellsworth, take Route 1 north to Gouldsboro, then head south on Route 186. For the Blue Hill Peninsula, Deer Isle, and Isle au Haut, from Ellsworth take Route 1 south to Route 172, then in Blue Hill, Route 15 south to reach Stonington and the boat to Isle au Haut.

BAR HARBOR AIRPORT

The most convenient air access to Acadia is **Hancock County-Bar Harbor Airport** (BHB, 207/667-7329, www.bhbairport.com). It's located 12 miles from downtown Bar Harbor, and despite its name, the airport is located in Trenton, just north of Mount Desert Island. This isn't a big-jet airport, in case you're squeamish about small planes. Alaska Air-partner **PenAir** (800/448-4226, www.penair.com) and Jet Blue-partner **Cape Air** (866/227-3247, www.capeair.com) provide summer service to Bar Harbor from Boston. Flight time from Boston to Trenton is about 80 minutes. Driving time from Boston to Trenton would be a minimum of six hours, usually longer.

Suggested Driving Routes

Lucky you; this one's quick and easy. Take Route 3 west for Mount Desert Island and Bar Harbor (just take a left when exiting the airport). For the Schoodic section of the park, head east on Route 3 to the junction with Route 1 in Ellsworth, then north on Route 1 to Gouldsboro, then south on Route 186. For the Blue Hill Peninsula, Deer Isle, and Isle au Haut, take Route 3 east through Ellsworth to Route 172, then in Blue Hill, Route 15 south to reach Stonington and the boat to Isle au Haut.

Car Rentals

Hertz (207/667-5017 or 800/654-3131, www.hertz.com) provides on-site rental cars year-round. **Enterprise** (207/667-2662 or 800/325-8007) operates seasonally. In summer, be sure to reserve a car well in advance.

Bus

The free **Island Explorer** (207/667-5796, www.exploreacadia.com) stops at the airport late June-early October. Connections serve most of Mount Desert Island, including Bar Harbor, Southwest Harbor, and Acadia National Park.

Getting Around

How will you get around once you get here? Europeans are always shocked at Maine's minimal public transport. Among less-populated areas, Mount Desert Island stands out, thanks to its fare-free, propane-fueled **Island Explorer** bus system, subsidized by your park fees, Friends of Acadia, L.L.Bean, and local businesses. It serves most of the island as well as Bar Harbor Airport in Trenton. The good news is that it's a very efficient network; the bad news is that it runs only late June-mid-October. So try to come during the Explorer's season, when you can rubberneck all you want from the comfort of a bus seat. No missed turns, no near misses; less pollution, less frazzle. If you've arrived by car, leave it at your lodging and hop on the bus.

The Island Explorer also circulates around the southern end of the Schoodic Peninsula, from Winter Harbor to Prospect Harbor, with a loop through the park. It meets the passenger ferry that connects Bar Harbor to Winter Harbor, so you can visit the Schoodic section of the park from Mount Desert Island without needing a car.

The outer islands are also accessible from

Mount Desert Island. Great Cranberry has a free, summer golf-cart shuttle, something others islands hope to copy. Most islands can be explored on foot or bicycle (rentals are available in Bar Harbor and Southwest Harbor). Passenger ferries from Southwest Harbor and Northeast Harbor cruise to the Cranberry Isles. A state car ferry serves Swans Island and Frenchboro. From Stonington, a passenger ferry connects Deer Isle to Isle au Haut.

You'll need a car to explore the other regions covered in this book: Blue Hill Peninsula, Deer Isle, the Schoodic region beyond the Island Explorer's reaches, and Ellsworth, although there are some regional bus services with limited schedules.

DRIVING

Almost all gas stations in Maine are self-serve. Pumps are marked "Self"; at those marked "Full," you'll pay more to have an attendant pump the gas for you. Most now allow you to pay at the pump with a credit card. Many also have ATMs, but you'll usually have to pay a bank surcharge.

Important Driving Regulations

Seat belts are mandatory in Maine. Unless posted otherwise, Maine allows right turns at red lights, after you stop and check for oncoming traffic. *Never* pass a stopped school bus in either direction. Wait until the bus's red lights have stopped flashing and all children are well off the road. Maine law also requires drivers to turn on their car's headlights any time the windshield wipers are operating. Keep right on multilane roads except to pass.

Roadside Assistance and Road Conditions

Since Maine is enslaved to the automobile, it's not a bad idea for vacationers to carry membership in AAA in case of breakdowns, flat tires, and other car crises. Contact your nearest AAA office or **AAA Northern New England** (425 Marginal Way, Portland, 207/780-6800 or 800/482-7497, www.aaanne.

com). The emergency road service number is 800/222-4357.

For real-time information on road conditions, weather, construction, and major delays, dial 511 in Maine or 866/282-7578 from out of state, or visit www.511maine.gov. Information is available in both English and French.

BUS SERVICES

Hancock County, including the Blue Hill Peninsula and Deer Isle, Ellsworth and Trenton, Mount Desert Island, and east to Gouldsboro, is served by a patchwork of local transportation systems designed for commuters, seniors, and residents without access to a vehicle. Providing an umbrella for it all is **Downeast Transportation** (207/667-5796, www.downeasttrans.org), with maps and schedules online. You can piece the region together, but each acts independently. Check online for details, as bus drivers require exact change.

MAPS

Request a free state map through the **Maine Office of Tourism** (888/624-6345, www.visitmaine.com). Acadia National Park maps are available at the visitors centers. Most local chambers of commerce have free local maps.

The Maine Atlas and Gazetteer

Peek in any Mainer's car and you're likely to see a copy of *The Maine Atlas and Gazetteer,* published by DeLorme Mapping Company in Yarmouth. Despite an oversize format inconvenient for hiking and kayaking, this 96-page paperbound book just about guarantees that you won't get lost (and if you're good at map reading, it can get you out of a lot of traffic jams). Scaled at one-half inch to the mile, it's meticulously compiled from aerial photographs, satellite images, U.S. Geological Survey maps, GPS readings, and timber-company maps, and it is revised annually. It details back roads and dirt roads and shows elevations, boat ramps, public lands, campgrounds and picnic areas, and trailheads. DeLorme products are available nationwide in book and map stores, but you can also order direct (800/452-5931, www.delorme.com). The atlas is $19.95 and shipping is $4 (Maine residents need to add 5 percent sales tax).

Travel Tips

FOREIGN TRAVELERS

Since 9/11, security has been excruciatingly tight for foreign visitors, with immigration and customs procedures in flux. For current rules, visit www.usa.gov/visitors/arriving.shtml. It's wise to make two sets of copies of all paperwork, one to carry separately on your trip and another left with a trusted friend or relative at home.

For information on what can be brought into the United States, check the website of the Customs and Border Protection division of the Department of Homeland Security (www.cbp.gov).

Money and Currency Exchange

Since Maine's Down East (geographically, northeast) coast borders Canada, don't be surprised to see a few Canadian coins mixed in with American ones when you receive change from a purchase. In such cases, Canadian and U.S. quarters are equivalent, although the exchange rate may be different. Most services (including banks) will accept a handful of Canadian coins at par, but you'll occasionally spot No Canadian Currency signs.

Other foreign currencies are not easily convertible (without losing in the exchange) at the small local banks on Mount Desert Island. Acadia National Park has no ATMs within its boundaries, but there are ATMs in Bar Harbor and other communities on Mount Desert Island.

For the most current exchange rate info, visit www.xe.com.

ACCOMMODATIONS

For all accommodations listings, rates are quoted for peak season, which is usually July-August but may extend through foliage season in mid-October. Rates drop, often dramatically, in the shoulder seasons and off-season at many accommodations that remain open. Especially during peak season, many accommodations require a 2-3-night minimum.

For the best rates, be sure to check Internet specials and ask about packages. Many accommodations also provide discounts for members of travel clubs such as AAA and to seniors, members of the military, and other such groups.

Unless otherwise noted, accommodations listed have private baths.

A note about B&Bs: If you've never stayed at a B&B, begin by putting aside any ideas you may have about them. No two are alike, but all are built on the premise that your experiences will be richer if it's easy to meet other travelers. That said, many provide private tables for breakfast—ask before booking—if you're just not up to being sociable first thing in the morning. The shared breakfast table does provide an opportunity to trade experiences with other guests. Some also provide afternoon refreshments, another opportunity to chat. Many B&Bs are quite exquisite and decorated with antiques and fine art, which means they're often inappropriate for young children. Others are equipped with in-room TVs, CD players, VCRs or DVD players, air-conditioning, phones, and other modern conveniences. A number of Mount Desert Island B&Bs are in grand historic cottages that survived the fire, providing a taste of that lifestyle and a peek into those rambling homes. Most B&Bs are operated by folks who live here year-round (some for generations), so they are able to provide recommendations based on their in-depth knowledge. B&Bs, especially, reflect

Maine Food Specialties

Everyone knows Maine is *the* place for lobster, but there are quite a few other foods that you should sample before you leave.

For a few weeks in May, right around Mother's Day (the second Sunday in May), a wonderful delicacy starts sprouting along Maine woodland streams: **fiddleheads,** the still-furled tops of the ostrich fern *(Matteuccia struthiopteris)*. Tasting vaguely like asparagus, fiddleheads have been on May menus ever since Native Americans taught the colonists to forage for the tasty vegetable. Don't go fiddleheading unless you're with a pro, though; the look-alikes are best left to the woodland critters. If you find them on a restaurant menu, indulge.

As with fiddleheads, we owe thanks to Native Americans for introducing us to **maple syrup,** one of Maine's major agricultural exports. The syrup comes in four different colors and flavors, from light amber to extra dark amber, and inspectors strictly monitor syrup quality. The best syrup comes from the sugar, or rock, maple *(Acer saccharum)*. On Maine Maple Sunday (usually the fourth Sunday in March), several dozen syrup producers open their rustic sugarhouses to the public for "sugaring-off" parties—to celebrate the sap harvest and share the final phase in the production process. Wood smoke billows from the sugarhouse chimney while everyone inside gathers around huge kettles used to boil down the watery sap. (A single gallon of syrup starts with 30-40 gallons of sap.) Finally, it's time to sample the syrup every which way—on pancakes and waffles, in tea, on ice cream, in puddings, in muffins, even just drizzled over snow. Most producers also have containers of syrup for sale. For a list of participating sugarhouses, contact the Maine Department of Agriculture (207/287-3491, www.getrealmaine.com).

The best place for Maine maple syrup is atop pancakes made with Maine **wild blueberries.** Packed with antioxidants and all kinds of good-for-you stuff, these flavorful berries are prized by bakers because they retain their form and flavor when cooked. Much smaller than the cultivated versions, wild blueberries are raked, not picked. Although most of the Down East barren barons harvest their crops for the lucrative wholesale market, a few growers let you pick your own blueberries in mid-August. Contact the Wild Blueberry Commission (207/581-1475, http://wildblueberries.maine.edu) or the state Department of Agriculture (207/287-3491, www.getrealmaine.com) for locations, recipes, and other wild blueberry information, or log on to the website of the Wild Blueberry Association of North America (www.wildblueberries.com), headquartered in Bar Harbor.

The best place to simply appreciate blueberries is Machias, an easy day trip from most anywhere in the Acadia region and site of the renowned annual Wild Blueberry Festival, held the third weekend in August. While harvesting is under way in the surrounding fields, you can stuff your

their owners, so expect any of them to be different than described if ownership has changed.

FOOD

Days and hours of operation listed for places serving food are for peak season. These do change often, sometimes even within a season, and it's not uncommon for a restaurant to close early on a quiet night. To avoid disappointment, call before making a special trip.

ALCOHOL

As in the rest of the country, Maine's minimum drinking age is 21—and bar owners, bartenders, and serving staff can be held legally accountable for serving underage imbibers. If your blood alcohol level is 0.08 percent or higher, you are legally considered to be operating under the influence.

SMOKING

Maine laws ban smoking in restaurants, bars, and lounges as well as enclosed areas of public places, such as shopping malls. Only a handful of bed-and-breakfasts and country inns permit smoking, and increasingly motels, hotels, and resorts are limiting the number of rooms where smoking is permitted. Some

Don't forget to try a Maine wild blueberry pie.

face with blueberry everything—muffins, jam, pancakes, ice cream, and pies. Plus you can collect blueberry-logo napkins, T-shirts, fridge magnets, pottery, and jewelry.

Another don't-miss while in Maine is Maine-made **ice cream.** Skip the overpriced Ben & Jerry's outlets. Locally made ice cream is fresher and better, and it often comes in an astounding range of flavors. The big name in the state is Gifford's, along with regional companies Shain's and Round Top. All beat the out-of-state competition by a long shot. Even better are some of the one-of-a-kind dairy bars and farm stands. Good bets are Morton's in Ellsworth and MDI Ice Cream and Ben & Bill's, both in Bar Harbor.

Finally, whenever you get a chance, shop at a **farmers market.** Their biggest asset is serendipity—you never know what you'll find. Everything is locally grown and often organic. Herbs, unusual vegetables, seedlings, baked goods, meat, free-range chicken, goat cheese, herb vinegars, berries, exotic condiments, smoked salmon, maple syrup, honey, and jams are just a few of the possibilities. For a list of all the markets, including those in inland areas, visit www.getrealmaine.com.

accommodations ban smoking anywhere on the property, and most have instituted high fines for smoking in a nonsmoking room. If you're a smoker, motels with direct outdoor access make it easiest to satisfy a craving.

TIME ZONE

All of Maine is in the eastern time zone—the same as New York, Washington DC, Philadelphia, and Orlando. Eastern standard time (EST) runs from the first Sunday in November to the second Sunday in March; eastern daylight time (EDT), one hour later, prevails otherwise. Surprising to many first-time visitors, especially when visiting coastal areas, is how early the sun rises in the morning and how early it sets at night.

If your itinerary also includes Canada, remember that the provinces of New Brunswick and Nova Scotia are on Atlantic time—one hour later than eastern time—so if it's noon in Maine, it's 1pm in these provinces.

TRAVELING BY RV

Bringing a recreational vehicle (RV) to Mount Desert Island and Acadia National Park creates something of a conundrum. No question, the vehicles are convenient for carting kids and gear, but they're a major source of traffic problems on the island, and especially within the park. All of the island's roads are two lanes, and even though the island offers more designated bike lanes than almost anywhere else in Maine, bikes and RVs often have to share the road. RV parking is very limited, and even banned in some locales (such as downtown Bar Harbor). Ideally, you should consider bringing an RV to Acadia only between late June and Columbus Day—when you can park the vehicle in one of the island's dozen commercial campgrounds and travel around the island via the Island Explorer shuttle service.

Incidentally, be aware that the maximum trailer (or RV) length in the national park's two campgrounds is 35 feet, maximum width is 12 feet, and only one vehicle is allowed per site. Neither park campground has water or electric hookups.

TRAVELING WITH CHILDREN

Acadia National Park isn't a turn-the-toddlers-loose kind of place—there are too many cliffs and other potential hazards—but for school-age youngsters and cooperative teenagers, it's a fabulous family vacation destination. Enroll kids in the Junior Ranger program and participate in the Acadia Quest scavenger hunt. There are family-oriented kayak tours, park ranger tours, whale-watching trips, hiking and biking trails, carriage rides, and boat excursions. There's saltwater swimming (literally breathtaking for adults, but not for kids) at Sand Beach and freshwater swimming at several lakes and ponds. Incredibly, McDonald's and Burger King haven't invaded Mount Desert Island (although Subway has), but Bar Harbor and other towns have plenty of pizza and lobster joints, as well as two cinemas (one year-round, one seasonal) and several museums for rainy days.

Be forewarned that in-line skates and skateboards are not allowed anywhere within the park. The island communities surrounding the park are small and—especially at the height of summer—congested. In-line skates can come in handy, but use them sensibly; skateboards, on the other hand, are a major hazard in these villages (Bar Harbor does have a skateboard park). Bikes are not allowed on any of the park's hiking trails, but the car-free carriage trail network is ideal for biking.

How about doing a family volunteer stint? Consider spending a morning on a trail-maintenance crew (8:20am-12:30pm Tues., Thurs., and Sat. June-Oct.). You'll help cut back vegetation along trails and carriage roads, rebuild walls or drainages, clean up, and participate in other such activities. Bring water, insect repellent, and a bag lunch for a post-work picnic—the camaraderie is contagious. It's advisable to dress in layers, and do wear sturdy shoes. The nonprofit Friends of Acadia organization chalks up more than 8,000 volunteer hours every year. Check the website (www.friendsofacadia.org) before you come, or call 207/288-3934 when you get here for the recorded schedule of work projects. Volunteer crews meet at park headquarters (Rte. 233/Eagle Lake Rd.).

Earn a BA in Family Fun

Every summer, College of the Atlantic opens its doors to families, offering five sessions of its **Family Nature Camp** (800/597-9500, www.coa.edu/summer). This hands-on, participatory, naturalist-led program provides plenty of fodder for those "What I Did on My Summer Vacation" essays. The weeklong sessions are designed to cure nature-deficit disorder, and they include activities such as whale-watching, tidal pool exploration, wildlife-viewing expeditions, and more. Minimum age is five; extended family is welcome. The fee is around $950 per person for age 16 and older, $480 per person age 15 and younger. Camp runs Sunday afternoon through Saturday morning and includes campus lodging (bring your own sheets and towels), meals, and all scheduled field trips.

TRAVELING WITH PETS

If you're used to traveling with your cat or dog, you should be accustomed to playing by the rules. In Acadia National Park, dogs are allowed only on leashes, and they are banned from several park locations: Sand and Echo Lake Beaches, Duck Harbor Campground on Isle au Haut, park buildings, and any of the "ladder" hiking trails, which have iron foot- and handholds. (When you see the ladder trails, you'll understand why pets are forbidden.) Don't take pets on the park ranger tours, and do not leave your dog unattended, especially in an RV at one of the campgrounds. Be considerate of your pet as well as of other visitors. Of course, guide dogs are exempted from the pet rules.

To make the best of a visit to Acadia—so you can hike and bike and kayak without worrying about your pet—you might want to reserve kennel space for part of your stay. Mount Desert Island has the **Acadia Woods Kennel** (Crooked Rd., Bar Harbor, 207/288-9766, www.acadiawoodskennel.com), which offers both overnight and day boarding. In July-August, be sure to call well in advance for a reservation. If you'd prefer to have a dog-sitter come to your hotel or campground, contact Wendy Scott at **Bark Harbor** (150 Main St., Bar Harbor, 207/288-0404, www. barkharbor.com). She'll recommend someone who can help. If at all possible, call before you arrive to make arrangements, and when you get here, visit the store—a Toys "R" Us for pet owners. Bark Harbor maintains a list of pet-friendly restaurants and accommodations. Another resource is *Downeast Dog News* (www.downeastdognews.com), a free monthly tabloid available at pet-friendly locations and also online. It has a calendar of events. Also available is *Dog Parks, Beaches & Trails of Maine* (order online, $5), a booklet listing dog-friendly parks, beaches, and trails throughout the state as well as info on public transportation, emergency veterinary clinic numbers, and other useful tidbits.

SENIORS

Age does have its privileges. U.S. citizens and permanent residents age 62 or older can purchase a **Senior Pass,** valid for admission to more than 300 national parks (including Acadia), historic sites, and monuments for $10, a one-time fee. It also entitles you to half-price camping. Many lodgings and many attractions and sights offer discounts to seniors. It never hurts to ask. Age varies; some begin their discounts for those as young as 55

Keep your pet leashed when traveling, especially in the park, where it's the law.

(egad!). In any case, you'll need proof of age, such as a driver's license or passport.

Age also often brings achy knees and hips or other such maladies. Many of the accommodations in this area are small inns and B&Bs. If you have mobility problems or difficulty carrying your luggage up a flight of stairs or two, you'll want to make sure that your lodging has either first-floor rooms or elevators.

ACCESSIBILITY

Acadia National Park has been conscientious about providing as much accessibility as possible to people with disabilities. For a start, the Hulls Cove Visitors Center (the park's spring, summer, and fall information center) has a special parking area for easy wheelchair access, bypassing the 52 steps from the main parking area. When you get into the center, request an **Access Pass,** which provides free lifetime entry to any national park and half-price camping at park sites for any citizen or permanent resident who is permanently disabled (if you've broken your leg or have another temporary disability, you're not eligible). The passport is also available at the park's two campgrounds, at park headquarters, and at the Sand Beach and Bar Harbor Village Green ticket booths.

Also at the Hulls Cove Visitors Center, pick up a copy of the *Acadia National Park Accessibility Guide,* which provides detailed accessibility information—including parking, entry, restrooms, pay phones, and water fountains—for the park's visitors centers, the two campgrounds, picnic areas, beaches, and gift shops as well as carriage rides, some boat cruises, and nonpark museums on Mount Desert Island. A few of the park ranger programs are wheelchair-accessible, as are all of the evening programs at the park's two campgrounds. Access to the carriage road network depends on your ability (there are some steep grades); even the easiest trails may require some assistance. Each of the Island Explorer shuttle buses—operating late June-Columbus Day—has room for at least one wheelchair.

Parking lots at some of the park's most popular locales (such as Thunder Hole, the Cadillac Mountain summit, and Jordan Pond House) have designated accessible parking spaces.

Wheelchair rentals are handled by **West End Drug** (105 Main St., Bar Harbor, 207/288-3318).

To plan your Acadia trip in advance, order an Access Pass online, then download the accessibility information from the park's website (www.nps.gov/acad/accessibility.htm). If you're reserving a campsite at the Blackwoods Campground online (www.recreation.gov), you'll need the Access Pass beforehand.

For additional accessibility information, call 207/288-3338 (voice) or 207/288-8800 (TTY). For emergencies in the park or elsewhere on Mount Desert Island, dial 911.

While newer properties must meet the strict standards of the Americans with Disabilities Act, older and historic lodgings and restaurants often don't have accessible rooms or facilities. It's wise to ask detailed questions pertaining to your needs before booking a room or making a restaurant reservation.

Health and Safety

There's too much to do and see in Acadia National Park to spend even a few hours laid low by illness or mishap. Be sensible—get enough sleep, wear sunscreen and appropriate clothing, know your limits and don't take foolhardy risks, heed weather and warning signs, carry water and snacks while hiking, don't overindulge in food or alcohol, always tell someone where you're going, and watch your step. If you're traveling with children, quadruple your caution.

Even though Maine's public transportation network is woefully inadequate, and the crime rate is one of the lowest in the nation, it's still risky to hitchhike or pick up hitchhikers.

MEDICAL CARE

In the event of any emergency, dial 911.

Blue Hill and Deer Isle

The hospital in this region is **Blue Hill Memorial Hospital** (57 Water St., Blue Hill, 207/374-3400, emergency 207/374-2836).

Acadia and Schoodic Region

Hospitals are **Maine Coast Memorial Hospital** (50 Union St., Ellsworth, 207/664-5311 or 888/645-8829, emergency 207/664-5340) and **Mount Desert Island Hospital** (10 Wayman Ln., Bar Harbor, 207/288-5081).

Alternative Health Care

Nontraditional health-care options are available on Mount Desert Island as well as on the Blue Hill Peninsula and Deer Isle. After some overambitious hiking or biking expeditions, a massage might be in order. Holistic practitioners as well as certified massage therapists and acupuncturists are listed in the yellow pages of local phone books, and most accommodations can make referrals. Also check the bulletin boards and talk to the managers at local health-food stores. They always know where to find homeopathic doctors.

Pharmacies

The major pharmacy chain in and near Acadia is **Rite Aid;** Hannaford supermarkets also have pharmacy departments; and some towns have an independent drug store, such as **West End Drug** (105 Main St., Bar Harbor, 207/288-3318). All carry prescription and over-the-counter medications. There are no round-the-clock pharmacies. Some independent pharmacists post emergency numbers on their doors and will go out of their way to help, but your best bet for a middle-of-the-night medication crisis is the hospital emergency room.

If you take regular medications, be sure to pack an adequate supply as well as a new prescription in case you lose your medicine or unexpectedly need a refill. It's also wise to travel with a list of any prescriptions taken, in case of emergency.

AFFLICTIONS

Insect Bites and Tick-Borne Diseases

If you plan to spend any time outdoors in Maine April-November, take precautions, especially when hiking, to avoid annoying insect bites and especially the diseases carried by tiny deer ticks (not the larger dog ticks; they don't carry it): **Lyme disease, anaplasmosis,** and **babesiosis. Powassan,** carried by the woodchuck tick, is so far extremely rare. Mosquito-borne **eastern equine encephalitis** has been found in mosquitoes in southern Maine, but as of 2013 had not yet been diagnosed in humans.

Wear a long-sleeved shirt and long pants, and tuck pant legs into your socks. Light-colored clothing makes ticks easier to spot. Buy insect repellent with DEET at a supermarket or convenience store and use it liberally; apply permethrin to clothing. Not much daunts the blackflies of spring and early summer, but you can lower your appeal by not using perfume, aftershave lotion, or scented shampoo and by wearing light-colored clothing.

After any hike or prolonged time outdoors in the woods, thick grass, overgrown bushes, or piles of brush or leaves, check for ticks—especially behind the knees and in the armpits, navel, and groin. If you find one, there's a good chance the tick was infected with Lyme disease, a bacterial infection that causes fever, head and body aches, and fatigue and can lead to joint pain and neurological and heart problems. It usually takes 24-48 hours before an attached tick begins to transmit the disease. About 80 percent of Lyme patients get a bull's-eye rash that appears within a month of being bit. Anaplasmosis and babesiosis also exhibit flu-like symptoms. Anaplasmosis can, in rare circumstances, lead to encephalitis/meningitis; babesiosis can cause anemia and dark urine and is especially problematic for those with weakened immune systems or who have had their spleen removed.

If bitten by a tick, wash the area thoroughly with soap and water and apply an antiseptic, mark the date on a calendar, then monitor your health. If you suspect any of these diseases, see a doctor to be diagnosed and treated immediately; don't put it off. For more information, contact the **Maine Center for Disease Control** (800/821-5821, www.mainepublichealth.gov).

Rabies

If you're bitten by any animal, especially one acting suspiciously, head for the nearest hospital emergency room. For statewide information about rabies, contact the **Maine Center for Disease Control** (800/821-5821, www.mainepublichealth.gov).

Allergies

If your medical history includes extreme allergies to shellfish or bee stings, you know the risks of eating a lobster or wandering around a wildflower meadow. However, if you come from a landlocked area and are new to crustaceans, you might not be aware of the potential hazard. Statistics indicate that less than 2 percent of adults have a severe shellfish allergy, but for those victims, the reaction can set in quickly. Immediate treatment is needed to keep the airways open. If you have a history of severe allergic reactions to *anything*, be prepared when you come to the Maine coast dreaming of lobster feasts. Ask your doctor for a prescription for EpiPen (epinephrine), a preloaded, single-use syringe containing 0.3 mg of the drug—enough to tide you over until you can get to a hospital.

Seasickness

If you're planning to do any boating in Maine—particularly sailing—you'll want to be prepared. (Being prepared may in fact keep you from succumbing, since fear of seasickness just about guarantees you'll get it.) Talk to a pharmacist or doctor about your options.

Hypothermia and Frostbite

Wind and weather can shift dramatically in Maine, especially at higher elevations, creating prime conditions for contracting hypothermia and frostbite. At risk are hikers, swimmers, canoeists, kayakers, sailors, skiers, even cyclists.

To prevent hypothermia and frostbite, dress in layers and remove or add them as needed. Wool, waterproof fabrics (such as Gore-Tex), and synthetic fleece (such as Polartec) are the best fabrics for repelling dampness. Polyester fleece lining wicks excess moisture away from your body. Especially in winter, always cover your head, since body heat escapes quickly through the head; a ski mask will protect ears and nose. Wear wool- or fleece-lined gloves and wool socks.

Special Considerations During Hunting Season

During Maine's fall hunting season (Oct.-Thanksgiving)—and especially during the November deer season—walk or hike only in wooded areas marked No Hunting, No

Trespassing, or Posted. And even if an area is closed to hunters, don't decide to explore the woods during deer or moose season without wearing a hunter-orange (eye-poppingly fluorescent) jacket or vest. If you take your dog along, be sure it wears an orange vest too. Hunting is illegal on Sunday.

During hunting season, moose and deer are on the move and are made understandably skittish by the hunters invading their turf. Moose are primarily found inland, but deer are everywhere, and even the occasional moose strays into coastal areas of Maine. At night, particularly in wooded areas, these huge creatures often end up alongside or on the roads, so ratchet up your defensive-driving skills. Reduce your normal speed, use high beams when there's no oncoming traffic, and remain extra alert. In a moose-versus-car encounter, no one wins, and human fatalities are common. An encounter between a deer and a car may be less dangerous to the humans (although the deer usually dies), but some damage to the vehicle is inevitable.

Sunstroke

Since Acadia National Park lies above the 44th parallel, sunstroke is not a major problem, but don't push your luck by spending an entire day frying on Sand Beach or the granite shoreline. Not only do you risk sunstroke and dehydration, but you're also asking for skin cancer down the road. Early in the season, slather yourself, and especially children, with plenty of PABA-free sunblock (PABA can cause skin rashes and eruptions, even on people not abnormally sensitive). If you're in the water a long time, slather on some more. Start with 15-30 minutes of solar exposure and increase gradually each day. When you're hiking, carry water. If you don't get it right, watch for symptoms of sunstroke: fever, profuse sweating, headache, nausea or vomiting, extreme thirst, and sometimes hallucinations. To treat someone for sunstroke, find a breezy spot and place a cold, wet cloth on the victim's forehead. Change the cloth frequently so it stays cold. Offer lots of liquids—strong tea or coffee, fruit juice, water, or soft drinks, and no alcohol.

Information and Services

MONEY

Typical banking hours are 9am-3pm Monday-Friday, occasionally with later hours on Friday. Drive-up windows at many banks tend to open as much as an hour earlier and stay open an hour or so after lobbies close. Some banks also maintain Saturday-morning hours. Automated teller machines (ATMs) are found throughout Maine.

Credit Cards and Travelers Checks

Bank credit cards have become so preferred and so prevalent that it's nearly impossible to rent a car or check into a hotel without one. MasterCard and Visa are the most widely accepted in Maine, and Discover and American Express are the next most popular;

Carte Blanche, Diners Club, and EnRoute (Canadian) lag far behind. Be aware, however, that small restaurants (including lobster pounds), shops, and bed-and-breakfasts off the beaten track might not accept credit cards or nonlocal personal checks; you may need to settle your account with cash or travelers check.

Taxes

Maine charges a 5.5 percent sales tax on general purchases and services; 8 percent on prepared foods, candy, and lodging/camping; and 10 percent on auto rentals.

Tipping

Tip 15-20 percent of the pretax bill in restaurants.

Taxi drivers expect a 15 percent tip, more if handling luggage or handling special requests; airport porters expect at least $1 per bag, depending on the difficulty of the job.

The usual tip for housekeeping services in accommodations is $1-5 per person per night, depending upon the level of service. It's not necessary to tip at bed-and-breakfasts if the owners do the housekeeping.

Some accommodations add a 10-15-percent service fee to rates.

TOURIST INFORMATION

The Maine Office of Tourism has established an excellent website: www.visitmaine.com. You'll find chamber of commerce addresses, articles, photos, information on lodgings, and access to a variety of Maine tourism businesses. The state's toll-free information hotline is 888/MAINE-45 (888/624-6345). The state also operates **information centers** in Calais, Fryeburg (May-Oct.), Hampden, Houlton, Kittery, and Yarmouth. These are excellent places to visit to stock up

on brochures, pick up a map, ask for advice, and use restrooms. All, except Hamden, offer free Wi-Fi.

The **Maine Tourism Association** (207/623-0363, www.mainetourism.com) also has information and publishes *Maine Invites You* and a free state map.

PHONE AND INTERNET

Maine still has only one telephone area code, 207. For directory assistance, dial 411.

Cell phone towers are now sprinkled pretty much throughout Maine; only a few pockets—mostly down peninsulas and in remote valleys and hollows—are out of cell-phone range. Of course, reception also varies by carrier, and getting reception often requires doing the cell-phone hokey pokey—putting your left arm out, your right leg in, and so on to find the strongest signal.

Internet access is widely available at libraries and coffeehouses. Most hotels and many inns and bed-and-breakfasts also offer Internet access.

Resources

Glossary

alewives: herring

ayuh: yes

barrens: as in "blueberry barrens," fields where wild blueberries grow

beamy: wide (as in a boat or a person)

beans: shorthand for the traditional Saturday-night meal, which always includes baked beans

blowdown: a forest area leveled by wind

blowing a gale: very windy

camp: a vacation house (small or large), usually on fresh water and/or in the woods

chance: serendipity or luck (as in "open by appointment or by chance")

chicken dressing: chicken manure

chowder: (pronounced "chowdah") soup made with lobster, clams, or fish, or a combination thereof; lobster version sometimes called "lobster stew"

chowderhead: mischief- or troublemakers, usually interchangeable with "idiot"

coneheads: tourists (because of their presumed penchant for ice cream)

cottage: a vacation house (anything from a bungalow to a mansion), usually on salt water

culch: (also cultch); stuff, the contents of attics, basements, and some flea markets

cull: a discount lobster, usually minus a claw

cunnin': cute (usually describing a baby or small child)

dinner: (pronounced "dinnah") the noon meal

dinner pail: lunchbox

dite: a very small amount

dooryard: the yard near a house's main entrance

downcellar: in the basement

Down East: with the prevailing wind; the old coastal sailing route from Boston to Nova Scotia

dry-ki: driftwood, usually remnants from the logging industry

ell: a residential structural section that links a house and a barn; formerly a popular location for the "summer kitchen," to spare the house from woodstove heat

exercised: upset; angry

fiddleheads: unopened ostrich fern fronds, a spring delicacy

finest kind: top quality; good news; an expression of general approval; also, a term of appreciation

flatlander: a person not from Maine, often someone from the Midwest

floatplane: a small plane equipped with pontoons for landing on water; the same aircraft often becomes a ski plane in winter.

flowage: a water body created by damming, usually beaver handiwork (also called "beaver flowage")

frappé: a thick drink containing milk, ice cream, and flavored syrup, as opposed to a milk shake, which does not include ice cream (but beware: a frappé offered in other parts of the United States is an ice cream sundae topped with whipped cream!)

from away: not native to Maine

galamander: a wheeled contraption formerly used to transport quarry granite to building sites or to boats for onward shipment

gore: a sliver of land left over from inaccurate boundary surveys. Maine has several gores; Hibberts Gore, for instance, has a population of one.

got done: quit a job; was let go

harbormaster: local official who monitors water traffic and assigns moorings; often a very political job

hardshell: lobster that hasn't molted yet (more scarce, thus more pricey in summer)

hod: wooden "basket" used for carrying clams

ice-out: the departure of winter ice from ponds, lakes, rivers, and streams; many communities have ice-out contests, awarding prizes for guessing the exact time of ice-out, in April or May.

Italian: long, soft bread roll sliced on top and filled with peppers, onions, tomatoes, sliced meat, and black olives and sprinkled with olive oil, salt, and pepper; veggie versions are available.

jimmies: chocolate sprinkles, like those on an ice cream cone

lobster car: a large floating crate for storing lobsters

Maine Guide: a member of the Maine Professional Guides Association, trained and tested for outdoor and survival skills; also called a Registered Maine Guide

market price: restaurant menu term for "the going rate," usually referring to the price of lobster or clams

molt: what a lobster does when it sheds its shell for a larger one; the act of molting is called "ecdysis" (as a stripper is an ecdysiast).

money tree: a collection device for a monetary gift

mud season: mid-March-mid-April, when back roads and unpaved driveways become virtual tank traps

nasty neat: extremely meticulous

near: stingy

notional: stubborn, determined

off island: the mainland, to an islander

place: another word for a house (as in "Herb Pendleton's place")

pot: trap, as in "lobster pot"

public landing: see "town landing"

rake: hand tool for harvesting blueberries

rusticator: a summer visitor, particularly in bygone days

scooch: (or scootch) to squat; to move sideways

sea smoke: heavy mist rising off the water when the air temperature suddenly becomes much colder than the ocean temperature

select: a lobster with claws intact

selectmen: the elected men and women who handle local affairs in small communities; the First Selectman chairs meetings. In some towns, "people from away" have proposed substituting a gender-neutral term, but in most cases the effort has failed.

shedder: a lobster with a new (soft) shell; molting generally occurs in July-August, making shedders more common then, thus less expensive than hardshells.

shire town: county seat

shore dinner: the works: chowder, clams, lobster, and sometimes corn on the cob; usually the most expensive item on a menu

short: a small, illegal-size lobster

slumgullion: tasteless food; a mess

snapper: an undersize illegal lobster

soda: cola, root beer, etc., referred to as "pop" in other parts of the country

softshell: see "shedder"

some: very (as in "some hot")

spleeny: overly sensitive

steamers: clams (before or after they are steamed)

sternman: a lobsterman's helper

summer complaint: a tourist

supper: (pronounced "suppah") evening meal, eaten by Mainers around 5pm-6pm, as opposed to flatlanders and summer people, who eat dinner around 7pm-9pm

tad: slightly; a little bit

thick-o'-fog: zero-visibility fog

to home: at home

tomalley: a lobster's green insides; considered a delicacy by some

town landing: shore access; often a park or a parking lot, next to a wharf or boat-launch ramp

upattic: in the attic

whoopie pie: a high-fat cake-like snack that only kids and dentists could love

wicked cold!: frigid

wicked good!: excellent

williwaws: uncomfortable feeling

Suggested Reading

CARRIAGE ROADS

Abrell, D. *A Pocket Guide to the Carriage Roads of Acadia National Park.* 3rd ed. Camden, ME: Down East Books, 2011. A dozen excellent carriage-road loops ranging 1.2-11.1 miles for hiking, biking, or horseback riding—presented in a portable format.

Roberts, A. R. *Mr. Rockefeller's Roads.* 2nd ed. Camden, ME: Down East Books, 2012. The fascinating story behind Acadia's scenic carriage roads, written by the granddaughter of John D. Rockefeller Jr., the man who created them.

CHILDREN

Evans, Lisa Gollin. *An Outdoor Family Guide to Acadia National Park.* Seattle: The Mountaineers, 1997. An excellent resource for hiking, biking, and paddling with kids in Acadia.

Robson, Gary D. *Who Pooped in the Park.* Helena, MT: Farcountry Press, 2006. A sweet story centered on a family exploring the park and learning about the animals through scat and tracks.

Scheid, M. *Discovering Acadia: A Guide for Young Naturalists.* Bar Harbor, ME: Acadia Publishing, 1990. A delightful book for children—as well as the adults who accompany them.

HISTORY

Collier, S. F. *Mount Desert Island and Acadia National Park: An Informal History.* Revised ed. Camden, ME: Down East Books, 1978. An oft-cited source for island and park history.

Dorr, G. *The Story of Acadia National Park.* 5th ed. Bar Harbor, ME: Acadia Publishing, 2012 (reprinted, combining 1942 and 1948 originals). How Acadia began, and the roller-coaster struggles involved, as related by George Dorr, "the Father of Acadia."

Duncan, R. F., E. G. Barlow, K. Bray, and C. Hanks. *Coastal Maine: A Maritime History.* Woodstock, VT: Countrymen Press, 2002. Updated version of the classic work.

Helfrich, G. W., and G. O'Neil. *Lost Bar Harbor.* Camden, ME: Down East Books, 1982. Fascinating collection of historic photographs of classic turn-of-the-20th-century "cottages," most obliterated by Bar Harbor's Great Fire of 1947.

Judd, R. W., E. A. Churchill, and J. W. Eastman, eds. *Maine: The Pine Tree State from Prehistory to the Present.* Orono, ME: University of Maine Press, 1995. The best available Maine history, with excellent historical maps.

Morison, S. E. *The Story of Mount Desert Island.* Yarmouth, ME: Islandport Press, 2011 (reprint of 1960 book). A quirky, entertaining little history—from Native Americans to 20th-century Americans—by the late maritime historian, a longtime Mount Desert summer resident.

Shettleworth, E. G., and L. Vandenberg. *Bar Harbor's Gilded Century: Opulence to Ashes.* Camden, ME: Down East Books, 2009. A pictorial history of Bar Harbor before the Great Fire; includes 250 photos, some not published previously.

Workman, A. K. *Schoodic Point: History on the Edge of Acadia National Park.* Charleston, SC: History Press, 2014. Examines the history of Schoodic Point from settlement through the creation and evolution of the park.

LOBSTERS AND LIGHTHOUSES

Caldwell, W. *Lighthouses of Maine*. Camden, ME: Down East Books, 2002 (reprint of 1986 book). A historical tour of Maine's lighthouses, with the emphasis on history, legends, and lore.

Corson, T. *The Secret Life of Lobsters*. New York: HarperCollins, 2004. Everything you wanted to know—or perhaps didn't want to know—about lobster.

Stander, Bella. *Maine Lighthouses—Illustrated Map & Guide*. Rhinebeck, NY: Bella Terra Publishing, 2013. An illustrated map and guide providing history and descriptions, directions on how to locate all Maine beacons, and information on lighthouse cruises and ferries as well as maritime and lighthouse museums.

Woodward, C. *The Lobster Coast: Rebels, Rusticators, and the Struggle for a Forgotten Frontier*. New York: Viking, 2004. A veteran journalist's take on the history of the Maine coast.

NATURAL HISTORY AND NATURE GUIDES

Butcher, Russell D. *Field Guide to Acadia National Park, Maine*. Lanham, MD: Taylor Trade Publishing, 2007. A detailed, illustrated guide to Acadia's flora, fauna, and geology, including some trail descriptions with what to look for along the way.

Conkling, P. W. *Islands in Time: A Natural and Cultural History of the Islands of the Gulf of Maine*. 3rd ed. Rockland, ME: Island Institute, 2011. A thoughtful overview by the president of Maine's Island Institute.

Gilman, Richard A., C. A. Chapman, T. V. Lowell, and H. W. Burns. *The Geology of Mount Desert Island*. Maine Geological Society, 1988. An introduction to the "geological processes which formed the island's spectacular scenery."

Gregory, Linda L., Sally C. Rooney, Jill E. Weber, and Glen H. Mittelhauser. *The Plants of Acadia National Park*. Orono, ME: University of Maine Press, 2010. A comprehensive guide to the plants found in and around Acadia National Park.

Grierson, R. G. *Acadia National Park: Wildlife Watcher's Guide*. Minocqua, WI: NorthWord Press, 1995. You're not likely to see any creature in the park that isn't mentioned in this handy guide.

Kavanaugh, J., and R. Leung. *Acadia National Park Wildlife: A Folding Pocket Guide to Familiar Species*. Phoenix: Waterford Press, 2008. An easy-to-carry laminated guide.

Kendall, D. L. *Glaciers & Granite: A Guide to Maine's Landscape and Geology*. Unity, ME: North Country Press, 1993. Explains knowledgeably why Maine looks the way it does.

Newlin, William V. P., K. S. Cline, R. Briggs, A. Addison Namnoum, and B. Ciccotelli. *The College of the Atlantic Guide to the Lakes & Ponds of Mt. Desert*. Bar Harbor, ME: College of the Atlantic Press, 2013. Tips for exploring Mount Desert Island's more than 25 lakes and 40 streams.

Perrin, S. *Acadia's Native Flowers, Fruits, and Wildlife*. Fort Washington, PA: Eastern National, 2001. This handy reference to the park's flora and fauna runs chronologically through three seasons (spring-fall). It's not a complete field guide but rather a selective collection of photos in a portable square format.

OFFSHORE ISLANDS
Cranberry Isles

Eliot, C. W. *John Gilley: One of the Forgotten Millions*. Bar Harbor, ME: Acadia Press,

1989 (reprint of 1904 book). Poignant story of 19th-century life in the Cranberries, as told by the Harvard president who was instrumental in the establishment of Acadia.

Frenchboro (Long Island)

Lunt, D. L. *Hauling by Hand: The Life and Times of a Maine Island*. Frenchboro, ME: Islandport Press, 1999. A sensitive history of Frenchboro (aka Long Island), eight miles offshore, written by an eighth-generation islander.

Isle au Haut

Greenlaw, L. *The Lobster Chronicles: Life on a Very Small Island*. New York: Hyperion, 2002. Essays on Isle au Haut life, warts and all, by the talented writer and lobsterwoman who first gained fame as a swordfishing skipper in *The Perfect Storm*.

Pratt, C. *Here on the Island*. New York: Harper & Row, 1974. An appealing, realistic portrait of life on Isle au Haut several decades ago.

PICTORIAL

Blagden Jr., T., and C. R. Tyson Jr. *First Light: Acadia National Park and Maine's Mount Desert Island*. Englewood, CO: Westcliffe Publishers, and Bar Harbor, ME: Friends of Acadia, 2003. A gorgeous, large-format book with spectacular photographs.

Wilmerding, J. *The Artist's Mount Desert: American Painters on the Maine Coast*. Princeton, NJ: Princeton University Press, 1995. A respected art historian's perspective on Mount Desert's magnetic attraction to such American artists as Thomas Cole, Frederic Church, and Fitz Hugh Lane.

RECREATION GUIDES
General

Monkman, J., and M. Monkman. *Discover Acadia National Park: A Guide to Hiking,*

Biking, and Paddling. 3rd ed. Boston: Appalachian Mountain Club Books, 2010. Well-planned and well-written guide, in the Appalachian Mountain Club tradition, including a foldout map.

Biking

Minutolo, A. *A Pocket Guide to Biking on Mount Desert Island*. Camden, ME: Down East Books, 1996. A third-generation islander's expert advice; this book covers the whole island, not just the park.

Birding

Duchesne, B. *Maine Birding Trail: The Official Guide to More Than 260 Accessible Sites*. Camden, ME: Down East Books, 2009. Authorized guide to the Maine Birding Trail.

Pierson, E. C., J. E. Pierson, and P. D. Vickery. *A Birder's Guide to Maine*. Camden, ME: Down East Books, 1996. An expanded version of *A Birder's Guide to the Coast of Maine*. A valuable resource for any ornithologist, novice or expert, for exploring Acadia and the rest of Maine.

Cruising Guides

Bilder, J. *A Visual Cruising Guide to the Maine Coast*. Camden, ME: Ragged Mountain Press, 2006. A spiral-bound guide, with 180 aerial photos providing visual guidance.

Taft, H., J. Taft, and C. Rindlaub. *A Cruising Guide to the Maine Coast*. 5th ed. Peaks Island, ME: Diamond Pass Publishing, 2008. Don't even consider cruising the coast around Acadia without this thoroughly researched volume.

Hiking

Gillmore, R. *Great Walks of Acadia National Park & Mount Desert Island*. Revised ed. Goffstown, NH: Great Walks, 2004. Two dozen trails in Acadia, some stretching the limits of their definition of "walks."

Kish, C. *Maine Mountain Guide: AMC's Comprehensive Guide to Hiking Trails of Maine, Featuring Baxter State Park and Acadia National Park.* 10th ed. Boston: Appalachian Mountain Club Books, 2012. The definitive statewide resource for going vertical, in a handy format.

Kong, D., and D. Ring. *Hiking Acadia National Park.* 2nd ed. Guilford, CT: Globe Pequot/FalconGuides, 2012. Excellent hiking guide, with useful, accurate descriptions of 94 trails on Mount Desert Island, Isle au Haut, and the Schoodic Peninsula. The authors include a list of their 25 favorites and advocate the Leave No Trace philosophy.

St. Germain Jr., T. A. *A Walk in the Park: Acadia's Hiking Guide.* 10th ed. Bar Harbor, ME: Parkman Publications, 2013. The book includes plenty of historical tidbits about the trails, the park, and the island. Part of the proceeds go to the Acadia Trails Forever campaign to maintain and rehabilitate the park's trails. The book is updated regularly; ask for the most recent edition.

Kayaking and Canoeing

Brechlin, E. D. *A Pocket Guide to Paddling the Waters of Mount Desert Island.* Camden, ME: Down East Books, 1996. Registered Maine Guide Brechlin recommends 17 places to paddle your kayak or canoe—in saltwater as well as freshwater ponds and lakes. This little handbook (64 pages) includes locations for parking and launching areas as well as route maps.

The Maine Island Trail Guidebook. Rockland, ME: Maine Island Trail Association, updated annually. Available only with MITA membership (www.mita.org, annual dues $45), providing access to dozens of islands along the watery trail, including many in the Acadia region between Schoodic Point and Deer Isle.

Miller, D. S. *Kayaking the Maine Coast.* 2nd ed. Woodstock, VT: Countryman Press/Backcountry Guides, 2006. Thoroughly researched guide by a veteran kayaker; good maps and particularly helpful information.

Wilson, A., and J. Hayes. *Quiet Water Maine: Canoe & Kayak Guide, Maine.* 2nd ed. Boston: Appalachian Mountain Club Books, 2005. Comprehensive handbook, with helpful maps, for inland paddling.

REFERENCE

The Maine Atlas and Gazetteer. Yarmouth, ME: DeLorme, updated annually. You'll be hard put to get lost on the roads in this region or anywhere else in Maine if you're carrying this essential volume; it contains 70 full-page (oversize format) topographical maps with GPS grids.

Internet Resources

ACADIA NATIONAL PARK INFORMATION

Acadia National Park
www.nps.gov/acad
A comprehensive site with extensive, detailed information about Maine's only national park. Download natural and cultural history articles, accessibility charts, a list of hiking trails, FAQs, maps of the park and its outlying sections (Isle au Haut and the Schoodic Peninsula), and the latest issue of the *Beaver Log*, the park's seasonal newspaper. Also included is a link for online reservations at park campgrounds.

Friends of Acadia
www.friendsofacadia.org
A very active nonprofit organization that acts as a financial safety net for the park and also organizes frequent volunteer work parties for various maintenance projects in the park. Its newsletters are posted on the website, as is information about where and when you can volunteer.

Island Explorer Bus System
www.exploreacadia.com
Everything you need to know about using the propane-fueled, fare-free Island Explorer buses (late June-early Oct. on Mount Desert, late June-early Sept. on the Schoodic Peninsula). Included are suggestions for getting to Mount Desert without a car as well as for exploring the park with the bus.

Schoodic Institute
www.schoodicinstitute.org
An active nonprofit supporting science and research on Acadia National Park's Schoodic section. Sponsors lectures, ranger-led programs, and other activities.

GENERAL INFORMATION

State of Maine
www.maine.gov
Everything you wanted to know about Maine and then some, with links to all government departments and Maine-related sites. Buy a fishing license online, reserve a state park campsite, or check the fall foliage conditions via the site's Leaf Cam. (You can also access foliage info at www.mainefoliage.com, where you can sign up for weekly email foliage reports in Sept. and early Oct.) Also listed is information on accessible arts and recreation.

Maine Office of Tourism
www.visitmaine.com
The biggest and most useful of all Maine-related tourism sites, with sections for where to visit, where to stay, things to do, trip planning, packages, and search capabilities as well as lodging specials and a comprehensive calendar of events.

Maine Tourism Association
www.mainetourism.com
Find lodging, camping, restaurants, attractions, services, and more as well as links for weather, foliage, transportation planning, and chambers of commerce.

Maine Emergency Management Association
www.state.me.us/mema/weather/weather.htm
Five-day weather forecasts broken down by 32 zones.

Maine Archives and Museums
www.mainemuseums.org
Information on and links to museums, archives, historical societies, and historic sites in Maine.

Maine Department of Agriculture
www.getrealmaine.com
Information on all things agricultural, including fairs, farmers markets, farm vacations, places to buy Maine foods, berry- and apple-picking sites, and more.

Maine Travel Maven
www.mainetravelmaven.com
Moon Acadia National Park author Hilary Nangle's site for keeping readers updated on what's happening throughout the state.

PARKS AND RECREATION

Bicycle Coalition of Maine
www.bikemaine.org
Tons of information for bicyclists, including routes, shops, events, organized rides, and much more.

Department of Conservation, Maine Bureau of Parks and Lands
www.parksandlands.com
Information on state parks, public reserved lands, and state historic sites as well as details on facilities such as campsites, picnic areas, and boat launches. Make state campground reservations online.

Island Institute
www.islandinstitute.org
The institute serves as a clearinghouse and advocate for Maine's islands; the website provides links to the major year-round islands.

Maine Audubon
www.maineaudubon.org
Information about Maine Audubon's environmental centers statewide. Activity and program schedules are included.

Maine Birding Trail
www.mainebirdingtrail.com
A must-visit site for anyone interested in

learning more about birding in Maine; includes news, checklists, events, tours, and more.

Maine Campground Owners Association
www.campmaine.com
Find private campgrounds statewide.

Maine Department of Inland Fisheries and Wildlife
www.state.me.us/ifw
Info on wildlife, hunting, fishing, snowmobiling, and boating.

Maine Island Trail Association
www.mita.org
The mission and activities of MITA as well as information on becoming a member and receiving the annual guidebook to the island trail.

Maine Land Trust Network
www.mltn.org
Maine has dozens of land trusts statewide, managing lands that provide opportunities for hiking, walking, canoeing, kayaking, and other such activities.

Maine Professional Guides Association
www.maineguides.org
Find Registered Maine Guides for sporting adventures, including sea kayaking, hunting, fishing, and recreation (such as canoeing trips and wildlife safaris).

Maine Trail Finder
www.mainetrailfinder.com
Searchable database of trails statewide with interactive maps, descriptions, images, and trip reports.

The Nature Conservancy
www.nature.org/wherewework/ northamerica/states/maine/
Information about Maine preserves, field trips, and events.

TRANSPORTATION

Explore Maine
www.exploremaine.org

Explore Maine is an invaluable site for trip planning, with information on and links to airports, rail service, bus service, automobile travel, and ferries as well as links to other key travel-planning sites.

Maine Department of Transportation
www.511maine.gov

Provides real-time information about major delays, accidents, road construction, and weather conditions. You can get the same info and more by dialing 511 in-state.

Index

List of Maps

Acknowledgments

This book is dedicated to all the underappreciated tourism workers throughout the Maine's Acadia region: the volunteers and lowly staffers, the waiters, waitresses, gatekeepers, park rangers, traffic cops, ferry attendants, deck hands, housekeepers, hostesses and front desk workers, tour guides, and everyone else who has contact with visitors. You make the region sing. You're the real face of Maine. Thank you.

Although I've lived in Maine since childhood (yes, I will always be a "from away"), and have traveled extensively in the state for both work and pleasure, every time I revisit a place, I find something new or changed, sometimes subtly, other times dramatically. Restaurants open and close. Outfitters change their offerings. Inns are sold. Motels open. New trails are cut. Museums expand. Hotels renovate. And on it goes. Which all goes to say, I couldn't have done this without the help of many people who served as additional eyes and ears.

I'll start with the folks at Avalon Travel who shepherded me through the process: Bill Newlin, Grace Fujimoto, Kevin McLain, Sierra Machado, Elizabeth Hansen, and most especially my team on this edition: editor Nikki Ioakimedes, graphics coordinator Darren Alessi, and map editor Albert Angulo. Also thank you to publicists J.T. Fales and Larissa Hageman, and to all the behind-the-scenes worker bees at Avalon Travel Publishing. I'm also eternally in debt to Kathleen Brandes, who wrote the original 2004 edition of this book and whose friendship I valued and whose work and dedication I respected long before I began with second edition.

More heartfelt thank-yous are due to those who shared insider info, sheltered me along the way, fed me, helped with arrangements, verified information, called with updates, or simply encouraged me: Park Planner John Kelly, Sam Coplon, Mark Berry, Jeff Folsom, Rosemary and Gary Levin, Nancy Marshall, Charlene Williams, Sally Littlefield, Sarah Pebworth, Julie Van de Graaf, Jack Burke, Isle au Haut Ranger Alison Richardson, Marshall Chapman, Devin Finigan, Anne and Peter Beerits, Bill Haefele, Jim Ash, Liane Wood, Helene Harton and Roy Kasindorf, Jim Ash, Susi Homer, Charles and Sue Starr, Richard Reith, and all of the ANP rangers and volunteers who answered my endless questions.

I save my biggest thanks for my husband, Tom, who drove me everywhere and didn't complain (too much) when I made him backtrack two or three times along the same stretch of road while seeking an elusive address; who waited patiently while I visited practically every restaurant, inn, and bed-and-breakfast from Isle au Haut to Corea; who let me order for him in restaurants; who tackled research projects; and who supported me in every way possible throughout the entire process, all while shooting photographs for the book. I couldn't have done it without him.

Big thanks are also due to my alternative faithful travel companions, my frequent sidekick Martha Kalina who is always up for an adventure (and always brings chocolate), my dear friend Sarah Wills, and, on occasion, my dog, Bernie, my resident expert on pet-friendly accommodations.

And you, dear reader, thank you for using this book to plan your visit to Maine's magical Acadia region. Please, do me a favor, will you? Provide feedback to help make the next edition even better. Visit www.MaineTravelMaven.com to know what's new, changed, or happening in Maine and please, drop a line to share your thoughts and finds.

MAP SYMBOLS

≡≡≡≡ Expressway	○	City/Town	✈	Airport	⚲	Golf Course
═══ Primary Road	◉	State Capital	✈	Airfield	🅿	Parking Area
─── Secondary Road	⊛	National Capital	▲	Mountain	◢	Archaeological Site
═ ═ ═ Unpaved Road	★	Point of Interest	✦	Unique Natural Feature	⸸	Church
──── Feature Trail						Gas Station
─ ─ ─ Other Trail	•	Accommodation	🝙	Waterfall		
·········· Ferry	▼	Restaurant/Bar	▲	Park	⬡	Glacier
═══ Pedestrian Walkway	■	Other Location	🅣	Trailhead		Mangrove
▥▥▥ Stairs	Λ	Campground	⛷	Skiing Area		Reef
						Swamp

CONVERSION TABLES

°C = (°F - 32) / 1.8
°F = (°C x 1.8) + 32
1 inch = 2.54 centimeters (cm)
1 foot = 0.304 meters (m)
1 yard = 0.914 meters
1 mile = 1.6093 kilometers (km)
1 km = 0.6214 miles
1 fathom = 1.8288 m
1 chain = 20.1168 m
1 furlong = 201.168 m
1 acre = 0.4047 hectares
1 sq km = 100 hectares
1 sq mile = 2.59 square km
1 ounce = 28.35 grams
1 pound = 0.4536 kilograms
1 short ton = 0.90718 metric ton
1 short ton = 2,000 pounds
1 long ton = 1.016 metric tons
1 long ton = 2,240 pounds
1 metric ton = 1,000 kilograms
1 quart = 0.94635 liters
1 US gallon = 3.7854 liters
1 Imperial gallon = 4.5459 liters
1 nautical mile = 1.852 km

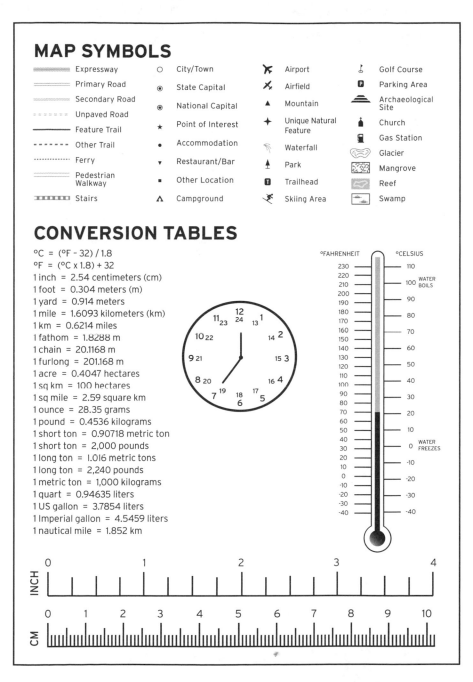

MOON ACADIA NATIONAL PARK
Avalon Travel
a member of the Perseus Books Group
1700 Fourth Street
Berkeley, CA 94710, USA
www.moon.com

Editor: Nikki Ioakimedes
Series Manager: Sabrina Young
Copy Editor: Ann Seifert
Graphics Coordinator: Darren Alessi
Production Coordinator: Darren Alessi
Cover Design: Faceout Studios, Charles Brock
Moon Logo: Tim McGrath
Map Editor: Albert Angulo
Cartographer: Kat Bennett
Indexer: Rachel Kuhn

ISBN-13: 978-1-63121-023-5
ISSN: 1546-8062

Printing History
1st Edition — 2004
5th Edition — May 2015
5 4 3 2 1

Text © 2015 by Hilary Nangle
Maps © 2015 by Avalon Travel.
All rights reserved.